THE RE-EMERGENCE OF CHINA

THE NEW GLOBAL ERA

THE

RE-EMERGENCE OF CHINA

THE NEW GLOBAL ERA

MICHAEL LLOYD
GLOBAL POLICY INSTITUTE, UK

BOB SAVIC
GLOBAL POLICY INSTITUTE, UK & UNIVERSITY OF NOTTINGHAM, UK

World Scientific

NEW JERSEY • LONDON • SINGAPORE • BEIJING • SHANGHAI • HONG KONG • TAIPEI • CHENNAI • TOKYO

Published by

World Scientific Publishing Europe Ltd.
57 Shelton Street, Covent Garden, London WC2H 9HE
Head office: 5 Toh Tuck Link, Singapore 596224
USA office: 27 Warren Street, Suite 401-402, Hackensack, NJ 07601

Library of Congress Cataloging-in-Publication Data
Names: Lloyd, Michael (Economist) author. | Savic, Bob, author.
Title: The re-emergence of China : the new global era / Michael Lloyd, Global Policy Institute, UK, Bob Savic, Global Policy Institute, UK & University of Nottingham, UK.
Description: Hackensack, NJ : World Scientific, [2022] | Includes bibliographical references and index.
Identifiers: LCCN 2021039117 | ISBN 9781800611269 (hardcover) | ISBN 9781800611276 (ebook) | ISBN 9781800611283 (ebook other)
Subjects: LCSH: Economic development--China--21st century. | China--Economic policy--21st century. | Information technology--China--Management. | China--Foreign relations--21st century. | China--Foreign relations--United States. | United States--Foreign relations--China. | China--Commerce--21st century. | China--Politics and government--21st century.
Classification: LCC HC427.95 .L596 2022 | DDC 330.951--dc23
LC record available at https://lccn.loc.gov/2021039117

British Library Cataloguing-in-Publication Data
A catalogue record for this book is available from the British Library.

For any available supplementary material, please visit
https://www.worldscientific.com/worldscibooks/10.1142/Q0332#t=suppl

Desk Editors: Balamurugan Rajendran/Michael Beale/Shi Ying Koe

Typeset by Stallion Press
Email: enquiries@stallionpress.com

Preface

The twenty-first century will see vast social, economic, scientific, and political changes, but none more influential than the re-emergence of China on the world stage.

The staggering economic growth of China over the past 30 years is impressive yet not surprising. What is perhaps more surprising, and for some in the West disturbing, is the technological and geopolitical challenge being presented by China.

However, the presentation of China in Western political, media, and many academic circles is less than objective, and often obscured by lack of knowledge and a distorted Western ideological perspective. This book attempts, as far as possible, to avoid a specific political, cultural, and philosophical viewpoint. It therefore starts by challenging the prevailing Western approach of assuming the universal validity of liberal individualist politics and neoliberal market economics. The aim is to produce a non-judgemental picture of China, as it has now rapidly re-emerged into the modern global polity.

Importantly, we will be exploring the unique vision that China has of the world, which is not simply that of a new global economic and political power. There is a sense in which China views the outside world, not simply from the nationalist perspective of a large nation-state, but also that of China as a civilisation spreading outwards, centred perhaps in East Asia, but extended outwards to Russia, Europe, and Africa. This is not a proselytising mission, China does not wish (as for instance does the United States, and in earlier times Britain, Spain, and other European powers) to impose its culture on others, but one of economic and political partnership. In reflecting this position, the re-emergence of China in global affairs affords an opportunity to understand and explore the role that China might play in this changing and challenging century.

We intend to examine the 'Chinese phenomenon' from a variety of angles. These will include, *inter alia*:

- The historical background to China's rise since 1990
- The nature of the economic development over the same period
- The emphasis placed by China on technological innovation and investment as an engine of economic growth
- The cultural challenges faced by China, both internally and externally
- The political philosophical traditions, ancient and modern, which inform the cultural and political development of China
- The geoeconomic and trade profile of China from 1990 to 2020 and the potential evolution of China within a changing international economic and financial order
- The various geopolitical contexts involving China with other national and regional players
- Bilateral and multilateral resolutions of existing and potential conflicts
- The growing geopolitical struggle between China and the US based on two opposing theories of political economy, and differing political philosophies of socialist collectivism and liberal individualism.

About the Authors

Michael Lloyd MA (Cantab), DSS (Oxon), DLL (Plymouth), is Senior Research Fellow and Associate Director, Global Policy Institute, and former Visiting Fellow, Newcastle University. Michael was educated at Oxford and Cambridge, following which he entered professional life as an applied economist, working, *inter alia*, as an official of the European Commission, as Economic Adviser to the European Parliament, and as an independent economic consultant, based in the United Kingdom and Brussels, Belgium. From 1982 to 1984 Michael was Director of International Affairs for British Shipbuilders. He has written extensively on European and global political and economic affairs, including on federalism. In 2020, he published *The Federalist Revolution*, which followed a previous book on political philosophy, *The Revolution of Civil Society*, in 2017. His latest book, *British Business Banking*, was published in February 2021. He has had a keen interest for many years in issues surrounding the UK and other national constitutions, including China. Michael currently lives in the rural county of Northumberland, UK, and writes poetry as a relaxation from his other writing.

Bob Savic is currently a Senior Research Fellow at the Global Policy Institute in London and a Visiting Professor with the University of Nottingham's Asia Research Institute where he specializes in International Relations and Politics. Bob also contributes regularly to the *South China Morning Post, the Diplomat, Bangkok Post, Asia Dialogue, China's World, China Oil and Gas, International Energy Law Review, International Trade Law & Regulation* and numerous other international media on Chinese political and economic issues.

Professionally, Bob has worked for over 30 years in China and across Asia, including with Deloitte China, Ernst & Young Singapore, Horwath Hong Kong, Asia Law & Practice and Asian Finance in Hong Kong. Currently, Bob is a Senior Consultant with Asia-based legal and accounting services firm, Dezan Shira, where he also writes for the firm's online platforms such as China Briefing, Silk Road Briefing and ASEAN Briefing on cross-border trade and investment matters, in addition to his contributions on the firm's 'Identifying Opportunities Within the Belt & Road Initiative' 2021 business guide.

Contents

Introduction

The West, led by an increasingly agitated United States (US), appears, in 2021, to be intent on waging a new Cold War with China. However, until the 1980s the West was essentially untroubled by China, as most of the twentieth century, until 1980, had seen increasing turmoil in China.

In the first half of the century, the collapse of Imperial China, struggles between various factions prior to the Second World War, and the invasions and occupations by Japan before and during the War were mainly of interests to sinologists. However, the post-War defeat of the Kuomintang nationalists by the Chinese Communist Party (CCP), the declaration of the People's Republic of China, followed by the intervention of the CCP in the Korean War (Zhou 2015) led to Western concerns. Nonetheless, the damaging impact of the long rule of Mao Zedong and the Cultural Revolution, until his death in the late 1970s, meant that most Western observers did not expect any rapid re-emergence of China as a major geopolitical force.

However, it perhaps should have been anticipated. China has been the site of many ancient civilisations. Chinese empires ran from the earliest recorded Zhou Empire from 1046 to 256 BC until the final Qing Empire from 1644 to 1912 (we will briefly consider the long evolution of the Chinese empires in Chapter 5). China is unique in many other ways. From a cultural perspective, its neo-Confucian, Buddhist, and Taoist heritage and practice — given its 1.4 billion population — means that in philosophical-religious terms this adherence could be said to rival Christianity, Islam, and Judaism. Its large geographical area (three times larger than India), in combination with housing one-fifth of the global population (four times larger than the US population), is unequalled. Since 2014, according to the International Monetary Fund statistics (IMF 2021), China's GDP in purchasing power parity terms is larger than the US. Moreover, the 'century of humiliation' from 1839 to 1949 still informs the thinking of Chinese elites in relation to China's role in the modern world (Kaufman 2010).

This unique combination of disparate statistics and issues should be borne in mind when attempting to assess China's current and future role in the world. Viewing China from almost any perspective entails considering its singularities in global terms.

China and the US in the Post-Cold War Era: A Snapshot

The US had made initial contact with Mao's China in 1972 with the visit of then-US President Richard Nixon. In 1979, Mao's effective successor, Deng Xiaoping, was invited to visit the US. Deng's economic reforms were seen by the US as heralding a potential move towards political democracy in China. This somewhat complacent approach received a stern shock in 1989 with the military suppression of student protests in Tiananmen Square and the deaths of many Chinese citizens in the surrounding streets. However, the relative tolerance of this event by the then-US President George HW Bush indicated a contemporary US administration view that perseverance of 'constructive engagement' would eventually bring rewards. The future was seen in terms of a continued move towards further economic reform and a degree of democratic easing of autocracy in China.

Since 1990, until recently, this had been the positioning of the US administrations. The positioning of Congress, however, was more hostile to China, especially on human rights issues. In 2008, the year before Barack Obama took office, there were 30 anti-China trade measures before Congress. Greater concern about the potential global economic and political threat further emerged under the Obama presidency.

Nonetheless, in 2008, China had hosted a successful Olympic Games. Its global profile had been enhanced. The relations between the US and China during the eight years of the Obama presidency started cautiously and proceeded relatively harmoniously, although with the US becoming increasingly wary of China's strengthening global economic profile.

Motivated by the military intelligence lobby in the US, the US administration made a 'Pivot to the Pacific' in its foreign policy and subsequently developed a tougher, Indo-Pacific foreign policy, characterised as the 'containment of China'.

Meanwhile, with internal foreign investment and via its increasing economic expansion externally into the rest of the world, China was emerging as a considerable economic and trading powerhouse, increasingly rivalling the dominance of the US. It was also developing rapidly as a technological power in certain sectors.

The Obama second term of office from 2012 saw increasing interaction between the US and China, but one now characterised by mutual suspicion, with both acting like sumo wrestlers circling each other. On occasions China would over-react and push the US into a more confrontational posture. US military intelligence obsession with cybersecurity threats from China (even though whatever infiltration may have taken place was linked more with industrial espionage) would be retaliated by China reasserting its rights in the South China Sea, followed by US condemnation. The direction of causality here is difficult to establish.

There is little doubt that under the Xi Jinping presidency, since 2013, China's foreign policy has become more extensive and robustly focused on what China perceives as its intrinsic interests. Nonetheless, during the period, China did attempt to advance negotiations on a US-China bilateral investment treaty. This treaty became enmeshed in the attempts to finalise an agreement on the Trans-Pacific Partnership (TPP), from which, unreasonably, China had been excluded. This trade agreement, given the increasing US concern about China's growing influence in East Asia, was a further attempt at 'containing' China (Perlez 2015).

Subsequently, with US withdrawal from the TPP, the then-US President Donald Trump abandoned the earlier approach in favour of his 'America First' policy initiative. Arguably, though, even if Obama had succeeded in arriving at a TPP agreement prior to Trump's election, it would not likely have been approved by the Republican-led US Congress at the time.

Trump's subsequent inchoate attempts at foreign and trade policy, linked to an idea of 'doing deals' with leaders such as Xi, led to a trade war between the US and China, which Trump was incapable of bringing to a resolution while in office. Moreover, relations between the US and China, under Trump, only further deteriorated, exacerbated by the ideological stance often taken by then-US Secretary of State Mike Pompeo in promoting the administration's national security policy of viewing China as a 'strategic rival' in economic terms. This deterioration in relations is not, however, simply attributable to the Trump administration and is not confined to the arena of US-China trade relations. The disenchantment with China — stimulated by the Western intelligence services and political ideologues in academia and various US-funded, or influenced, 'think tanks' and amplified by national media narratives — is now prevalent in a group of English-speaking nations. These include the US, the UK, Australia, Canada, and New Zealand, and other countries in the Western ambit. This development in the West appears to be leading to a new ideological and geostrategic Cold War, led by the US.

Peaceful Coexistence or New Cold War?

Notwithstanding the above picture and naval skirmishes in the South China Sea, the global rise of China in the 30 years since 1990 has been peaceful. As a developing country, it has indicated a new and successful way to industrialise and to modernise. Whatever the development of market capitalism within its boundaries, currently it remains a country committed to demonstrating a desire to develop a Chinese socialist future. This is beginning to be recognised by the West, but, if an intensifying ideological conflict is established, then this may sabotage the potential to achieve 'peaceful coexistence'. In this context, it is important that China transmits its broad societal values in a manner to which the international community can respond positively but which does not threaten the West. We will return to this issue in the concluding chapters.

During the next 30 years, the world faces a perilous future dominated by climate change, more pandemics, and significant population movements. Humanity's fraught relationship with the natural world and humanity's relationships between its various nation-states, large and small, will influence our political, economic, and societal survival and the nature of its evolution.

Intensifying the friction between the West and China is not the way forward. There needs to be established effective communications mechanisms to enable an ongoing and fruitful global dialogue. Moreover, a clear and close relationship between the state and the people across all countries will be required to deal with these future challenges: ensuring that we cooperate more closely to prevent engaging in damaging zero-sum competition.

In reflecting on these issues, the re-emergence of China in global affairs affords an opportunity to examine — both from China's unique perspective and from the external observation and reactions of, particularly Western, critics — of the role that China will play in this changing and challenging twenty-first century. To enable this examination to be made from a balanced perspective, it will be imperative to first provide a non-judgemental assessment of China, across its economic, technological, financial, political, and internal and external societal and policy landscapes. Moreover, it will be important to recognise how, perhaps uniquely, China's foreign policies should be viewed as intrinsic extensions of its interior cultural and political development. This complex task is the *raison d'être* of the book.

Brief Overview

The first chapter will be one in which we 'set the scene', providing a short analysis of the 30 years since the advent of the 'reform and opening up' of China launched by Deng Xiaoping in 1979. It will also examine the various staging posts on the road to the re-emergence of China as a major global power in 2021, as well as contemporary events and attitudes towards China.

This will be followed by an examination of the technological development and economic growth in China between 1990–2020 and its drive for technological excellence and global leadership. Also examined will be China's current external economic actions and policy, linked to its economic development, with special reference to the Belt and Road Initiative (BRI).

This description of the motivation and policies to move China to a leading economic position in the world will be followed by a discussion of how China attempts to extend its 'soft power' influence on the world beyond its physical borders. An assessment will be made of how successful or otherwise China is being in this endeavour, and in resisting severe Western criticism. The BRI will be briefly revisited in terms of its ability to extend a 'benevolent' expression of Chinese values along its expanding connectivity.

An examination will follow of the political-philosophical positioning of China, referencing this to the past and present traditions and trends, including the basis of 'socialism with Chinese characteristics' and how it might be interpreted. There will be an examination of the practicality or otherwise of the apparent desire of Xi Jinping to marry the conceptual approaches on Marxism and Confucianism and their praxis in the governance of China.

An analysis of the cultural and social development of China will follow, with reference to these characteristics as being embedded in a centuries-long, historical context, but translated into modern China. *Inter alia*, this will include an examination of the role of Chinese 'community identity'. This will include its links to the Chinese diaspora across East Asia, together with the involvement of the latter in the early 30-year economic development of China.

The book will then turn to the geopolitical issues which encompass China. The first chapter in Part II will explore China's potential role in meeting the various geopolitical challenges faced by the world, including climate change, pandemics, and others. It will explore the urgent need, in each of these areas, to bring countries together to agree and to implement global solutions, including the participation of China.

The next three chapters will explore a variety of foreign policy dimensions of China's geopolitical relations with various parts of the world and individual countries. An exploration will be made of China's bilateral and multilateral involvement with countries and regional groupings such as the EU. This will be followed by a discussion of China's anchor role in East Asia, the political and economic relations of countries in this neighbourhood region, and China's involvement with ASEAN. Finally, an examination will be made of China's external relations with two major other countries, Russia and India.

The final chapter, Chapter 11, will review how China and the US — themselves encapsulated in differing global political and economic dimensions juxtaposed against one another in geographic terms such as 'West', 'East', 'North' and 'South' — might attempt to positively alter the current unstable geoeconomic and geopolitical rifts. The review will present an alternative, optimistic reconciliation scenario to the current intensifying 'Cold War' rhetoric and diplomatic conflict between the US and China: one which may involve the potential for interlocutory roles for others as well as direct US-China reconciliation. The chapter concludes by urging the need for a better understanding of China by the West, and especially the US, and an avoidance of political positioning which simply assumes that the West's liberal individualism, pluralistic party electoral democracy, and free market capitalism is inherently superior to China's political philosophy and praxis. The chapter will reiterate the importance of Western commentators adopting a non-judgemental view of China's cultural values and political philosophy as a key to understanding and accommodating current differences, and achieving peaceful coexistence between China, the US-led West, and the rest of the world.

PART 1

China's Twenty-First Century Rise

Chapter 1

Setting the Scene

We will start with the event which immediately preceded the period 1990 to 2020. The Tiananmen Square 'story' is notorious in Western eyes. The event, and its aftermath, illustrates the reactions to a modernising China as it began to re-emerge in global terms. It also demonstrated the complexity of the events themselves; the evolution of the ultimately hard-line decision taken by the Standing Committee of the CCP Politburo and, despite the widespread international condemnation of the military action, the recognition by the US Administration at the time, if not by the US Congress, of the need to maintain a constructive dialogue with China.

Tiananmen Square

The suppression of the Tiananmen Square protests (Public Broadcasting Service 2019) is routinely condemned as an example of a ruthless, dictatorial regime willing to kill its own people simply for protesting. Leaving aside that this condemnation ignores the fact that other countries, including the US, have been alleged to have been behind similar atrocities, it is nonetheless worth discussing further the reasons for the abrupt, drastic, and violent action in China in 1989. This examination is not in any way to excuse or to justify the actions taken but to explain the contingent circumstances surrounding the Tiananmen Square protests and the reaction of the Chinese government.

One underlying issue, in 1989, was the general discontent in China with the inadequate economic benefits of the earlier Deng reforms. Adding to this discontent was the difficulty of there not being organisations through which protest could be made, including the absence of open civic associations, independent trade unions, and non-state student associations. Had such civic associations existed, then they may have been able to carry to the CCP leadership the level of discontent with the socio-economic situation at the time. This dialogue may have prompted reforms and dissipated the anger felt by some in the general population, and especially by university students, who were all constrained in their ability to protest. These various factors — added to the Leninist political nature of the CCP Politburo — influenced the final decision to impose martial law, with the almost inevitable consequences.

Earlier, in 1986, there had been student protests, supporting wider calls for reform from Fang Lizhi — a professor returned from the US — which many students had supported. During these particular protests, there was a willingness to compromise from both sides — the CCP and the students. In 1989, the student protests started in mid-April. Unfortunately, on this occasion, both sides were riven by factions advocating different strategies. A hard-line Politburo faction, concerned at the student unrest spreading nationally, simply wanted the protests to cease. An editorial in the *People's Daily* on April 26th, 1989 (Tan 1990), effectively the voice of the CCP, called on the protests to end on the basis that they were 'challenging the Party and the State'.

There were attempts to accommodate the students' views, especially by then-General Secretary Zhao Ziyang (Bader 2019). He took a moderate view and made two speeches on April 30th, 1989, effectively disavowing the *People's Daily* editorial. After his intervention, the student protests began to subside outside Beijing.

In celebration of the May 4th protests of 1919 (Dictionary of World History 2020), 50,000 to 100,000 students, on May 4th, 1989, marched into Tiananmen Square and occupied it. During the next two weeks, potential dialogue between the students and the government was still possible. However, splits in the student movement frustrated attempts at dialogue and the student faction wanting confrontation appeared to win out.

It should be said that the students, in 1989, were also not a united group, and the competing factions stretched from moderate to extreme. Later in May of that year, when the Square was occupied by the students on hunger strike, the Beijing Workers Autonomous Federation accused the students of elitism. The Workers Federation was also heavily involved in the protests but had more prosaic concerns, though no less important, about inflation and corruption and were unsympathetic to the narrower student demands (Walder and Gong 1993).

On May 13th, 1989, the students began a hunger strike which gained popular support, not simply among students, but across the country. Despite some contact with the government, the combination of an increasingly hard-line Politburo and the inability of the students to agree on a single policy line resulted in Martial Law being declared on May 20th, 1989. It is not clear what the position of Deng was on the strategy to handle the student protest. However, in 1989 he was Chair of the Central Military Commission, so the final decision was his to implement (China. Org 2010).

Between June 1st and June 3rd, the protests were characterised and publicised, by the CCP, as being counter-revolutionary. By now, of course, in Hong Kong in particular and around the Western world, there was mounting support for the students. This further facilitated the CCP's definition of the 'problem' as a threat to the Chinese state.

Once this decision had been taken — and unless the students in the Square and beyond agreed to concede, leave the square, and abandon their protests — defeat was inevitable. At first, the People's Liberation Army (PLA) was denied entry to the inner area of Beijing by the people sympathetic to the students, but eventually, on June 3rd, the PLA gained access. A complicating factor was that the PLA was not then equipped with non-lethal riot equipment. Hence, in any violent clash, lethal weapons were going to be used (Jencks 1989). Violent clashes on the streets between residents of Beijing and the PLA resulted in up to 300 deaths. There were also many thousands of injuries among the civilian population. Ironically, there were no deaths in Tiananmen Square itself.

There can be nothing other than moral condemnation of the violent suppression of the protests and the killing of civilians. However, it should be noted that the events came at a time when the Soviet Union was beginning to fracture. *Glasnost*,[1] whatever its merits, was failing to preserve the Communist system and Gorbachev's version of *Perestroika*, economic reform, was proving inadequate. It was ironic therefore that Gorbachev had paid a state visit to China from May 15th to May 17th, 1989. Aware of events in the Soviet Union, Deng was not going to make the same mistake of allowing democratic challenges to disturb his economic reforms.

[1]*Glasnost*: allowing a greater degree of political freedom and democracy.

His fear of allowing an unmonitored *Glasnost*, and the collapse of CCP control, was linked to a very Chinese concern rooted in its Confucian history and culture, namely the pervasive fear of *luan* or chaos. The fear is linked to its obverse, the desire to maintain social harmony and collective solidarity, the prime motivation of contemporary Chinese governments.

Youth, including specifically university-educated students, are of course less likely to succumb to the fear of chaos. Political protests everywhere tend to be led by the young, well-educated student populations. For this age group, change is to be welcomed. The inchoate nature of the Chinese autonomous student movement was also testimony to the emotional politics which inhibited tactical awareness and the need to accept constraints on what the student protest was likely to achieve. All these deficiencies were demonstrated among the Chinese student protesters in 1989.

However, there are also lessons for the CCP Politburo. Some figures, such as Zhao, wished to consider the grievances of the protesters and perhaps to make some minor concessions. Others argued that the protest situation — especially when it began to re-emerge after a week or so in mid-May, after quietening after the end of April — required strong action to prevent the protests from spreading and deepening in urban centres across China. The moderates were probably correct to urge conciliation and patience, but to an extent they were thwarted by the recalcitrant faction among the students. In the end, the hard-line core of the CCP Politburo determined the tragic outcome of the protests (Skidmore 2020).

Post-Tiananmen

The year 1990 has been chosen as the starting point for the book, partly because it *was* the year following the brutal suppression of the Tiananmen Square protests. Viewed from the West, this event seemed climactic, being linked to the emerging revolutions in Eastern Europe, and there was intense media coverage and demonstrations against China in many Western countries.

There was also widespread US condemnation of the action and Congress passed legislation imposing sanctions. US sanctions were imposed on sales of military equipment, crime control equipment, and technology transfers. The US government also argued for restricting loans to China by international financial institution, and direct contacts of senior US diplomats with Chinese officials were halted, though such direct contacts did occur in secret (*The New York Times* 1989).

Then-US President George H.W. Bush was concerned to avoid a diplomatic rupture with China, and in the immediate aftermath of the events, he stated at a press conference that this was the time for 'reasoned, careful action that takes into account our long-term interest and recognition of a complex internal situation in China' (Bush 1989). The US needed, he stressed, 'time to look beyond the moment to the important and enduring aspects of this vital relationship'.

Importantly, in relation to trade relations, the annual extension to China of 'most favoured nation status' (MFN) was maintained, despite the US House of Representatives passing legislation removing it. Moreover, despite the intention of President Bill Clinton, who became president in 1993, to cancel the MFN extension, it remained in place. Across East Asia, responses to the events surrounding the Tiananmen Square protests were muted, and though sanctions were reluctantly imposed by Japan, they were soon revoked.

It is worth indicating at this point — to be considered in more detail when subsequently examining Chinese cultural differences to those of the West — that the muted reaction in East Asia, in 1989, towards events in Tiananmen, reflects the cultural characteristics of countries within the region, including China itself, which may appear alien to the Western tradition of liberal individualism.

This philosophical tradition is not shared to the same extent in East Asian countries, including China and Japan. Civic society in these countries is not based especially on individual rights, as in the West, but on identification with a series of collectivities, running from the family up to the State. Moreover, this characteristic is linked to the desire to protect social stability and social harmony, and not just among the ruling elite. This desire for social harmony, combined with an appreciation of collective interests, is also deeply ingrained in the populace. This is a key theme that will run through much of this book.

The muted reactions to the events at Tiananmen, and indeed to the more recent situation in Hong Kong, from most other East Asian governments, also reflects the foreign policy positions of these countries. This involves rarely commenting on the internal affairs of other sovereign states, a form of diplomacy institutionalised by the member countries of the Association of Southeast Asian Nations (ASEAN).

This well-modulated response stands in stark contrast to the outrage among the current Western political class and the media, across a range of countries, about the imposition on Hong Kong of a national security law from Beijing.

This contemporary furore is despite the fact that a similar statute was successfully legislated by Macao in 2009 — a much smaller territory but one in the same position as Hong Kong — in relation to its hand over back to China by Portugal in 1999. In 2003 (Human Rights Watch 2003), Hong Kong was unable to implement a similar, but weaker, statute because of internal opposition.

During the protests against the more recent attempted introduction of such a law, there were no Western media reports of the fact that a Hong Kong government petition was circulated with apparently some 3 million voters (50% of those eligible to vote) approving of a new security law. A new security law was eventually imposed by Beijing in line with Article 23 of the Basic Law (The Basic Law 2020).

The relative equanimity involved of China in apparently dismissing the state violence and deaths involved in ultimately suppressing the student protests in 1989 may seem to demonstrate a rigid utilitarian attitude in China. Not that it is unknown, historically and contemporaneously, in Western governmental political actions, in circumstances when societal stability appears to be threatened! The nature of the suppression of the Black Lives Matter protests in some US states and the even greater violence exhibited by some authorities in the US Civil Rights demonstrations in the 1960s are but two examples. Ultimately it is a matter of degree, not of qualitative difference in potential suppressive action.

Deng and the Push for Economic Change from 1990

The initial impetus for the economic changes began with Deng Xiaoping in 1979 during the post-Mao period. By 1982, the programme of reform initiated by Deng (Kobayashi *et al.* 1999) had begun to show material improvements in both agricultural and industrial production. The reform process was broadened to cover 'reform and opening', that is, reform of the domestic economic system and opening the economy to foreign trade. The fruits of this reform drive only started to become evident in the 1990s, especially in the gradual development of agricultural land reform and the developments of agri-businesses. Though there were reports of some protests over the land reform, it has been argued that traditions of social protests as means of achieving resolution of the negative impacts of reform are characteristic of China, and should not necessarily be considered as socially dysfunctional (O'Brien and Li 2006).

In 1992, buoyed by the relative success of the initial approach, Deng made a renewed push for market reforms, stating that China's key task in the 1990s was to create a 'socialist market economy'. Over the period 1990 to 2004, China's economy grew at an average rate of 10% per year.

Deng had spent 50 tumultuous years in the CCP before becoming China's pre-eminent leader from 1978 to 1989. On reaching the top, Deng became convinced that China needed modernisation and technological innovation (initially much of this might need to be imported). He saw an opportunity to creatively reform much of the chaotic economic system he had, ironically, helped Mao to build. He was also willing to authorise the violent suppression of the Tiananmen protests, where others in the CCP leadership saw the potential of protests widening to threaten the stability of China. It might be argued that Deng's concern was more focused on protecting his economic reforms.

Deng never held the official high office of China's President — simply being known as the 'Paramount Leader'.[2] He retired in 1992 and died in 1997. Following his departure, his socialist market economy reforms continued under President Jiang Zemin from 1993 to 2003. Another important economic reformer during the post-Deng period was Zhu Rongji. Zhu had made a name for himself as a widely-celebrated and dynamic Mayor of Shanghai from 1987 to 1991. Later, he was appointed as Vice Premier, and then China's Premier from 1998 to 2003. The reform process, perhaps more subdued, continued from 2003 to 2013 when Xi Jinping took power as President, General Secretary, and Paramount Leader.

Economic Growth and Global Emergence: 1990 to 2013

During this period, China's development was characterised by the three-pronged Deng approach of modernisation, technological innovation, and

[2]The designation 'Paramount Leader' is informal, but indicates that there is one pre-eminent politician in China. It should be noted that Deng Xiaoping never held either of the two highest offices of the CCP — General Secretary or President. Deng and Xi Jinping held/hold the position of Chair of the Central Military Commission.

openness to foreign trade and foreign corporate investment, albeit on terms ensuring majority control by the state and state companies. Economic growth, under the successors to Deng, continued to accelerate, despite some cyclical variation.

The opening of China in global economic terms, the demonstrable increase in the comparative size of its economy, and its gradually increasing weight in terms of global trade, meant Western companies, including major US companies, became increasingly involved with China. Joint companies were set up, though always with majority control by the Chinese partner. This involvement, and China's US-supported participation in international fora (it joined the WTO[3] in 2001, following a decade of attempts to do so), was proof of the apparent success of Deng's initiative.

The accession to the WTO was not an unmitigated blessing for China. The terms of accession were harsh for a developing country. The US, supported by the EU, imposed unprecedented conditions on China. As Garten (2001) indicated at the time, Beijing committed to tariff rates lower than any other developing country, and it was not permitted the use of key subsidies that the WTO normally permits for developing countries. China allowed other governments to shut out its goods with much less justification than required under existing international trade law. Other developing countries were permitted to retain import restrictions on textile and clothing products.

The decision by China to join the WTO, despite the harsh terms imposed for its accession, represented a significant milestone in China's development as a global trade player, with considerable implications for its domestic economic development policy. There had, nonetheless, been considerable debate among the Chinese governing elites, at provincial and local levels as well as centrally in the CCP, as to the costs and benefits of acceding to the WTO, given the onerous terms which were eventually agreed.

In 1997/98, China's apparent backwardness in shunning the development of financial markets and liberalising its capital account, unlike many of its Southeast Asian neighbours, had turned into an advantage. It escaped the ravages of the Asian financial crisis, essentially because, given the stage of its economic development, most inward investment in China was

---

[3] The WTO, set up in 1995, is an intergovernmental organisation that is concerned with the regulation of international trade between nations.

principally physical direct investment rather than portfolio investment. Four major East Asian economies — South Korea, Thailand, Indonesia, and Malaysia — allowed their principally foreign-owned (mostly private) debt to balloon. Debt/GDP ratios rose by two-thirds, from 100% in 1993 to around 167% by 1997. The use of private capital to fuel exaggerated and unsustainable real estate investment was then followed by the sudden withdrawal of foreign capital, leading to substantial financial crises in these countries.

The question being asked by internal CCP critics, in respect of WTO membership, was whether opening-up to the West might yet prove damaging to China? However, given China's then reliance on export-led growth, the reasons for joining the WTO became clearer. Two-thirds of its exports in the early 2000s went to the three key developed country markets of the US, Japan, and the EU.

Nonetheless, during the 1990s and early 2000s, though strong exports generated economic growth and lowered inflation, domestic demand remained sluggish. Despite this, a key figure in the central governing elite — the economic reformer Zhu Rongji (Naughton 2001) mentioned previously — became Premier in 1998. He strongly argued for a continuation of a moderate path to liberalisation and continued, if careful, opening to the world, and oversaw both market reforms and a vastly improved banking structure. Despite his privatising and banking reforms, Zhu supported strong, centralised over-seeing of the economy and business. In some ways he anticipated the later 're-centralising' approach of Xi Jinping, following a loosening of central control between 2003 and 2013.

China's Changing Trade Growth Patterns

Over time, the pattern of Chinese trade has grown and changed. By 2019 it was the world's largest exporter by value and represented, in US dollar terms, 13% of total global exports. About half (49%) of Chinese exports by value in 2019 was delivered to fellow Asian countries (with 5.7% going to Japan), while 16.8% were sold to the US. Another 19.9% went to clients in Europe. If we look at Chinese imports in 2019, then 55.4% of China's total imports by value in 2019 were purchased from fellow Asian countries. European trade partners accounted for 18.1% of imported goods bought by China. Of overall Chinese imports,

North America contributed only 8%. Electrical machinery and mineral fuels accounted for 40% of total imports (World Top Exports 2020).

Hence, leaving aside the, to an extent, problematic statistical issue of Hong Kong trade,[4] the changing pattern of trade is clear. There has been a substantial shift in trade focus towards Asian countries. Given the size of China's exports and imports, this phenomenon means that the centre of gravity of global trade is shifting substantially to this area of the world, though interestingly only 3% of China's exports go to India.

In relation to the US-China trade conflict, from 2005 to 2013, the Renminbi appreciated by 34% on a nominal basis against the dollar and by 42% on a real (inflation-adjusted) basis, via a tacit agreement between the US and China (Congressional Research Service 2011).

Finally, it needs to be understood that since 2006 China has steadily been reducing its dependence on trade — from 65% of GDP in 2006 to 36% in 2019 (World Bank 2019b), as its own personal consumption and public consumption gradually expanded, reaching 38% and 18% respectively in 2019 (Paribas 2019).

China Replaces Japan as Principal US 'Trade Adversary'

In the 1980s, it was Japan that challenged US trade and also US technological dominance. The US, unwilling to accept industrial inferiority, engaged in a trade war with Japan — one as serious as the current industrial technology battle with China. The missing dimension was the absence of a major ideological challenge. While Japan's statist approach to its economic development *was* strongly criticised by the US, essentially, Japan was simply a more efficient and aggressive capitalist competitor. Japan was subject to a further charge of currency manipulation by the US. Various adversarial trade disputes occurred during the 1970s, 1980s, and the 1990s, involving textiles, automobiles, and computers. Voluntary export restrictions were introduced by Japan, and there were continuing disputes over the use by Japan of regulatory restrictions on automobile parts. Pressures from the US led to Japanese companies setting up in the US and sourcing US auto-parts, despite their being higher-cost than Japanese parts (Satake 1999).

---

[4]Around 17% of Chinese goods going to Hong Kong are re-exported to other countries.

A significant dollar appreciation of the Yen against the US dollar was the subject of the Plaza Accord[5] reached in 1985 between the members of the G5 — the US, Japan, West Germany, France, and the UK. Germany was also accused of currency manipulation, but the D-mark against the dollar did not appreciate as substantially as that of the Yen. This currency accord paved the later 2004 currency accord between the US and China, which led to a similar appreciation of the Chinese currency against the US dollar and it being tied to a basket of currencies, including the dollar. There seemed no real evidence that Chinese currency manipulation was the reason for the US trade deficit (Morrison and Labonte 2009).

From 2004 onwards, China gradually became the main country to which the US turned its attention, and it began to regard China as an increasing threat to its technology and trade pre-eminence. Earlier engagement gradually moved to containment. Containment was the principal policy towards China during the 2012–2016 Obama administration.

From Containment to Challenge

A decade and a half from the engagement policy of 2004, China is now regarded as a far wider threat to US political influence in Asia, and as a potential ideological enemy. A more aggressive US foreign, trade, and defence policy has emerged over the past four years. There are still a minority in the US who support an engagement policy, but their voices are drowned out by those who support a stronger stance towards China. This has been especially marked under Trump's erratic, blundering approach towards China. In 2020, as is argued later, a committed ideological attack on China is being mounted by the US, though partly cloaked in the thinly veiled guise of achieving 'fair competition'. There seems little likelihood of a major change of policy direction under President Joe Biden's administration.

Within the US defence, security, and foreign policy establishments, the containment policy appears to have been overtly abandoned in favour of political challenge, confrontation, and direct resistance to

---

[5] The Plaza Accord was a 1985 agreement among the G-5 nations — France, Germany, the United States, the United Kingdom, and Japan — to manipulate exchange rates by depreciating the US dollar relative to the Japanese yen and the German Deutsche mark.

China's current trade, external economic development, and technological progress. China is now regarded as an existential threat to US geopolitical hegemony.

This increasing hostility towards China by the US has coincided with a more assertive Chinese foreign policy, under Xi, towards the US, though carefully modulated. This policy has been accompanied by the expansion of China's Asian financial and trade interventions, such as the Asian Infrastructure Investment Bank (AIIB), and the development of the Belt and Road Initiative in Southeast Asia and beyond.

Whether or not justified by China's actions, the current trade war with China, which Trump initiated, also includes the use of financial and trade sanctions against not only China but also US nominal allies and, indeed, often US companies operating in China and elsewhere. Aggressive trade and industrial policies are accompanied by an aggressive overall foreign policy towards China, which was promulgated in 2020 in an ideological manner by Mike Pompeo (ex-CIA Director) as then-US Secretary of State for Foreign Affairs. In practical trade policy terms, the Biden administration is likely to pursue a similar policy, although with perhaps a change of tone.

Politics and Technology

An example of the 'aggressive trade strategy' in the area of technology is the US position on the use of Huawei 5G equipment being ordered by various European countries. It was demonstrated in the case of the UK, where the British government had already decided in 2019 to continue with Huawei telecommunication equipment. The ostensible, albeit invalid, reason is the suggestion that Huawei posed a national security risk to the UK, and thereby to the US. The UK eventually succumbed to intense pressure from the US and has now completely excluded Huawei from its developing 5G networks at a cost estimate removal of around £1 billion (Lloyd 2020).

Leaving aside the underlying political motivation of the US in launching a trade war on China, and its blatant attempt to damage Huawei (see Chapter 2) by whatever means possible, it seems evident that the commitment of the US to capitalism and market forces does not extend to international trade competition. Maybe, except for its relatively brief period of global trade dominance, it never did? Any student of the latter quarter of the nineteenth century will instantly recognise the protectionist instincts of the US (Lloyd 2020).

Aside from the blatant abuse of US commercial power, this and other measures risk further damaging the integrated global trading system at a time when the world economy is undergoing a significant global downturn during the COVID-19 pandemic. Yet this is precisely what the US is accusing China of doing. It should be noted that despite US criticism of China not being open to competition within China itself, Huawei's two main rivals Ericsson[6] and Nokia[7] have both been awarded 5G contracts in China.

The world is one where companies are part of integrated supply chains that support the global economy. The problem with the US approach is that the strong economic position of China in the global integrated environment and its likely strong, though usually carefully calibrated response, may push China into a less open trading approach in relation to Western technology companies.

If these actions were simply a matter of commercial 'bullying' by the US, one might hope for a less autarkic, post-Trump era in US trade policy. However, US commercial policy appears to be partly driven by a wider and deeper political concern — emanating from the political establishment in Washington DC — at the increasing global economic and political influence of China. Insofar as this is an attempt to defend the US geopolitical empire, in an era when a multi-polar world appeared to be emerging, this is both foolish and dangerous.

Notwithstanding the recent assertive responses of China to the Huawei ban from a Chinese Foreign Affairs spokesperson, the global polity requires, from President Biden and from President Xi, a return to constructive engagement. At a minimum, the trade war initiated by Trump which has enveloped Huawei, TikTok, and other Chinese companies needs a truce, if only to protect the rest of the world's trading nations and technology companies (including major US companies) and the progress of global innovation, in relation to 5G and other technology areas.

---

[6]Ericsson wins 5G contracts with China Mobile, China Telecom, and China Unicom (Ericsson 2020).

[7]Nokia announced that it has signed a five-year networking infrastructure and big data analytics agreement with leading real estate group Central China Holdings Co Ltd. (Nokia 2020).

However, such a re-engagement with China to avoid further damage to global trade and to take advantage of China's technological lead in certain areas, seems highly unlikely at this point in time.

Politics and Human Rights: Hong Kong

Another arena in which the US and Western resistance policy towards China is deployed is in relation to human rights. However, in China and indeed in many other Asian countries, civic society is not based on the individual or on individual rights to the degree it is in the West, but on identification with a series of collectivities, running from the family up to the State.

Moreover, this characteristic is linked to the desire to protect social stability and social harmony, above freedom to dissent. This position will be discussed in philosophical and cultural terms in Chapters 5 and 6. For the present, it will be useful to illustrate the point by briefly discussing Western attitudes to the Chinese position on Hong Kong.

First, the situation in Hong Kong is being used to accuse China of suppressing the right of peaceful protest and using a new draconian security law to prevent further protests. This position is supported by the Western media interviewing dissidents who have been forced to flee Hong Kong. Others, it is said, are in hiding. A few protesters, one waving an independence flag, were initially arrested under the new law, though others have been subsequently charged with offences.

It should be observed that the imposition of the new security law does not, as some have alleged, breach Hong's Kong's mini-constitution, known as 'the Basic Law', which was agreed by China at the time of the handover from British rule in 1997. This constitution underpins international legal provisions, such as the 1984 Sino-UK Joint Declaration on Hong Kong during the 50-year transition period of 'one country, two systems'. Accordingly, the Constitution does make provision for a Chinese national security law to be introduced for the territory, just as it was put into place for Macau in 2009 without any disruptions.

The characterisation by Western governments of the Hong Kong authorities' actions to stem the protest movement as breaching human rights ignores some other salient points. Since July 2019, there have been protests that rapidly escalated into riots, with rioters throwing petrol bombs into shops, police stations, and at the police. Throughout the chaos, not a single rioter was killed by the police. This outcome might be contrasted with the Black Lives Matter protests in the US, which led to a number of deaths.

The Hong Kong democratic movement, currently substantially made up of student activists, is highly organised. Its activists appear to be trained and well-equipped, from executing propaganda, forming alliances with the press, to tactical warfare with the police. The protest movement was well-funded, with financial support of between US$600,000 to US$800,000 from the US National Endowment for Democracy (NED 2020), as their website confirms. The NED has been active in Hong Kong for some years.

Contemporary complaints, from the UK, about a lack of democracy in Hong Kong ring rather hollow. Throughout its 150-year colonial rule of Hong Kong, including when Britain was promoting democracy around the world during and after the Cold War democracy was never implemented in Hong Kong.

In June 2020, Chinese media (Xinhuanet 2020d) reported that 2.9 million people signed a petition supporting the new national security law, though most Western media did not report the event. Given Hong Kong's social problems relating to job security, unaffordable house prices, and high rents are not resolved, it seems likely that a majority of its residents' priorities are likely to lie in resolving these problems, rather than engaging in violent protests aimed increasingly at subversion of the position of Hong Kong as part of China.

The political issue here is related to two issues: a) how representative of Hong Kong society are the (principally) student protesters and b) how constrained are the freedom of assembly and freedom of expression by the terms of the law.

First, given that the grievance is purported as one affecting the whole Hong Kong population, if reports of the petition are correct, it does not appear that the violent protests can necessarily be perceived to be representative of a significant part of the population. Against this point it may be argued that during the past two-to-three years, pro-Beijing candidates have performed poorly in district elections. However, there does appear to be external foreign influence being exerted by the US, as indicated above with reference to the NED.

Second, in relation to the national security law,[8] the law covers the offences of secession, subversion, and organisation and perpetration of

[8]The Basic Law of The Hong Kong Special Administrative Region of The People's Republic of China (2020). Published by the Constitutional and Mainland Affairs Bureau Hong Kong Special Administrative Region Government.

terrorist activities or actions endangering national security. It is difficult to argue that these are unusual. They are standard national security offences included in the laws of many countries.

In defining the legal position, the issue of human rights is covered by Article 4 of the new law.

> 'Human rights shall be respected and protected in safeguarding national security in the Hong Kong Special Administrative Region. The rights and freedoms, including the freedoms of speech, of the press, of publication, of association, of assembly, of procession and of demonstration, which the residents of the Region enjoy under the Basic Law of the Hong Kong Special Administrative Region and the provisions of the International Covenant on Civil and Political Rights and the International Covenant on Economic, Social and Cultural Rights as applied to Hong Kong, shall be protected in accordance with the law'.

Perhaps the initial subsiding of the violent protests — especially advocacy of full independence from China — will remove some of the 'oxygen' fuelling the Western 'hysteria' about Hong Kong. However, any event which may occur and is capable of being manipulated to support the resistance to China policy will no doubt be so used. Western, and especially US, antagonism towards China has deeper roots than criticising China's introduction of the national security law for Hong Kong and the handling of the Hong Kong student protests since the law's inception in June 2020.

Current US Policy for China

The previous reference to the US-led attacks on China regarding trade and technology issues (paralleling similar attacks on Japan in the 1980s), which clearly move the US position from 'Containment to Challenge', would seem to be a conventional, if unjustified, declaration of a trade war. This might be so argued but for the public announcement issued by the White House in May 2020 and titled 'United States Strategic Approach to the People's Republic of China'. The paper (White House 2020) argues that:

> 'The PRC's rapid economic development and increased engagement with the world did not lead to convergence with the citizen-centric, free and open order as the United States had hoped. The CCP has chosen

instead to exploit the free and open rules-based order and attempt to reshape the international system in its favour. Beijing openly acknowledges that it seeks to transform the international order to align with CCP interests and ideology. The CCP's expanding use of economic, political, and military power to compel acquiescence from nation states harms vital American interests and undermines the sovereignty and dignity of countries and individuals around the world'.

The 16-page paper clearly indicates that the US intends:

> 'To respond to Beijing's challenge, the Administration has adopted a competitive approach to the PRC, based on a clear-eyed assessment of the CCP's intentions and actions, a reappraisal of the United States' many strategic advantages and shortfalls, and a tolerance of greater bilateral friction'.
>
> and
>
> 'We aim to: 1) protect the American people, homeland, and way of life; 2) promote American prosperity; 3) preserve peace through strength; and 4) advance American influence'.

The US position may be understandable, given its perceived weakening geopolitical position. Its judgement — which it has always held since it began the process of 'engagement' with President Nixon in 1972 — is that the Chinese political system and political philosophy is diametrically opposed to the US version of a liberal individualist and democratic, pluralist party system. The US honestly believes its political ideology to be universally superior and that it should be adopted by not only the West but by all countries in the world.

US willingness to engage with China suggests the paper:

> 'Was largely premised on a hope that deepening engagement would spur fundamental economic and political opening in the PRC and lead to its emergence as a constructive and responsible global stakeholder, with a more open society'.

This policy of engagement is now abandoned by the US.

It is, in fact, always naïve for the US political elites to believe that the People's Republic of China would abandon its pursuance of 'socialism with Chinese characteristics', in Deng's phraseology and now reiterated by Xi. For a period, while China was preoccupied with managing its quasi-capitalistic development, the US appeared to believe that fundamental political change was possible. The advent of the accession of Xi Jinping — who, in practice, appears to be not more despotic than Deng in his governance approach — has persuaded the US that the 'democratic' changes they sought are not going to happen. Hence, the switch by the US to an apparently analogous position adopted in the long and ultimately successful ideological Cold War against the Soviet Union.

The problem for the US is that China is not the Soviet Union. It does not proselytise for Communism in the same manner as the Soviet Union; there are no sister Chinese Marxist Communist parties in the US and elsewhere; its foreign policy demonstrates a partnership approach and its military policies are defensive in nature (as the US accepts, see Chapter 11); and, above all, its pre-eminent concern is the continuation of China's own economic development.

Moreover, China's population is one-fifth of the world, it is the second-largest global economy after the US, and it has a dynamic, technological company sector. Its preoccupation is with developing and safeguarding its economic development at home and abroad, not seeking to impose a hegemonic global dominance.

For these reasons, the new US strategy, though understandable, is unlikely to be successful in either converting or engendering China's collapse. The hope is that for the foreseeable future (though the potential impact of climate change renders any prediction uncertain), the US and China should be seeking to avoid further conflict, including ideological conflict, which could potentially slide into military conflict. The aim should be to achieve peaceful coexistence. The possibility of this latter objective being realised is discussed in the final chapter of the book.

Chapter 2

Technological Development

Introduction

China's commitment to rapid technological development, especially over the past decade, has been sustained on the Chinese government's view that technology development is the key to future global strength. Technology, it believes, is the way to maintain continued rapid internal economic growth and to deliver the advancement of a distinctive representation of China in the modern world.

It is recognised, even by the US, that in certain areas of technology and science, China has an outstanding record of both development and, importantly, implementation. Indeed, part of the US strategy towards China is to damage the international capability of prominent Chinese technology companies such as Huawei, and to hinder Chinese technological progress in whatever ways it can. For China, on the other hand, technology development is seen as both facilitating an increasing pace of national economic growth and prosperity and of presenting an external vision of China to the world as a country and economic system to be respected and emulated by the developing countries of the world.

Interestingly, on China's technology and economic front in relation to US reactions, there are strong similarities between the positions of Japan (in the 1980s) and China (now), and between Toshiba (then) and Huawei (now). In the 1980s, the US accused Japan of 'state capitalism', technology theft, an artificially depreciated value of the Yen, and unfair trade practices, especially dumping.[1] This conflict was resolved via the Plaza Accord (Frankel 2015). The difference was that, in military and security terms, Japan was a US 'satellite state', and therefore its resilience in the face of the US attacks was far less than China's is now. Ironically, in 2020, Japan still has a trade surplus with the US and is the third-largest economy in the world.

One positive aspect of the US trade and technology attacks on Japan was that the external pressure enabled it to overcome internal resistance to structural change, and the country was able to introduce 'technology networks' into Japan. US trade and financial pressure could likely lead to increased efficiency and performance of Chinese companies. Meanwhile, in the US, substantial and sustained state investment via the defence budget may enable the US to maintain global leadership in the key semiconductor design and production sectors!

China's progress in technological development and innovation is substantial but, like Japan in the 1980s, there is some need for structural change, especially in state-owned enterprises (SOEs) (Naughton 2007). Nonetheless, in the space of 10 years, China has doubled the size of its digital economy — taking account of all associated sectors involved and not simply the digital sector itself — from 15% in 2008 to 30% in 2018. However, this still leaves China behind Japan, the UK, and the US (59%) (Zhang and Chen 2019).

There are a variety of technology development tasks that China has set for itself. In 2015, the 'Made in China 2025' Plan; in 2017, the 'New Generation Artificial Intelligence Development Plan'; and, in 2020, the 'Digital Transformation Partnership Action Plan', are all indicators of this development.

Concerning the manufacturing of integrated circuits, the crucial base component of the digital revolution, the application of the National Integrated Circuits Plan 2018, known as the 'Guidelines to Promote National Integrated Circuit Industry' and with a fund of US$150 billion attached, is the main driver.

The various plans are all focused on applying the technologies to 10 strategic manufacturing sectors and securing the global leadership of China in advanced industries such as AI, robotics, aviation, electric vehicles, biotechnology, among others. The plans are driven by investment in

---

[1] Dumping occurs when a country or company exports a product at a price that is lower in the foreign importing market than the price in the exporter's domestic market.

research and development by both state and private sector companies, research institutes, and universities.

One aim is the development of smart manufacturing, combining the internet with wireless sensors and robotics to improve manufacturing efficiency, quality, and productivity. China intends to move up the value-added chain, repositioning itself from being a low-cost manufacturer to being a direct competitor to nations like South Korea, Japan, and Germany (Zhang and Chen 2019).

The ambition is clear. It is worth exploring what progress is being made in achieving these objectives, and how China is attempting to deal with the barriers to technology development recently erected by the US.

Research and Innovation (R&D)

The average R&D intensity (defined as the ratio of R&D investment to total sales revenue) of all sizeable Chinese companies was around 3%, only half of company average spending in the US. However, among the world's 2,500 most-R&D-intensive companies, R&D spending by Chinese companies grew 18.8% in 2017, compared with 7.2% in the US and a 3% decline in Japan, suggesting that Chinese companies are catching up rapidly (European Commission 2017). It is, however, crucial for success that China enhances the capacity of all its indigenous companies to be able to absorb incremental technological improvements. Improving the managerial capacity of Chinese firms is critical for enhancing the quality of patents, innovation, and technological upgrading. Such capacity is vital through process and product innovation, R&D, patenting, and firm competitiveness and productivity.

In East Asia's newly industrialised economies, the organisational and managerial capacity of firms to acquire, learn, and apply technology appear to be more important than conventional R&D in promoting innovation. At least 30% of the differences in total factor productivity (TFP) among countries appear to be related to variations in management quality (OECD 2018).

Chinese top firms are among the largest in the world. However, none made the list of Thomson Reuters Top 100 Global Technology Leaders (Thomson Reuters 2018), which was led by mainly US and Japanese firms. How much of this ranking may be down to unconscious bias is unclear, but the rapid growth of these sizeable Chinese companies, based on a large, captive home market, suggests that managerial competence may take more time to catch up with international peers. Areas that are important for continuing innovation include long-run strategic planning and human resources management.

However, there is also evidence, in respect of the key issue of the diffusion of innovation throughout sectors, that it is the overall national or regional 'systems innovation' response which is of crucial importance. Here, China's combination of state and business collaborative structures should provide a strong basis for future action.

In the Systems Innovation (SI) (Edquist 2001) approach, innovation does not take place in isolation. A variety of actors within the system, interact, cooperate, and learn. Institutions and 'hard' motivators (regulations, laws, executive orders, and such like) and 'soft' motivators (cultural norms, values, and so on) modify economic behaviour and performance, and formulate the 'rules of the game'. Hence, under the SI approach, asymmetries of information and behaviour are encouraged, unlike neo-classical economic theory, where the objective is eliminating asymmetries and seeking perfect information and market equilibrium.

Within the system, mechanisms to support the diffusion of new and existing technologies will be required. These will range from broad management extension services to more sophisticated R&D institutions, technology information and collaboration platforms, and public-private co-operations.

Some examples of this approach can be found in Europe. For instance, technology centres, such as those in Catalonia, Spain, arose from public-private partnerships established to solve technological problems and develop solutions for specific industrial sectors or clusters. The centres tend to specialise in specific technologies and are managed as a network. A similar approach is used in Germany with the Fraunhofer Institutes[2] in Germany — a network of 60 private non-profit research institutes which undertake contract research for the government and for private business organisations.

In this manner, China's top-down approach to promoting innovation, which is already being piloted, could be complemented with a more collaborative, coordinated systems approach.

China could also derive lessons learned from the EU's 'smart specialisation' concept (European Commission 2016). Smart specialisation is

[2]Fraunhofer Institutes and Research Units: www.fraunhofer.de› institutes.

about prioritising public support for innovation in economic activities that may not yet be fully 'visible' yet have the largest developmental potential based on an economy's current comparative advantages.

China has already reaped huge benefits from expanding its international R&D cooperation. China is active in the Human Genome Project,[3] which has resulted in Chinese enterprises and academics collaborating with the world's leading geneticists, moving the country to prominence in global genomics research. This has been clearly demonstrated in relation to COVID-19 research (Nature 2020). China could therefore benefit further from participation in the Human Frontier Science Programme[4]. The programme has been operating since 1990, with a Secretariat based in Strasbourg, France.

Finally, besides China's drive for innovation, it will at the same time need to prepare for growing technological disruptions through the combination of policies linked to the promotion of R&D-based and non-R&D-based innovation. In this context it will be essential to provide for continuous upgrading of skills, side by side with the innovation, as part of the system process.

IP Rights and Patents

Over the past five years or so, Chinese companies have become a growing issuer of patents while taking advantage of other companies' patents. This is a useful indicator of R&D activity. However, there are signs of slowing in the past couple of years: 'utility' patents have hitherto represented a large proportion of the patents filed in China, where the majority of the world's patents are filed (World Intellectual Property Organisation 2016). The past use of utility patents has been valuable for China in the 'catch-up' phase of industrial development, even though most of these types of patent (61%) survive no more than five years. In its current development phase, a further decline will be expected, as the need for them in more advanced manufacturing is reduced.

As China's technological lead in certain areas of technology matures, it is expected that the revenue it will derive from issuing patents will increase considerably. Patents (Adcock and Ordish 2008) are an area

[3] Human-genome-project: www.genome.gov

[4] Human Frontier Science Program: www.hfsp.org

where there is a considerable international dimension. China, aside from its commitments under the WTO, is also a signatory to the Berne Convention on copyrights.

Chinese patent law operates under the 'first to file' principle — that is, if two people apply for a patent on an identical invention, the first one to file the application will be awarded the patent. Intellectual Property Rights are covered by the Chinese Patent Law. The law's design rights provisions are similar to those for utility models, with protection for a maximum of 10 years.

The main options for enforcing IP rights in China include administrative action, customs seizure, and civil litigation, while the State may prosecute offenders under criminal law. However, negotiation and mediation are very much a part of the Chinese business practice. Many IP disputes are solved through dispute resolution, either before or after going to court. International arbitration rights and practice are now incorporated into Chinese law. Hence, remedies are available to foreign firms in case of contractual disputes (see Chapter 5).

Digital Adoption Rates

China's digital adoption rate is higher than the average for upper-middle-income countries, according to the World Bank's Digital Adoption Index (World Bank 2016a). There is also a large gap between China and OECD countries in the extent of digital adoption among businesses, and it has lower shares of business websites and overall lower internet access. For example, the percentage of enterprises with a website is highest in Shanghai, at 62%, but this is still lower than in 26 of the 33 OECD countries (World Bank 2016a) countries. These statistics may partly be a function of high mobile access in China, as opposed to the use of computers. On the other hand, digital adoption in the state sector is around the average OECD adoption rate. This is not surprising given the importance placed on the provision of online public services and core government administrative services.

Digital adoption, however, has a broader definition and covers the adoption of digitisation across the production of investment and consumer goods, as well as personal communications and business to business communications. Indeed, China is committed to developing global leadership in the adoption and use of digital technology throughout its domestic economy and beyond, as in the Digital Silk Road (DSR) to be discussed in subsequent chapters.

However, the ability of China to adopt digitisation widely in the future will also depend on the ability of China to develop its own digital design and production facilities. This is important in the short-run insofar as US sanctions are now being applied to some of its leading digital players. For this reason, it is worth taking a close look at the progress China is making on this frontier and examining the industrial area of integrated circuits production (sometimes referred to as 'chips').

Integrated Circuits: Design and Production

As indicated, integrated circuits (IC), and semiconductors which are the components of the circuits, represent the essential underpinning of China's digital revolution (Lapedus 2020). Success in this area of technology is crucial in making progress towards achieving the technological dominance objectives set by China under Xi Jinping. Hence, this sector will be examined in some detail.

Between 2014 and 2018, Chinese total IC revenue grew by a compound annual growth rate (CAGR) of 25% and accounted for some 20% of the global total. The revenue from electronic design automation (EDA) accounted for 39% of total Chinese IC revenue; the revenue from integrated circuit manufacturing accounted for about 28%; the revenue from integrated circuit packaging and testing, the low-value end of the semiconductor industry, was 34%.

In addition, China remains dependent on IC imports — in 2018 these accounted for 84% of domestic demand while 80% of onshore production was in the hands of foreign companies, with Chinese output also concentrated in the lower end ICs. Here the vulnerability of the Chinese tech sector has been exposed by US sanctions that limit Chinese access to American technology, elements of which are utilised by the key producers of high-end ICs and their semiconductor components. In turn, this threatens the underpinning of the whole Chinese tech sector and its digital revolution. However, US companies have been putting pressure on their government to relax the rules. Qualcomm and AMD have, in November 2020, been granted licences to supply Huawei with 4G chips but not 5G. Intel also has been granted a licence to supply laptop and server processors.

In 2018, the import volume of integrated circuits in China was 417.60 billion units, increasing by 11% annually; the export volume was 217.10 billion units, increasing by 6% annually. In value terms, China's trade deficit in integrated circuits reached US$227.40 billion in 2018.

However, the US sanctions are a double-edged sword. In 2018, Chinese enterprises contributed more than half the sales revenue of major US chip enterprises such as Qualcomm, Broadcom, Micron, and Marvell. US sanctions also imply serious economic damage for such major IC suppliers to China as Taiwanese-based Taiwan Semiconductor Manufacturing Corporation (TSMC) and pose major political questions for that island's government. The collateral damage of American attempts to sabotage Chinese IC production will adversely affect the IC integrated global value chains. The chip industry is by far the most complex and globally integrated of any industry, with multiple stages and repeated border crossings. This integration explains the reluctance of US ICT companies to follow the lead of the US Trump government. The Biden administration may be more susceptible to the lobbying by US corporates.

Nonetheless, while China is becoming a major IC production player, it has significant deficiencies in all stages of IC production, out of line with its high domestic demand. In 2018, China only accounted for 10% of global capacity in design companies, 12% in assembly and testing, and only 7% in early-stage manufacture (Deloitte 2020b).

Essentially, there are four types of IC companies: design companies, manufacture companies, assembly and testing companies, and integrated device manufacturing companies (IDMs). There is no sign yet of a Chinese integrated circuit design and manufacturing (IDM) company along the lines of Intel.

The cause of the inadequate productive capacity in China, given its large current and future internal demand for ICs, lies in its current heavy reliance for the majority of its capacity on imports. The other route is through company association agreements to manufacture inside China, for instance, with US and Taiwanese companies. The damaging impact of US sanctions will provide further problems for China, though the impact will also accelerate the rate of growth of the areas where China has some capacity. But overall, they may slow the development of China's indigenous IC industry, and mean reliance on other countries, who are likely to be caught themselves by US sanctions, including Taiwan.

Irrespective of the attempts by the US to sabotage China's prospects of developing its own IC capacity, China's plans and latest updates indicate a strong defensive strategy to expand in key areas of the IC industry beyond what is indicated above. For instance, Liu Dai, the rotating chairman of the China Semiconductor Industry Association noted: 'The industry has registered steady growth over the past few years as its scale and competitiveness increased' (Xinhuanet 2019a).

Statistics from the association showed that the industry's total sales revenue surged 20.7% year on year to reach Chinese Yuan (CNY) 653.2 billion (about US$91.7 billion) in 2018, in the face of booming demand. Indeed, the sheer size and growth rate of the Chinese market is both a major engine of growth for the industry and a vehicle for rapid technical progress. Liu also noted that:

> 'Only twenty percent of the domestic demand for IC products and services have been met by Chinese IC companies, more efforts can be made to cater to booming domestic demand, which in turn will become another growth engine for the companies'.

The challenge for China's IC industry is clear. The industry's current reliance on global and especially US players has to be reduced. Whatever China's genuine commitment is to being a willing participant in the global trading order, a more autarkic position will have to be sought in this area of technology.

Electronic Design Automation Tools

Up to 33.6% of Chinese IC companies specialise in IC packaging, which makes wafers into independent computer chips. This ratio, in line with the global average, indicates that China is continuing to make progress in this area, admittedly a low-value sector. Moreover, though currently a low-value area of IC production, innovation in chip design for applications will require system architects to explore physical, electrical, and thermal design options at the system level before committing to final architectures, including packaging. In addition, this will provide opportunities for electronic design automation (EDA) tools, already an identified priority for China, given the potential growth in this market, albeit from a low base of around 2% within the IC total industry market. The EDA market is driven by the end-market for a wide range of appliances (Global Market Insights 2016).

A major strength of China lies in the sheer size of its domestic market. This means that the demand from China's large number of consumer and home appliances and system manufacturers can demonstrate the need for improvements in chip design in relation the application of AI. This process can, in turn, further develop AI, creating a virtuous circle. One such appliance company is Gree Electrical Appliance Inc[5], the world's largest residential air-conditioner manufacturer. The company offers two types of air conditioners: household air conditioners and commercial air conditioners. The company also produces electric fans, water dispensers, heaters, rice cookers, air purifiers, water kettles, humidifiers, and induction cookers. This demand will facilitate the expansion of the IC supply sector. Another important driver of demand in the consumer electronics market is the need to increase the battery life of devices, such as smartphones, wearables, smart home devices and so forth.

Although the global EDA market is currently dominated by three major players — Synopsis, Cadence, and Mentor (owned by Siemens), there are many companies involved. China's strategy is to combine, under state-supervision, the current Chinese EDA companies to increase their manufacturing capacities and abilities to compete with foreign rivals. Through this consolidation, which will be provided with any necessary state funds, new Chinese semiconductor giants are emerging. They will be able to jointly and substantially augment domestic production, with an anticipated 10% growth rate per annum between 2020 and 2025, thereby reducing China's reliance on imports.

The task is formidable. Currently, 95% of China's EDA market is controlled by foreign enterprises. This is because of the nascent nature of the Chinese industry, notwithstanding its high relative growth rate. For instance, Empyrean Software — the leading EDA supplier based in China — was 10 years old in 2019, and the global EDA industry is approximately 60 years old. China is likely to take at least another 10 years to be one of the dominant EDA players (Global Market Insights 2016).

The problem is concretely and significantly presenting itself in relation to the chips used in Chinese smartphones, where Huawei is a major supplier. The IC in the Huawei phones is made by a Huawei subsidiary Hisilicon. But the architecture design used by Hisilicon is licensed from UK-based company ARM, which is owned by Softbank, a Japanese conglomerate. Softbank has accepted an offer to buy ARM by Nvidia, a US

---

[5] Gree Electric Appliances Inc of Zhuhai: global.gree.com

technology company and competitor of Intel and AMD. If the sale goes through, it appears unlikely that Nvidia will be allowed by the US administration to continue with the licensing of the ARM design architecture to Huawei/Hisilicon. At the time of writing, there have already been objections from Chinese regulators, and UK, Japan, EU, and US regulators may also raise objections to the deal. Even if these barriers are overcome, it seems unlikely that the deal will be concluded for another 12 months or so.

Product Design

The situation for semiconductor manufacturing equipment is problematic. Advanced IC equipment and the use of licences have been banned by the US for use by China. If the availability of production equipment and design licenses remains a US bargaining counter in global trade disputes, how is China to increase the local rate of semiconductors?

One actively pursued mechanism to improve the quality of indigenous designs is that of actual or virtual vertical integration, in which the end-using company/domestic consumer supplier is involved with the IC or EDA company from the outset of the design process. In this manner there is likely to be more rapidity and certainty of end-use, avoiding time-consuming trials.

Unfortunately, though this may speed up the development of Chinese IC and EDA companies, it does not directly resolve the current problems of the impact of US sanctions. China could attempt to use WTO procedures to challenge US actions and this may be a route that China takes. It would signal to the world that it is the US and not China which is damaging the global trade order. The difficulty is that the WTO remedial process is slow, legalistic, and subject to political pressure.

Engineering Talent

In terms of future development of a competitive Chinese semiconductor industry, there is a crucial requirement for a strong pool of talented engineers at all levels. Huawei has always been regarded as one of the most attractive Chinese companies for talents. However, it is the only domestic electronics company with salaries comparable to other international giants. The problem of matching salary levels for other Chinese tech companies is exacerbated by the principal locations of the IC industry being in areas of high living costs, such as Beijing, Shanghai, and Shenzhen.

One further problem, discussed in Chapter 3, is the current inadequacies in the primary and continuing education sectors, linked also to problems with the *hukou* system of household registration (see Chapter 3), which leads to gaps in ensuring an adequate supply of technicians available and willing to work in IC companies.

In the interim, and as a potential means of partially resisting the damage to current leading companies posed by US sanctions, the recruitment of engineering talent by Huawei needs urgently to be matched by other Chinese IC companies. The recruitment approach is already being attempted, but the living cost constraints also need to be addressed.

Recent 2020 State Support for the IC Industry

In addition to the national semiconductor fund of CNY204.2 billion (US$28.9 billion) support to the IC industry, the State Council (2020) issued a circular, Guo Fa No. 8 [2020], in August 2020 on policies promoting the high-quality development of the IC and software industries (China Briefing 2020d). In the circular, to further optimise the business environment for the development of the IC and software industries, policy measures are put forward in eight areas, including fiscal as well as investment and financing. Companies having an operation period of more than 10 years are exempt from enterprise income tax in the first and second years and then will pay enterprise income tax at the reduced rate of half the statutory rate of 25% from the third to fifth year.

Compared with the policies introduced in 2000 and 2011, the new policies are more generous and broader and include, besides a series of tax incentives, streamlined domestic listing procedure; financial support from government-invested funds; improved intellectual property rights (IPR) protection, as well as policies to promote related research, trade, education, market application, and international collaboration.

However, though in the first half of 2020, China produced more than 100 billion IC chips, up 16.4% year-on-year, the nation still lacks the ability to produce the most advanced chips — the current state-of-the-art 7nm process can only be made by overseas foundries, such as TSMC and Samsung Electronics, and possibly made by Intel in about 12 months

(China Briefing 2020d). Indeed, the measures announced are to support chips down only to the 28nm size, again demonstrating the IC production gap which China has to bridge in terms of fully indigenous production facilities. For example, in the association with TSMC, China plans to produce 16nm fin field-effect transistor (FinFET) at a new 'fab' in Nanjing, in addition to the production of 20nm integrated circuits that it has been producing in commercial quantities at its site in Shanghai. This is part of a phased plan to eventually migrate to 12nm integrated circuits. This is a significant development for China's semiconductor production.

Yangtze Memory Technologies Co. (which is owned by the state-backed Tsinghua Unigroup) expects to triple production of its own 128-layer NAND flash memory chip to 60,000 wafers a month, or 5% of world output, by the end of 2020 at a new US$24 billion plant in Wuhan. However, even in this case, Yangtze is around six to nine months behind their international competitors — Samsung, Micron, and SK Hynix.

Nonetheless, it is the US fear that China, which already has a lead in other high-tech areas is likely to catch up in IC production which, as with Japan in the 1980s, is leading to US charges of state subsidies and security concerns.

On the issue of China's 'unfair' state-supported investment, it is worth noting the path which the US pursued, after effectively sabotaging the Japanese electronic capability. US double standards can be easily demonstrated. In 1987, the US's diminishing competitive position in relation to Japan in semiconductor development was considered a national security issue. This concern prompted the US government, together with 14 US firms in the semiconductor sector, to establish the Semiconductor Manufacturing Technology consortium. Over five years, Sematech (Irwin and Klenow 1996) received public subsidies from the US Department of Defense (DoD), via the Defense Advanced Research Projects Agency (DARPA), totalling US$500 million. Until very recently, the US government was still financing almost half of Sematech's roughly US$200 million annual budget. Whether directly or indirectly via supporting US IC companies, this state financial support policy led to the US eventually overtaking Japan in the semiconductor sector by around 2000.

However, given the sheer size of China's IC industry investment and, especially its huge domestic market for electronic products, one likely escape scenario for China is the development of a separate East Asia IC industry trading and economic ecosystem, involving China, Japan, South Korea, and other Southeast Asian countries.

This view is supported by industry analysts:

> 'At present, the global industrial system is dominated by the United States, and there may be a parallel ecosystem … where the United States is not dominant. This is very unfavourable for the long-term development of the U.S. industry' (CNBC 2020).

5G Technology and Challenges

China has described 5G as a key technology under its 13th five-year plan (Koleski 2017). It plans to invest US$411 billion to upgrade its telecommunications systems to 5G between 2020 and 2030. China also leads the way in 5G patents, and by 2025, it is expected that China will have the largest market with 430 million users (Dace 2020).

Huawei, China's major telecommunications equipment manufacturer and network provider, has been largely responsible for China's success. Its state-sponsored programme offers cheap finance, which means that Huawei has been able to offer significant discounts on its base stations. As a result, the company has already shipped 200,000 units to 50 telecoms operators in Europe and Asia, despite earlier sanctions from the US. Huawei's superiority in global terms presents a challenge for the US, similar to the one they faced from Japan in the 1980s. This superiority has led to specific negative public relations and damaging trade and technology sanctions applied to Huawei. In 2019, the UK government appeared to have taken the decision, advised by its security services, to use Huawei to provide around 35% of the 'non-core' 5G network equipment. The UK had insisted that Huawei would not be involved in the 'core' provision (Lloyd 2020).

Given almost 20 years of using Huawei equipment, as far as security directly is concerned, it was not surprising that an audit carried out by the UK security services initially found that any potential threat to UK cybersecurity from Huawei was minimal. There had been no national security breaches or any detected evidence of malicious Chinese state cyber activity through Huawei since the inception of the UK National Cyber Security Centre (NCSC) in 2014.

The key issue was the potential future role of Huawei in relation to security. It is alleged that Huawei, as a Chinese company, albeit private, could ultimately be influenced or even directed to provide sensitive national security information to the Chinese government. However, the wording of Article 77 in the Chinese security law (National Security Law 2015) appears to exclude 'enterprises' from such collaboration.

Aside from the blatant abuse of US commercial power, this and other measures risk further damaging the integrated global trading system at a time when there is a significant global downturn because of COVID-19. The world is one where companies are part of integrated supply chains which support the global economy. The problem with the US approach is that the strong economic position of China in the global integrated environment, despite its usually calibrated response, may push China into a less open trading approach, at least in the semiconductor market.

However, there is evidence emerging that Huawei will be able, at least partially, to circumvent US sanctions. Samsung and Huawei are considering a deal (Goldman 2020), under which the South Korean giant would fabricate advanced 7nm chips for Huawei's 5G equipment, and Huawei would in effect cede a substantial amount of its smartphone market share to Samsung. Mobile phones are Samsung's flagship business, but they are a relatively small contributor to profits at Huawei, whose core business remains telecommunications equipment. Another advantage for Samsung is the stable guaranteed market which would be provided by Huawei.

If the US actions were simply a matter of commercial 'bullying' by the US, one might hope for a less autarkic, post-Trump era in US trade policy. However, US commercial policy, always protectionist, appears to be partly driven by a wider and deeper political concern — emanating from the political establishment in the US — at the increasing global economic and political influence of China.

The UK succumbed to the international and internal Conservative Party lobbying and cancelled the Huawei contract, at a considerable price, both in terms of delay in rolling out 5G (two to three years) and in terms of higher alternative supplier costs and the cost of removing Huawei equipment (Lloyd 2020). The direct financial costs incurred are likely to exceed £1 billion.

The security issues given were an excuse, linked to the extreme sanctions imposed on Huawei by the US. As the US altered the supply chains involved, it therefore, ostensibly, led to alternative components not being able to be verified by the UK security service, who had previously rejected security concerns. It is unclear as to the precise technical nature of these concerns.

The real issue at stake is the broader industrial technology strategy being deployed by the US and some of its allies against China. To further elucidate the point being made here, it is worth explaining the broad parameters of 5G technology (Lloyd 2020). It is important to recognise that the essence of 5G is a telecommunications network, and unlike 4G, its network architecture is virtual and is mediated principally by vendor proprietary software. It is important to recognise that 5G will not 'replace' 4G for some considerable time (until the late 2030s) but will, effectively, overlay it and be integrated with it. Huawei, although it manufactures and sells mobile phones, is primarily a telecommunications network provider. It is currently the leading global provider of 5G networks. Its technological lead is significant because of the early roll-out in China compared to 4G, and the wide use of mobile technology in China, for instance in payment systems. It has also benefited from Chinese government R&D support, as happens in various ways, some overt and some less so, in other countries. The US, for instance, has always used its defence procurement as well as direct R&D support to provide backing to private companies.

Interestingly, 5G was launched in the US in 2018 and has wide coverage. If this is so, one might question why the US is getting so excited about Huawei? The answer is that the US system is currently based on a non-standalone (nsa) network which is most useful for enhancing broadband mobile voice and data coverage on an upgraded 4G system across the US. The top US suppliers are Verizon and AT&T, together with T-Mobile and Sprint. The Huawei network is a standalone (sa) system with a new radio access system and new core architecture (to which nsa networks, as intermediate systems, will transition, in time). The sa system is necessary for the sophisticated data use in industrial and public, including government, settings, e.g., the 'Internet of Things', remote robots, public transport control, and driver-less cars. This difference explains Huawei's current technological lead and US fears.

It is these latter applications, in sectoral economic areas and also public health and finance areas, which is driving China's use of 5G and associated technologies to achieve its China 2025 economic development vision. A drive, significantly reinforced in the context of COVID-19, which has seen the announcement of major technological upgrading, including the 'industrial internet' and the launching of the Digital Transformation Partnership Action Plan 2020 (Fitch Solutions 2020).

Currently, there are three major companies capable of supplying 5G networks, software, and hardware. These are Huawei, Ericsson, and Nokia, though other major companies are involved in the various supply networks involved in establishing 5G networks. These companies include, for instance, patent licenses provided by the US firm Qualcomm and the Taiwanese advanced chip supplying firm TSMC.

Comparison about the relative positions of the major supplying companies in their telecommunications network business and their mobile technology business is difficult to assess with absolute certainty. None of the major companies involved are particularly transparent, not just Huawei (Morris 2020). The generally accepted ranking is Huawei, Ericsson, and Nokia in terms of market share.

The global power reach of the US and China, in the struggle to influence the business and trade outcomes of the new Cold War (of which the Huawei issue is simply one dimension, albeit an important one) is easier to assess. The international financial and technological reach of the US, built up over many decades, gives it considerable power to influence matters. This power is used in a ruthless manner, by wielding extraterritorial influence and constraining the ability of companies and governments to independently pursue selected investment and policy routes.

A minor but crucial example is the recent US decision to tighten Commerce Department rules to prevent Huawei from buying components made with US technology, even where they are made outside the US. This will, for instance, prevent Huawei from using equipment in its mobile phones and in its cellular 5G base stations from key Taiwanese supplier, TSMC, which is probably the world's leading supplier of advanced chips. There are reports from Taiwan that TSMC is already restricting shipments to Huawei. This punitive action will cause some economic damage to TSMC, which is unlikely to receive any favours from the US in terms of trade or technology, except that TSMC is planning a new 5nm factory in the US, starting production in 2024 (The Register 2020). Taiwan appears to be 'keeping a foot in both camps'.

China could retaliate, for instance against Apple or Qualcomm, who are US firms operating in China. In the short run, Huawei may switch to Samsung in South Korea, and in the longer-run develop more rapidly its own chip-making capacity. Alternatively, another Chinese company will establish capacity to supply the advanced, decreasing-in-size chips. TSMC is already investing in a 3nm production facility in Taiwan! China's Semiconductor Manufacturing International Corporation (SMIC) chip company was planning to start production of 7nm chips by the end of 2020. However, it is not clear how independent of the US the production process will be, given how events have unfolded.

This strategy points to another US market fear which is related to its own telecommunications industry (Lloyd 2020), namely the monopoly-hold that AT&T, as a vertically integrated telecommunications company, had on the US market; though the hold is only destroyed relatively recently. Huawei is a similarly vertically integrated company, which could, as some US commentators believe, lead to an analogous global dominance by Huawei. This scenario is unlikely, but its credibility does not matter if Trump or now Biden believes it!

As has been suggested, there is competition in the 5G market, with Ericsson and Nokia as the main rivals of Huawei. This competition has driven innovation and is linked to the ongoing process of telecommunications standards, via 3GPP, the mobile standards body which the US has only recently joined.

One US multinational which might become a credible 5G provider is Cisco Systems. However, it manufactures in China and thus may face countermeasures. Qualcomm is another US firm, one of whose major customers is Huawei, so it will lose revenue from the US attacks on Huawei. The problem for any US action is the complex, inter-related nature of the software, mobile radio, and telecommunications industry, which operates across the world. The law of unintended consequences operates in this area and it may not leave US companies unscathed. In the short-term, the US technology attacks on Huawei may have some limited success. In the medium-term, as with Japan, the US is unlikely to be the overall victor.

China's success in developing and rolling out 5G will have wider consequences for its digital economy. By enabling massive device connectivity, 5G is facilitating progress in other areas, such as the 'Internet of Things', smart cities, telesurgery, and virtual reality. 5G will also enable advances in self-driving cars and industrial robotics. From an economic perspective, it is likely to trigger significant competitive advantages for China (Lloyd 2020).

Moreover, the move towards a digital industrial economy is not limited to Huawei. President Xi recently announced the creation of 20 showcase examples of digital networks, including all China's large telecom and internet operators. For instance, one of China's leading internet operators, Alibaba Cloud, has been constructing 10 industrial internet platforms for various industry sectors, including textiles, clothing, food and beverage, processing, home appliances, electronics, and textile printing and dyeing. According to Wei Wei, head of Alibaba's Cloud Industrial Internet Platform (Savic 2020b), the newly-applied technology provides for integrated product development, manufacturing, sales, logistics, warehousing, and energy management — essentially creating a singular digital service ecosystem. Wei says the dyed-spinning industry 'can now realise lean sales, procurement, and warehousing management, so that goods and services across the supply chain are standardised and online, while transaction data is transparent and open'.

Digitalisation and Robotics

The importance of digitalisation cannot be over-emphasised as it substantially enhances total factor productivity growth. This has been the experience of China over the past decade. Though there has been both a growth in employment in the industries impacted by digitalisation and a displacement of jobs, the net impact on employment has been positive, see discussion in Chapter 3.

The area where there is the largest prospect for digital growth is in the application of robots. In China, more than 40% of the country's manufacturing workers are employed in firms with automation equipment and some 10% are employed in firms with robots. For example, there has been a 500% increase in the annual installation of robotic upgrades since 2012. This rate is staggering, especially when compared to a rate of just over 100% in Europe (Shoham *et al.* 2018), equating to more than double the number of robot installations in China than Europe.

By 2015, China had become the world's largest user of robots. Industrial robots, which accounted for 27% of new robots globally, are projected to constitute 40% of global sales by 2019. It is argued by the World Bank (Artuc *et al.* 2018) that robot density — the number of industrial robots per 10,000 workers in manufacturing jobs — is still low in China (49) compared with Korea (531), Singapore (389), Japan (305), Germany (301), the United States (176), and the United Kingdom (71). However, given the size of the low tech manufacturing sector and the size of the workforce, this statistic is hardly appropriate, save to underestimate China's dominance in robotics.

E-Commerce

China is the world leader in e-commerce, accounting for 40% of global transactions, with a 15% penetration of retail sales as compared to the US figure of 10% (Zhang and Chen 2019). It is also the global leader in FinTech, accounting for 70% of corporate valuations, and its mobile payments transactions are 11 times that of the US and three times faster.

According to the 'Statistical Report on Internet Development in China' (Red Digital China 2020), by the first half of 2019, the number of online Chinese shoppers in China was at around 640 million. Meantime, annual online retail transactions hit US$5.5 trillion.

In contrast to bullish data on China's e-commerce expansion, from 2015 to 2020, the roll-out of e-commerce internet platforms has been a relatively recent phenomenon relative to most countries in the developed world, and even some more open emerging economies. Beijing's adoption of e-commerce has been cautious. There has also been a notable deficit in the provision of effective legal and non-statutory guidance for its governance.

In part, this can be attributed to China's initial gradualist investment in basic network resources. Since 2015, though, this has been growing exponentially compared with China's main comparators including the United States, Japan, and South Korea (Yue 2017). Still, internet penetration among China's population, as a whole and particularly in the lesser developed regions of the west and north, remains at a relatively low level. What has made up for some of the laggard growth has been the accelerating provision of a mobile e-commerce internet which has bridged, to some degree, the internet penetration deficit in recent years (UNCTAD 2020).

Despite China's slow start in the e-commerce space relative to its international peers the rate of growth in e-commerce transactions has been in double digits over several years, for instance, in mid-2019, rising by over 13% from the same period in 2018 (Dudarenok and Zakkour 2019). From that time onwards, particularly as Chinese shoppers have been avoiding physical retail since the advent of the coronavirus crisis in early 2020, the trend of online shopping has been increasing even more steeply. In support of this trend, China's government has launched a broad array of fiscal incentives designed for accelerating the use of e-commerce by the small and medium enterprises (SMEs) sector (UNCTAD 2020).

The most pronounced expansion in e-commerce has been in online shopping. To meet soaring demand by households, the Chinese business sector has substantially expanded its network of mobile terminals. As a result, the use of mobile phones for online retail has surged, becoming a major driver in the roll-out of online shopping. This flourishing aspect of China's business to consumer 'B2C' phenomenon has further contributed to the overall expansion of the country's e-commerce (Zhang and Hu 2020).

From 2020 onwards, the pace of China's e-commerce sector expansion is anticipated to gradually decline. Even so, by 2025, the total market volume of e-commerce transactions will be over US$1.63 trillion per year (Statista 2020).

In terms of business-to-business 'B2B' transactions, China's B2B e-commerce sector accounts for the bulk of B2B transactions across all industry sectors. In 2019, B2B e-commerce deal flow accounted for over two-thirds of the volume of transactions. Meanwhile, B2C e-commerce made up around 29% of that sector's total.

In terms of China's e-commerce corporate presence on the equity markets, China had 66 publicly-listed e-commerce companies by end-2019. Of those enterprises, 28 were in retail, 21 in services, 10 in the industrial sector, and 7 were engaged in cross-border e-commerce.

The regional distribution of publicly-traded e-commerce companies was heavily weighted towards Beijing which had 22 businesses, accounting for about a third of the national total. Another 12 enterprises were headquartered in Shanghai, while the city of Hangzhou hosted nine e-commerce ventures; each city constituted 18% and 14%, respectively, of China's e-commerce businesses.

In 2019, there were five cities and provinces which emerged as the lead centres of China's e-commerce sector. According to the national e-commerce development index of China's provincial administrative regions, these centres included Guangdong, Zhejiang, Jiangsu, Beijing and Shanghai. Each of these districts continue to innovate and facilitate conducive environments for investment in the sector, enabling their ongoing dominance over other competing and upcoming parts of the country's e-commerce development. As examples of their lead in e-commerce, individually, these regions comprised 72% of the national online retail sales in 2019, whereas the top 10 regions accounted for 86% of transaction value.

In respect of the new centres of e-commerce, the provinces of Shandong, Fujian, and Sichuan have been gaining ground on the top five e-commerce hotspots. These three regions now constitute a second tier of

China's e-commerce sector. Even a nascent third tier is beginning to mushroom in the four widely dispersed and lesser developed provinces of Heilongjiang, Gansu, Guangxi, and Xinjiang. China's other provinces are currently looking at investing in local e-commerce opportunities.

The pattern of e-commerce growth has been most evident in China's east, which is also the most developed and wealthy region of the country (Alibaba 2019). The western half of China has seen the least development in the sector since 2010, although the westernmost province of Xinjiang has appeared on the e-commerce development map. The main driver of this trend can be attributed to central government direction of provincial authorities in priming the province for trading opportunities along the westwards-oriented Belt and Road Initiative and the emerging Digital Silk Road (Han 2018).

As a reflection of China's marked regional disparities, the eastern, central, western, and north-eastern areas made up 83%, 9%, 6%, and 2%, respectively, of online retail sales across the country in 2019. However, the eastern part of China also exhibited the only decline in growth among all four regions, decreasing by 0.7% in 2019 from the previous year. The other regions all experienced sharp growth given their significantly lesser developed e-commerce status.

Social media e-commerce has been flourishing as a major by-product of China's e-commerce revolution. Popular social networking sites such as Weibo and other network media act as communications channels in transacting goods through social interaction and user-generated content. The platforms enable social interaction such as information sharing and group communication. Hence, social media and e-commerce, as two separate digital developments, have converged in China to form a social-business interchange of ideas and commercial transactions.

According to most observers, China's social media e-commerce has entered a period of high growth, fuelled by Chinese consumers' preferences for online deals. This is in contrast to flagging demand for physical retail, given that the coronavirus pandemic has visibly changed households' habits. China's social media-related advertising spending in 2019 was US$21 billion (FBIC 2020).

As a reflection of this striking new trend in online shopping, the social media e-commerce revolution is anticipated to expand rapidly over 2021. This should reach in excess of 30% of overall e-commerce retail sales for that year and a likely higher proportion in the coming decade. Much of the reason for this spending surge is based on a number of key components.

These include increasing internet access by China's large population and its highly active social media users. This will be further supported by the expected large volume of online transactions, the involvement of high-profile product opinion-makers, the large number of businesses participating, and the sector's ongoing creativity.

A range of innovative business models has also come into being which have further contributed to the social media e-commerce growth patterns. Some of these Chinese business formats have been characterised by low-priced markets, thereby attracting strong demand. There has also been a growing differentiation of lower end and higher-quality products, which has encouraged the development of niche domestic markets quickly satisfied by the market entry of low-cost and entrepreneurial SMEs (Chiu *et al.* 2012). While most e-commerce is conducted by Chinese companies, certain key sectors have in recent years been gradually opened to foreign investment, such as platform-type e-commerce.

As more economic categories enter the arena of e-commerce, this will further advance the diversification and expansion of the sector. Additionally, China's broad variety of internet resources amid the ongoing entry of new e-commerce platforms is also likely to have an enduring influence on the expansion of the country's e-commerce sector for years to come.

Cross-border e-commerce involving foreign firms has also developed, but in practice many foreign companies find it challenging to compete against well-resourced Chinese competition. An illustrative example is the recent acquisition of ride-hailing app Uber's Chinese operations by Didi Chuxing, a Chinese company, though Uber retains a minority 15% shareholding. Moreover, the Chinese government will be scrutinising the industry to ensure all transactions are conducted in accordance with fast-evolving Chinese law.

In April 2016, for instance, the authorities issued a new policy regulating cross-border e-commerce (CBEC) (Marketing to China 2019). The policy raised concerns because of its requirement for a wide range of products, including cosmetics, health foods, infant formula, and medical devices, to be registered with authorities. The policy sparked panic in the CBEC market and CBEC revenue fell by almost one-third. Fortunately, China's Ministry of Commerce (MOFCOM) has since stated that it aims to promote the stable development of CBEC in China, and has adjusted the policy's requirements to mitigate its disruptive market effects.

The various Chinese authorities at the table want to develop the CBEC sector but are anxious to balance its growth with consumer safety. Indeed, the authorities will increasingly monitor safety risks in CBEC products and look to optimise their supervision.

Furthermore, the Deputy Director-General of the Financial Department of the Ministry of Commerce (2019) clarified that CBEC enterprises will shoulder responsibility for the quality and safety of CBEC products and will be personally responsible for informing and warning consumers when issues arise. Accordingly, companies are being advised to continue to prepare for filing and registration for their products — if such products are being shipped in commercial quantities — and to monitor the situation regularly.

Clearly there will be opportunities for foreign investors to leverage Chinese cross-border e-commerce as a result of the industry's rapid development. However, given that these sectors are likely to continue experiencing dramatic adjustments in regulation, foreign entrants will need to carefully monitor regulatory changes.

Recent Regulatory Changes

In November 2020, the withdrawal of the US$37 billion Initial Public Offering (IPO) of Ant Group, an Alibaba affiliate company, from the Shanghai stock exchange was characterised by *The Wall Street Journal* as a decision taken directly by Xi Jinping (Skinner 2020). Concerns about a potential decision had prompted an outburst by Jack Ma, the founder of Ant, at a banking industry convention, when he said that Basel Accords were created by 'an old people's club' and banks have a 'pawnshop' mentality. Ma's speech was given at the International Bund Summit in Shanghai, held between October 23rd to 25th, 2020. At the same event, Zhou Xiaochuan, a former Chinese central bank governor, said that some young people are borrowing and spending too much. In another contribution, Zou Jiayi, a vice finance minister, said that the authorities should prevent fintech companies from enabling excessive consumption of financial services. The Chinese financial regulatory authorities obviously were taking a different position from Ma. The withdrawal of the IPO should not have been a surprise for him.

The decision not to go ahead with the Ant IPO was actually taken by China's State Administration for Market Regulation (SAMR), which had issued draft regulations aimed at preventing ICT platforms from dominating the market or from adopting methods aimed at blocking fair competition. The regulations would apply to a number of e-commerce sites, including Alibaba's Taobao and Tmall marketplaces, JD.com, payment services like Ant's Alipay or Tencent, food delivery platforms like Meituan, and WeChat Pay. The platform companies involved have known about the potential for regulation for some time. In 2019, SAMR called more than 20 platforms to a meeting to ask them to stop requiring merchants to sign exclusive cooperation agreements.

The publication of the draft regulations came after China's Financial Stability and Development Committee, a cabinet-level body headed by Vice Premier Liu He, emphasised in October 2020 (Bloomberg 2020c) the need to improve mechanisms to ensure fair competition and to strengthen anti-monopoly law enforcement. Independent of the SAMR draft regulations (approved on November 30th, 2020, following public consultations), China's internet regulator, the Cyberspace Affairs Commission, together with SAMR and the national tax authorities, recently held a meeting with 27 internet companies — including Meituan, TikTok owner ByteDance, Alibaba, JD.com, and Trip.com, during which they discussed online economic practices.

Ant Group runs China's ubiquitous payment app, Alipay, and facilitates investments for its customers' savings, sells insurance, and originates short-term loans. Ant provides just a small amount of the money it lends. The bulk of the funds come from more than 100 commercial banks that it has partnered with and from the sale of securities. Ant collects fees for facilitating the transactions. The company takes an average 30%–40% cut of the interest on loans it facilitates, according to analysts' estimates, without bearing such products' credit risks. However, the company covers only 2% of the total loan amount, most banks would need to cover a minimum 30% (Reuters 2020a).

Separately, China's central bank and banking regulator published draft fintech, micro-lending rules (Skinner 2020) which seek to increase the bar for micro-lenders to be able to provide online loans directly to consumers or jointly with banks, while limiting the amount they can lend. The draft required small online lenders to provide at least 30% of any loan they fund jointly with banks, which is widely considered to be a key rule that will hurt the profitability of Ant's current business model.

The rules insist that fintech, micro lending companies must now have:

- minimum capital of CNY1 billion (was CNY50 million). Nationwide lenders need CNY5 billion capital;
- fintech must fund at least 30% of every single loan (none before);
- leverage is capped at 16–17x of capital;
- loans to individuals cannot exceed a) CNY300,000 or b) one-third of average annual income in the past three years; and
- corporate loans cannot exceed CNY1 million.

These rules confirm that easy credit has given rise to increasing household debt and has drawn concern from experts and regulators.

China's 'state capitalist' approach is argued by US observers as avoiding the stringent financial regulation applicable in the US. However, the approach of SAMR and of China's central bank proves otherwise. China is clearly concerned to avoid the problems arising from the lax regulation that precipitated the Global Financial Crisis of 2007/2008.

China's Central Bank Digital Currency

China's interest in potentially establishing a central bank digital currency (CBDC) goes back to 2014 when a study of such a currency was initiated by the People's Bank of China (PBOC) (Higgins 2016). In 2017, China's State Council approved the PBOC, in cooperation with commercial banks, to design the CBDC. This work was done by a Digital Currency Research Institute under the aegis of the PBOC. The aim is to design a Digital Currency/Electronic Payment (DCEP) system that will function much like a digital form of cash. For retail payments it will operate principally through smartphones.

The reason for the link with electronic payments is because China is the world's leading country in terms of smartphone payments and technology. This is largely thanks to mobile payment platforms like Alibaba's Alipay and Tencent's WeChat Pay, which act like digital wallets that allow users to make purchases in stores, pay bills, and transfer funds to other individuals.

According to a PricewaterhouseCoopers study (China Banking News 2019), 86% of people in China used mobile payment platforms to make purchases in 2019. This was well ahead of Thailand, which had the second-highest percentage of mobile payment users (67%) and more than twice the global average (34%).

In May 2019, PBOC Governor Yi Gang stated that 'top-level design' of DCEP had already been completed and announced that initial pilot projects would take place in Chengdu, Shenzhen, Suzhou, and Xiong'an. In April 2020, DCEP pilots were initiated in the four designated cities. In Suzhou, for example, some government workers were told to download a digital wallet app for DCEP. Images of what was claimed to be the digital wallet circulated widely on the Chinese internet at that time. In May 2020, government workers in Suzhou began getting paid portions of a transportation subsidy in the form of DCEP (Pan 2020b).

Although the concept of a CBDC was proposed decades ago (Tobin 1987), attitudes about whether central banks should issue them have changed noticeably since 2019.

A tipping point for all central banks was the announcement in 2018 of Facebook's digital currency (DC) — Libra, intending to be tied to a basket of international currencies. Although earlier DCs, such as Bitcoin, had been developed, these were principally for investment with no link to other currencies. The announcement of Libra initiated a negative response from central banks. China had, in any event, earlier blocked Bitcoin investments in China. Bitcoin is not able to act as a unit of account and only to a very limited extent as a medium of exchange. It does act as a store of value, though as an extremely volatile investment asset.

The general concern for central banks, including the PBOC, is that the introduction of a sizeable, global, private payments DC, such as Libra, could eventually mean that they might lose control over the issuance of their currencies, including cash, as a medium of exchange. It is already the experience in China that the substantial move to cashless payments has meant that individuals have been losing direct access to the Renimbi as China's sovereign currency. The introduction of a CBDC would not only resolve this problem, but monetary policy could be then directly transmitted to the general public (BIS 2018).

Several major companies are also making plans to use the new digital currency. The ride-hailing app Didi Chuxing has entered into a 'strategic partnership' (*SCMP* 2020) with the PBOC that could eventually allow its 500-plus million users to pay for rides with DCEP. US companies operating in China such as McDonalds, Starbucks, and Subway are likewise to be included in testing the new digital currency.

Although China has not yet formally launched the digital Yuan nationally, it is far ahead of other major countries in rolling out a CBDC for significant testing purposes at scale; some 100 million digital Yuan have been issued (Iwomoto 2021). As Beijing moves to launch DCEP, it will be aided by rolling out across digital payment platforms, as well as the country's state-led economic structure.

Chinese consumers may adopt it relatively easily, given their familiarity with existing mobile payment platforms. It only took a few years for mobile payments to go from a novelty to widespread use. According to data from the PBOC, the amount of money that changed hands in China via mobile payments grew from CNY11.7 trillion (US$1.9 trillion) in 2013 to a staggering CNY347.1 trillion (US$51.8 trillion) in 2019.

DCEP is expected to operate without the need for a bank account, which could bring new sources of economic growth and opportunities for greater financial inclusion. DCEP could open up new avenues for institutions to provide services for borrowing, saving, and investing to individuals. Moreover, DCEP can attract new users to China's thriving e-commerce market.

Beyond China's borders, DCEP could help facilitate the internationalisation of the Yuan. According to the Society for Worldwide Interbank Financial Telecommunication (SWIFT), the world's largest international electronic payment system, the Renminbi was only used in about 1.9% of all international payments in July 2020. By comparison, the US dollar and the euro were used in 38.8% and 36.5% of transactions, respectively. These figures may underestimate the use of the Yuan, but it is not as acceptable in payments globally as the dollar or the euro. However, interestingly, a joint venture involving the PBOC and SWIFT was set up at the beginning of 2021 (Rolfe 2021).

Alongside the pilot projects within China, there is evidence that use of the digital Yuan is for external as well as domestic purposes. A suggestion recently arose from 10 members of the Chinese People's Political Consultative Conference (Pan 2020a) for the digital currency to be used as a cross-border payments network, supporting a free trade agreement between China, Japan, South Korea, and Hong Kong. Here the link with SWIFT will be important.

The planned regional digital currency will be backed by a basket of the four currencies, the ratios of these in the 'stablecoin' will be determined by the economic weight of the associated economies, according to the proposal. Thus, the Yuan and the Yen would account for more than 60% and 20% of the guarantee, respectively.

The proposal is clearly in line with China's drive to increase the use of its currency internationally, initially in East Asia (Iwomoto 2021). With the US successively barring dollar-based transactions as a sanction against adversarial countries, China is rushing to build a payment network independent of the dollar, which so far has been indispensable for international business transactions.

China has accelerated studies on the digital Yuan after seeing the Libra digital currency plan, based on a basket of currencies, announced by Facebook in June 2018 as a rival. The recently updated Libra by the Libra Association, now known as the DIEM Association (Digital Electronic Money Association 2020), in April 2020 is proposed to be linked only to the US dollar.

However, unless there is a link to the US Federal Reserve, it is not clear how Libra would be able to guarantee a stable value, but such a public function link would limit, but not completely prevent, profit-taking by Libra. To China, the updated version of the Libra, linked directly to the US dollar (and possibly, again directly, the euro), seems no different from a digital dollar disguised as a currency basket. Hence, China has taken the actions indicated above.

It should be noted that payments systems tend to be regionalised. The US dollar may be by some distance still the world's reserve currency, but the euro, for instance, remains the principal currency in which payments are made across the currency union and the wider euro area across Europe. The suggestion by China for a free trade area covering Japan, South Korea, and Hong Kong, if accepted, would then mean that China's digital currency, backed by an appropriately weighted basket of currencies, would become the regional payments currency across that free trade zone. It is not yet clear how such an initiative would fit with other currency union suggestions made over the past decade within areas covered by ASEAN-plus Three (Randhawa 2020).

The rapidly evolving development of the DCEP demonstrates two aspects of China' combined technological and political policies. The sheer speed of the implementation of innovation is demonstrated clearly in the arena of central bank digital currency progress. The suggested expanded use of the DCEP as a payments system within the core free trade agreement between China (including Hong Kong in trade currency terms), Japan, and South Korea is an independent Chinese initiative. However, it may eventually stimulate progress on the various ASEAN initiatives over the past decade that proposed currency unions involving various Asia-Pacific trading country groupings (Inui *et al*. 2020). The problem for such a wider development, as with any proposed currency union, is the degree of economic, political, and institutional alignment of the groups of countries concerned.

Artificial Intelligence (AI)

One area of technology in which China is already a leading global player is AI. Moreover, it aims to be dominant in this area over the next decade. In July 2017, China's State Council announced its 'New Generation Artificial Intelligence Development Plan' (China Science and Technology Newsletter 2017) which set the goal of creating a US$150 billion AI market and becoming a global leader by 2030.

But AI development will not be predominantly central- or state-driven. Major Chinese businesses, as well as a myriad of SMEs, will be involved. However, broad central direction will be provided via a national team by leading the research and development in a handful of designated strategic areas.

Already, the central government and Chinese industry have been launching AI initiatives one after another. In one of the latest moves, China will build a US$2.1 billion AI technology park in Beijing's western suburbs, as reported by the state news service (Xinhuanet 2018d). The overarching aim of the policy, as articulated by the Artificial Intelligence Development Plan (AIDP), is to make China the world centre of AI innovation and make AI 'the main driving force for China's industrial upgrading and economic transformation' (China Science and Technology Newsletter 2017). The AIDP also indicates the intention to use AI in a broader range of sectors, including defence and social welfare, and focuses on the need to develop standards and ethical norms for the use of AI.

China aims to maintain competitiveness with other major powers and optimise its AI development environment. In monetary terms, China intended in its 2017 plan to create an AI industry worth more than US$150 billion by 2030. But, given the current growth rate of almost 50%, this figure seems likely to be exceeded by a considerable margin. In 2019, its estimated size was CNY21 billion or almost

US$3 billion. China is also seeking to establish initial ethical norms, policies, and regulations for vital areas of AI.

By 2025, China aims to have achieved a 'major breakthrough' (as stated in the AIDP document) in basic AI theory and to be world-leading in some applications ('some technologies and applications achieving a world-leading level'). China also targets an increase in the worth of AI industry to over CNY400 billion (US$58 billion) and plans to expand upon and codify, in law, ethical standards for AI.

By 2030, China seeks to become the world's innovation centre for AI. By then, growth in the core AI industry is expected to more than double again and be valued at CNY1 trillion (US$150 billion). Further upgrades in China's regulations and technology standards are also to be expected to deal with newly emerging AI technologies.

AI in Businesses and Provinces

Emphasising the collaborative and decentralised nature of the AI programme, the business element of the plan implementation will be led initially by three of China's largest private sector companies — Baidu, Alibaba, and Tencent (Jing and Dai 2017). Collectively, they are known as the BAT, and they are integral to the well-capitalised AI plan. In October 2017, for instance, Alibaba announced plans to invest US$15 billion in research over three years to build seven labs in four countries that will focus on quantum computing and AI (Business Wire 2017).

These 'AI national champions' are mandated by the government to focus on developing specific sectors of AI. For example, Baidu has been tasked with the development of autonomous driving, Alibaba with the development of smart cities, and Tencent with computer vision for medical diagnoses (Jing and Dai 2017). Being endorsed as a national champion involves a deal whereby private companies agree to focus on the government's strategic aims. In return, these companies receive preferential contract bidding, easier access to finance, and sometimes market share protection.

Subsequent documentation has emphasised the importance of strengthening organisation and implementation, including between provinces and ministries. The Tianjin Municipal Government in 2018 announced a US$16 billion fund to support the development of the AI industry (*SCMP* 2018a). The announced expenditure from the Tianjin government does not appear to be annualised, but it is a substantial sum from within one province.

In 2019, China hosted the World Artificial Intelligence Conference (WAIC) for the first time in Shanghai to promote AI innovation globally. At the conference, IBM China signed a three-year agreement with the Shanghai Zhangjiang Group to set up the first Watson Build Artificial Intelligence Innovation Centre in the country (Xinhuanet 2019d). The centre is anticipated to be hugely beneficial to technology companies as it will potentially serve 500 domestic and foreign companies, and it enhances Shanghai's role as perhaps the principal AI pole in China.

It is important also to recognise the global aim of China in relation to its strong focus on AI as an all-encompassing horizontal sector which represents one of the most important socio-economic pillars of future society. Leadership in this area would cement China's role in the new twenty-first century global era.

AI Military Applications

Attempts to use technologies to compete with US military power are nothing new within China's military strategy. Since the late 1990s, the country has been following a policy of '*shashoujian*', which roughly translates as 'trump card' (Bruzdzinski 2005). Rather than directly competing with the US, China has sought to develop asymmetric capabilities that could provide a critical advantage in warfare. The overall aim is to use defence expenditure, including on AI, to modernise the military, rather than any futile attempt to outspend the US, or for that matter over-burden the public purse with excessive expenditure on defence. China's defence capability and deployment is discussed in further detail in Chapter 11.

Social Governance and AI

It is important to note that the term 'social governance', though used in English translations, may be misleading. The Chinese text (社会建设) directly translates to 'society/community' and 'build/construction'. Hence, 'community building' may provide a clearer insight into the positive purpose of the policy actions involved, rather than the pejorative interpretation placed on 'social governance' by Western commentators.

The Chinese government, with high-level officials including President Xi, has advanced the objective of establishing a 'minimum moral standard' within society (He 2015). This goal is not limited to ensuring 'good' governance in the traditional sense; it extends to regulating the behaviour of citizens and enhancing their moral integrity, which is considered a task within the government's remit (Pan 2020b). As will be discussed in Chapter 5, this mission has a link with China's Confucian and Daoist/Taoist past.

In the view of the Chinese government, AI can be used in the service of policy action aimed at raising moral standards in the context of creating stronger solidarity within communities. The echoes of Confucianism are evident here. This approach may be seen as placing a greater emphasis on social responsibility and group and community relations, with relatively less focus on individualistic rights, as is the case in the West.

AI and Social Credit

An example of social governance which represents one of the more disturbing issues from a Western standpoint, has been the planned national introduction of the social credit system — already operating, with regional differences in various cities and provinces — by the end of 2020. Media coverage in the West of the social credit system has been negative and often hostile.

For instance, in March 2019, it was reported that 'according to the National Public Credit Information Centre, Chinese courts banned would-be travellers from buying flights 17.5 million times by the end of 2018 (*The Guardian* 2019). Citizens placed on blacklists for social credit offences were prevented from buying train tickets 5.5 million times'. The report said that 'once discredited, limited everywhere'.

The social credit system aims to incentivise 'trustworthy' behaviour through penalties as well as rewards. According to a 2014 government document about the system, the aim is to 'allow the trustworthy to roam everywhere under heaven while making it hard for the discredited to take a single step'.

Social credit offences range from not paying individual taxes or fines to spreading false information and taking drugs. More minor violations include using expired tickets, smoking on a train or not walking a dog on a leash.

China's National Development and Reform Commission said it would begin banning people on public transport for up to a year (Reuters 2018). The report also said that 128 people were prevented from leaving China because of unpaid taxes. Officials believe the system is working. The report said that 3.5 million people or companies paid taxes or debts they owed because of the social credit system.

A year earlier, the US journal *The Atlantic* (2018) published a more hostile article:

> 'The Chinese genius, if you can call it that, was to take credit scoring as a tool of social discipline to its logical conclusion, building a formal public-private partnership around it. This move extends dominion across the entire range of interactions any member of modern society is more or less compelled to pursue by the very style and structure of contemporary life. Each and every Chinese citizen would henceforth bear this index, in perpetuity'.
>
> 'The scheme is fused to a repertory of existing techniques the Chinese state retains to guarantee control, including the *hukou* system of internal passports that restricts the free movement of individuals, right up to detention, incarceration, and execution. What emerges is a marriage of database and truncheon — a vision of supple, gleaming technology at the surface of everyday life, working hand in hand with the oldest and most brutal forms of oppression'.

In an article in *Wired*, Hoffman (2019), a non-resident fellow at the Australian Strategic Policy Institute stated that:

> 'There are no genuine protections for the people and entities subject to the system. In China there is no such thing as the rule of law. Regulations that can be largely apolitical on the surface can be political when the Communist Party of China (CCP) decides to use them for political purposes'.
>
> 'If solving problems was the real goal, the CCP would not need social credit to do it. China's social credit system is a state-driven programme designed to do one thing, to uphold and expand the Chinese Communist Party's power'.

She added that social credit is a tech-enabled way to tie political power to social and economic development that has been discussed in the country since the 1980s, an automation of Chairman Mao's Mass Line — a term to describe how the party's leadership shaped and managed society.

> 'In Mao's China, the Mass Line relied on ideological mass mobilisation, using Mao Zedong's personal charisma to force participation'. 'The CCP could no longer, after the Mao era, rely on ideological mobilisation as the primary tool for operationalising social management'.

Given this level of concern, it is worth examining the social credit system in some detail, and also because it illustrates some of the Chinese cultural values discussed in Chapters 5 and 6.

China's social credit system was formally announced in 2014 but has existed on a regional level since 2009. While many elements of the social credit system are operational already, the aim is to provide a fully functional system — enabling the ranking of all Chinese citizens and businesses — by the end of 2020. Currently, businesses are being categorised based on their compliance standards as well as their audit and financial records. More than 33 million businesses in China have been given a score (China Briefing 2019), and many companies have already been blacklisted.

The system has the capability to carefully monitor and control individual behaviour. People are rewarded or punished based on their scores, and people's scores can increase or decrease based on their individual behaviour. Individuals may be banned from flying or getting on a train, or from purchasing business-class tickets. Some hotels have also banned people with low scores. A bad score can mean that a person may be denied the ability to perform work in a big bank, executive job, or at a state-owned firm. Businesses may be excluded from public procurement projects. The government keeps a public list of individuals and businesses with a poor score and these can be published as a way of publicly shaming miscreants.

People in the UK or the US are used to credit checks. Credit rating agencies, such as Experian, track debt payments and give a score that is used by lenders and mortgage providers. There is also social-style scores. When shopping online with eBay, there is a rating on shipping times and communication. Uber drivers and passengers both rate each other; if the score falls too far, transactions may be blocked. The contemporary discussion of the potential use of vaccine passports for admission to entertainment venues, premises in the domestic market, etc., is a form of social control, however justified they may appear to be.

Moreover, Chinese society does have trust issues. These include food quality scandals, pollution, employers not paying their workers, and regular cases of poor product quality. Companies need to be sanctioned for this kind of bad behaviour. Indeed, the question of whom to trust, and social trust more broadly, is one that is relevant to every modern society, not just China. Although Western critics, as shown previously, often see the system as an intrusive state surveillance apparatus, there is a different perception among the Chinese population. Over 60% of Chinese view the social credit system as a project that will strengthen public morality and that will increase trust in society (Wang 2019b).

The idea of someone being 'trustworthy' (*chengxin*) has long existed in the Chinese traditional Confucian moral system. It is widely believed this was fundamentally damaged in the past 50 years, starting with Mao's Cultural Revolution (1966–76), now seen as a period characterised by the 'breakdown of public morality' (Wang 2019b).

In former times, and still in rural areas, the close proximity of social acquaintances enabled these smaller collectivities to be able to establish mutual trust. The Chinese concept of '*guanxi*' (loosely translated as social relation) doesn't only refer to social connections but is a more sophisticated concept that refers to a trusted social relation within which an individual's value is endorsed. Clearly, the rapid urbanisation and the insertion of market transactional relationships in China led to the breakdown of these 'circles of trust'.

Further, the concept of *tian* essentially resembles independent laws of nature (especially in Daoism/Taoism, one of the religious traditions of China). *Tian* resembles the sky or heaven in that it can observe everyone's deeds and thoughts. *Tian* therefore is regarded as a fair judge, basing its decisions on observation. Whether it is appropriate for the state to play the role of *tian* is a question which will be examined in Chapter 5 when exploring Chinese political philosophy. However, the social credit system could be regarded as a mundane way of attempting to replicate the relationship between human beings, society, and *tian*.

Interestingly, the anthropologist Wagner argues that Chinese people traditionally view life itself as a credit system (Wagner 2014). One can earn points by doing good deeds, but these can also be easily squandered through bad ones (this view echoes the notion of 'karma', a concept in another Chinese religious tradition, Buddhism).

The introduction and development of the social credit system is a massive social experiment. Obviously, it can be viewed in hostile Western eyes as yet another manifestation of Chinese communist party oppression and societal control. However, seen from a less ideologically critical position, it may equally be viewed as a mechanism for renewing traditional trust and for justly rewarding good behaviour and penalising bad behaviour in this life. The judges will be the Chinese people: for the time being their position is relatively positive.

AI in Health Care

This societal approach may be demonstrated in connection with the use of AI in relation to healthcare. In the West, where electronic healthcare data are predominantly focused on individual health treatments, AI techniques are thus considered crucial to unlock 'personalised medicine' (Nittas *et al.* 2018). By contrast, in China, healthcare is predominantly focused on the health of the population. In this context, the ambition of AI is to liberate data for public health purposes.

As part of China's 'Made in 2025' plan, 130 companies, including 'WeDoctor' (backed by Tencent, one of China's AI national champions), signed cooperation agreements with local governments to provide medical check-ups, comprised of blood pressure, electrocardiogram (ECG), and urine and blood tests, free of charge to rural citizens (Hawkins 2019). The data generated by these tests were automatically (that is, with no consent from the individual) linked to a personal identification number and then uploaded to the WeDoctor cloud, where they were used to train WeDoctor's AI products.

These products include the 'auxiliary treatment system for general practice', which is used by village doctors to provide suggested diagnosis and treatments from a database of over 5,000 symptoms and 2,000 diseases. Although this and other similar practices often do involve anonymisation, Western critics point out the contrast with the European and US approaches to the use of medical data, which prioritise individual autonomy and privacy rather than social welfare. Given the anonymity of the data, such criticisms, usually from US commentators, are unsustainable.

This over-hasty ideological attitude is evident in Western responses to the actions of biophysics researcher He Jiankui. He revealed in November 2018 that he had been successfully genetically modified babies using the CRISPR method to limit their chances of ever contracting HIV

(Cohen 2019). The announcement was met by international outcry, but He's experiment was immediately condemned by the Chinese government at the time and he was subsequently severely punished (Cyranoski 2019).

There are issues of ethical philosophy surrounding the potential of CRISPR gene-editing techniques in medical research, and they will need to be discussed as we move through the 'twenty-first century of biology' (Lloyd 2017). But these issues need to be discussed at a global level and should involve China, the US, and other countries. Given the unenthusiastic US attitude to the WHO, it is not certain that the US would be prepared to discuss the ethical issues involved.

However, Western commentators often go on to suggest improperly that the drive for China to be seen as a world leader in medical care, combined with the promise gene-editing offers for the treatment of diseases, suggest that a different response to that taken by the Chinese government may be possible in the future (Cyranoski 2019). It is concerning that when discussing Chinese research and policies, even Western academic commentators appear incapable of removing ideological undertones in their responses. One might equally argue that the US 'free market' ideology poses a similar, if not greater, threat.

Health expenditures have increased rapidly as China has developed its system of universal health coverage. Double-digit health spending growth surpassed the rate of economic growth, and as a result, health spending absorbs an increasingly larger share of the total economy. Increasingly this will require spending on health and elderly care to be efficient and effective.

The use of AI directed at public healthcare — addressing lifestyle determinants of health and promoting healthy ageing — is the direction of government policy. Engineering the health system to concentrate on disease-prevention, together with ensuring equitable access to rapidly changing medical technologies, are crucial objectives. The demographic factors to be discussed in Chapter 3 indicate the need to provide long-term care for the elderly through the public health system. This public health preventative approach will be a substantive way for China to avoid unsustainable increases in the direct provision of both acute and chronic care.

One of the associated benefits of better public healthcare, again a factor dealing with the adverse demographic impacts of a decline in the normal working-age population, is to enable an extension of working lives (just as in Japan which has similar serious demographic problems). There should also be benefits in reducing pressure on future pension payments.

Smart Cities and AI

China has been at the forefront of the development of smart cities, with many of the world's smart cities located within China. The majority of AI resources that have gone into developing these cities have so far tended to focus on surveillance technologies, such as facial recognition and cloud computing for ordinary policing (Anderlini 2019).

According to international accounting firm Deloitte's 'Super Smart City' management consulting report, there are currently more than 1,000 smart cities launched or under construction worldwide. In terms of the number under construction, China ranks first with several large-scale smart-city clusters having been formed (Deloitte 2020a).

Deloitte China says: 'China has become one of the most active countries in the construction of smart cities in the world. With the advancement of refined urban management, the government increasingly pays more attention to urban residents and workers. With improvements in the living and working environments, the application of smart cities will enter a new stage of development'.

In respect of China's 13th Five-Year Plan (NDRC 2019), the Chinese government set out new objectives and conditions for the development of a revolutionary form of smart-city. This blueprint defines the development of a smart-city as sharing information and data, and being open and flexible in its cooperation between public and private partners engaged in its joint construction. To this end, each new urban tech centre will also be oriented towards the advancement of culture and community development.

While China's smart cities are mushrooming and gradually evolving in their development, the majority have encountered various drawbacks in relation to their design, construction, maintenance, and operational efficacy. As a result, there is a claim that these cities are more urban technological zones rather than functioning as 'smart cities' in the real sense of the term.

Observers have remarked that for the concept of a smart-city to fully evolve into an environment that adopts broad and deep connectivity across all sectors of society (ScienceDirect 2020), there are several layers of functionality which need to be fully applied, including universal reach and participation, openness and transparency, autonomous control, real-time application, amid all-encompassing artificial intelligence. On another higher level, these essential components of a smart-city need to seamlessly combine to create a genuine platform such that a smart-city becomes a living ecosystem for its population. As a result, the smart-city's residents can fully avail themselves of its recreation, work, travel, security, education, and green environment. This multi-participant collaboration will achieve maximum outcome with the efficient use of the city's governance infrastructure, communities, and businesses.

Smart city development is not subject to an overarching strategy of design and implementation. Rather, municipal and regional authorities have become involved in the integration of local requirements into a smart city's construction so that a region's unique characteristics can be fully absorbed into the enhancing of socio-economic engagement for its residents.

For instance, among China's top tier one and tier two cities, a majority have progressed well in attuning to the concept of smart cities through the high adoption of artificial intelligence in their commercial and governance operations (Ekman and de Esperanza Picardo 2020). As a result, Chinese cities have made significant gains in the networking of expansive smart-city AI systems and applications. On the other hand, there is still a high degree of potential for these maturing AI-ingrained urban centres to engage in the roll-out of higher-end strategic and innovative value-added planning.

Ever since the launch of China's 13th Five-Year Plan, the programme of smart-city development has been coordinated alongside the provision of big data, cloud computing, e-government, and smart transportation (KPMG 2016). Under the guidance of the central government, China's major urban municipalities have been intensifying their construction of smart-cities. The policy of smart-city expansion has also been extended to capital cities and economic core urban areas of dispersed Chinese provinces.

Various ministerial-level Chinese institutions have been tasked with developing the smart-city programme. These include China's Ministry of Housing and Urban-Rural Development which created smart-city lists to identify 290 pilot cities (Atha *et al.* 2020). In 2019, smart-city-related pilot schemes were set up by the Ministry of Computing Technology, the Ministry of Industry and Information Technology, the National Bureau of Surveying, Mapping and Geographic Information, and the National Development and Reform Commission (Wang *et al.* 2019).

The benefits of smart-city-related policy projects have been released by the government on an ongoing basis since their inception. Its resulting payback has been the increase in substantial levels of social capital for urban residents. According to the 'Global Semi-Annual Smart City Spending Guide' (IDC 2020), China's smart-city technology-related investment in 2018 and 2019 was US$20 billion and US$22 billion, respectively.

The overall scale of China's smart logistics investment has continued to expand. The groundwork for the information construction of China's logistics industry has also experienced solid growth. In turn, Chinese logistics operators have attached importance to effective modes of management, including supply chains, business processing, and customer resources. In 2019, the amount of investment in smart logistics technology was in the region of US$5 billion (Deloitte 2020a).

Since the country began to promote the construction of smart cities, the number of smart-city pilot projects have exceeded 700, as of September 2019. Increasingly, the 'smart city' concept is taking root across the length and breadth of China's town planning communities — permeating Chinese government policymaking, ranging from technology engineers and architects based in local and municipal authorities, to regional and provincial decisionmakers, and up to the master planners in Beijing. China's smart city developers must surely be aware that the ongoing evolution and expansion of the nation's smart city program — within the context of the largest urbanisation program in mankind's history — will clearly have consequences not only for China's vast population, but for the uptake of smart cities across the entire developing world in years to come.

With the continuous development of China's technology and ongoing improvements in levels of urbanisation, the scale of China's smart-city market will expand in future. The rapid development of technological outcomes such as the Internet of Things and cloud computing has laid a solid foundation for the further construction of smart-cities in China. Taking cloud computing as an example, the key technology has reached international leading levels and can support complex application scenarios such as substantial concurrent, hybrid cloud and multi-cloud management.

In coordination with the expansion of smart cities, China's intelligent transportation systems have managed to achieve advanced international levels (Huang *et al.* 2017). This has been propelled by a range of government polices to support upscaling of the intelligent transportation industry. Its principal benefits have been manifested in the form of integrated applications, such as for Beijing, Shanghai, Guangzhou, and Shenzhen's transportation management systems.

In particular, the Electronic Toll Collection 'ETC' — a highway network electronic service system — is currently the only nationwide application in China (PR Newswire 2020). It has independent intellectual property rights and unified standards, forming a comprehensive industrial intelligent transportation system.

In coping with the relentless expansion of megacities and the negative impacts of their urbanisation over the twenty-first century, China has been seeking to turn around its often over-polluted impersonal urban environments. In the promotion of smart cities, Chinese urban planning — formerly geared for mass-scale production — has seen an effort to steer urban living away from industrial production and large-scale government housing in favour of private household development and community cohesion. China's smart cities may become a giant leap forward in the upgrading of social and work patterns of urban lifestyle, not just for China but for the world.

One of the major challenges for humankind in the twenty-first century is how to cope with the negative effects of urbanisation, exacerbated by the growth of cities, especially megacities. Humanising these vast urban conglomerations of people, occupational activities, transport networks, and domestic and leisure lives is going to require global efforts to substantially improve urban design and retrofitting. China may be able to contribute greatly to this endeavour.

Data Protection

This is a policy area where China is criticised in the West for having no controls in place. Whatever may have been the case earlier, the Cybersecurity Law (Network Security Law) came into effect in June 2017 and changed the landscape for data protection in China. It states core principles on the collection and use of personal information, requires data on consumers in the areas of 'key information infrastructure' to be stored within the country, and bans the export of 'personal and important data' that could threaten national security or the public interest.

According to a Linklaters report (2020) entitled 'China publishes revised personal data protection guidelines', China's State Administration for Market Supervision and State Standardisation Administration released the revised Information Security Technology: Personal Information Security Specification 2020 Guidelines — the '2020 Guidelines'.

As such, the 2020 Guidelines cover the country's standards concerning various areas of a Chinese individual's privacy of information. This would include how information is collected, stored, shared, disclosed, transferred, and otherwise utilised. Although the 2020 Guidelines are not legally binding, they have been designed to incorporate 'best practice' relying on international sources of data protection. In practice, this should mean that Chinese-based commercial and government organisations being required to handle personal data in accordance with globally recognised norms. In particular, this could include employing aspects of robust data protection regimes such as the European Union's General Data Protection Regulation (GDPR).

Of equal importance, since the enactment of China's Cybersecurity Law in 2017 (China Briefing 2020c), there has been greater focus on government information security also becoming subject to a comprehensive and centralised set of guidelines. This trend towards consolidation of data governance has increasingly substituted China's more fragmented nature of regulation in this sphere. As a result, the previous emphasis on regional and local information control and data protection-related regulations will, in future, become administered at the national level. With this in mind, the 2020 Guidelines incorporate several recent pieces of cybersecurity legislation, including China's E-commerce Law (Melchers 2018) and Cryptography Law (Covington 2019).

Other features in the new guidelines take account of advances in information technology such as those emanating from the Cybersecurity Law. These include guidance on personal data security for internet service providers, among various other organisations and commercial entities, utilising state-of-the-art emerging technologies.

Most Chinese internet-related enterprises hold, process, and commercially utilise large quantities of personal data. This has meant enabling sensitive data being subject to third-party access and its facilitation of individualised presentational platforms. Chinese authorities have become increasingly conscious of the growing manipulation of data by independent operators. As a result, they have pushed for greater controls over its implementation in practice.

The 2020 Guidelines have also been upgraded to deal with the creation and import of significant updating technology. This includes the emergence of facial recognition software and its manipulation of personal data in a biometric format.

The new guidelines are also designed to advance the expansion of increased transparency by personal data holders and providers. This area of coverage has become particularly relevant following surveys of Chinese consumers' attitudes towards information security issues. These have indicated an ongoing shift in changing attitudes towards the need for stepping-up the protection of personal data.

The ramification for commercial enterprises is the expectation that they should facilitate increasingly robust and detailed personal privacy policies. For example, this would involve expanding communications tools by which individual users are made aware of how their personal data is being collected and generally used. The applicable forms of communication by holders and exploiters of that information could include messaging such as targeted pop-ups or other effective measures of knowledge-sharing.

Going beyond technology-based solutions for the protection of privacy is an expansion in the application of legal rights in favour of individuals. This involves including and upgrading the drafting of contractual provisions between data controllers and suppliers of personal information. For instance, enabling the application of limitations to which an individual's consents can be bundled into conditions of service by data providers, given such bundles may be difficult for most individual users of technology to comprehend.

The 2020 Guidelines have been introduced with the purpose of beefing up the tools available for official regulators to more effectively monitor and remedy situations of misuse of personal data. This includes online misappropriation of individuals' private information. Therefore, the overall trend in the level of Chinese data protection and enforcement appears, at least in theory, to be moving in the overriding direction of greater information security for individual users of internet and high-technology systems.

Concluding Comments

The motivation for this chapter in providing extensive coverage of technology has been because the governing elites in modern China view technology as a fundamental driver of the internal development of China and, importantly also, its external development and a distinctive global presentation of China in the twenty-first century.

The chapter has explored the undoubted technological strengths of China as it delivers on its latest five-year plan, though it also has some weaknesses and areas where it lags behind. Some of the areas raised by Western observers as concerns have also been explored, such as data protection and privacy and societal management issues. The overall conclusion is that the acceleration of technological change in China will certainly match that of the West and, in some areas, China will lead the world in the beneficial application of technologies and their export to the rest of the world.

The internal transformation of the most advanced regions and cities of China, its impressive modernity, may be viewed as presaging an exciting new global societal future by some, while others may see these developments as a regrettable 'brave new world'. What is clear is that China is leading the way in transforming many aspects of our lives. The ethical values that underlie our handling of this transformation are clearly important. How these values are perceived in China raises issues that are discussed in detail in Chapters 5 and 6.

Chapter 3

The Dynamics of Economic Growth

Patterns of Economic Growth

China's overall labour force continued to grow until 2017, and is now falling in size. Despite increased labour productivity, the shift of surplus labour from rural areas dominated by agriculture to a manufacturing economy appears to have slowed in recent years, partly due to improved agricultural methods and technology. The contribution to GDP from agriculture in 2020 is estimated to be between 7% and 8%; it is relatively high by developed country standards, but below that of India whose comparable figure is 14%.

Rural Areas and Agriculture

However, the employment situation in rural areas, where 45% of China's population live and much agricultural production is located, is complex, especially because of the substantial amount of off-farm employment. While a substantial proportion of the population is employed on the farms, some of which are corporate, most are household farms. The Household Responsibility System originated in the 1970s. Reformed, it was also used to initiate agricultural reforms in the 1980s and 1990s (Lei *et al.* 2016). Currently, a large proportion — over 60% of the rural population are either self-employed or employed in private SMEs and half of the total are employed in town and village enterprises (TVE) — engage in off-farm activity, including rural tourism (CEIC 2020). It is important to recognise, as discussed in connection with the *hukou* registration system, that holders of agricultural residency have land-rights for both farming and residence. These have become increasingly valuable, as a continuing social/cultural identification with their birthplace for rural migrants moving to cities, and as physical wealth which can be traded since land has become more valuable in China.

Hence, though surplus labour from agriculture is transferred to enable low-tech industry to develop, rural areas have not been neglected. The emergence of farm-mechanisation service providers has enabled small-scale farmers to quickly mechanise their cultivation activities without heavy capital investment. Mechanisation has reduced the labour input required for farming and also increased the time available for engaging in off-farm income opportunities in rural areas.

Latterly, a high penetration of internet and mobile networks in rural areas has accelerated the application of information and communications technology. E-commerce platforms such as Taobao have been essential in connecting farmers to end-consumers and have oriented agriculture to be more demand-driven. E-commerce has played a significant role in maintaining food supply chains during the COVID-19 pandemic.

The growing engagement of tech-companies in rural development is providing a new model of development led by the private sector. Despite this progress, the per capita incomes of rural households remains less than half that of urban households.

Manufacturing and Services

Over the period from 1990, three other national development patterns have emerged. First was the growth of the low-tech and now medium-tech manufacturing sectors, enabled by the surplus labour transferred from an increasingly productive agricultural sector. Second was the phenomenal growth of the high-tech sector in recent years. This dual economic pattern has been supplemented by a third pattern, a rapid shift towards a services sector which now occupies more than 50% of the total Chinese economy (Investopedia 2020).

In this movement from a low-income economy to an upper middle-income economy, the development and application of technology has had an important role to play in maintaining economic growth rates and ensuring that real wages have grown, though not yet evenly across the population. A continuation of high growth rates is likely, though probably lower than the 10% annual rates managed between 1979 and 2010 or the 7.5% annual growth rates between 2010 and 2019 (OECD 2019).

Some commentators argue that maintaining these high levels of growth is particularly important for China due to 'the implicit trading by citizens of political freedoms for economic growth and embourgeoisement' (Balding 2018). It remains to be seen whether this harsh and effectively untestable ideological judgement can be maintained in the future.

Guiding Economic Development

It is clear that not only is China's economic growth rate extraordinary over the past 30 years, but the nature of China's socio-economic development has also been distinctive. The distinctive nature of the development — described by the CCP as a 'socialist' development 'with Chinese characteristics' — departs from Western economic development, which is based on the assumptions of individuals acting in a 'rational' manner and 'individuals aggregating into civil society'. The collectivism which underlies Chinese socio-economic market development is ethnographically distinguishable from Western liberal market development, underpinned by individualism. To an extent, the Chinese model is similar (though not identical) in respect of the collectivist and statist economic development experienced by Japan and other East Asian economies (Morishima 1982).

These characteristics lead to a distinctive role for the Chinese state and its link with a collectivist civil society. Hence, the role of the CCP, in the Chinese state, in 'guiding' socio-economic development is a mechanism to rapidly mobilise the collective will of the Chinese people. This approach is not unknown in Western liberal countries, for instance in times of war. In practical terms, the mechanism involves the publication of a series of overlapping 'plans' which are qualitatively and quantitatively different from detailed, centralised Soviet command planning. These plans are essentially similar to a private corporation's strategy documents, and indeed, mesh closely with the Chinese private sector company strategic plans.

It is undeniable that the use of this 'strategic guidance' approach in China has enabled — and continues to enable — significant economic and technological growth, and increasingly demonstrated global technological leadership in key areas (as indicated in Chapter 2). However, it has also enabled a continuous increase in per capita income and in the overall welfare of Chinese citizens. It should be said that it has also led to the creation of an elite group of extremely wealthy citizens. The inequality, of course not unknown in the West, is an issue which will have to be resolved, as it has also been linked to high-level corruption in some cases.

Economic Growth: The Key Role of Technology

Chapter 2 illustrated the importance placed on technological development by China. It is important to appreciate how this element of economic growth relates to other complementary human elements in that growth.

A report by PricewaterhouseCoopers suggested that China is the country that has the most to gain economically from the application of AI, with a boost in GDP of up to 26% by 2030 (PricewaterhouseCoopers 2017). Estimates also suggest that AI could facilitate an increase in employment by 12% over the next two decades (PricewaterhouseCoopers 2018).

Because of these potential benefits, President Xi has frequently spoken of the centrality of AI to the country's overall economic development (Hickert and Ding 2018). China has been pursuing the potential economic benefits of AI concretely and proactively for some time. One major impact of AI will be in stimulating an increase in the application of automation in the middle-tech sector.

Automation and Its Economic Impacts

There is considerable disagreement over the impact of automation on employment. However, in the West, evidence shows that jobs are displaced by innovations such as robotics. It seems unlikely that increasing the number of robots in Chinese industrial sectors will be any different. The issue is how this and other aspects of automation and its management are viewed. China appears to be preparing better than other middle-income countries to deal with the longer-term challenges of automation (Roberts *et al.* 2020).

Two aspects of the impact of the application of automation on employment have attracted a broad consensus. First, the impacts will alter, in some cases radically, the tasks performed by humans in providing inputs and exercising skills in all sectors from manufacturing to personal services. A set of tasks make up a job, so it is the design of jobs which is the immediate change, depending on a variety of factors across the economy, including the availability of skills. The second area of agreement is the need for an overall strategy, and one in which the government has a major planning, financing, and guidance role. The impacts of automation need to be continuously assessed and managed.

China appears not only to be aware of these two crucial points but to be moving forward to implement the strategies and actions required. Given the crucial importance placed on technology as a key driver of future economic growth, the policy approach is well-advised.

But China has a lot of catching up to do to compete with the world leader in the preparations required to manage automation, South Korea. Interestingly, two large Chinese systems integrators, Guangzhou Mino and Dalian Auto, are currently cooperating with German premium producers (*China Daily* 2018) and have established their first bridgeheads in Europe and North America. These types of international collaboration have enhanced progress on various engineering and technology fronts in the past and are increasingly utilised by Chinese companies.

The Economist Intelligence Unit (EIU) Automation Readiness Index (2018) measures progress in three key aspects of readiness to manage automation in major countries across the world. These are the innovation environment, education policies, and labour market policies. For a middle-income country, China scores highly. The latest figures available in 2018 show that China is ranked tenth for its innovation environment, fourteenth for its education policies, seventh for its labour market policies, and twelfth overall.

The labour market and education system are both areas that require substantial relative improvement. It is clear that, despite having made great strides in education, certainly at higher and advanced levels, greater emphasis needs to be made in the areas of primary and secondary level education and continuing education for adults, especially in technical education.

China has taken steps towards building a lifelong education system but its progress on this front is behind that of other wealthier countries. For instance, the EIU Index ranks China's workforce transition programmes for vocational training in twenty-first place. This ranking is well behind Singapore, which offers funding for employee training at small and medium enterprises, and Germany, which funds up to 80% of fees for human resources transformation projects. This issue is now being taken seriously by the Chinese government, as indicated in the section below on vocational education.

As indicated, there is no consensus on whether automation will result in a net loss or a net gain of jobs. Nonetheless, McKinsey (2017) estimates that automation could push 375 million workers globally to switch occupations by 2030. For China, the estimate is that automation could displace up to a fifth of all manufacturing jobs, forcing nearly 100 million workers (around 12% of the current total Chinese labour force) to find new work. This is merely one estimate, which is disputed by others, including the World Economic Forum and PricewaterhouseCoopers.

That job losses will occur as automation proceeds is demonstrated by figures from the China Development Research Foundation (CDRF 2018), which show that automation has replaced up to 40% of workers in some companies. For example, one of China's most popular beverage brands, Wahaha, trimmed an assembly line workforce of 200–300 workers down to just a handful of individuals. Foxconn — a company based in Taiwan with factories across the Chinese mainland — replaced 400,000 jobs with robots between 2012 and 2016.

However, from a Chinese perspective, one important aspect of the drive for automation is to compensate for the future reduction in the available workforce. The PricewaterhouseCoopers estimate of job loss/gain (PricewaterhouseCoopers 2017) suggests that agriculture will probably show a net job loss, industry will probably remain in balance overall, while it is the services sector, where jobs are being increasingly created in China, which is likely to show a net gain in jobs.

As these various studies indicate, China's service, construction, and industry sectors, as well as agriculture, are likely to experience positive net job creation from AI and related technologies. The agriculture sector, however, will see permanent job loss as some of China's automation programmes are looking to eliminate human labour. For instance, Jiangsu Province launched a pilot programme in 2018 that employs unmanned tractors, rice-transplanters, pesticide-applicators, and fertilisation equipment aided by a navigational satellite, replacing human labour (China Power 2019).

China appears to be well-set to increase the pace of its move towards increasing automation (as we saw from the acceleration of robotics installations). The main issue now is to improve in the two key areas measured by the global EIU Index, with a particular emphasis on continuing education and preparing workforces for the significant changes ahead.

However, unless the deficiencies in these areas are addressed, the pace of automation will not achieve that required by the 2025 strategic plan. The education system needs to be capable of delivering a) a better-educated technician workforce, and b) a managerial cohort to provide the leadership required to implement automation across agriculture, manufacturing, and the services sector. Moreover, a flexible labour market, which encourages re-skilling and occupational movement and is linked to an active regional policy, may help obviate some of the labour market problems discussed in relation to the *hukou* system discussed below. Given the importance of education, it is worth exploring the latest educational reform plans.

Education and Economic Growth

There is a clear policy link in China between technological advancement, economic growth, and the developing education system. China now has one of the world's largest tertiary education systems, with 27 million students in its universities and colleges (including 16.1 million in technical or specialised short-cycle programmes), 2 million in graduate schools and research institutes, and 5.8 million in 284 tertiary institutions for adult education. The tertiary education participation rate is 56.1% (Statista 2019). This compares favourably with 37% across the EU and 50.2% in England.

Public higher educational institutions, where 86% of students are enrolled, are overseen by either the central ministries or the provincial authorities. All the institutions under the central ministries are full universities; the majority of the most prestigious universities are overseen by the Ministry of Education.

As university enrolments in China continue to increase, the number of young college graduates (ages 25 to 34) with tertiary degrees in China is projected to rise a further 300% by 2030, compared with an increase of about 30% in Europe and the United States (World Education News + Reviews 2019).

In 2013, China already accounted for 17% of all young college graduates across OECD countries, the largest share among all countries. This share is expected to reach 27% by 2030. China's contribution to the pool of scientists and skilled technicians will be even greater; its share is projected to reach 37% by 2030 (OECD 2015).

The main gap in China's education provision is continuing education for adults linked to workforce adaptation. Unfortunately, despite its popularity following the Deng reforms, vocational education has declined in popularity since 2000. This situation of dwindling interest from students in vocational school education has been the obverse of the massive investment in, and attractiveness of, higher education. Between 1998 and 2008, the number of vocational secondary education schools dropped by 35% and by another 27% by 2016 (Yi *et al.* 2018). Funding used to be a problem as well. In 2013, for instance, vocational secondary schools received only 10% of the total budget for secondary education, while academic schools received about 90%.

Since 2014, and again in 2019, the Ministry of Education has recognised the economic *raison d'être* of investment in adult and vocational education. In 2010, it set the goal to boost enrolments in vocational schools to 23.5 million by 2020, although this objective would be hard to achieve. In fact, in 2018, the number of vocational secondary schools decreased by 4% from the previous year. There were 10,200 vocational secondary schools nationwide in that year.

In March 2014, a China Dual Track Education Programme was announced in a speech by Vice Minister of Education Lu Xin at the China Development Forum (Liu 2014b). The policies announced in the speech were officially published by the Ministry of Education, slightly modified, in the Modern Vocational Education Development Strategy 2014–2020. According to the strategy, the priority areas for vocational education are modern agriculture, advanced manufacturing, service industry, strategic industries, energy, transportation, ocean industry, social management, and the creative and culture sectors.

The policy documents aim to support the development of a world-class modern vocational education system that meets China's needs by 2020. According to the policy documents, the Tertiary Vocation Education and Training (TVET) system should contribute to the development of a highly qualified workforce, promote career development, and develop skills and talents that are competitive in the international market. Moreover, the policy documents support the involvement of other stakeholders in providing and developing TVET. It states that the proportion of medium and large enterprises participating in running vocational education schools should be above 80% by 2020. By the end of 2014, 26 major companies were involved in providing and developing vocational education.

In 2019, the government put forward a comprehensive National Vocational Education Reform Implementation Plan (Xinhuanet 2019b), which is intended to boost enrolments in vocational secondary schools from the current ratio of 40% to 50% by 2022. The Ministry of Finance has earmarked additional funding for scholarships and financial assistance and other incentives to bolster vocational education.

The government is also piloting a new so-called 1+x certificate system under which graduates of both secondary schools and universities can earn a vocational skills certificate in fields like information technology, transportation logistics, or elder care.

Despite some missteps and a need to accelerate the development of technical and vocational training, especially in a continuing educational context, the Chinese government is now committed to moving forward at a rapid pace. The strategy of setting a goal that more than 80% of large and medium-sized companies will become 'providers of TVET services' by 2020 is one of the ways. The strategy includes the option of providing TVET for employees that will not only be institutionalised but will also become a legal responsibility of companies.

It is also envisaged that provincial governments will play a key role. A recent priority of the Ministry of Education is to push provincial governments to establish mandatory funding for the TVET sector based on the number of students in TVET. Provincial governments will be given greater financial flexibility on how to spend their TVET budget. They would have more autonomy in adapting central guidelines according to local circumstances, especially on accrediting and assessing TVET schools. This would also include identifying prioritised provincial lists of professions taught in schools, using localised course materials, and designing local curricula based on cooperation with local industries.

Finally, in an attempt to shift the focus from academic qualifications, a new player will be the Universities of Applied Sciences (UAS) which will issue bachelor degrees (World Education News + Reviews 2019). UAS are mentioned in the strategy as 'a key component of the higher education sector, equal with academic universities', but 'administrated separately and differently'. As the strategy states, universities that aim at 'providing labour force to the service industry and supporting local economic development' are encouraged to transform themselves into Universities of Applied Sciences.

One might question whether these various strategies will all be entirely successful, but clearly the shift in focus amid financial and other commitments are evident and necessary.

Demography, Employment, and Socio-Economic Development

The 10% economic growth rates achieved by China between 1990 and 2010 were substantially driven by the availability of a sustained increase in the labour supply from rural to urban industrial areas. However, *adverse* demographic factors have recently become considerable concern in China. China's labour force grew until 2017, but having reached a peak, it is now falling. Moreover, the age profile is shifting towards the older generational segments.

There are a variety of demographic factors at play in China. It is worth summarising them and then providing an analysis of the relative positive and negative impacts on economic growth over the next two decades.

First, in common with many East Asian countries and many other parts of the world, China has been experiencing a decline in fertility rate. In the case of China, this fall was exacerbated by the one-child policy in force from 1979, which was intended to ameliorate the pro-birth policy of the Mao era.

The statistics are startling. The ratio of people under the age of 15 to those in the 15 to 65 age group declined from 70% in 1975 to 22% in 2012. Nonetheless, during roughly the same period between 1978 and 2010, the age group of 15 to 65 increased from 58% of the population to 74%, contributing substantially to China's economic growth during this period. The inevitable reduction of availability of labour may lead to reductions in China's hitherto extraordinary high annual economic growth rates. Some estimates suggest an achievement of only 4% until around 2027, though the International Monetary Fund (IMF) put it at 5.7% from 2021 to 2025 (IMF 2019). However, the continuation of these comparatively high rates — but not super high growth rates as before — will depend far more on increases in productivity driven by technology. Hence, the priority being placed on technology by the Chinese government.

Second, accompanying these figures, UNDP projections suggest that between 2015 and 2040, China's post-65 years population will increase from 135 million to 340 million, a growth rate of 3.7% per annum (Eberstadt 2019). This trend will provide further challenges in providing pensions and other incomes and service provision for this large cohort. One positive factor is that this group should be the best-educated and healthiest in Chinese history, and they are likely to be less economically dependent on their children than previous generations.

Linked to this change is going to be the impact of the one-child family structure on the traditional extended family structure. With a high proportion of male children leading to a reduction in marriages, there will be a higher proportion of single and male households. Given the importance of family in the social and moral life of Chinese society, this development will have social, welfare, and even political significance, as well as economic impact, in the future.

Third, the above factors may be partially offset by migration policies, internal and external. As far as migration to China is concerned, the average annual influx between 2010 and 2020 is around 130,000. This is compared to a US figure of around 630,000 over the same period — a number five times larger with a population three and a half times less than China. One economic solution to China's demographic problem would be to increase the inflow of migrant workers from other countries.

But there is also significant internal migration in China. Internal migrants, at 18 million, formed less than 2% of the population in 1990. In 2017, this was 286 million where they formed 18% of the population. Internal flows from 2013 to 2017 were between 4 to 5 million persons per year.

The 2017 National Bureau of Statistics (NBS) survey also found that most rural migrants still prefer the eastern region in China, but there has been an increasing growth of migrant workers in the western and central regions. The eastern region accounted for 36.4% of the total number of rural workers; the central region accounted for 33%; the western region accounted for 27.3%, an increase of 3.3% from the previous year; and the northeast accounted for 3.3%, an increase of 3.1%.

These migrant flows are motivated by a number of factors, including to seek higher wages, job opportunities, and better basic education and medical services. The search for better education and medical services is, however, constrained by the problem that in the inflow cities, usually the larger cities, migrants cannot enjoy the same public services as local residents because of the constraints of the *hukou* system (to be discussed in the next section).

It is likely that the movement of the rural population to the cities will continue over the next two decades. United Nations' estimates suggest that the proportion of the population living in cities and other urban centres is projected to rise from over 50% in 2017 to well over 70% in 2037 (UN

2018). This projection may not be validated, especially if real wages in China's rural areas continue to rise.

Hukou System

The *hukou* (household registration) factor is closely linked to the nature of internal migration which has supported industrial growth in China. In turn, the availability of this source of labour is related to the essential need to reform the *hukou* system. The system links every Chinese resident with their birthplace. Residents can only fully access their health care, pension, and education for their children in their birthplace (Song and Smith 2019).

The *hukou* system has ancient roots in China, but in formal, legislative terms it dates from 1958 in the Mao era. Essentially, at that time, it divided the registration of citizens into agricultural residents and non-agricultural residents.

Agricultural *hukou* holders (rural residents) have land rights[1] but no social welfare services, and non-agricultural *hukou* holders (urban residents) had access to social welfare services but no land rights. The economic aim was to drive industrial development in urban areas. As agriculture gradually became mechanised and required less labour, there was a movement of labour from rural areas to urban areas for jobs in the industries. Various subsequent reforms were made — accelerating during and following the Deng era — to introduce more flexibility in the overall *hukou* system to provide greater access rights to public services for rural migrants coming into cities and urban areas.

In 2014, a State Council policy initiative — 'Opinions on Further Promoting *Hukou* Reform' (Refworld 2015) — marked a new era in reforming the *hukou* and managing internal labour mobility and migration in China. This policy initiative had five key aspects:

1) adjusting *hukou* conversion policy;
2) unifying the urban and rural *hukou* registration system;
3) introducing a residence permit system;
4) establishing a national basic population database; and
5) increasing the coverage of basic public services to the residential population in cities.

[1]As discussed later on, the possession of land rights is an important issue.

The 2014 *hukou* policy explicitly sets different limits for *hukou* conversion by city size; the larger the size of a city, the higher the threshold of *hukou* conversion. As a result, the *hukou* has been liberalised in medium and small cities. This allows for education for migrant workers' children, but the 'threshold' to increase migrants' rights for large cities and megacities remains high, in turn discouraging migration from rural areas and constraining labour mobility.

While important strides are being made on *hukou* reforms, more actions are needed to meet the government's ambitious plan to settle 100 million people in cities (Xinhuanet 2018b). Local governments have been piloting various 'quasi *hukou*' status categories as a transitional solution that provides partial access to urban public services and welfare. The goal is to establish a fully residence-based *hukou* system, which would not need a separate residence permit system.

But *hukou* restrictions in large cities and megacities remain problematic. *Hukou* conversion rules in large cities and megacities only allow highly qualified migrants to move in. Early research by Zhang and Pi (2016) found that the attraction of urban regions to rural migrant labour is closely related to the ownership structure of the urban economy which affects wage structures.

After the 1990s, rural labour that migrated to the cities tended to work outside of the traditional system, and few could squeeze into state-owned enterprises. The *hukou* system's discrimination was not only reflected in wages but also in job opportunities. Based on survey data on Beijing, Wuxi, and Zhuhai and referenced by Zhang (2010), it was discovered that *hukou*-based discrimination reduced job opportunities for the migrant population and increased the costs that they bore while job hunting and unemployed. Therefore, although short-term migrants may mainly work in jobs that locals are unwilling to do, they change jobs less often and only when they have stayed in the city long enough to have accumulated enough savings.

Not all public services do or can exclude migrant workers, such as open green spaces and public transport. However, without the local urban *hukou*, local public schools in large cities will not in general admit children of migrant workers; if they do, the fee tends to be higher. Schools for migrant children have opened, but funding is limited.

The issue of access to education is important as there is evidence of its importance for China's economic growth rate — termed by economists as endogenous human capital investment. In plain words, this means the contribution that parents make by investing in the education of their children.

Later evidence indicates the continuing nature of the problems still being faced by migrant workers. According to the China Labour Bulletin (2019), in 2018, only 35.1% of migrant workers had a work contract, 22% had basic pension or medical insurance, 27% had work-related injury insurance, and only 17% had unemployment insurance.

A further important contribution that migrant workers make is by transferring payments back to their rural homeland. These remittances are large enough to be a source of income growth for undeveloped rural regions, thereby alleviating poverty and assisting with rural households' medical expenses (Liang and Ma 2004). In a poor Sichuan township in the mid-1990s, the money posted back home by migrant workers every year was five times greater than that of the town government's fiscal revenue.

Despite these problems, some progress has been made since the *hukou* reforms were announced in 2014. Other problems are related to the failures of local governments to deliver on the national policy approach. For instance, rural migrant workers should be allowed to decide whether they want to keep or sell their land rights if they change their *hukou* status. If they sell the land rights, then adequate reimbursement should be made (Andreas and Zhan 2016). These solutions serve as part of the continuing efforts to systematically reform the *hukou* system across Chinese cities.

In April 2019, the National Development and Reform Commission (NDRC) announced that local governments of cities with an urban population of 1 million to 3 million residents should eliminate all restrictions for *hukou*. The NDRC also said 'governments of cities with an urban population of 3 million to 5 million should also ease restrictions for farmers-turned workers who have lived there for more than five years, as well as technicians, college, and vocational school graduates and people who have obtained overseas degrees' (Cheng and Shen 2019).

As indicated in the above reports, the Ministry of Public Security (MPS), NBS, and NDRC have worked together to help implement the process nationally, to evaluate the progress that has been made or not made, and to continue further reforms of the *hukou* system. The MPS is managing the *hukou* application process and ultimately delivering the urban *hukou* to interested migrant workers. The NBS is providing an annual evaluation of the results of the *hukou* reform process by surveying the rural migrants themselves.

Ironically, given the reputation that China has as a 'centralised authoritarian state' in the eyes of the West, the conclusion is that the fragmented response to the *hukou* reforms needs to be more centrally integrated across the urban centres and cites of China. Many of China's problems are, ironically, caused by unconstrained decentralisation rather than by top-down, centralised government instigated by the CCP — a Western myth!

Social Development

One area of policy where the Chinese socialist system appears to lag behind various developed countries in a number of aspects is its social security system. Notwithstanding certain problems, including the *hukou* issue, China's record in terms of attempting to ensure social development is that it keeps pace with economic development.

Pension provision is an issue, as it is indeed in Western countries. In terms of coverage, China has managed giant strides over the past decade. The strategy proposed by the 18th National Congress of the Communist Party of China (NCCPC) aimed at establishing pensions for all in the form of basic security. This approach drove the extraordinary extension of pension coverage in China, from 360 million people in 2010 to 858 million people in 2015, representing an average annual increase of 19%. The International Social Security Association gave the prestigious Award of Outstanding Achievement in Social Security to the Chinese government for this unprecedented extension of pensions. The problem of pension stratification, however, remains unresolved. In China, 80% of the retired population receives a pension, but the stratification means that the majority, just over 60%, receive only the basic social pension, the URRSP (Urban-Rural Resident Social Pension). Civil servants, at 5.6% of pensioners, receive the most generous occupational pensions, followed by state-owned enterprise pensioners (5.5%) and private company pensioners (7.7%) (Zhu and Walker 2018).

The problem for China's current provision is this extreme stratification of the scheme, substantially as a result of the proportion of the population who live in rural areas, especially in the north and west, receiving only the URRSP or no pension at all, amid the legacy of being an emerging economy.

The problem is alleviated by income transfers from children, which, though falling as a proportion of pensioners' income, was still at 40% of the elderly population's incomes in 2005. The existence of this contribution alleviates poverty and also strengthens social solidarity between generations. Benefit levels for employment pensions are increasing along with economic development. The levels of the Enterprise Employee Basic Pension (EEBP) have increased at a rate of 10% every year since 2005, and 8% in 2016 (Keyong and Donghyun 2019).

A World Bank report (2019a) suggested a more sustainable pension system with an automatic balancing mechanism, (i.e., effectively a 'funded model' with some redistribution). The report argued that adequate pension levels, via a funded scheme, could reduce precautionary savings, boost domestic consumption, remove fiscal pressure, and promote macroeconomic stability. In 2014, the total social insurance contribution rate was over 40% in China and among the highest in the world. Lowering that rate would increase disposable income, which, in turn, would promote higher household consumption. A move in this direction, suggested the report, may become increasingly important as China is rebalancing towards greater growth reliance on consumption.

However, it is not clear that China will follow this advice nor that it would be appropriate to move in the direction suggested. This is partly explained by the nature and intrinsic value of the Chinese mandatory social security system. In relation to the basic state pension, the scheme is that of 'pay as you go', which could continue to be funded from taxation, with an enhanced redistributive element. The majority of Chinese workers have no access to funded schemes through private pension providers.

Funded models generally provide higher benefits for individuals, dependent on the size of the fund and the state of the stock market when cashed. Given the collectivist approach of China, it is easy to see that a funded scheme would more likely worsen rather than improve the stratification of the pension structure in China.

China's Regional Development Strategy

The optimisation of spatial growth in any economy is a key factor in reaching national growth potential. This is no less the case in China where regional planning and development have a high priority in the national economic strategy, especially since China's reform and opening up policies from the 1980s (Dunford and Bonschab 2013). Four regional strategies — Western Region Development, Northeast Region Revitalisation, Rise of the Central Region, and Leading Development in the Coastal Region — were initially deployed as national strategies to optimise spatial development, cultivate new growth poles, and foster territorial cooperation.

The key early elements of the regional policy were a massive investment in transport infrastructure (especially rail) using the 'reform and opening' strategy to develop manufacturing and its port infrastructure in China's southeast. It also encouraged substantial ongoing movement of population from rural and agricultural areas to urban areas. Subsequently, and especially in recent years, the intensity of the transport infrastructure construction has been reduced in favour of a substantial increase in digital infrastructure to further develop connectivity.

Since China's Third Plenum in 2012 (Nelson 2013), four further major regional strategies have been proposed to complement the original four: the Jing-Jin-Ji Coordinated Development, Yangtze River Economic Belt, the Belt and Road Initiative (BRI) and the more recent Greater Bay Area Initiative.

Jing-Jin-Ji Coordinated Development

The Jing-Jin-Ji Coordinated Development or 'Jing-Jin-Ji plan', otherwise known as the Beijing-Tianjin-Hebei Integrated Development Plan (China Briefing 2018), is a multi-regional urban developmental cluster with Beijing as its central focus. The capital city will also provide a pivotal framework for the cluster's regional coordination and reconstruction.

The Jing-Jin-Ji plan aims to set out a variety of regional areas which can develop their individual comparative advantages. This way, each area complements another, while their shared benefits are integrated to achieve maximum effect.

Sub-regions falling into the Jing-Jin-Ji plan are assumed to already possess different relative advantages in particular areas. As an example, Beijing is the nation's political, educational, cultural, and R&D powerhouse; Tianjin is northern China's logistics hub, having one of the world's busiest ports; whereas Hebei is a region surrounding Beijing and parts of Tianjin, containing concentrations of heavy industry such as steel.

Altogether the conurbation is home to over 100 million inhabitants and encompasses a zone exceeding 200,000 square kilometres. The Jing-Jin-Ji plan will act as China's new dynamo to power domestic national innovation services and manufacturing-led economic expansion (Huang 2014). It will also be a showcase for environmental greening and ecological upgrading.

Other than intensive environmental management, the other key areas for modernisation in the coordinated Jing-Jin-Ji master plan will be industrial re-design and renovation, amid the extensive and efficient integration of a state-of-the-art transport system.

Among the scheme's new features, one of the most important objectives will be to deal with the resolution of the regions' social and economic problems coming off the back of a re-orientation towards a post-industrial economy. Correspondingly, the plan will set out the groundwork for high environmental standards involving heightened levels of focused investment designed to foster the creation and maintenance of value-added industrial assets (Preen 2018).

As such, the Hebei region will move towards becoming a state-of-the-art industrial cluster while shifting away from its traditional heavy industrial base. Tianjin will evolve into a highly-advanced research and development zone for manufacturing. It will also serve as a launchpad for attracting domestic and international financial innovation and technology. The Tianjin Free Trade Zone (TFTZ) will support the city of Tianjin in this transition into a modern high-tech services-centred economy (Jing 2018). Its role will be as an area for implementing a flexible regulation regime and policy liberalisation.

In entering this transitional phase, various productive capacities which are no longer benefiting from previous comparative advantages have been migrated out of Beijing. These include industrial plants, food, and agricultural wholesale markets. Such assets have also been shifted out of Tianjin into less developed areas of Hebei.

One objective of this migration of industry and basic resources from Beijing has been to remedy the city's pollution and traffic congestion. Therefore, to make the whole region's economic development more sustainable, Hebei will become a key ecological protection zone (World Bank 2016b), endowed with natural environments including dedicated national parks and forests circling the capital.

Alongside the focus on nature development, several new areas known as 'urbanisation demonstration zones' will be created around Beijing. These will offer opportunities for the commercial sector to provide innovative services in the form of social and public provision to facilitate and promote de-urbanisation and de-industrialisation.

As the Jing-Jin-Ji plan rebalances and integrates regional resources, the end result would be to foster the development of consumer markets and raise aggregate demand from the higher incomes anticipated to arise from the transition to a services-led, consumption economy.

The Yangtze River Economic Belt

The Yangtze River Economic Belt encompasses 11 provinces and a multitude of cities in China (Xinhuanet 2019c). It spans the three major regions including the Yangtze River Delta city cluster in the country's east, and the vast hinterland located in the central and western regions. The Yangtze River, commonly referred to as the 'golden waterway', boasts the largest inland waterway in the world. While the land area around the Yangtze River Economic Belt covers only just over one-fifth of the country's territory, it hosts a disproportionate share of the population — roughly 43% of China's inhabitants. In 2018, it accounted for up to a quarter of the nation's GDP and is an important element of the country's economic growth (PricewaterhouseCoopers 2019). In 2014, the State Council announced the 'Guiding Opinions on Relying on the Golden Waterway to Promote the Development of the Yangtze River Economic Belt' (*China Daily* 2014). This programme entailed development of the region into a globally significant inland river economic system. It would be promoted internationally through a pilot development zone dedicated towards upgrading ecological conservation along the country's eastern coastline and the banks of the Yangtze River.

The region would also benefit from interactive cooperation between developed eastern China and fast-developing western China. However, integration is still expected to be challenging due to its scale and ambition, not least due to the obstacles in overcoming the tradition of provincial and prefectural governments competing for projects and investment opportunities. The project has also been designed to tap the sizeable domestic demand potential in the upper and middle reaches of the surrounding hinterland.

It will also be an overarching structure in narrowing the development gap between China's disparate and vast eastern, central, and western regions. The principal connection will be the construction of a new land-sea two-way corridor. Businesses located on the eastern coast will be able to more easily migrate westwards, benefiting from the latter region's lower wages and various financial incentives provided by the Chinese government's 'Go West' strategy (*China Daily* 2016).

By these means, the government envisages a gradual transfer of industrial capacity from the Yangtze River Delta region to further inland.

For the traditionally industrialised Delta, the outbound migration of its heavy industries will make space for the development of more environmentally sustainable and higher value-added industry sectors. In support of the project, President Xi has emphasised that it should focus on environmental sustainability over rapid economic growth.

The Yangtze River Economic Belt will also link the Yangtze River Delta region to the central Chinese city of Chongqing (China Briefing 2018) at the intersection of the national east-west crossroads of the BRI — a region which lacks highly developed and interconnected infrastructure and currently hosts inefficient railway and highway linkages.

Given the details outlined above, the Yangtze River Economic Belt project is clearly one of China's most ambitious and challenging grand re-designs of the country. To a large extent, the obstacles it faces are probably greater than China's other two aspiring internal developmental clusters — the Greater Bay Area of southern China's coastal provinces and the Beijing-Tianjin-Hebei region. No matter how challenging the prospects, China has become almost unique, in the modern era, to dare embark on such mammoth extravaganzas, alongside developing a critical eye for planning detail and excellence in resources management.

Nonetheless, in a recent speech at a symposium, President Xi urged all parts of the region to prioritise key technologies, and hence to foster the development of micro and SME businesses in the industrial sectors of integrated circuitry, biomedicine, and artificial intelligence applications (*China Daily* 2020).

With high-level manufacturing, strong consumption power, and an advanced export-oriented economy, the Delta region would be able to set a national example for the future development of city clusters in the context of the 'dual circulation' development pattern — integrating domestic and foreign industrial production — which will form the framework for the next five-year plan.

On January 16th, 2020, the Anhui Provincial Development and Reform Commission released a plan on regional integration (*China Daily* 2020), indicating that the province, which is home to many prominent universities and institutions, will work with Shanghai to bolster research in cutting-edge technologies with an aim to elevate the country's overall innovative capacity.

Businesses have already benefited from the integrated development of the Yangtze River Delta region. Zhang Xiaojun, vice-president of smart wearable devices maker Huami Corp, which is headquartered in Hefei, said that the integrated development of the Yangtze River Delta region has already brought about more favourable changes for small and medium-sized companies, including a larger talent pool from which to recruit staff.

Belt and Road Initiative (BRI)

Although there will be substantial regional impacts of the BRI in and across China, the BRI is also an investment and technology programme extending far from China's borders along the ancient Silk Road trading routes. However, its internal regional economic development impact should not be ignored.

The external dimension of this major two-pronged economic and diplomatic initiative was launched by President Xi Jinping. The 'Silk Road Economic Belt', being the overland component, was announced towards end-2013 when President Xi visited Kazakhstan. The sea route, known as the '21st Century Maritime Silk Road', was unveiled during his visit to Indonesia one month later. The BRI has been interpreted as China's new strategy to further integrate itself with surrounding countries and regions. On a more sceptical level, it has been viewed as a scheme to reshape the world's political and economic landscape by leveraging its recently attained economic power.

All told, the BRI embraces a growing list of countries, which by end-2020 numbered over 135 officially signed up states. The initiative's area of coverage exceeds 40% of the world's entire land mass and over 4.5 billion people, making up three-fifths of the global population. By 2019, the combined value of BRI-affiliated economies amounted to US$28 trillion — close to 40% of global output. Needless to say, these figures are subject to constant change, given the ongoing and expanding coverage of the BRI around the world, particularly as it reaches out across continents even in the face of the economically debilitating coronavirus pandemic.

The BRI's principal geographic corridors spread out through a couple of major tributaries. The land corridor connects China via Central Asia and Russia mainly to southern and eastern Europe. It also links China, via Central Asia and parts of South Asia, to the Persian Gulf, East Africa, and the eastern Mediterranean. Meanwhile, another major sub-corridor connects China, via Southeast Asia's subcontinental IndoChina peninsular, to various parts of South Asia and the Indian Ocean.

The other major route is mainly a sea route which runs from China's eastern and southern coastal ports across the South China Sea, along the Southeast Asian island-chain archipelago, then on to the Indian Ocean. Another sub-corridor extends across the South China Sea and into the South Pacific.

The BRI's key land-enabling platforms include major global cities that often serve as financial service centres, and the construction of state-of-the-art industrial, technology, and business parks. Its sea connections include key ports as nodes on a pan-continental trading network.

China has been jointly constructing transportation channels with other countries as key partners. The BRI's web of regional and pan-continental interconnections essentially rely on existing bilateral and multilateral mechanisms between China and relevant countries and on developing existing and proven regional cooperation platforms.

In this regard, the Chinese government have made reassurances that the BRI will neither overlap nor compete with existing international and regional cooperation groupings that intersect with its corridors, including the Eurasian Economic Union, the European Union, the African Union, the Gulf Cooperation Council, and the ASEAN Economic Community among other international formal regional groupings. Instead, it will work with other formats of international cooperation in a complementary and non-divisive way and as a means of injecting *new* funding and economic vitality into these forums, where agreed with their constituent member states.

The fact that the initial BRI model was fairly land-based, being dominated by projects like Jakarta-Bandung high-speed railway in Indonesia, Abuja-Kaduna railway in Nigeria, and Vientiane-Boten railway in Laos, posed substantial challenges to improving connectivity for China, with its projects spreading all across the globe.

This was the reason for the emphasis on the maritime dimension as a second, key element in the construction of the BRI. Its sea connections include key ports operating as nodes on the extended trading network, which is the means of avoiding the historic maritime constraints which China has long had to endure. For China, this grand maritime logistics plan is not aggressive and expansionist; it is inclusive and mutually developmental in nature for all countries participating.

ASEAN-plus Three (APT), which was set up in 1997, strengthens initiatives such as the BRI because it cooperatively links China, Japan, and the Republic of Korea with the other 10 nation-states of the Association of Southeast Asian Nations (ASEAN).

As recently as February 2020, the APT leaders adopted a Joint Statement reaffirming the importance of solidarity and working collectively together in the fight against COVID-19 and to contain the pandemic and protect their populations (ASEAN Secretariat 2018). They also reaffirmed commitment to ensure macroeconomic and financial stability by keeping markets open for trade and investment. This included ensuring cross border supply chain movements, particularly for the flow of essential goods such as medical supplies, medicines, and food. We will revisit this regional cooperative framework in more detail in Chapter 9.

In general, the BRI sets out five principal objectives to be achieved between countries, regions, and across continents:

- policy coordination;
- infrastructure connectivity;
- free and fair trade;
- financial integration; and
- people mobility.

Since its official inception, the BRI has raised financing of US$2.4 trillion by 2020, according to Refinitiv. This has taken shape in the form of debt and equity investments. Much of this investment has been largely channelled into infrastructure development for ports, roads, railways, airports, power plants, and telecommunications networks, but increasingly for manufacturing plants, technology, and digital service centres.

Digital Silk Road (DSR)

One other outstanding feature of the BRI is the development of digitisation along the routes: namely the DSR (Fitch Solutions 2019; Kitson and Liew 2019).

The first iteration of the DSR in 2015 included a broad set of ICT infrastructure investments that supported the BRI strategy, including but not limited to laying fibre optic cables and creating data centres. The DSR development includes network equipment, technology, and facilitating software in the form of 5G networks (Pointe Bello 2019). Since 2019 a new focus is on building smart ports that incorporate integrated smart management and operations technologies. Moreover, China is also establishing along the routes its own technological standards and principles of cyber-sovereignty, though it also works within international standards bodies to establish these as international standards.

The DSR incorporates telecoms, media, and technology to develop the BRI across Asia, the Middle East, Europe, Africa and Latin America, and uses these corridors to enable major Chinese technology companies to export smart-city sensors and data platforms across its own digital highway with its own standards. An example here is the agreement between Algeria and China to build five industrial and port infrastructure projects, increasing the two countries' cooperation in railways, steel, engineering, and petrochemicals.

The size of this digitisation programme is immense. It involves the building of approximately 30% of the existing fibre optic cables in Asia and 54% of planned cables. In a global sense, China itself owns or supplies 11% of existing cables and 24% of planned cables. The domestic BeiDou[2] satellite navigation system is now supported by more satellites (35 in total) than the US-aligned GPS navigation system; 30 BRI nations have signed up to use the BeiDou satellite navigation network (Beidou 2020).

The emerging DSR platform appears to be creating a new East-centred trade world, capable of competing with the US-led West. It is imperative that digital integration and interoperability is achieved with the Western US-led system. However, recent actions have suggested that the US is apparently only interested in continuing domination, not collaboration. The global aim should be reducing total costs of supply chain movements through optimal asset utilisation, lowering inventory costs in the form of efficient cargo management, and ensuring open access to the entire value chain from manufacture to end user.

The US and some other governments in the West view the BRI development as a direct Chinese challenge to the US-dominated neoliberal international order. The alternative view is that China, now re-emerging as a world power, is willing to emancipate itself within a growing array of strategic partner countries. This new agglomeration is challenging the hegemonic rule of the US with an alternative structure, but one which is open to global collaboration both technologically and politically.

[2]On August 3, 2020, a news conference was held at the State Council Information Office, announcing that the BeiDou Navigation Satellite System BDS-3 was formally commissioned.

In fact, it is not an assertion of a desire by China to replace one hegemony with another. We will revisit this geopolitical dimension of the BRI and the DSR specifically in the next chapter and in Chapter 11, challenging a pervasive view in the West that China is attempting to establish a new, structural hegemonic world order.

Concluding Comments

This chapter has described how the patterns and dynamics of economic growth in China have influenced not only its urban and rural development but also its overall internal population movements. It has also looked at how China is further adjusting its technology and its education system to facilitate a continuation of its growth beyond that of a middle-income country. The suggestion has been made that the distinctive and rapid nature of socio-economic development of China is related to its key ethnographic difference — to an extent shared with other East Asian countries — linked to its collectivist approach, and which is markedly different from the Western liberal market approach.

Despite adverse demographic trends, future technological development, environmental challenges, and the current external concerns from a US-led Western coalition of countries, China's economic development and continuation of increasing prosperity for its people seems set to continue, though probably at a more modest pace than before.

The BRI is deployed as a partnership programme (with, admittedly, side-benefits to the Chinese construction and technology sectors). One key aim is to connect and protect trade routes and projects of strategic trade and investment importance to China. The BRI should be understood, principally, as a project connecting China to the rest of the world and defending its trade and other interests. It is not — as it was not historically with Imperial China — an attempt to create a new world order or to exert apolitical or cultural global hegemony.

Chapter 4

Projecting Global Influence

Introduction

Insofar as China has sought global influence — related to its increasing technology excellence and dominance in some areas, and to its economic and trade 'weight' in the world — its approach represents a different style and substance of the approach taken by the US in the second half of the twentieth century. China is not attempting to establish a global 'moral' and ideological hegemonic leadership, as did, and still does, the US. As we have seen in relation to the BRI and will explore further in this chapter, China's approach is different.

Nonetheless, there is little doubt that the Chinese CCP leadership is as convinced of the superiority of its 'socialism with Chinese characteristics' as US proponents are of 'liberal individualist democracy'. The difference is indicated by the 'Chinese characteristics' qualifier. China does not seek to impose its political system on other countries: contrary to the US elites' belief that liberal individual democracy is a universally applicable system. Insofar as the China elites believe this to be the case, it is indifferent as to whether other countries wish to follow a socialist path.

However, China does not define boundaries in strictly defined physical terms. This does not imply that it wishes to alter physical boundaries by the use of unilateral force.[1] Moreover, its economic, technological, and financial expansion should not be characterised as 'twenty-first century

[1] It may be argued that it is attempting such action in the maritime boundaries within the South China Sea, but this is misleading, see Chapter 11.

colonialism', as it is by some opponents. China constantly refers to the 'partnership relations' underpinning the development of the BRI, and the initiative is perhaps the best example of China's most successful projection of 'soft power'.

For contemporary and ancient China, the driving force is to expand its influence by connecting with others. It wishes to be admired as an extended civilisation, but not to dominate: to be respected, but not to convert. This approach may be seen in relation to the BRI and its overall foreign relations approach.

The BRI as Soft Power

The successful pursuance of the BRI project relies on the strong engagement of the considerably different partner countries and regional groupings along the corridors/routes of the BRI. Insofar as China's aim is a major political-economic shift of global territorial transport and communication structures to influence the economic geography of the global capitalist system, then this is intended to be done without imposing Chinese values on other country participants. Indeed, China has no interest whatsoever in so doing. The BRI is not a twenty-first century colonial enterprise. It is intended, however, to improve the connectivity of China with the partner countries along the various routes. It is a soft power initiative, not a colonial takeover (Sharma and Singh 2019).

In economic terms, the BRI should be regarded as an organic growth corridor. Its various geographical nodes stimulate further transport and telecommunications networks and industrial development, reaching into the interiors of the territories involved. This organic development will both be aligned with the economic profiles of the countries concerned and to their resource endowments. Obviously, movements of goods along the main route and its various branches will stimulate the movement of people, especially artisans and artists, as did the ancient Silk Road.

Yet, because of the deep suspicion engendered by ideological Cold War rhetoric, though now more overt, China will want to avoid too high a national profile. Instead, China stresses the economic principles behind the various projects, large and small. The BRI must appear as enhancing the current world order, not attempting to transform it, and certainly not in terms of advertising Chinese socialist values. Other countries along the BRI routes will require even more attention from China to avoid resentment based on potential misperception and conflicts with distinctively different cultures. There is, perhaps, another area where care needs to be exercised, namely in relation to creating Chinese standards, such as technical standards, which do not become *de facto* international standards to be imposed on other countries. In this regard, China has a clear and positive approach to the setting of open international standards and will eventually publish a China 2035 Standards Plan. In 2020 it published a preliminary paper, '2020 Standardisation Key Areas of Work in China' (Deutsche Gessellschaft fur Internationale Zussammenarbeit 2020).

The involvement of East Asian countries in the BRI 'partnership' programme, though not without its problems, should — by virtue of geographical proximity, strong trade links, and similar cultural traditions — exhibit greater mutual understanding and perhaps induce less suspicion of China. Though even here, historical rivalries and current geopolitical concerns play their part in raising stumbling blocks.

The BRI thus has implications for the Asia-Pacific regional order and for the world order more generally, as will be discussed in Chapter 9. If successful, from China's perspective, the initiative may help create a well-integrated, extended economic 'sphere of influence' driven by Chinese capital, expertise, and philosophy, and strengthen China as a respected economic partner for its neighbours and other countries along the BRI routes. Ideally, from China's perspective in the East Asian context, it could enhance a complementary set of new institutions, such as the AIIB, based on shared Asian interests and values, amid other ASEAN initiatives linking with the BRI investments in East Asia. More widely, for instance in Africa, it may be able to demonstrate the validity of a non-colonial development model without the constraints imposed by current Western-led international organisations and funding agencies.

Difficulties for China on BRI

Despite the golden scenario painted above, the BRI presents significant problems for China. The current sets of international institutions are informed by so-called 'Western' values. One may agree or disagree with these values, but the national and international elites, led by the US elites, that hold them perceive China and its values as threats. This arises not only in geopolitical terms but also in the general global acceptance of these 'universal' values. In this context, China tends to be regarded as an outlier. China has no interest in 'converting' other countries to its set of values. It is interested only in defending the territorial integrity of China and, in terms of political values, its 'socialism with Chinese characteristics'. Nevertheless, its actions, including the BRI project, tend to be viewed with suspicion, including by some of the beneficiary BRI countries.

However, even setting aside Western influence and propaganda, China has considerable work to do to eliminate potentially damaging negative impressions of its economic and technological expansion. In part, this is because of the, albeit limited, security installations in some parts of the BRI which give the impression of the creation of a wider, albeit defensive, security architecture beyond China's recognised international borders. In practice, only one concrete example can be adduced, in the form of the PLA Djibouti Support Base, opened in August 2017. China continues to refer to it as a logistics facility intended solely to support peacekeeping, counter-piracy, and humanitarian missions around the Horn of Africa and in the Gulf of Aden, and to defend Chinese nationals (Yang and Yang 2018). Despite these claims, Western analysts suggest that satellite imagery and unofficial reports indicate the base has military infrastructure that would render it more than a mere logistics facility (Zheng 2017).

Other issues have been raised in relation to the potential fiscal burden placed on some developed countries, including Bangladesh and Pakistan, by the need to repay the loans made by China. China has made clear that these loans are not a form of development aid and, as such, should be repaid, preferably with a modicum of interest. We may not have any evidence of actual outcomes for some considerable time.

A clue may perhaps be gleaned from the financing of the Hambantota port in Sri Lanka. Western suggestions of the potential 'debt trap' aspect of the BRI are based principally on the Hambantota Port investment in Sri Lanka. However, Sri Lanka's entire foreign debt is around US$55 billion, of which only US$6 billion is accounted for by Chinese loans, which is around 11% of the total. It is important also to note that the Chinese loans do not come with restrictive market economic conditions attached, as do World Bank and IMF loans.

An analysis by Calinoff and Gordon (2020) indicates that the financial terms applied and the burden of financing are both modest and cost-effective. Similar views are shared by Jones and Hameiri (2020). Moreover, with Chinese management support, the port has operated profitably since 2016 following initial losses, aided by extra investment on cranage, technically qualified staff, among other resources required following the port's completion in 2014. The port, focused on roll-on, roll-off operations, doubled its business with a 136% increase over two years in the volume of ro-ro vessels handled by the operators.

Jones and Hameiri (2020) argue that the accusation of the BRI 'debt trap' is connected to the wider misperception of BRI investments. In many cases these investments, though agreed and supported by China, are frequently not initiated by China. Instead, the recipient governments are the demandeurs and the BRI investment projects are 'heavily recipient-driven'. This characterisation was certainly the case of the Hambantota port project.

Initially, the port was losing money, but an agreement between China and Sri Lanka resulted in a renegotiation of the investment and a 99-year lease agreement on the port and 15,000 acres of surrounding land. China Merchants Port Holdings has taken an 85% stake in the Hambantota International Port Group to run the port and its terminals. The rest is held by the Sri Lanka Ports Authority. China's payment for the lease was US$1.1 billion, the proceeds of which were used by Sri Lanka to pay down its debt and boost its foreign currency reserves. The original loans remained in place and will have to be repaid. A second company, Hambantota International Port Group Services Co with a capital of US$606 million, will be set up to oversee security operations. The Sri Lankans will hold a 50.7% stake and the Chinese 49.3%.

Hambantota is an ideal location to invest in storage tanks, refineries, and LNG bunkering facilities with higher capacity to support the global ship fleet. Moreover, the International Maritime Organisation's (IMO) Internal Green House Gas strategy aiming to decarbonise the industry by 2100 would give fresh opportunities for the Hambantota International Port to operate as a 'Green port' in the region (Ranaraja 2020).

Western/US Views on the BRI

Potentially problematic aspects of the BRI have given rise to various serious concerns in Western commentators, notwithstanding the Hambantota Port project. These concerns are promulgated, even when not accompanied by Cold War-style ideological rhetoric. For instance, an informative discussion of the BRI in a paper written for the Asia Society Policy Institute (ASPI) by Russel and Berger (2020) suggests that:

> 'Beijing's win-win rhetoric about the peaceful and benign nature of BRI notwithstanding, a deliberate military and strategic functionality seems clearly entrenched in the initiative. But the security challenge to United States or regional interests does not lie in the risk of a String of Pearls-type chain of overseas coastal fortifications from which the PLA can wage war and that it will defend. There is little evidence so far of Beijing

> constructing full-blown overseas military bases on the U.S. model, but there is abundant evidence it is developing a network of strategic strong points that can significantly raise the costs of any U.S. military intervention and lower the willingness of BRI host governments to offer access or assistance to the United States. This network, embedding the military within the civilian, harnesses financial, technological, trade, and development tools in service of strategic and defence goals. It directly supports PLA power projection through enhanced operational, logistics, and information network capabilities centred on BRI platforms. It aims at creating an environment conducive to China's interests and inhospitable to America's. The gains to China from BRI-related leverage come largely at the expense of the United States. They are, as a former U.S. defence official put it, "a suite of capabilities that are intended, clearly [...] to defeat American [...] power projection"'.

This quotation is selected as representative of Western/US perception of the underlying Chinese logic of the BRI. It is by no means extreme in the position it takes overall on BRI projects. It is of course correct to suggest that part of the motivation for the BRI is to enhance China's defensive capabilities, especially around the South China Sea.

As Russel and Berger (2020) insist, there is no evidence of aggressive intent on the part of China. Moreover, it is unclear why 'aiming at creating an environment conducive to China's interests and inhospitable to America's should be regarded as reprehensible from an independent observer's viewpoint.

The ASPI published paper goes on to argue that:

> 'The nascent trend seems to be towards an increasingly Chinese dominated political, economic, technological, and strategic ecosystem in the Indo-Pacific. If there is a challenge posed by BRI for the United States, therefore, it lies not in enhanced PLA capabilities per se, but in Beijing's enhanced ability to project its sovereignty, rules, or undue influence over international space based on a unilateral assertion of core interests. This power will challenge the U.S.-led open, rules-based international order. Should Beijing be successful in leveraging BRI for pre-eminence in Asia, America's role as the guarantor of regional peace and stability would be undermined'.

Given the behaviour of the US Trump administration in terms of destroying the rules-based, international trading order and creating substantial collateral damage when targeting China, the above argument is a little thin. Also, it is not clear where the US action in Vietnam in the 1960s can be placed in the paper's regional peace narrative.

In the medium-term, the problems for Beijing's Southeast Asian, South China Sea/Pacific soft power extensions of the BRI are: a) to ensure that other East Asian powers, especially Japan, are reassured about China's intentions and behaviour, and hence do not side strongly with the US, and b) that the modalities of the strategic joint investments, including debt repayment problems, do not create problems for some countries, such as Pakistan.

Indeed, if one wanted to criticise the BRI programme, one might conclude, as do Jones and Hameiri (2020), that China has not applied due diligence to some of these projects:

> 'Thus, rather than debt-trap diplomacy, bumps on the Belt and Road are typically caused by the intersection between powerful interests and associated governance shortcomings on the Chinese and recipient sides. Chinese SOEs' desperate need for contracts, and weak governance of development financing, coupled with poor planning or venal interests in recipient countries, are generating badly conceived projects that replicate China's surplus capacity crisis'.

To assist in rectifying these problems and avoiding such issues in the future, the China International Development Cooperative Agency (CIDCA) was established in 2018 to improve inter-agency coordination.

The BRI is one example of China's expansive use of soft power. However, it is essential, from a soft power viewpoint, that problems of execution surrounding BRI projects are resolved between China and its BRI partners. In a wider sense, one handicap of soft power for China is that it constitutes a complex mixture of policies projecting internally and externally as a means of constructing a united, attractive image of China in both directions.

We may now turn to a more general exploration of China's exercise of conventional soft power in this dual context.

Conventional Soft Power

The exercise of conventional soft power communications strategy externally by China is an important mode of interacting with the world, but it also has internal dimensions. We will examine the geopolitical implications of China's foreign policy and its specific interaction with the US and its Western allies in Chapter 11.

In this section of this chapter, we will first try to assess how soft power deployment reflects back into the domestic scene in China, and how it has developed in relation to the creation of China's self-image. In so doing, we will use the term 'ideational'. The concept was coined by Althusser to describe how the state disseminates a specific ruling ideology, utilising a variety of communication channels, including political, educational, religious, cultural, legal, and others (Althusser 1971).

The CCP has, since 1978 in the Deng 'new' era, amended Marxist-Leninist orthodoxy with an updated theory featuring a more pragmatic worldview, relying on a more articulated ideational approach that is aimed at internal as well as external legitimisation.

Anne-Marie Brady, an ideological though well-informed critic of the CCP, argues that the CCP's contemporary 'thought-management' (*sixiangguanli*) has successfully used mass communications, media, and the cultural economy to create a 'market-friendly, scientific, high tech, and politics-lite' form of propaganda conducive to 'stability, harmony, and happiness' (Brady 2012).

In China, a de-emphasis on economic and political messaging has resulted in a new stress on culture. Hence, the CCP regards 'the economy is the flesh and blood, politics is the skeleton, and culture is the soul of a society' (China Cadre Learning Network 2016).

As all states legitimise and maintain the integrity of their countries in this manner, it is not clear whether this development should be regarded as reprehensible! The cultural dimension of the ideation communication process is further illustrated and defined by Shen Haixiong, deputy-director of the Xinhua News Agency, in 2014. The CCP, he argues, maintains that China's national culture consists of four strands: 'traditional culture', 'ethnic culture', 'red culture', and 'contemporary culture' (Klimes 2017).

The linking of these strands can be seen in the use of the term 'moderately prosperous society' by Xi in referring to the economic aim of China. This term relates directly to the ancient Confucian vision of the 'ideal society' which uses the same term 'moderate prosperity' (*xiaokang*) in the *Record of Rites*, where it is translated as 'peaceful' or 'happy'.

Internally, the aim of Beijing's leadership is for China's self-image to be one of being culturally confident and proud as well as technologically and economically strong. By the same token, externally, its image to the world is intended to be one of projecting stability and trustworthiness.

Hence, China is to be regarded as a reliable economic partner and as a responsible member of the international community. Currently, there is a long way to go to achieve these objectives.

In a number of speeches between 2013 and 2016, Xi has attempted to set out his cultural reform agenda (Wilson Center 2016). In essence, these could be said to indicate four cultural priorities: promotion of socialist core values; careful promotion of its traditional, historical culture; development of the cultural industries; and strengthening of ideational education in universities (N.B. Cultural industries can make up to 10% of the GDP in many Western countries, with 12% in the UK and 25% in the US. In China, it is a mere 4%) (Xi 2016).

Xi elaborated on the ideational education construct by emphasising that 'patriotic, collectivist, and socialist' education should be revised so that people have a 'correct view' of history, nation, state, and culture, and so that they strengthen their confidence in being Chinese. Thus, each individual citizen out of the 1.4 billion population should become a disseminator of Chinese culture, as well as of traditional, Marxist, and socialist values.

Linking the internal and the external exercise of soft power, Xi's position emphasises that:

1) The historical traditions, cultural resources, and essential national conditions of every nation are different; therefore, the respective national paths to development are also different.
2) Chinese culture accumulates and nourishes the spiritual aspirations of the primordial and advanced Chinese nation.
3) Traditional Chinese culture is the precious asset of the Chinese nation and the source of its cultural soft power.
4) Socialism with Chinese characteristics is rooted in the fertile soil of Chinese culture. It reflects the Chinese people's aspirations, suits the requirements for the development and progress of China, and has ancient historical origins and an extensive practical basis.

The aim for the CCP is to strive to promote China as:

1) a civilised power possessing a long history, an ethnically diverse yet unified national identity, and a heterogeneous yet harmonious culture;
2) an oriental power boasting clean politics, economic development, splendid culture, stable society, a united people, and natural beauty;

3) a responsible power that contributes to humankind by effecting peaceful development, promoting common development, and safeguarding international justice;
4) a socialist power that is increasingly open, approachable, optimistic, and energetic.

This approach has been followed since 2016, together with further thinking and action. One may enquire whether, certainly externally since 2016, the exercise of soft power using the BRI is failing, at least in terms of the West not perceiving China as it wishes to be seen.

Two explanations for this seeming failure of soft power may be given. The first, from ideological opponents:

> 'The CCP's approach, however, differs from that of democratic states in that it sees legitimation as the most important function of culture, in that this legitimation is used to justify an unattractive non-democratic regime, and in that the party monopolises domestic visions of national culture and history, while simultaneously suppressing alternative interpretations. Domestic cultural work is a vital part of ideational and propaganda work in instilling internal ideational order and garnering acceptance for the CCP's rule, while cultural diplomacy seeks to establish cultural soft power and win international acknowledgement of the regime' (Klimes 2017).

Perry (2015) calls the CCP approach 'cultural nationalism' and concludes that the effort:

> 'Commingle revolutionary and pre-revolutionary symbolic resources, as though there were no inherent contradiction between Confucian "culturalism" and modern "nationalism", is but the latest twist in a complicated and circuitous process aimed at justifying the Communist Party's right to rule'.

Perhaps more sympathetically, others have identified Western hegemony in the global media discourse, the lack of credibility in China's reporting, and the apparent lack of appeal of China's values as the principal problems surrounding China's public diplomacy. One academic has specifically commented that China's cultural diplomacy does not address the problem of 'liking traditional China, but not contemporary China, liking Chinese culture, but not Chinese politics, and liking Chinese people, but not the Chinese government' (d'Hooghe 2014).

The problem is compounded by a combination of sometimes naïve attempts to emulate the transmission of hegemonic Western liberal-democratic messaging — a mistaken direct engagement with Western media outlets and a failure to appreciate how deep is the rejection among Western, particularly the US, populations of any suggestion of 'socialism'. Any intellectual discursive messaging probably needs to be through academic engagement in the social sciences as well as natural sciences, especially given the objective of presenting a case for socialism in countries beyond China.

There are also deeper philosophical problems related to how cultural activity is perceived and treated in the West. Culture in the West often tends to be regarded as an intangible expression of individual free will. China is perceived as a country where expression of individual views is suppressed in an unfree polity. The West tends to assume a too individualistic view of culture. Such a view tends to ignore the underlying collective nature of artistic outputs and, more importantly, downplays the societally embedded nature of all of us as individuals. Culture is not derived from a vacuum. It is a societal concept.[2]

Nonetheless, there are instances where individual artist/writers are interpreted as challenging the political status quo in China, leading to an unnecessarily 'paranoiac' reaction by the authorities. These instances receive publicity in the West and give the impression that the suppression is more frequent than it is. However, the 'chilling', deterrent effect on artists/writers is also likely to be damaging.

The CCP is not, as we have indicated, a monolithic entity. There is probably far more scope than some in the CCP leading echelons imagine to explore culturally diverse messaging in China and to dilute the perceived 'China threat' externally. Using non-state cultural networks and avoiding overly constraining central control at home and abroad would be likely to improve the efficacy of soft power, thus enhancing China's self-image and its external image in the eyes of the world.

[2]These issues will be explored in Chapter 5.

Western Criticism

There is little doubt when reading Western academic literature, and the manner in which it dictates the global political and media discourse, that the attempted exercise of soft power internally by China is regarded as an ideological and ideational approach to controlling the political and societal discourse in China. The sole aim is being attributed to securing the Marxist agenda of the CCP inside China and defending its position outside China. Interestingly, though, there is a stress on socialism in the internal discourse, but socialism is rarely mentioned in the external projection of China.

At one level, it is difficult to disagree with the prevailing Western academic discourse about China in relation to internal 'propaganda'. We might, however, observe that China's objective is precisely paralleled by the political and ideational agenda of all Western governments. The approach may be more sophisticated and proceeds *sotto voce*, but the agenda is the same. At this point, it is worth quoting the introduction to a set of academic essays in *Ideology, Propaganda, and Political Discourse in the Xi Jinping Era* (Klimes and Marinelli 2018):

> 'Before we started working on this project in 2015, scholars were in agreement that, despite the more pragmatic and rationalized policy agenda pursued by the CCP throughout the reform era in a new governing paradigm, ideology remained at the core of the PRC's political system. It serves as a belief system, which conveys a particular worldview and an outlook on an ideal society, and as the guide to the CCP's actions, which enables the party-state to legitimize and operationalize various practices, institutions, and organizations.
>
> Propaganda is the "life blood" of the Chinese party-state as it remains one of the key means by which it secures popular support, which in turn is the source of the CCP's authority to govern in the post-revolutionary era. By means of propaganda, the party not only controls the dissemination of information and ideas, but also tailors its response to emerging socio-political challenges associated with modernization and globalization, thus preventing other actors from undermining the CCP's legitimacy and challenging its official narrative.
>
> Through meticulously devised and controlled discursive practices, language use, and recourse to key vocabularies, the party-state aims to

> manage the complex ongoing transformations in China's politics, society, culture, and other realms. It can be argued that ideology, along with propaganda and political discourse, as well as efficient party-state organization, continue to hold together the PRC's "vast building made of different kinds of brick and stone" in much the same way as examined some fifty years ago by (Schurmann 1966) in his pioneering work *Ideology and Organization in Communist China*'.

The authors find, however, that the general trends of Xi's era do not present paradigmatic shifts but rather an overall reassertion of previous uses of ideology, propaganda, and political discourse of the Maoist and post-Maoist eras. This collection of articles thus corroborates the argument that the innovation of governance terminology under Xi does not necessarily mean a revision of basic patterns and techniques of governance, thus rejecting the alternative Western criticism that Xi's 'regime' is qualitatively different from what went before, and, implicitly, worse.

One might differ from these conclusions concerning the Maoist era, but, as has already been observed, the links between the views and modus operandi of Xi pay closer attention to the post-Maoist era of Deng and his successors than is the general Western view (Brown and Bērziņa-Čerenkova 2018). The more general problem, however, for any writer attempting to portray the various approaches and actions of the CCP from a 'neutral perspective', is that much of the criticism and analysis of Chinese soft power is couched in these terms. In some cases, it is even stronger, as in (Brady 2018). Against this background, any attempt to provide a non-judgemental appraisal of China's soft power is problematic.

It would be disingenuous not to accept that the motivation of China's propaganda is to project, albeit subtly for the most part, in external messaging to the outside world a positive perception that socialism, with national characteristics, is a choice that countries can make if they wish. Though such a choice would be welcome, it is not a demand. The opposing US propaganda projects — though not necessarily subtly — a position that liberal individualist democracy is a choice that all countries should adopt, especially as practised in the US.

However, it may be argued with some credibility that China's socialist messaging inside China is also somewhat formulaic, simplistic, and robotic. Then again, internal messaging to the general population in all large countries is also formulaic. This is partly a result of an inadequate basic education system in some large Western countries, thereby putting a premium on simplistic messaging.

What is certainly correct to say is that to some outside observers, the internal messaging about the political and cultural success of the socialist system in China is dependent on continuing eradication of the 'yawning wealth gap and low social mobility, where hundreds of millions of people are concerned more with survival than with culture' (Klimes and Marinelli 2018). For these Western observers, the Chinese internal messaging that cultural confidence complements 'confidence in the path, theory, and system of socialism with Chinese characteristics' is rejected as facile.

How far the view on income distribution can be confirmed depends on two factors. First, whether the suggested 'yawning gap' is, albeit slowly, reducing regional developmental gaps in the Chinese economy. A significant fall in regional economic disparities did occur between 2008 and 2015 (Westmore 2017). During this period, the Gini coefficient, an internationally reputable measure of economic inequality, fell from 49 to 46. It has risen since then, principally because the income tax system in China is not effective in redistributing income. However, once housing costs are accounted for, the regional disparities in China have still been reduced substantially (Reinbold and Wen 2018). International statistics showing a 15.6% GDP per capita increase from 2017 to 2019 (Macrotrends 2020) also appear to confirm that overall per capita incomes in China are increasing, and that progress is being made to raise these incomes to that of a moderately prosperous country over the next decade to 2030.

Second, independent public opinion polling in China consistently suggests high levels of satisfaction with government across the population (Feng 2020a). This phenomenon does not of itself prove that, in political cultural terms, the Chinese people endorse the view that it is the socialist nature of the governance system which is the key element in achieving the progress which generates the high satisfaction levels. However, it does mean that one cannot simply assert without proof, as some Western critics do, that there is substantial hidden discontent with the CCP governance role, when measured against Western liberal metrics.

Comments about the maldistribution of income and of wealth, whatever the relative position of China, are somewhat hypocritical coming from Western countries. This criticism is especially pertinent in the case of the US — with significant relative income and wealth disparities — in the absence of developing country problems still faced by China.

External Messaging

In relation to the external messaging of China, the difficulty is that — given that the Xi administration appears to be attempting to articulate an international communications strategy, which includes offering to the world the 'China model' as a potential exemplar — the distinctive characteristics of China have encountered the barrier noted by Shambaugh (2013). He notes that China's national-image building may fail because the essence of soft power projection is 'to possess national attributes that transcend one's own country and appeal to others. Here, China seems to have few responses other than peace and harmony'. However, it should be noted that the social harmony position is one shared with other East Asian societies, particularly those of ASEAN countries.

From a Western viewpoint, Shambaugh's point is well-made, but there is an implicit, unstated premise — other countries' soft power projections, such as the US's, fulfil this 'transcendental' condition. It is not clear if the US aggressive attempt to export its neoliberal-individualist model to other countries is received everywhere with acclamation.

It is not the purpose here to provide advice to the Chinese government, and even less to the CCP, as to how they might improve their external communications strategy as part of their soft power projection policy. However, advice has been offered internally in China, as Klimes notes, by Zhao (2015).

Zhao sees the limitations of China's current public diplomacy as follows:

1) Excessive role of government in drafting and implementing cultural diplomacy objectives and the lack of innovative input from institutions, commercial subjects, and social organisations. The main actor should be society, and government should play only an auxiliary role.
2) Overemphasis on traditional culture and disregard for contemporary popular culture.
3) Confinement of cultural exchange to the elite layers of society and its inaccessibility to people with limited finances or possibilities.
4) Lack of foreign communication methods and perspectives on China. China's cultural diplomacy should respect the values of other cultures and should deemphasise the official institutional perspective and state interests.

Zhao's position is clear. There is too strong a directional role for the CCP elite leadership; the communications methods are unprofessional, and there is a lack of feedback as to how China is perceived by other countries in order to frame more appealing messages.

Zhao's sound advice appears to have been ignored. He did go into more detail in his paper, but this does not need to concern us. However, Barmé writes that 'attempts by governments or cultural authorities, regardless of whether elected or self-appointed, to define or articulate cultural nationhood and boundaries can be deadening' (Barmé 2012).

The task for China is that much greater, given their messaging is challenging a wider and longer-lasting political and philosophical dialogue between Western countries and other countries. For China, it may be more practical and fruitful to convince East Asian countries (where similar collectivist societal approaches and values exist) and where China's messaging may be more likely to resonate. The messaging may possibly also be received more favourably in African developing countries that have suffered, not only from Western colonial rule and exploitation but also from international organisations subscribing to the Washington Consensus (Williamson 2004). Moreover, China's successful economic development model will have some appeal.

The exercise of soft power and its modalities is linked to the overall political philosophy of China. Some elements derive from traditional neo-Confucian routes, while others owe their lineage to current Chinese Marxist socialist theory, promulgated via the theoretical basis of CCP policies.

Alternative External Deployment of Soft Power: The BRI Approach

China is clearly under ideological attack from the US and its allies in the West, though this position is not supported by all countries, including some under the broad ambit of the West. To challenge this sustained attack, China will continue to enhance and deploy its 'soft power' by working with partner countries. It would, in any case, be ill-advised for China to respond in kind to the US aggressive approach. The hard-line taken by the US is likely, over time, to be seen not to serve US interests well.

The BRI is a classic example of how China will increasingly deploy its soft power. This will not be aimed directly at influencing the politics of the nations it encounters in the BRI construction but to enter into economic partnerships with those countries. There will of course be benefits to the Chinese companies involved, but the benefits, both economically and politically, will also be delivered to the partner countries.

This foreign policy positioning is in sharp contrast to US foreign policy — sometimes imitated by the UK — which is not only aggressive and proselytising, but also appears to take the view that its liberal individualism and neoliberal market economics are not only the best, but the only basis for the global political economy. How successful China will be in this BRI soft power venture remains to be seen. It looks more capable of influencing countries to take a positive view of China than its attempts to deploy conventional mediated propaganda messaging.

Concluding Comments

In this chapter we have explored some of the ways in which China attempts to use soft power to project a self-image of what it means to be a Chinese in a socialist country in the twenty-first century. There is also an examination of how Beijing is using the projection of a modern China to seek partners in the modern global context. As we have suggested, the development of conventional soft power, essentially in the form of propaganda, has not been especially successful. Aside from standard Western criticisms, it is too formulaic internally and generally lacking in incisiveness externally.

However, against these deficiencies in the CCP's internal and external imaging, there is practical success. Internally, the continuing economic success and significant growth in GDP per capita, and a gradual rebalancing between rural and urban areas as indicated in Chapter 3, have been welcomed by the Chinese people.

Externally, despite Western criticisms (mainly misconceived), the ongoing construction of the BRI and China's partnership approach within the BRI have projected a positive and supportive image of China in many countries along the BRI route, such as Sri Lanka and African countries. The exercise of China's economic and partnership diplomatic soft power is more successful than its conventional soft power. It presents and promotes the positive cooperative, non-hegemonic image that China wants to project. Which is perhaps why it attracts so much US/Western criticism.

However, understanding the basis of the Chinese elites' approach to the political manifestation of their social and political core ideas in a modern global arena is perhaps best illustrated by a detailed consideration of Chinese political philosophy: past and present, Confucian and Marxist.

Chapter 5

Political Philosophy: Past and Present

Introduction

There is a fundamental divide between Chinese and Western conceptualisations of society and the external world. Not appreciating the nature of this difference is at the root of the potentially dangerous ideological conflict between the West and China. We need, therefore, to seek to understand this difference from a political-philosophical approach. As will be indicated, this in practice is not simply a divide between the US and China, but in some respects, a wider global 'fault line' between East and West. However, in both cases there are variations in the political governance structures and operations, reflecting, *inter alia,* cultural values in individual countries in the East and the West.

In comparing Chinese political philosophy with Western modes of thought, there are differences both in the historical evolution of Chinese political-philosophical positions and in its explicit rejection of the broad, liberal-individualistic basis of Western political philosophy since the Western 'Enlightenment', dating from the seventeenth century.

The Antecedents of Modern Chinese Political Thought

The *Analects* of Confucius (Lexis PSL 2020) — mostly written after his death in 479 BCE — form the early basis of Chinese political thought. There is disagreement among Confucian scholars as to how integrated the ethical elements of Confucianism thought and its political thought are. However, the consensus appears to be that it is possible to separate out the political thought content and therefore its influence on issues of governance.

However, the problem is that Confucianism, like Christianity — though Confucianism is not a religion as such — has over centuries been appropriated and reinterpreted by the State and by commentators to justify historical choices of governance structures and practices. Hence, it is best regarded as a malleable framework enabling many variations in governance and their justifications.

In terms of governance, the Confucian position as expressed in the *Analects*, when its ethical recommendations are emphasised, may appear close to that of the Western concept of a 'benevolent dictator'. Hence:

> 'Lead them with government and regulate them by punishments, and the people will evade them with no sense of shame. Lead them with virtue and regulate them by ritual, and they will acquire a sense of shame — and moreover, they will be orderly'.

The suggestion is that, as the family will follow the lead of a good father, so will the people follow a good ruler and be transformed into a single state-wide 'family'. As imperial rule was the norm for most people in recorded history, this injunction is perhaps not surprising. Notwithstanding the obvious fact that the creation of empires was achieved by violence, and not all emperors had been 'benevolent' dictators!

Dynastic Empires

The first authenticated dynasty in China was that of the Shang, which lasted from 1600 BCE to 1046 BCE. This dynasty was overthrown by a subject people, the Zhou and King Wu became the emperor. It is the Zhou dynasty — 1046 BCE to 476 BCE — which left records of its systems of governance and political thought. As a means of justifying the overthrowing of Shang, Wu developed an analogous concept of the Western 'divine right of kings', but with substantial differences. The concept was the well-known 'Mandate of Heaven' (MoH) and it became embedded in Chinese polity and culture (Cartwright 2017).

The MoH

First, Chinese religion at the time was polytheistic. The easiest comparison is with the Ancient Greeks in which there was a 'senior god', Zeus;

in China, the name of the senior god was 'Shangdi'. The MoH was therefore granted by the heavens, a supernatural community.

Second, the MoH could be conferred on anyone, that is, any individual from any strata of society. The emperor did not have to be of royal or noble birth; he/she only had to be fit to rule.

Third, and most significantly, the MoH held the emperor accountable to certain standards. He was answerable to Heaven for the wellbeing of the Chinese people. This introduced the era of the Confucian ideal of inner sage-hood and associated kingship — the 'sage-king' (Chen 2009). However, if the emperor and his government failed to govern responsibly, mistreated the people, or abused their power, their authority to rule could be withdrawn.

However, the Zhou dynasty began to fracture and during the period of the Warring States between 475 BCE and 221 BCE, there was a development of thinking. We can also see the emergence of the notion of bureaucracy. Hence, Creel observes that Shen, the Chancellor of the state of Han, favoured:

> 'A system of administration by means of professional functionaries, whose functions are more or less definitely prescribed' (Buhai, p.55 cf. Creel 1974).

We see the emergence of notions of standards (effectively rights) and rituals as a method of 'training' the people to maintain order. However, though standards are important, they will often conflict like rights and will therefore require modification from time to time.

The end of the period of the Warring States was followed by a short-lived, 15-year Qin dynasty. It was notable for the development of a philosophical movement later named 'Legalism', which argued that people were motivated by self-interest and strict laws were needed to constrain behaviour.

In 206 BCE, the 400-year Han imperial dynasty was established. For a period, the Han dynasty continued with the policy of Legalism. In 141 BCE this approach was abandoned, and Confucianism returned as the underpinning of the cultural and governance systems.

This resuscitation led to the development of political thought. Firstly, it sought to bring together thought and practice (praxis) to devise institutional structures aimed at realising socio-economic goals. Secondly, a system of centralised schools was established to ensure that entry into the bureaucratic elite was by professional examination. A system is still in place today, though in a less strict and formalised framework, and it is indeed copied in France via the *grandes ecoles*.

There were also further initiatives taken in standards-based governance. The standards were to be developed in line with the disposition of the people. Hence, a Han normative system of governance was based on social harmony in line with the prevailing Confucian edicts. Part of the rationale for the emphasis on social harmony was to avoid the problem of too many competing factions, which would be destructive to attempts to seek consensus. To Western eyes that are wedded to liberal individualism, this emphasis can seem aimed at eliminating dissenting views. However, in governance decision-making contexts in the West, there is generally an attempt to seek consensus, though if this fails then the majority view prevails.

In the early Chinese context, the central role which Confucianism placed on benevolence — required in the behaviour of both the governed and the rulers — should be noted. This is in contrast to a similar Japanese Confucian-based system which makes no mention of benevolence. It is interesting to note that this injunction for benevolence applied also to the Chinese military. It was replaced in the Japanese military with 'loyalty', defined as loyalty to the Emperor, unlike China which exerted civil control of the military to a soldier's conscience (Morishima 1982).

The neo-Confucian period covering the Tang and the Song dynasties, which succeeded the Han dynasty and lasted from 618 CE to 1271 CE, witnessed further development of governance praxis. Moreover, the Song dynasty also saw the rise of an intellectual elite, termed the literati, as part of the governing class. But perhaps of crucial importance, though it was lost to an extent in the following more despotic dynasties, was the notion of decentralised power which was instituted via the 'prefectural' system of regional governors. This political process amounted to an injunction to 'think globally, act locally'. This was necessitated, of course, by the huge population and geographical extent of the country, just as in modern China.

However, problems arose in the practice of government for Confucian ministers. The problems arose because of the generation of factions (*pengdang*) within the governing circles. One view is that if the set of 'superior' educated people form a faction they will be able to dominate. However, the alternative view is that factionalism is dangerous and should be suppressed. In practice, a third view prevailed. This third view argued that factionalism is inevitable, though it may be overcome by 'vertical loyalty' to a wise and strong ruler.

In the later Song dynasty, Zhu Xi — a scholar who was Prefect of Nanking for a short period of time — successfully promoted the first proposition and advocated the idea of a 'faction of superior people', to which the emperor should also belong.

The idea of an intellectual elite being uniquely qualified to govern has echoes of Plato's 'guardians'. The idea was taken up by the Donglin faction during the Ming dynasty (1368 to 1844) (Theobald 2016). Unfortunately for this faction, their publication of a strongly worded letter accusing a senior palace official of 'gross moral turpitude' (a phrase still used in British academic circles) led to the death of key Donglin figures and the dissolution of the faction.

During the post neo-Confucian period of the Qing dynasty (1844 to 1912), leading eventually into the modern era, another debate ensued. This concerned the relative importance of the role of character (a combination of ability and ethical character) against the role of institutions (sets of traditions, laws, rules, and regulations) in determining the efficacy of governance.

To an extent, this is an unresolved issue which still preoccupies modern political philosophers. In earlier times, the philosopher who attempted a resolution was Huang Zongxi (Theobald 2013). He lived in the late Ming and early Qing period. His argument was that what gives rulers legitimacy is the purpose for which they are fashioned. Moreover, he suggested that if rules/laws are designed with the interests of the people in mind, they tend to be loose and open-ended; the aim is not just to control human behaviour, but also to cultivate virtues. The danger is that laws which are too tightly drawn and coercive may not be obeyed, and lead to a vicious circle of increasing coercion.

However, the above debate leaves unanswered the question of — even assuming a set of rules of societal governance which attempts to adhere to Huang's dictum — what if the governance structure ceases to provide the social harmony required to maintain a stable society. How may the people be able to alter the situation? In Imperial China, the solution was achieved by the mantle of the MoH (Jiang 2011) being passed to another Emperor, often via violent overthrow. In effect, the only solution was revolution.

In many Western countries, their past history of governance systems — beyond perhaps 200 years — is of little relevance to modern political thought and practice. (We might make exceptions for the UK where the constitutional practice of modern Britain is still locked in the seventeenth century!).

In China, the past not only still matters, but it informs the present day. The system of political thought underlying China's governance system owes more to the past than is the case in Western liberal individualistic governance regimes; it is also significantly different from them. Whether this is a good or a bad thing is to be debated.

These reflections about a past political philosophy are not to deny the modernity as it has been manifested in China over the past 100 years (Xiang 2016). As we have seen in previous chapters on technology and economic growth, modern China shares common experiences with Western and other developed countries. However, a strong emphasis on meritocratic governance and a collective sense of morality appears to pervade the consciousness of Chinese elites and the population more generally. These characteristics are also found in other East Asian countries, but certainly not contemporarily and explicitly in Western countries, with perhaps the exception of France.

The above discussion has concentrated on the influence of neo-Confucianism on Chinese political thought. This will be discussed in the section on Modern Chinese Political Thought — together with its attempted 'appropriation' by Chinese Marxism, certainly since the time of Deng and now Xi — as a strand of modern political thought and praxis in China. However, it would be misleading to suggest that the two other East-Asian religious/philosophical influences of Buddhism and Daoism have not also left their mark on Chinese societal behaviour. Certainly, the Buddhist notion of 'karma' and the pantheism of Daoism remain influential in terms of societal behaviour in China, as suggested in the discussion in Chapter 3 of the social credit system in China.

Modern Chinese Political Thought

The post-Imperial period from 1912 brought not only domestic upheaval, but also an invasion of ideas — democratic reform through universal suffrage, the Western liberal tradition, and Marxist revolutionary praxis.

However, aside from the CCP's specific interpretation of Marxism, which we will discuss in the section on universal human rights, another major influence on Chinese political philosophy was that of New Confucianism (together with elements of Buddhism). The main exponent of 'New Confucian' political thinking was Mou Zongsan and his followers (Schmidt 2011). Mou died in 1995, but his copious writings are extant in China. Mou was a Chinese nationalist and took the view that Chinese philosophy was superior to Western philosophy, though he was a strong admirer of Immanuel Kant and translated some of Kant's work into Chinese. Though born in China, Mou was opposed to the Communists and spent most of his life as a university lecturer in Taiwan and in Hong Kong.

For Mou, politics and political virtue develop out of morality, but have an independent, objective existence, albeit based on the Confucian idea of an intuitive understanding of virtue and harmony. Hence, on human rights, Mou argued that although they must have a basis in morality, they should also be measured via separate constitutional legal standards.

Mou's approach has been taken up by liberals in China, Taiwan, Hong Kong, and around the world. In this form, it is now termed 'Progressive Confucianism' or 'PC'. There is a strong emphasis here of elements of Western liberal democratic thinking.

PC does not strictly follow the teachings of Mou (Angle 2011). It seeks to embed the notion of a universal morality, based on Western conceptions of moral progress, liberal individualism, pluralistic democracy, individual human rights, and the rule of law. In its total opposition to authoritarian governance, PC departs from any endorsement of the Confucian ideal of inner sage-hood and associated kingship (the 'sage-king') as the basis of the 'ideal' society. Morality is served solely by adherence to constraints of constitutional democracy and its accompaniments, including regular and popular elections, a 'free press' among other practices of modern democracy.

In abandoning the associated endorsement of a meritocratic, elitist governance structure — the core of original Confucianism, with its emphasis on achieving social harmony and maintaining social solidarity and respect for a wise leader, PC appears to disavow some key aspects of Confucianism. As an attempt to appease criticism of China in the US (it is not clear how much, if any, influence this position has had on US thinking), it leads on to a wider discussion.

Governance and Democracy in China

One obvious difference between the two governance systems — the West and China — lies in the absence, in the latter, of pluralistic political parties and 'externalised' democracy through elections of the governing political elites based on universal suffrage. In China there is only one political party, the Chinese Communist Party (CCP).

Democracy in China is 'internalised' through the mechanism of the 'collective presidency' within the CCP Politburo, supported by traditional elected and appointed administrations of government at various levels based on the Chinese constitutional order. The Western liberal view is that this exercise is best conducted external to the organs of the state. The Chinese socialist view is that this exercise is best conducted internal to the organs of the state.

These differences in view between the West and China — in some cases encompassing views shared with other East Asian countries — should not be an excuse for ideological conflict, but instead for political and philosophical debate and discussion. In this context it is worth examining, in more detail, what we mean when we use the term 'democracy', and specifically how democracy may be said to operate within China. Democracy is clearly linked with governance. This is true whatever the size of social group of adults we are discussing, including from families, clans, villages up to the 1.4 billion people in China.

Democracy may thus be defined as 'egalitarian collective decision-making' (Lloyd 2017) in relation to the system of governance. The structure of decision-making may be imposed, for example, in some cultures, in families by the father, or in a dictatorship by the despotic leader. Alternatively, the structure may be by the consent of all members of the group/population. How this democratic consent is arrived at is complex and changes over time (including representative government, qualified voting, universal suffrage, voting systems, role of referenda, etc).

In smaller groups, for instance in Chinese villages or in communes and cantons in Switzerland, direct democracy may prevail. In larger collectivities there will be a hierarchical/elite structure, achieved through a combination of indirect democracy and appointment (bureaucracy/technocracy). In any large collectivity at the level of the nation-state — whether China or the US — there will always be a governing elite; the issue for democratic participation is how the governed are able to elect, approve, and remove the elite.

The key questions for any system of governance are therefore: a) on what basis the governing elite is either elected, selected, or appointed, b) the term of office of the elite and how the elite shall be removed, and c) most importantly, during its term of office, how elite decisions shall be reviewed (and by whom), endorsed (either positively or by default), and, if deemed necessary, amended or reversed.

The above 'universal objectives' will require complex sets of necessary and sufficient democratic rules and laws. The precise content of the set of rules will be dependent on the historical and cultural context of the collectivities concerned. Hence, though the above objectives are universal, their application in specific national, confederal, or federal political structures will vary. Another issue, closely related to the differences in the views of democracy between the West and China, relates to the importance of individual rights, including the right to vote in political elections.

Early Confucian and Buddhist perspectives started from the social group, not the individual. For this reason, collective rights have a rating higher than individual rights. This is not intended to undervalue the individual, but simply to see an individual as an inextricable part of society. It is for this reason that in China, and more widely in East Asia, individual human rights are not seen as being universal. This position has impacts not only internally in China, but also externally in how this view is regarded in a world politically dominated by the West.

How Universal are Universal Human Rights?

This raises the question of acceptance of the universality of individual human rights. As will be indicated, underlying the Asian value system is an identification of collective rights and the importance of social solidarity/harmony.

In an article for the International Peace Institute, Shaheed and Richter (2018) attempted to tackle this question and defended the charge that universal human rights are, in fact, a 'Western Concept'. Their defence was not based on any philosophical analysis; rather they argued that:

> 'The international expressions of rights themselves claim no philosophical foundation, do not reflect any clear philosophical assumptions, and "articulate no particular moral principles or any single, comprehensive theory of the relation of the individual to society". They are the outcome of diplomatic initiatives, involving political strategy and negotiated agreements'.

This position may be diplomatically and politically convenient, but it surely cannot stand as an unchallengeable philosophical position.

Nonetheless, it does accurately reflect the way in which the human rights issue has been operationalised in the West. To fully understand the position of China on human rights, we need to explore the various issues involved from a philosophical standpoint to appreciate the position of China. In so doing, we will reveal the underlying cultural and political issues which is one reason for the fundamental disagreement between the West and China, and to an extent between Western values and Asian cultural values more generally. The aim is to explicitly distinguish the Western liberal philosophical tradition from the older Eastern collectivist philosophical tradition. Readers will have their own views.

It is generally accepted that, whatever has developed in modern times (since 1945), the concept of human rights is derived from the French and US revolutions in the seventeenth century around the time of the 'Enlightenment'. The US Bill of Rights, part of the US Constitution, was also adopted in the same year as the French Constitution, 'the Declaration of the Rights of Man and the Citizen' in 1789. In fact, the US Bill of Rights was based on the earlier formulated Virginia Bill of Rights. It is worth quoting the first Article of this latter Bill of Rights as it sets in context the link between rights and their attachment to the individual, as opposed to the general concern in the US Constitution with republican democracy (Lloyd 2017).

> 'That all men are by nature equally free and independent, and have certain inherent rights, of which, when they enter into a state of society, they cannot, by any compact, deprive or divest their posterity; namely, the enjoyment of life and liberty, with the means of acquiring and possessing property, and pursuing and obtaining happiness and safety'.

The interesting feature of this definition, which stems from English philosophers Thomas Hobbes and John Locke, is the idea that individuals 'have inherent rights' (of which) 'when they enter into a state of society'. This conceptualisation of individual pre-dating society, when used by Hobbes (1651), was a purely analytical device. If taken literally, it is nonsense. Our individuality is defined by our being part of society since we are born. However, this is precisely what is done in the above US definition. The position has been carried through ever since by many Western thinkers, but not by Eastern philosophers.

The implication of abandoning this notion of the individual being defined outside society, is that human rights, if the term is to be used at all, are not attached to individuals, but must be defined as collective rights, as in China and widely across East Asia. This division, between the individualist conception of society — defined as an aggregation of interacting individuals with properties attached, finds its apogee in neoclassical economics based on individuals each possessing in-built preferences (Lloyd 2017) — and the collectivist conception of society, is at the root of the difference in cultural perception between the West and the East. In the case of China, this societal conception is overlaid by its adherence to socialism, and in the US by its adherence to neoliberalism.

For any society, it is the sustaining of a harmonious network of relationships within the population which define an appropriate set of social rules and laws. In defining ethical rules, we do not start from the individual, but from the social system. For instance, Mead (1964) argues that individuation depends on socialisation, and hence any anthropologically valid system of morality must protect not only the integrity of individuals, but also the web of social relationships and the cultural forms of life on which individuals depend for their moral development. We need now to explore the implications of this view and the suggestion that it may be held in the strongest sense, thus implying necessity as well as contingency in relation to the position in China.

The position defined above insists that all individual action is, in practice, societal and it is the seeking of a cohesive society which is the societal objective. The role of the state is therefore to consolidate, at all levels, the universal and cooperative bonds which preserve a cohesive society. This position underlies ancient Chinese philosophy and, whatever view one may take about its implementation by the contemporary Chinese governing elites, it informs some of their policy actions. Liberty and democracy, interpreted as above, are understood in China to be the essential means by which a self-sustaining, cooperative society is established, and are continuously maintained with the support of the state in creating an appropriate institutional framework.

The creation of the Han Chinese ethnic concept, to which an overwhelming majority of Chinese belong to (perhaps questionably), appears to be used to establish and to maintain an overarching Chinese identity. It may be argued that this nationalistic ethnic objective is crude, and possibly incorrect in ethnic terms. Insofar as it is imposed, without regard to other valued ethnic identities, it is liable to produce serious damage to collective rights in China.

In relation to the so-called 're-education' of the Uyghurs in the Xinjiang region — even if one accepts that the underlying objective is to promote a coherent national Chinese civic identity — the policy appears to breach collective human rights.

The Chinese Conception of Collective Human Rights versus Western Individual Human Rights

Notwithstanding the point made in the preceding section, it is worth exploring at some length the conceptualisation of collective rights which underpins the Chinese viewpoint. Its position, which is rarely fully articulated in philosophical terms, underpins both China's social practice and law in the social sphere. It will first be necessary to elaborate the problems inherent in the familiar but rarely explored Western conceptualisation of individual human rights, as a contrasting viewpoint.

The definition of human rights as individual rights rather as collective rights leads to the establishment of modern laws in the Western conception on the basis of the general liberal individualistic view of a set of self-regarding activities (Mill 1859). These are said to form a core set of individual freedoms. These freedoms may then also be designated as individual human rights and hence the purpose of laws to secure these rights.

It may be argued that this is not only an inappropriate basis on which to model law-making, but that it also concedes too much to the liberal individualism position. For instance, this integration of law and individual rights leads to further difficulties in developing a coherent philosophical and cohesive social interpretation of the relationship between society and the individual (and also the role of the state). One immediately obvious problem with individual human rights as the basis for laws, is that it allows for perennial disputes over what is or is not a fundamental human right and offers no way of resolving conflicts between one human right and another, except by arbitrarily interpreting one right as being above another.

Reinforcing this argument is a point is made powerfully by Hallpike (1995), an anthropologist, when he states that:

> 'For this reason, the idea of a right as inhering in a single person is as philosophically absurd as the idea of a coin with only one side. Society also comes before individuals in the practical sense that individuals can

> only develop their potential as individuals, intellectually, morally, and physically, by being brought up in human society from birth. We know from numerous studies of children raised by animals or in isolation that as a result they have no human qualities'.

In challenging the notion of individual human rights forming the basis for modern laws in the West, it is not suggested that the views or actions of the individual should be ignored. However, just as we may argue that liberty is a function of social group interactions and is not an attribute of the individual, so should 'rights' be similarly defined — as the obverse of societal rules. Using rights as attached to individuals is certainly more convenient for lawyers, but we do not actually require the concept of individual rights, leaving aside the potential 'category' error of attaching human rights to individuals.

It is sufficient to observe that societal interactions require rules to govern them — a point which all agree on. The rules will be defined in relation to putative actions by the individual in the context of the social group involved. The justification of the rules will be based on the impacts of the putative actions on social cohesion. The rules will therefore cover both rights and responsibilities. This formulation disposes of the problem of there being no generally accepted hierarchy of rights and the social rules will, of course, include responsibilities. To a large extent, this formulation underlies the Chinese position (shared by some East Asian countries) justifying their use of collective rights in relation to law.

To advocate this position may seem to be taking a giant step away from conventional Western thinking — that of entrenched individualism in current times; it is also taking a strong philosophical position on the existence of individual rights (sometimes referred to as 'inalienable'). This position has become embedded in Western cultural discourse over the past four centuries. The Chinese objection to this proposed 'universality' of the Western tradition was expressed in 'Document 9' (Drezner 2013).

The Chinese position is that the aim of social rules or laws in general is to maximise cooperative societal actions and to minimise conflictive societal interactions. This will mean that both rights and responsibilities will be covered. Laws and social conduct rules exist to encourage and stimulate good behaviour (their 'declarative' value) as well as prohibit and discourage bad behaviour (Lloyd 2017). China's societal belief system appears to subscribe strongly to this view, and certainly evident among older generational cohorts.

Collective rights should be viewed, therefore, as the obverse of the social rules established in relation to promoting cohesive societal interactions (Lloyd 2017). Despite this argument, it may well be argued by liberals that this approach will generally leave the individual at the mercy of the 'state', and hence no individual will have protection from 'state interference'. But this is not necessarily the case.

The state need not be regarded as separate from civil society; instead, certainly in China, it should be regarded as representative of society, but with clear constitutional boundaries. This is obviously a contentious argument, but it is one supported by the Chinese state. It is not necessary to accept the argument as valid, but in exploring China's position and policy actions, it needs to be understood.

Hence, though clearly the state may fail in its duty as representative of society, one should not automatically assume that the state *qua* state will be opposed to the interests of society and the individuals comprising society. To do so would undermine many Western governance structures as much as it would China's. Resolutions of contentious issues involving the state are a matter for constitutional courts. However, in China, as will be discussed in the section below on the law in China, the Supreme People's Court is not the final arbiter on constitutional issues.

In China, in general, constitutional matters which appear to raise issues going beyond the current constitution, as explained in the section on the law below, may ultimately be settled by the political authorities. This is a severe weakness, but the almost complete politicisation of the state does have the benefit of being able to adjust constitutional conventions going forwards, compared to say the 'arthritic' US constitution and its politicisation via the Supreme Court appointments process.

In China, the Supreme People's Court (SPC) is the highest court in China. According to China's Constitution, it exercises judicial power independently. But it is accountable to the National People's Congress (NPC) (Lin 2016). Only the SPC has the power to issue precedents that unify the legal interpretation of all courts. Nonetheless, even the SPC does not have the power of judicial review, and neither does any other court in China.

Returning to the issue of democratic governance structures, in China — bearing in mind the earlier discussion of political philosophy in China — how may we describe the Chinese system of democratic governance and how to assess how well it might be able to secure the objective of 'good governance'?

We are, of course, used to viewing democracy through the lens of a multiparty system; though in the West it is often restricted in terms of two major parties vying for power. There is no political party pluralism in China. So how does the single party structure, and the wider, complex governance structures in China, attempt to meet the objective of good governance and how far is democratic participation possible?

The One-Party System

Clearly, the effective, central governing elite in China is the CCP, supported by a system of elected officials at various national and regional levels and a bureaucracy. The CCP is a democratic centralist party, as is, interestingly, the British Labour Party. This hierarchical structure means that the layer/tier below is always subservient to the layer/tier above. The details of the structure are summarised later in this section.

Elections are held within the CCP, whose membership in 2019[1] was almost 92 million or 6.6% of the population. Their representatives or cadres are nominated/selected and then voted for by the tier involved. Under Xi, membership is now far more selective and controlled than previously, but the democratic structure of the party is maintained.

Political power in China in terms of governance at national level is therefore through the CCP, and especially through the Standing Committee (7 members) of the 25-member Politburo. Both the Standing Committee and the Politburo are nominally elected ('confirmed' would be a more accurate description) by the Central Committee of the CCP (205 member and 171 alternate members) as its formal ruling body.

The Standing Committee is an inner 'cabinet' and operates as a collective leadership, based on one person one vote. This exercise of power by the Standing Committee represents the CCP acting as a Leninist vanguard party.[2] Therefore, the CCP as a vanguard party is better understood, not as a conventional political party, but as an organisation which is part of the constitutional order of the state, even though CCP is not

---

[1]The Communist Party of China (CPC) had more than 91.91 million members as of the end of 2019, representing a net increase of 1.32 million (*The Tribune* 2020).

[2]The notion of the Communist Party as a vanguard was conceived by Lenin, following Marx and Engels, to create an intellectual, technocratic elite which would ensure the people followed the 'correct path'.

formally recognised in strict constitutional terms. It should be noted that neither are political parties in Western countries.

A Communist Party Congress (89,000 members) is held every five years (the last one was in 2017). There is also a Central Commission for Discipline Inspection (CCDI). Comprising 130 members which are elected by the Party Congress and having a national Standing Committee of 20 members, this body operates regionally and in the large cities and has around 2,000 employees. It is responsible both for party discipline and for operating anti-corruption actions. It now operates independently of the Central Committee, though its elected Chair is a member of the Standing Committee of the Politburo. The above structures may appear complex and cumbersome, though they should not necessarily be described as undemocratic.

One key issue is how the governing elite may be replaced. Clearly the term of five years set for the Party Congress go some way to establish an ability to change the elite, albeit only within the governing party. In the case of Xi, notwithstanding the constraints of a collective leadership, he is currently 'President for life', thus overruling Deng's attempt to enforce a term limit on the post. Xi actually holds three top posts on the seven-person Standing Committee of the Politburo: General Secretary, Chair of the Central Military Commission since 2012, and President since 2013 and confirmed for life in 2018. It will be interesting to see whether he holds on to all three posts. Since 2012/2013, he has also been 'Paramount Leader', as was Deng. Whether this quasi-permanent, supreme leadership role will remain the situation is perhaps an issue for debate, though as yet no apparent successor is emerging. An optimistic view might be that since he was 67 years of age in 2020, he would normally retire in 2021. However, he will be wishing to serve out the five-year term of General Secretary to 2022. In the interim, he will stay in post during 2021, the 100th anniversary of the CCP. But this is only speculation. Assuming good health, Xi is likely to be in power for some time.

However, the broader issue is whether one may define China as a democracy in conventional terms. This is especially the case given that the CCP is not a formal part of the Chinese constitution, and its decisions cannot be challenged constitutionally. It should be recalled that in constitutional terms, neither are Western political parties. One perspective on the situation is what political constraints, relative to those in practice in Western democracies, are able to be applied to the CCP when it is in power? (Backer 2014).

First, it is useful to examine the governance structures within the constitutional state in China. The People's National Congress (PNC) — separate from the CCP and recognised in the Constitution — has 3,000 members. Elections to the PNC are through a complex hierarchical structure of People's Congresses. Each congressional layer — at levels of towns, cities, provinces, and regions — elects a set of representatives to the congress above, up to the national level. The CCP tends to dominate in these elections but the dominance is not complete, though direct elections occur only at village level.

The elected President of the PNC nominates all the senior state official positions — including, notably, the Premier, the Chief Justice of the Supreme Court, and the Chair of the Central Military Commission — and these nominations are confirmed by the NPC. The Premier and the Chair of the Central Military Commission (who currently is Xi) normally become members of the Standing Committee of the Politburo.

Often ignored, though it is specifically referred to in the Constitution, is the Chinese People's Political Consultative Conference (CPPCC) (China.Org 2020). The majority or 60% of the CPPCC members are not members of the CCP but of various other political parties, mass organisations, industry leaders, and 'personages of various social circles'. Their role is to assist in the running of the state, in effect representing civil society elites who may or may not be members of the CCP.

According to the charter of the CPPCC, its major functions are to conduct political consultation, exercise democratic supervision, and organise its members from various non-CCP political parties, mass organisations, public personages from all walks of life, representatives of compatriots of Taiwan, Hong Kong, and Macao, as well as of returned overseas Chinese and other specially invited people.

The CPPCC takes part in the discussion and management of state affairs. In this context, it makes recommendations to the Party leadership. Its Chair is a full member of the Standing Committee of the CCP Politburo and the fourth ranking member of the CCP hierarchy.

The CPPCC works in collaboration with the United Front Work Department (UFWD), which is part of the CCP, and acts as an organ for promulgating party policies domestically to various socio-economic groups, regions, and territories, such as Tibet, Hong Kong, and Macao, and internationally, including to Chinese communities abroad.

Local committees of the CPPCC at various levels serve a term of five years. The way of organisation, responsibilities, and the setup of major working bodies of local committees reflect the overall representative structure of the national organisation. The CPPCC has been described as similar to some more formalised advisory bodies in other countries. 'Its role and powers are analogous to an advisory senate in other countries, and there have been proposals to formalise this role in the Constitution, making it a de facto national senate' (Backer 2014).

This internal democratic role clarifies that though the CPPCC operates under the general aegis of the CCP, other civil society and political organisations do have an input to policy making through this route.

The activities of the CPPCC do seem to fulfil, to an extent, the role of monitoring and also influencing the delivery of policies by the governing elite. A recent example is the launching by the CPPCC of the proposal that China's Digital Yuan could be used within the APT grouping (with the addition of Hong Kong) as a trade payments system (see Chapter 2).

However, the US and some other Western countries are concerned about the CCPPC operations outside China via its collaboration with the UFWD. The CPPCC is actively engaged in exchanges with foreign countries for the purpose of strengthening friendship with people in foreign countries. It has established friendly contacts with 105 national organisations in various countries and 4 international organisations.

Somewhat hypocritically — the US Congress provides substantial funding to the National Endowment for Democracy organisation which operates outside the US and attempts to influence populations in places like Hong Kong and Tibet — the US sees the United Front operations in the US and elsewhere as propaganda and spying operations. In practice, they are more concerned in positively influencing members of the large Chinese diaspora in other countries (see Chapter 6) as a way of exerting 'soft power'.

CCP Reform

In attempting to understand the Chinese one-party system, it is worth noting that in modern Chinese political thought, collectivism is a core concept and is not necessarily viewed as being imposed on the people by the CCP. The aim is to use the acceptance of a collectivist approach as an expression of the people's concordance with the collective views of the people (the so-called 'mass line'[3]). The collectivist approach is also

[3]The 'mass line' is the formalised societal mechanism for the governance role of the CCP to secure democratic legitimacy from the Chinese people. The intention is to build a policy

supposed to be expressed in the behaviour of collective decision-making in the Standing Committee of the Politburo (SCP) and of the Politburo itself. Decisions at this level are intended to be based on consensus, rather than on majority voting. In this respect, it is analogous to the decision-making processes of the European Commission, and generally, the European Council (and the British Cabinet).

The notion that the ruling elite of the CCP is purported to represent the demonstrable 'will of the people' may appear alien to the way of thinking in the West. However, it is in practice no different from the views of the governing elites in Western countries.

All governments adopt the perspective of the 'wise sage' to deliver what is best for the people. That after all is the reason governments are elected, directly or indirectly. Given the absence of formal political competition between political parties in China, it might be argued — based on well-attested opinion in verifiable polls (Harsha 2020) that a substantial majority of the Chinese population are satisfied with their governance — that the level of democracy, as measured in this manner, is high in China. Opinion polling in the West is used in an analogous way to ascertain the democratic popularity of governments and political leaders. However, this is not the only criterion which may be used to attempt to measure democracy.

In terms of overall governance structure, it is worth noting that China (unlike the US or the former Soviet Union) is a supranational unitary state, not a federal or even confederal state. In practice however, the sheer size and variety of the Chinese polity and its organisational expression entail considerable 'practical federalism', with provinces, autonomous regions, and large cities having significant devolved decision-making.

As a general proposition, it may be adduced that the smaller the collectivity, the closer one may approach direct democracy and consensus decision-making. In China, villages, as the smallest recognised level of political collectivity, utilise direct democracy. Given the necessity of functional analysis to derive the most appropriate level at which specific functions may be managed, there will be distribution of political and

---

response mechanism to ensure that public resources and national policies are always geared to meeting the fundamental needs of the people. The mechanism is nowadays focused on mass communication via conventional news channels and the internet and social media, and by mechanisms for testing the reactions of the populations at all levels to policies.

democratic control exerted at a variety of levels, up to the highest national level of the state. In China, this level will be the SCP.

However, there are many intermediate levels in China between the village council and the SCP: province, region, city, town, and others which exercise specific functions and have specific powers allocated to them. Hence, the quasi-federal structure of China suggests a greater degree of democracy than say England or France (though France has a greater formal level of decentralised powers than England). On this measure of democracy, China appears to outscore England.

In the context of the CCP itself, it would be possible to introduce greater intra-CCP democracy by allowing organised political groups within the CCP. This would, of course, create factions. However, as the debates among Confucian elites during the Song dynasty indicated, the negative aspects of factionalism are not new issues. Moreover, as the history of the CCP and for that matter of the Soviet Communist Party shows, factions exist in any event. The issue is whether and how to create a formal structure of factions which can be made acceptable and democratic within a one-party system.

The CCP defence of the current one-party, internal democratic system derives from the defence offered in the Song dynasty the subsequent Ming dynasty, and the final Qing dynasty. The maintenance of social harmony, based on collective interests, rests on acceptance of government by a meritocratic elite. This elite should only be removed if they fail to deliver on the commitment to bring about satisfactory progress in living standards and the maintenance of social harmony. In the modern era, this commitment also includes achieving external security in foreign policy, accompanied by being able to act as an exemplar in global terms.

Currently, Xi is the 'supreme meritocrat'. He is General Secretary of the CCP, but he is also, as Mao and Deng before him, 'Paramount Leader'. As paramount leader, Xi is expected to lead not only in government policy, but also in intellectual terms as far as political thought is considered, as was expected of Mao and of Deng. Insofar as Xi fulfils this wide mandate, then Xi is likely to remain in power perhaps until 2030.

This idea of staying in a position of political power is not unusual in the West. The most admired US President, Franklin Roosevelt served four successive four-year terms. It was only after this that the restriction of two terms was imposed on future US Presidents. Congressional members have no time limits placed on their tenure and often serve for many decades. The problems with this combination of long-term tenure and a one-party system are: how to decide if the leader has not fulfilled the mandate, and how shall the person be removed from office? With a 'paramount leader', unless like Deng you hold no other position, this is a serious problem. The holding of multiple senior CCP and military posts is perhaps a weakness of Xi's current position, not a strength.

But this is not the only problem with the one-party system. Nonetheless, it may be observed that moving away from a one-party system, such as in the West, may not achieve a great deal unless a proportional voting system is instituted. The US and the UK, with non-proportional voting systems for national elections arriving at a two-party system and with often long periods of one-party rule, are hardly much of a democratic advancement.

In China, there is a need to examine carefully the 'collective presidency' model (Backer 2014) as a potentially valid arrangement within a constitutional order. Insofar as the CCP is concerned, it should be considered as a governance mechanism which is consistent with the 1982 Chinese Constitution. Whether its operation is in conformity with the Constitution is a matter for empirical investigation based on analysis on the governance system in China. As has been observed, democracy or rather how democracy operates in practice is a subset of governance theory and analysis. Often in Western academic dialogue, democracy and governance are treated as if democracy is necessary and sufficient to define governance as adequate, *a priori*.

If we assume that the CCP is not going to relinquish the one-party rule, how can a system of effective, 'democratic factions' within the CCP work? Three minimum conditions need to be satisfied: first, the maximum and minimum size of the factions; second, the number of allowable factions; and third, the role of the factions in policy formulation. Meeting these conditions should not be especially difficult. It may be argued that, as the description of the complex structure of the CCP suggests, there is already scope for the 'natural' development of factions.

Whatever rationale is provided, it will not satisfy some Western liberals. Their real concern is ideological, that is, to demolish the socialist system in China. This position has been made clear in the underlying message of the White House paper published on May 26th, 2020.

The Future under President Xi Jinping

Some Western commentators have interpreted the ascendancy of Xi since 2013 and his various roles, including his ascription of 'paramount leadership', as having ushered in a dominant leader more in the mould of Mao than Deng. It is suggested that the Xi 'regime' is leading to a more assertive China on the world stage, intent on resisting US global domination. We will examine the external Chinese attitude towards the US, its regional neighbours, the EU, and major countries and blocs, and global challenges, in Part 2, Chapters 7 to 11. But here we examine the internal position and behaviour of Xi.

He is often portrayed in the West as a despot, exercising dictatorial powers over the Chinese people. There are undoubtedly some in China who also subscribe, at least partly, to this view. However, as public opinion polling reveals (Feng 2020a), this does not appear to be the general view of the Chinese people. Moreover, given his father's and his own negative experience during the Mao era, he is likely to be aware of the dangers of a personality cult and of instability (Chinafile 2015).

How then should Xi be characterised and where is he leading the Chinese people? His speeches, especially internal ones, provide some clues. In his first speech as de-facto paramount leader in 2013 (Xi 2013), he made clear that: 'Socialism with Chinese characteristics is socialism, not any other "ism".' He grounds this espousal in historical terms:

> 'Which ideological system a country implements depends on one crucial issue: can this ideology resolve the historical problems facing the country?' 'It includes promoting the comprehensive development of the people, gradually realising the common prosperity of all the people, and building a modern, prosperous, strong, democratic, civilised and harmonious socialist country — including adhering to the fundamental political system of the National People's Congress, a Communist Party led system of multiparty cooperation and political consultation, a system of regional ethnic autonomy, a system of grassroots self-government, a legal system with Chinese characteristics, and an economic system in which publicly owned enterprises are the principle part, which develop side by side with diverse forms of ownership'.
>
> 'We firmly believe that as socialism with Chinese characteristics develops further, our system will inevitably mature; it is likewise inevitable that the superiority of our socialist system will be increasingly

apparent. Inevitably, our road will become wider; inevitably, our country's road of development will have increasingly greater influence on the world'.

The influence of Deng on Xi is considerable and profound, in both practical and theoretical terms. Therefore, Xi should not be seen as a break from the post-1990 period in China but its continuation, evolving after Deng. The difference from Deng may be nuanced, as was Deng's approach which had different but understandable reasons, following Mao's rule and the latter's influence on the Chinese people.

Perhaps Deng was more likely to consult colleagues to achieve a consensus than Xi, but once the decision is made, both strongly drove forward the agreed action. Nonetheless, Xi appears to adhere to the concept of collective leadership which Deng adopted and to the concept of the 'mass line' of Mao. It should be noted that Xi became a member of the Standing Committee of the Politburo in 2007, six years before being selected as General Secretary of the CCP. That Xi is responsible for, or even involved in, every decision taken in China is a Western myth. Nonetheless, Xi is responsible for a more centralised approach in foreign policy matters and the internal campaign to reduce corruption at various levels in both public and private arenas.

However, in China's new twenty-first century socio-economic circumstances, there is a substantive alteration in the meaning and methodology of the use of the term 'mass line', as referred to in speeches by Xi. The CCP is now seeking to emulate the 'focus group' and political opinion polling introduced in the US by former US President Bill Clinton and in the UK by former Prime Minister Tony Blair. In this way, the CCP is attempting to ensure that the 'mass line' is as much 'bottom up' as 'top down'.

The other difference, in 2020, is that China is now more globally powerful in economic and political terms under Xi than under Deng. However, though this introduces opportunities in the foreign policy area, it also poses dangers of over-reach. Managing external relations with an often negatively perceived political system and set of values presents a unique set of foreign policy challenges for China. Whatever the West's views of Xi and the CCP governance role, it needs to be always recognised that China is a huge and diverse country in terms of populations and physical, political, and economic geography. Many decisions taken at local, city, and province levels are not under the direct surveillance of central governance.

It should be recalled that the delayed action in reporting the early stages of the COVID-19 epidemic in Wuhan were taken by local officials, who were subsequently disciplined. It is impossible for Xi to run a country of the population, geographical size, and socio-economic structure of China as a despot. Moreover, there are significant constraints, even within the CCP structure and the constitutional structures, to ensure that there is collective leadership in China. Obviously, as paramount leader, Xi has more influence than any other single person in China, but he is not an absolute ruler.

Pluralist democracy as operated in the West is not present in China, but this does not mean the absence of democracy. Xi and the CCP are perhaps more aware than Western governments of the need to seek and maintain the support of the people by democratic means, so as to secure the legitimacy of the system of governance from the people.

The Role of the Law in China

Introduction

Another issue which is raised — often as a criticism — is the operation of the rule of law in China, or rather the suggested abrogation of it. In practice, no country can be run without a complex and extensive set of social conventions and enforceable legal rules. China is no exception. Moreover, a significant portion of that codified law in China reflects a wide range of international legal norms and precepts. This section will describe, summarily, the three sub-divisions of law: criminal law, civil law (including corporate law), and constitutional law.

China is a 'civil law' country (Chang and Madison 2013) — a system of law also found in most continental European legal systems where court rulings do not enable authority by precedence, unlike Anglo-Saxon common law systems. China's civil law system largely entails the exercise of law primarily based on the interpretation of its constitution, along with statutes issued by an executive and adopted by a legislature, along with regulations and decrees made at ministerial levels.

The Chinese legal system therefore operates through various, albeit relatively limited, sources of law, and whose respective authority is based on a hierarchical basis, in order of importance as follows: the Constitution, national laws, administrative regulations, departmental rules, and provincial or other local regulations.

China's legal system came under heightened international scrutiny following the introduction in 2020 of a national security law designed also for application in the Hong Kong Special Administrative Region (SAR). The controversy arose over the new law's potential conflict with the SAR's constitution, the so-called 'Basic Law' which was set out by China alongside the Sino-British Joint Declaration of 1984. These sets of legal agreements guaranteed a high degree of autonomy for the territory after its handover to China in 1997, under the so-called 'one country two systems', over a subsequent period of 50 years. As a result of the incident, China's legal system has been subject to renewed criticism by various international circles over opacity in the practice and application of its domestic law (Wong 2015).

Criticisms have included claims that China's court system lacks judicial independence and impartiality. Consequently, the courts have been criticised for typically interpreting the law overwhelmingly in favour of the State and connected vested interests. Even though the Constitution subordinates the CCP to its legal authority, including all primary legislation which is required to comply with the principles of the Constitution, numerous observers have claimed that China's courts are politically-controlled, in all respects, by the CCP.

There have also been numerous allegations of corruption where the courts are accused of acting as tools for the CCP in silencing its critics or are used to settle scores for powerful personal and business interests.

Despite these severe flaws, China's legal system has been improving in recent years according to some jurists (Choukroune 2015), particularly in relation to increasingly upholding individuals' rights on issues of employment, health and safety, environment, housing, and other social matters. The most evident aspect of an incremental rebalancing between the state and the individual has been the Chinese legal system's focus on tackling corruption, especially targeting high-ranking CCP officials in provincial and local governments as well as large state enterprises (Liu 2019).

There is still some way to go before China's legal system can become genuinely independent of the CCP's political control. Even so, there is room for optimism that a consensus on collective rights between the state and its citizens will materialise in the medium to longer term. These forces will become more apparent as new economic policies lay greater emphasis on individuals' consumer power and privacy rights.

Criminal Law and Rights of Individuals

China's first post-1949 substantive and procedural Criminal Code was enacted in 1979. The 1979 Code followed the release of a new Constitution in 1978.

The present criminal code, *The Criminal Law of the People's Republic of China* (Wang 2017) is subject to the requirement that crimes and criminal sanctions may only be governed by national laws (as opposed to provincial laws or ministerial regulations).

The Criminal Procedure Law of China provides for all phases of the criminal process. This is distinct from the system of administrative punishments (including detention for periods of multiple years) and procedures which are governed under a separate system of laws and regulations. The criminal procedure law governs the conduct of investigations, including pre-trial detention, interrogation, surveillance, prosecution, and the conduct of trials and the defence of the accused.

However, the independence of the courts and institutions involved in the investigation, prosecution, and trial of criminal offences in China remains challenged by the structure of the China's government and public institutions. One example of the structural barriers to the independence of courts is the CCP political-legal committee system. In this case, the CCP has the power to instruct, monitor, or scrutinise courts regarding specific decisions of individual cases or categories of cases that attract attention from the CCP.

While various international jurists and legal observers have commented on widespread improvements governing China's criminal law and practice, the general consensus still holds that particular groups, including minority groups, migrant workers, and political dissidents, encounter multiple obstacles in receiving a fair trial and balanced justice (Wang 2018).

In such cases, there are numerous examples of defendants being denied legal representation or not being given the opportunity to put forward their defence. There are also numerous reports of convictions being made on the basis of weak evidence by which defendants are not permitted to challenge a court ruling or are denied the prospect of an appeal. These issues are exacerbated by the fact that China's criminal courts are seldom open to the public.

In many instances, Chinese lawyers are also unwilling to represent accused clients where they are viewed as directly challenging the authorities in court. The result has, in some cases, meant those lawyers becoming exposed to professional and even personal risks.

Commercial Law and Foreign Investment

The Civil Code governs the current company law regime. In 2019, the National People's Congress passed the Foreign Investment Law (FIL) (NPC Observer 2019) — a landmark legislation to regulate foreign investments in China and provide stronger protection for foreign investors. The FIL took effect from January 1st, 2020, repealing at the same time the prior laws governing Sino-foreign equity joint ventures.

The FIL guarantees that all foreign-invested enterprises (FIEs), whether as joint ventures or wholly foreign owned entities, will be governed by company law in the same way as all Chinese domestic entities.

Along with rapid economic growth, the number of commercial disputes submitted to litigation or arbitration in China has increased in recent years. In addition, as a result of the demands of China's own technological progress, disputes over intellectual property (including technology transfer, patent, trademark, copyright, IT, and software), especially disputes over foreign intellectual property, have increased rapidly.

Meanwhile, the issues faced by disputing parties have become more complex. China's courts at all levels are therefore exploring new ways to resolve disputes. Since 2017, China's court system has undergone a series of substantial changes, especially in the trial of intellectual property (IP) cases. As a result, the courts have endeavoured to improve the transparency of not only IP cases but also general civil proceedings.

Arbitration is also becoming a popular alternative to litigation as China has developed a well-established structure for resolution of disputes by this means (Pisacane *et al.* 2016). Arbitration bodies are set up in China at national and local levels. The China International Economic and Trade Arbitration Commission (CIETAC) is the best-known arbitration institute in China that handles international economic and trade disputes, including foreign investment-related cases.

China is promoting other diversified dispute resolution mechanisms (Fu and Palmer 2017). The United Nations Convention on International Settlement Agreements Resulting from Mediation (Singapore Convention on Mediation) signed in August 2019 (UNCITRAL 2019) is an important step, providing more dispute resolution options for parties involved in international commercial transactions. After the entry into force of the Convention, the settlement agreements reached between the parties with business operations in different countries will, in principle, be subject to direct enforcement mechanisms.

Arguably, the status of China's legal system is a reflection of its economic development. As its economy becomes more sophisticated, so does the legal system in supporting it. This is mirrored in the drafting of new legislation such as the FIL, or the revamping of old statutes to invoke greater depth and detail of legal expression. There is also greater clarity in the legal drafting than was previously the case, where many legislative terms were often left undefined and ambiguous, thus becoming prone to abuse in court rulings.

Beyond these general improvements, China's business law for foreign companies, in particular, is undergoing significant upgrades. These include a standardised and unified FIL which addresses many foreign investors' longstanding issues such as prohibiting forced technology transfers, greater protection for intellectual property rights, and ensuring equal treatment and protection between foreign and domestic players. The law also promises to protect foreign investors' rights and interests, based on principles which are closer to international legal norms. Indeed, as China further integrates into the global economy and modernises its own domestic economy, the legal system is expected to continue to incorporate international legal principles and practice in the coming years.

Constitutional Law and Judicial Review

The Constitution formally stipulates that political power is exercised by the people from the bottom up — through representative people's congresses from the local up to the provincial and national levels. In practice, policymaking and administration can at times be highly centralised and uniform in nature, and at others highly decentralised and diverse.

The National People's Congress (NPC) and its Standing Committee have the power to pass laws on behalf of the state. The NPC can amend the Constitution and enact and amend basic laws governing state departments and public, civil, and criminal matters. The Standing Committee of the NPC has the power to interpret, enact, and amend laws other than those which must be enacted by the NPC (Jiang 2003).

The Constitution is adopted by a two-thirds majority vote from all deputies of the NPC. Foreign investors are unlikely to encounter the Constitution in the course of commercial practice, although it sets the foundations for the principles to Chinese laws and the legal system.

Other national laws and amendments are adopted by a simple majority vote of all deputies of the NPC, or by its standing committee. National laws are utilised in a number of broad areas, such as crimes, fundamental civil institutions including property law, intellectual property law, and other civil law, basic economic systems, and basic systems of finance, taxation, customs, banking, foreign trade, litigation, and arbitration. Many national laws use general wording and only lay out broad principles.

Although it is not granted any formal legal status or powers in the Constitution and is technically separate from the government, the CCP parallels, overlaps with, and controls the government at all levels. This system helps the CCP to ensure a high degree of national uniformity and cohesion, but it also sets the CCP above the government which can make it difficult in practice to subject the CCP itself and its individual members to the rule of law. Moreover, the CCP has the power to instruct, monitor or scrutinise courts regarding specific decisions of individual cases or categories of cases that attract attention from the CCP.

The State Council of China (State Council) is the highest level of state executive administration and has the power to enact administrative rules and regulations consistent with law. Ministries and commissions under the State Council are also vested with the power to issue orders, directives, and regulations within their respective areas of competence. The State Council also submits legislative proposals to the NPC or its Standing Committee for enactment into law.

The People's Congresses and the governments of different provinces, autonomous regions, and municipalities directly under the central government also have the power to enact local regulations and administrative rules to implement national laws (Zhang 2012). These subsidiary forms of governance allow for the implementation of the laws in a way that takes into account the local political, economic, and cultural conditions. Despite the uniformity attributable to centralisation, there can be a great deal of variation in local practice and interpretation where central policy is silent or unclear.

The judicial power to apply the law in civil and criminal matters is vested in the people's courts at various levels — from the central Supreme People's Court (SPC), provincial High People's Court, municipal

Intermediate People's Courts, and local Basic People's Courts (Qi 2019a). People's Courts at different levels are not independent, though they carry out the judicial function in fairly close coordination with the courts, government, and the CCP at the same and higher levels.

As stated earlier, under China's civil law system, court cases do not act as binding precedents. However, many court opinions are published annually and may provide useful guidance for outcomes in similar cases. SPC decisions also provide non-binding judicial guidance for lower courts, and the SPC's detailed interpretations on the application of national laws are considered to have the force of law.

The CCP-controlled central legislative/executive/judicial structure is repeated at lower levels. Laws and regulations made at lower levels must not conflict with those made at higher levels, and generally only serve to implement central-level enactments. However, regulations, rules, or directives are occasionally enacted or issued at the provincial level in the first instance on a trial basis, and later enacted on a national basis after sufficient experience has been gained.

Concluding Comments

There are some distinguishing features of Chinese political theory and praxis from Western, especially US, political theory and praxis; in other areas, such as the legal system, there are similarities. The differences, similarities, or parallelisms may be summarised as the following.

First, the Chinese commitment to the collective interest is represented by the departure from the Western philosophical, liberal individualistic tradition derived from the Anglo-Scottish Enlightenment dating from the seventeenth century onwards. The philosophical tradition of collectivism in China (and broadly East Asia) — influenced by aspects of Confucianism and Marxism in China — is equally valid.

Hence, collective human rights rather than individual human rights are the prevailing tradition, though they may also be breached in China. From the Chinese standpoint, there is no prohibition on holding nonconformist, private views, which may significantly differ from prevailing societal positions. However, the expression of those views, if it destroys social solidarity and social harmony, is liable to breach the law. In practice, a greater degree of freedom to express unconventional views, without the danger of fomenting revolution, might well be permitted. Nonetheless, it is interesting that even in the US, the spreading of such views through social media is giving rise to concerns. These concerns have increased recently and seem likely to provoke tighter regulation.

In this respect, one is reminded of remarks reputed to have been made by former Soviet author Alexander Solzhenitsyn. He was asked why he returned to the Soviet Union after originally 'escaping' to the West and staying in the US for 18 years. His attributed reply was to the effect that 'in the West, unlike the Soviet Union, one is free to say what you like, but no one will pay any attention'. Freedom of speech, as opposed to freedom of thought, is never total.

Second, the importance of meritocracy in Chinese thinking, but linked not simply to intellectual attainment, but also ethical performance in post. In Western thought, the concept of meritocratic rule derives from the conceptualisation of Plato's 'guardians'. The West has gradually abandoned this line of meritocratic thought with the advent of popular democracy (except perhaps in France).

To an extent, this view is endorsed in China by the Confucian concept of the 'sage king'. This view has been reinforced by the Marxist-Leninism of the CCP, though the position departs from 'orthodox' Marxism. This approach does not imply that the Chinese governance system is undemocratic. The rejection of the pluralist, multiparty system that is familiar in the West does not mean that other views are not canvassed, such as through the CPPCC. Moreover, the need for the people to provide the government, in the form of the collective leadership of the CCP, with legitimacy is a key reason for the 'mass line' approach — attempting to ensure that the people's social and economic interests are continuously monitored and responded to as far as possible.

Third, despite much Western comment, the system of law in China is a civil law system, similar to that of continental European legal systems but dissimilar to the US and UK common law systems. The system of corporate law is nor far removed from that in the West, though ironically shareholders probably have more power in Chinese private companies than in, say, the UK. Data privacy and patents protection is another area where protection has been substantially increased over the last decade, as far as enhancing the ability of foreign companies to take action to enforce contractual terms in court.

Fourth, the Western concept of an independent constitutional legal system — which, for instance, formally sets out the relative roles of the governance units — is challenged on the basis that it restricts the flexibility required within governance structures as social and economic conditions change. China's Supreme People's Court has an important constitutional role but has no power of judicial review and ultimately is accountable to the National People's Congress. The Western position suggests that a constitutional court provides a guarantee against *ultra vires* activity outside the constitutional boundaries, though the certainty of this position varies between Western countries at the margin. However, there is a clear choice between politicising the constitution (the Chinese position) and judicialising the political order and process (the Western position).

There are costs and benefits associated with either system. Lord Jonathan Sumption, a retired UK Supreme Court judge, attacked what he perceived as judicial interference in political issues in the UK in his 2019 BBC Reith Lectures (Sumption 2019). The need to adjust written constitutions, as they inevitably ossify as the social, political, economic, and technological circumstances in a country change, suggests a positive benefit/cost ratio in favour of the Chinese position, although the requirement to avoid actions of the State imperilling the constitutional and collective rights of the population suggest an alternative positive benefit/cost ratio in favour of the Western position. Regular review and amendment procedures that are embedded in law would seem an appropriate resolution of the problems.

Some of these four explanations of Chinese positions may find support in the West. However, it will probably be maintained that the lack of recognition of individual rights and freedoms, including the ability to be able to choose in elections between differing policy views especially at central and national level, prevents political challenges from maturing. Against this argument, the Chinese position is that the recognition of collective rights provides an alternative and valid approach to developing a politically democratic governance system, possessing greater social solidarity and harmony. Equally, in respect of pluralism in terms of political parties, the Chinese position is that intra-party democracy may provide an equivalent mechanism to the electoral governance practice in some Western countries.

Chapter 6

Cultural and Social Development

Introduction

In the last chapter there was some reference to cultural and ethical issues, unavoidable when discussing political philosophy with reference to China. In this chapter, we will explore the cultural and social development of the Chinese people over the past 30 years. We will look inside China, but we will also explore the nature and roles of the Chinese community outside China — the Chinese diaspora, and the continuing cultural and financial influence of these groups, both inside as well as outside mainland China. This excursion will throw a light on the familial and clan nature of various Chinese societies inside and outside China, and some key links between ethnic Chinese communities across East Asia and those in mainland China.

We will explore some of the ethical, cultural, and religious issues of Chinese social policies and criticisms of China in these areas by Western commentators. We conclude with a discussion of the ethical issues which appear to divide China from the West.

Chinese Society in the Twentieth and Twenty-First Centuries

For the majority of the twentieth century, up till around 1990 at which this book effectively commences, China was in various stages of turmoil.

Before and After Mao

Given the time-frame which this book is covering, it is not intended to produce more than a summary discussion of the impacts of the Mao era on China's social and cultural development. Principally, this section is concerned with the post-Mao transition period during Deng's paramount leadership. However, this transition period needs to be set in the context of the years before 1977, the inaugural year of Deng's leadership (China. Org 2010).

From 1949 — following the departure of the Kuomintang to Taiwan — until 1990, there were five distinct, overlapping phases of China's revolutionary development, covering periods of turmoil and unnecessary loss of life (Knight 1982).

The first phase lasted from 1949 to 1958, during which 'New China' emerged as a 'revolutionary communist country' siding with the Soviet Union in the geopolitical 'Cold War' of the time. This positioning of China led to its involvement in the Korean War between 1950 and 1953. It enabled Mao to engage in revolutionary nationalist rhetoric in China and to cement his own position and policies. Around 160,000 Chinese soldiers lost their lives in the Korean conflict.

The second overlapping phase, from 1956 until 1976, followed China's split with the Soviet Union after then-Soviet Premier Nikita Khrushchev succeeded ex-Soviet leader Joseph Stalin. After Stalin's death, Mao began to develop his views on the need to initiate the 'Great Proletarian Cultural Revolution', arguing that China under Mao represented the true inheritors of Marxism, which should be based on permanent proletarian revolution and continuous class struggle.

The third overlapping phase, between 1958 and 1962, was known as the 'Great Leap Forward'. During this period, although there were some increases in agricultural and steel productions, there were other attendant problems including the famine in 1959/60. Hence, despite production increasing, there were only limited gains in agricultural productivity.

Western analysts estimate that the number of deaths connected to the famine ranges between 15 million and 40 million (Holmes 2009). As we are aware from the reporting of COVID-19 deaths, the problem is that the relevant statistic is 'excess deaths'. It seems likely therefore that the figure may be closer to the lower end of the estimated range.

The fourth overlapping phase, between 1962 and 1976, provided a second opportunity for Mao to present himself internally as a revolutionary nationalist. The Cultural Revolution began in earnest in 1966 and though Mao declared it over in 1969, its legacy of turmoil continued until 1977.

It is estimated that possibly up to 400,000 people were killed during the Cultural Revolution. Following the deterioration of Mao's health from 1972 and until his death in 1976, there were a variety of factional party struggles. Prominent among these was the faction known as the Gang of Four, which contained Mao's then-wife.

Despite criticising this faction, Mao secured their place within the Politburo. In 1976 they convinced the ageing Mao to purge Deng, albeit for a short time, prior to the 'Gang of Four' being removed from power.

The fifth phase, overlapping the period examined in this book, saw Deng regaining power in 1977. He would maintain control over Chinese governance for the next 20 years, initiating the market reform and the 'opening up' of China to the world and the consequential surge of economic growth from the late 1990s onwards.

Despite the grave mistakes, turmoil, and unnecessary and substantial loss of life, Mao's long period as Chinese leader was not without some measure of economic and social gains for the Chinese people.

The book, *The Battle for China's Past: Mao and the Cultural Revolution* (Gao 2008), credits him for raising the average life expectancy from 35 in 1949 to 63 by 1975. This brought 'unity and stability to a country that had been plagued by civil wars and foreign invasions'. It also laid the foundation for China to 'become the equal of the great global powers'.

Scholars, outside of China, also credit Mao for boosting literacy (only 20% of the population could read in 1949, compared to 65.5% thirty years later), doubling life expectancy during a period when the population nearly doubled, and developing China's industry and infrastructure, paving the way for its position as a world power (Ebrey 2010).

Moreover, it was under Mao that the rapprochement with the US was initiated, leading to the visit of then-US President Richard Nixon to China and the cordial meetings with Chairman Mao Zedong and Premier Zhou Enlai in Beijing during 'the week that changed the world' in February 1972.

The subsequent joint communique interestingly declared, *inter alia*, that neither country 'should seek hegemony in the Asia-Pacific region'. This initial US/China relationship facilitated Deng's later 'opening up' of China into the global marketplace and movement into the geopolitical arena.

Religion

China's fast-growing economic and social development has given rise to several waves of intensive religious revivals of traditional Chinese faiths alongside the birth of new faiths and spiritual practices over the last three to four decades (Pang 2019). The rapid expansion of urbanisation and the vast movements of people from rural areas into cities have further fuelled an expansion in religious worship. Moreover, the existence of nearly a billion internet users has also enabled China's vast population to access faith and religious practice on an unprecedented scale, both in China and abroad.

This religious revival reflects the broad diversity of China's society in the twenty-first century and is evident in the increased forms of both Eastern and Western religions found throughout the country. The five major, so-called 'patriotic', faiths — a term which means being officially sanctioned by China's government — include Buddhism, Catholicism, Islam, Protestantism and Taoism (Albert and Maizland 2020). Religious places of worship also have to be approved by the authorities. For those temples, churches, mosques, and other venues which are not given the official green light, such institutions tend to function in an uncertain religious environment, albeit tolerated.

As one would expect, the Buddhist faith and its network of temples has become the most popular faith in China, since the resurgence of Chinese traditional values following the CCP's acceptance of religious revival in the 1970s. Islam is evident in some of the western and central parts of China and has also flourished.

Perhaps surprisingly, the Protestant Christian denomination has, over recent decades, risen as the main form of religious worship in various provinces and counties across the entire breadth and length of China (Hunter and Chan 2010). Much of this may be attributable to Protestant missionaries and evangelism arising from America amid China's embrace of an open-door policy towards culture.

At the provincial level, Buddhism can be mainly found in the country's south (Kiely and Jessup 2016). This spans Tibet, in the southwest, to Fujian province, in the southeast. Other provinces hosting large communities of Buddhists include the southern regions of Guangdong, Guizhou, Hunan, Hubei, Jiangxi, Sichuan, and Yunnan. While Islam is the principal religion in the northwest province of Xinjiang, other concentrations of the faith can be found in the provinces of Gansu, Ningxia, and Qinghai.

Protestant churches have become especially numerous in Guangxi and Hainan provinces, but have also been spreading out across central, eastern, northern, and north-eastern areas, including Anhui, Heilongjiang, Henan, Jiangsu, Jilin, Liaoning, Shaanxi, Shandong, and Inner Mongolia.

In Shanxi, Taoist temples have become the majority of places of worship, while in Hebei Catholic churches outnumber other religious institutions.

There are also regional variations of these five main religions at the provincial, prefectural, and county levels, evidenced by the differences in architecture of structures and internal decoration of many religious sites.

Aside from the conventional faiths, there are also Confucian places of worship. For instance, there exists various cult orders which have deified the CCP founder Mao Zedong; there are also spiritistic or animistic practices typically associated with local folk beliefs. These forms of worship are not classified as official faiths, yet are tolerated and given a general unofficial acceptance that such beliefs contain some level of religious character of need to various communities in China (Dillon 2001).

More controversially, various sects or smaller faiths in China have been officially prohibited from exercising their beliefs. About 20 such outlawed forms of organised worship continue to exist in China, including the most internationally well-known and persecuted Chinese faith — Falun Gong (Sanghamitra 2013), also referred to in English as the Church of Almighty God.

Generally, religions in China are considered minority beliefs. This is because the CCP maintains atheism as an official ideology. Consequently, there are still many restrictions on the practice of religion and many faiths, including the five 'official faiths', are still monitored by the state's apparatus and officialdom. This is despite the fact that China's constitution guarantees freedom of religious worship.

In light of such a social and political context, the majority of Chinese citizens do not officially belong to any religion or claim a religious identity. Yet, according to limited region-based surveys, about 85% of the population either engage in certain religious practices or admit to holding religious or spiritual beliefs (Dueck and Han 2012). Comprehensive nationwide studies of religion in China still fall short on account of the lack of surveying and collection of empirical data.

Nevertheless, the above religious developments are contrary to the perceived global trend of religious decline amid processes of modernisation. China's religious revival and expanding interest in religion exist in spite of a state policy, which has been become more restrictive of varied forms of religious worship in recent years, especially as the CCP has been reviving its own authority and ideological certitude.

It is suggested that the fundamental problem in the relationship between the Chinese state and religion is that 'the party is willing to tolerate the emergence of religion as a purely private experience, but it is not willing to see religion expressed as a sort of collective authority' (Shakya 2009).

In conclusion, rapid changes in China's social, economic, and political landscapes over the late twentieth and early twenty-first centuries have brought about radical and extensive developments in the country's religious beliefs and worship. Further scholarly research and social surveys are necessary to comprehend the nature and scale of this religious evolution.

Civil Society and NGOs (Non-Governmental Organisations)

Civil Society

In the West, and certainly in modern texts, the term 'civil society' is variously used to describe societal activity as lying somewhere between the state and the market. The term became popular in political and economic discussions in the 1980s, when it started to be identified with non-state movements that were defying authoritarian regimes, especially in Central and Eastern Europe and Latin America.

The World Economic Forum (2013) defines civil society as the 'area outside the family, market, and state'. The European Union defines civil society as 'all forms of social action carried out by individuals or groups who are neither connected to, nor managed by, the State'. According to the World Bank, 'Civil society ... refers to a wide array of organisations: community groups, non-governmental organisations [NGOs], labour unions, indigenous groups, charitable organisations, faith-based organisations, professional associations, and foundations'.

An often quoted academic definition is by VanDyck (2017), who proposes a definition of civil society as an ecosystem of 'organised and organic social and cultural relations existing in the space between the state, business, and family, which builds on indigenous and external knowledge, values, traditions, and principles to foster collaboration and the achievement of specific goals by and among citizens and other stakeholders'.

What all these definitions, partly derived from the 1980s discussions, have in common is that civil society must lie outside the state. In fact, an earlier definition by Hegel did not make this distinction (Lloyd 2017), but considered civil society to be encompassed by the state. If one defines the state as excluding the government, then there is no reason to object to defining civil society — including all its economic, social, familial, and political activities — to be an integral part of the state. The people are the state. This is the definition we will adopt (Lloyd 2017).

Given the Chinese context, this definition has a higher explanatory value. Certainly, the CCP see the organisations, generally and broadly defined as NGOs, as part of the governance structures of the state, albeit outside of government.

NGOs

Over the past 30 years, the number and role of NGOs have increased and strengthened. This is partly because some of them are involved in delivering social services. Certain Chinese NGOs have developed to meet growing social needs linked to income disparities, while others often operate at the centre of significant and developing social issues, such as environmental protection, poverty reduction, and labour rights (Hsu 2014). Many Chinese NGOs also engage in advocacy and are formally consulted about policy formulation, acting as intermediaries between their constituencies and the governing authorities (Liu 2011).

To obtain legal status, NGOs need a governmental sponsoring unit. Thus, many NGOs prefer to register as business enterprises, research centres, or student associations (Xie 2012). However, many web-based groups that function as NGOs never register as formal organisations at all. Indeed, Chinese civic organisations have historically avoided the NGO nomenclature, preferring to call themselves people-based or social organisations so as to minimise government intervention in their activities (Yang 2005).

Although NGOs' activism occurs mostly within the boundaries defined by the political authorities, some NGOs have considerable sway, particularly in areas such as animal protection and environmental rights (Sima 2011; Sullivan and Xie 2009).

The use of social media by NGOs has increased in recent years, given its development in China. Several studies have examined how NGOs have embraced dialogical analysis, the building of online communities, as well as seeking of safe opportunities for both online and offline collective actions (Lo and Waters 2012; Yang and Taylor 2010). Notably, the communication practices of younger feminists reflect their interests in working with emerging, market-oriented media to create well-choreographed and dramatic stories, such as the 'Occupy Men's Toilet' movement to highlight gender discrimination.

Often, Western research attempts to analyse Chinese NGOs through the prism of the place of NGOs in Western countries, However, Wang (2015) made the striking point that it may be easier for some Chinese NGOs to function and better serve their constituents within the planned spaces and confines of Party-State surveillance than carve out alternative spaces. There are communication benefits from cultivating close relations with governing authorities because Chinese NGOs, which are closely tied to the government, may paradoxically have the highest degree of autonomy in their operations.

As China develops in an increasingly diversified manner, whether that is economically, regionally, or socially, the government alone cannot deal with the multifarious issues and concerns facing society. New institutions such as NGOs can mobilise large amounts of social capital that will be instrumental to China's social and economic development. To facilitate NGO development in China, the government needs to put in place a more constructive legal framework in which NGOs can function in partnership with the government, within society and the state.

Currently, the rigid legal structure in China recognises and endorses only a relatively small number of NGOs and leaves the rest in an either illegal or semi-legal position. This situation is detrimental to NGO development in line with the needs of societal governance. The CCP accepts and endorses the principle of the 'United Front', including NGOs. Therefore, the introduction of a flexible and clear legal framework would be a means of avoiding autonomous forces continually generating pressures for new NGOs. Given the propagandist use of the CCP United Front organisation, introducing separate, specific legislation for NGOs would permit them to fulfil the traditional roles of NGOs in acting as 'voices for policy reform', albeit within the overall political system and polity.

Marxism and Confucianism: Quo Vadis?

We have explored Chinese political philosophy in Chapter 5 and have commented there on some cultural developments over the past 30 years. We should now attempt to foresee how the intermingling of Marxism and Confucianism in the governance of China may evolve in cultural and social lives, as well as in political terms.

There are some Chinese scholars operating both in the West and in China who may argue that the Marxist-Leninist CCP is alien to how modern China should be governed. Notable among these is Lanxin Xiang. Xiang's communication to Western intellectuals and scholars about the culture, philosophy, and politics of China has added considerably to a more sophisticated view of China. This is valuable to the understanding of China, notwithstanding his view of the role of the CCP.

Clearly there have been, in the past and currently, aspects of the political governance emanating from an apparently narrow CCP elite, namely the Standing Committee of the Politburo, to which many outside China and some inside China might reject. Criticism of any government in any country is not unusual. Moreover, all governing elites have defined and strongly held views of their visions which they wish their countries to adopt, such as former US President Donald Trump's 'America First' and UK Prime Minister Boris Johnson's 'Brexit-A Sovereign Britain'. The uniqueness of the CCP's 'vanguardism' is that it regards a Marxist vision of communism as its ultimate vision — though its 'operational' vision is 'socialism with Chinese characteristics' — which cannot even be operationally defined. It is a vague destination, not a vehicle.

Xiang rejects the conventional view that the answer to China's governance 'problem' is Western democracy (Xiang 2019), but argues that Marxism and Confucianism are 'totally incompatible'. He accepts that 'Xi Jinping is attempting to restore Confucian legitimacy' — defined by Xiang as *hefa,* essentially the Confucian conceptual combination of law and morality — but argues that the current Chinese ruling system is 'derived from an alien source, Bolshevik Russia'. (As Marx and Engels first came up with the 'vanguard party concept', it is actually more German than Russian in origin).

Xiang's comment, however, is substantively misleading: the Chinese variant of Marxism, since Deng, has rejected the idea of classes and class consciousness — a view firmly held by Maoists and by orthodox Marxists in the West. In other words, Chinese Marxism is different, as it holds on to the Confucian notion of *hefa*, at least in theoretical terms. Finally, Xiang contends that the 'alien system' cannot be preserved, especially since Xi's cultural focus is on the Chinese Dream. Xiang may be correct from his own specific Chinese identification. However, he also advocates a shift to pluralist political parties for China. It would be equally valid in terms of political philosophy, including Xiang's own, to introduce greater democracy via reformed CCP intra-party democracy, plus a greater role for non-CCP political consultative organisations.

The 'democratic centralist' structure is a constraint on such a reform, though it does not render such a reform impossible to enact. Xiang also suggests adoption of the Swiss system of governance, at least on a local level. On this issue he is on strong ground, as he has spent part of his academic life in Geneva, the birthplace of Rousseau, who nonetheless believed in the necessity of elites (Lloyd 2019). However, Xiang seems to ignore the actual 'quasi-federal' structure of the Chinese state, where direct democracy happens at village levels, for instance.

For the leadership of the CCP, its version of Marxism is appropriate to the current stage of capitalistic development in China, accepted by both Deng and Xi. It is, as observed, 'socialism with Chinese characteristics'. Moreover, 'Communism' is undefined, except in the most general sense, as the ultimate destination. Its mention is more for rhetorical consistency, without any delineated path to its achievement. This much is clear from Xi's first major speech at the outset of his pre-eminence (Xi 2013):

> 'As long as we stick to our own path and unswervingly adhere to and develop socialism with Chinese characteristics, we will surely be able to comprehensively build a moderately prosperous society by the centennial anniversary of the founding of the Communist Party of China, and a prosperous, democratic, civilised, modernised, and harmonious socialist country by the centennial anniversary of the founding of New China'.
>
> 'Facts have repeatedly told us that Marx and Engels' analysis of the basic contradictions in capitalist society is not outdated, nor is the historical materialist view that capitalism is bound to die out and socialism is bound to win. This is an inevitable trend in social and historical development. But the road is tortuous. The eventual demise of capitalism and the ultimate victory of socialism will require a long historical process to reach completion. In the meantime, we must have a deep appreciation for capitalism's ability to self-correct, and a full, objective assessment of the real long-term advantages that the developed Western nations have

> in the economic, technological, and military spheres. Then we must diligently prepare for a long period of cooperation and of conflict between these two social systems in each of these domains'.
>
> 'We should educate and guide cadres and the broader mass of Party members so that we can unite our the common ideal of practicing socialism with Chinese characteristics together with our lofty ideal of securing Communism'.

What should be understood is that, irrespective of a distant and vague final socio-economic destination, the CCP experiment — to promote 'socialism with Chinese characteristics' — will continue to develop and evolve.

The 'experiment' might as well be called 'capitalism with socialist market characteristics' (the Marxist left in the West simply term it 'state capitalism'). Others might call it simply a 'mixed economy'. But this term covers all modern economies, including the so-called 'free market' economy of the US.

Chinese Marxism is clear on specific points of difference in its model, to both Soviet Marxism and the neoliberal market capitalism. All land is owned by the state, though it can be and is leased; the state either owns or controls the majority of companies in China, sometimes in partnership with Western, often US, companies; markets are strongly regulated; and the CCP is a Leninist vanguard party, whose role is pre-eminent in guiding the Chinese economy and society. Clearly, this is not a mixed economy, in the sense in which the term is normally employed. It is a socialist economy nominally, in transition towards China's objective of a substantially technology-based economy, capable of eradicating all but essential work.

The wider question for other countries, perhaps especially emerging economies, is whether this effectively domestic vision for China is capable of being a global model. Given the current structure of the global economy and polity and the current unattractiveness of the externally perceived Chinese value system, this currently seems unlikely.

There is frequent reference, including by Xi and Deng before him, to the importance of Confucian values in China, and the endorsement of these values by both Deng and Xi. There is less reference to Buddhism and Daoism, even though the values associated with these philosophies and religions are also entwined with values of collectivism and social harmony, evident in the older Chinese population.

Some Western observers either ignore or dismiss this thematic thread running through the Chinese leadership since Deng through Xi as manipulative propaganda. More sympathetic and knowledgeable Chinese scholars, such as Xiang, tend to dismiss Marxist-Leninism as 'alien' and therefore intrinsically incompatible with Confucianism.

The key issue here is how influential this potential confluence of traditional values, Marxist socialist values, and modern technological development will translate into China's current and future geoeconomic and geopolitical policies and actions, and how they will be perceived outside China.

There is a temptation in the West to view the rhetorical inter-twining of Confucianism and Marxism adopted by Xi as a mere instrumental tool to convince older Chinese that the modern socialist regime holds on to ancient Chinese values. However, this is to ignore the moral, collectivist, and social underpinning of Marxism, which has echoes of Confucianism.

Moreover, notwithstanding the tragic and horrendous mistakes of the Mao era, Mao's intentions were to benefit the Chinese people. The fact that religion is not only tolerated in China, but also that the desire for spiritual enlightenment appears to be as strong in China as in the West, is proof that a soulless atheism is insufficient in China. Other moral imperatives are shown by the growing number and influence of NGOs, both those which are formally recognised and approved and those which are tolerated.

Whether the confluence of Marxism and Confucianism in China is a valid prospective development is a matter for praxis and for future empirical evidence. To regard it as impossible or to suggest that the Chinese governance system should be replaced with a Western-style set of institutions and processes is a matter for conjecture and debate, certainly not an obvious prescription to be adopted.

The older cultural and religious values often linked to Confucianism and other Eastern religions certainly play a part in the cultural and social lives of many Chinese people, and are likely to find an echo in the many Chinese who live abroad either permanently or temporarily. The influence of the various segments of the Chinese diaspora, particularly those in Southeast Asia, has a significant impact on China's economic development over the past 30 years. It is worth exploring the familial and clan nature of the various external connections — between groups and individuals — and its effects on China's economic development. The next section will also explore the feedback mechanisms and familial, cultural, and financial characteristics which link ethnic Chinese outside and inside China.

The Bamboo Network: Overseas Chinese Role in China's Development

Size and Nature of the Diaspora

Former Malaysian Prime Minister Mahathir Mohamad once alluded to the international Chinese diaspora as the world's third largest economy (Mohamad 1999). With estimated wealth holdings currently around US$3 trillion (Oxford Economics 2010) versus estimated onshore Chinese wealth of US$8 trillion in 2020, the so-called 'Bamboo Network' is a complex cross-border and intercontinental web of family, intra-clan and community-wide ties intermingling with business and open access to domestic and international markets.

As each year passes, this stock of wealth, particularly from a number of major companies belonging to ethnic Chinese living in Taiwan, Hong Kong, Macau in Greater China and in Southeast Asia, North America, Australasia, Africa, and Europe, continues to grow in value.

As the world's largest diaspora population, people of Chinese ancestry living outside Mainland and Greater China are estimated to number around 43 million and distributed across 148 countries (Poston and Wong 2016). This diaspora is not evenly spread out; Asia, especially Southeast Asia, accounts for the largest share (73%), and North America, the second largest share.

China's government has extolled the virtues of its expanding overseas diaspora. In an address to the 12th World Chinese Entrepreneurs Convention in 2013, President Xi Jinping said: 'Thanks to their hard work and magnificent traditions, Chinese businessmen abroad live in harmony with people around the world and contribute to the global economy and social progress' (ECNS 2013).

Over the past several decades, given the low-profile characteristics enveloped in the family- and clan-centricity of the overseas Chinese, they have emerged tentatively onto the international arena, alongside the rapid expansion of China's economy.

Essentially, the spotlight is shone on this global community because of their substantial investments in mainland China, accounting for about 80% of all annual foreign investment there, reaching US$200 billion at its peak during the 1990s (Long 1998). While Hong Kong still accounts for about two-thirds of this annual direct investment, it mainly serves as a conduit for channelling other countries' investment flows, rather than as an originator of capital (Wang 2019a). While capital from Hong Kong and

Taiwan declined over the last decade, the share of overseas Chinese investments from the large ethnic Chinese business communities of Singapore, Malaysia, Thailand, Indonesia, and the Philippines has been growing (Suryadinata 2017).

In 1980, when Deng Xiaoping began the process of opening China by setting up Special Economic Zones (SEZs) — free market enclaves — in its southern provinces, he chose the ancestral homes of three of the most important groups in the Chinese diaspora: the Cantonese from Guangdong province, who also predominate in Hong Kong; the Hokkien from Fujian province, making up 85% of Taiwan's population and much of Singapore's; and less well known, the Teochew from around Shantou, on the border between Guangdong and Fujian, which include tycoons such as Li Ka-shing, Hong Kong's most renowned billionaire and the Ma family, which controls the Oriental Press Group there. Indeed, the Teochew also make up most of the ethnic Chinese in Thailand, including the Sophonpanich family who founded and developed the country's largest financial institution, the Bangkok Bank (Campden Wealth 2020).

Another southern Chinese group, known as the Hakka, can also lay claim as to the origins of three highly influential Chinese leaders at the end of the twentieth century. They are Deng Xiaoping, China's paramount leader; Lee Kuan Yew, the founder of modern Singapore; and Lee Teng-hui, the first popularly elected president of Taiwan (Liu 2014a) — all globally-renowned political leaders.

Sun Yat-sen, the first President and later de-facto ruler of the Republic of China, once famously said of the Chinese people 'as having only family and clan solidarity, lacking a national spirit and just a heap of loose sand'. Yet there is also a strong sense of ethnic solidarity, encapsulated in the Chinese word *huaqiao* for overseas Chinese, which implies 'an eventual return home'.

Speaking on behalf of the overseas Chinese character, late-Singapore Prime Minister Lee Kuan Yew praised the cosmopolitan Chinese character. He invoked the virtues of *guanxi* (connections) and said that for the Chinese, 'networking is the natural thing to do' — suggesting that from a business perspective, they were better at it than most other people anywhere in the world (Liu 2012).

Attitudes in Mainland China

In China itself, these networks transformed the official perception of the overseas Chinese. Traditionally, they were viewed with a high degree of disdain. In Imperial China, trading was among the least respected of professional activities. Those who had left to make their fortune elsewhere were seen as unpatriotic and selfish. But most of those who left in the large-scale exoduses of the late nineteenth and early twentieth centuries did so in desperation or under coercion. Their existence overseas was simply a reflection of the failings and weaknesses of China's fragmenting society and national decline.

During the Mao era, especially the Cultural Revolution of the late 1960s, overseas Chinese in some Southeast Asian countries played important roles in left-wing insurgencies supported by China (Reid 1995). However, the Chinese authorities stopped short of allowing overseas Chinese having any political influence within China.

As China withdrew support for overseas ethnic Chinese movements and cemented friendships with the governments of Southeast Asia, it also began to take a more tolerant and eventually welcoming attitude to the overseas Chinese business community.

Today's generation of elite overseas Chinese business leaders are often educated abroad, particularly in the West, as are those from China itself. As a result, both tend to have more westernised views, including in their conduct of business, than previous generations of overseas Chinese entrepreneurs and those from the mainland.

At the same time, allegiances to blood ties and kinship which transcend national borders have subjected overseas Chinese to criticism outside China. Suspicions are exacerbated by the Chinese diaspora tradition of shifting money into secretive and distant offshore tax havens. As much as US$120 billion may have been held offshore by ethnic Chinese Indonesians in the late-1990s (Long 1998), at around the time of the fall of then-Indonesian President Suharto. Even Li Ka-shing is reported to have transferred ownership of his corporate assets to the Cayman Islands in 2015 as a hedge against political risks in Hong Kong (Awai 2015).

Cultural Identities in the Chinese Diaspora

The reasons for overseas Chinese economic successes are often ascribed to their individual and community characteristics. Scholars tend to unify these aspects of the diaspora as the 'Chinese spirit' (Redding 1993).

On the other hand, as emigration occurred during different historical periods in China for varied reasons, combined with living in countries of diverse social and political systems, the overseas Chinese are also said to be highly heterogeneous. This was bolstered by political developments in the first half of the twentieth century, which served to consolidate the heterogeneity of disparate overseas Chinese communities. To counter this social diversity, the unitary identity of *huaqiao* was constructed for the global landscape.

However, this identity — based on political loyalty to China — became an issue when new nation-states arose in Southeast Asia after WWII. The agreement that Mao's China signed with Indonesia in 1955 symbolised a major shift in the Chinese government's policy toward overseas Chinese, that is, encouraging them to adopt the citizenship of their host countries.

In subsequent decades, most Chinese living in Southeast Asia became citizens of their countries of residence. In the US, Canada, Australia, and New Zealand, many Chinese became naturalised citizens. As a result, the majority of overseas Chinese are no longer considered *huaqiao*, instead taking up the identity of *huayi*, which means 'foreigners of Chinese ancestry'.

These formal changes did not result in the loss of a Chinese identity among diaspora Chinese. Just as the identity of *huaqiao* was a product of particular historical contexts, post-colonial politics in Southeast Asia and multiculturalism in Western societies have created new contexts in which the identities of overseas Chinese have been reconstructed.

To this extent, they are culturally and ethnically Chinese but are also nationals of their resident countries. For many people, being Chinese is more a cultural than territorial phenomenon. Although it means different things to different people in a range of contexts, being Chinese in a cultural setting is something that helps to define the identity of the Chinese diaspora.

The Chinese Merchant Class in Southeast Asia

The region of Southeast Asia became an important pillar of the overseas Chinese economy during the latter decades of the twentieth century (Suryadinata 2017). Historically, the Chinese dominated trade and commercial life in Southeast Asia and became an economically powerful minority living among Southeast Asian native majorities. Public attitudes towards ethnic Chinese in the Asian countries have therefore not been always positive.

With the rise of these twentieth century linkages across Southeast Asia, Hong Kong, Taiwan, and North America, the overseas Chinese and their personal and business connections have played an ever more prominent role in the growth of China's economy. In recent years, this has facilitated large-scale private investment, trade, and technological dynamism.

The launch of China's economy from 1990 as a global manufacturing and export powerhouse was significantly financed by networks of overseas Chinese as large-scale owners of capital. Territories and countries with the largest communities of overseas Chinese, such as Hong Kong, Taiwan, Singapore, Thailand, Indonesia, and Malaysia, accounted for the bulk of such direct investments in developing China's manufacturing sector.

Overseas Chinese networks have also served as important channels for promoting sales of Chinese manufactured output into international markets. Southeast Asia, also being closely connected to Hong Kong and Taiwan, was a favoured channel for further supply-chain expansion into international markets, building on the importance of blood ties and linguistic and cultural identities.

China's provincial governments have extensively invited overseas Chinese, descended from a town or local family in the province, to invest there. This was achieved by utilising communication channels through a broad overseas Chinese network which was formed to promote such economic benefits. It was further supported by information exchanges between the hometown and overseas Chinese communities and facilitated by local government sponsorship programmes. Major dignitaries from the diaspora hometowns were also included in the endeavours to attract overseas Chinese to invest, thereby taking additional advantage of personal networks.

Subsequently, the means by which all these efforts were organised increasingly involved more formal structures than those conducted through traditional family or clan networks, as overseas Chinese were offered these investment opportunities in China at government-sponsored global business gatherings both outside and within China.

Ethical Concerns

Many of the comments on China by Western political, academic, and media analysts — be it out of admiration of or displeasure at the technological and economic successes of China — have been ethical concerns about China's internal policies and actions, especially in the area of human rights and democratic governance. These concerns are based essentially on the Western philosophical basis of liberal individualism, derived from a Lockean perspective (Locke 1690).

Often, and misleadingly, these concerns are linked with democracy, or rather its absence in China: though we have argued in Chapter 5 that this view is misleading. In fact, democracy covers a subset of theories of governance. Hence, the Western ethical concerns will be discussed from the aspects of liberalism, individualism, and governance. The intention is not to 'take sides', but to clarify the substantive and subjective nature of the arguments generally deployed, including a challenge to the tendentious universalism often maintained by Western critics of China.

An example of Western ethical concerns may be illustrated by a few moderate paragraphs from the Conclusions of the AI & Society paper on the Chinese approach to AI (Roberts *et al.* 2020):

> 'The AIDP also promotes AI as a way to help deal with some of the major social problems, ranging from pollution to standards of living. However, positive impact in this area seem to come with increased control over individuals' behaviour, with governance extending into the realm of moral behaviour and further erosion of privacy'.
>
> 'With respect to privacy, a closer look exposes the many loopholes and exceptions that enable the government (and companies implicitly endorsed by the government) to bypass privacy protection and fundamental issues concerning lack of accountability and government's unrestrained decisional power about mass-surveillance'.
>
> 'In the same vein, when focusing on medical ethics, it is clear that, although China may agree with the West on the bioethical principles, its focus on the health of the population, in contrast to the West's focus on the health of the individual, may easily lead to unethical outcomes (the sacrifice imposed on one for the benefit of many) and is creating a number of risks, as AI encroaches on the medical space'.
>
> 'However, some ethical safeguards, constraints and desiderata are universal and are universally accepted and cherished, such as the nature and scope of human rights. They enable one to evaluate, after having understood, China's approach to the development of AI'.

On the surface, the concerns appear justified. However, the four ethical issues raised in the said paper, though familiar, are challengeable, once we abandon an individualistic perspective and view them from a no-less ethically valid, societal, or collectivist position. Moreover, when we examine them more closely, they are not even unknown in Western societal practice. The criticism deployed in the above paper are dealt with as follows.

'*increased control over individuals' behaviour, with governance extending into the realm of moral behaviour*'. The US government and the UK government both seek to influence moral behaviour in various ways, such as imposing penalties on drink-driving and other motoring offences, removing children from inadequate parents, and having zero tolerance for anti-social behaviour. All societies use various more or less severe methods to attempt to achieve social harmony. Achieving social harmony has a higher priority as an accepted social objective in East Asian countries, including China, than is the case in Western countries.

'*fundamental issues concerning lack of accountability and government's unrestrained decisional power about mass-surveillance*'. This lack of accountability is a real concern in China. However, the visibility of the surveillance renders the perceived lack readily challengeable. However, as has been argued in Chapters 2 and 5, there is an increasing degree of individual data privacy now being incorporated in legislation.

Moreover, a lack of accountability is also present in Western countries, but is far less visible, unless and until revealed either by whistle-blowers or by the publication of historical documents decades later (and even then, documents are sometimes substantially redacted). The Panama papers are an example where unaccountable practices were revealed. The unauthorised release of the Watergate papers was another. These instances do not, of course, justify government unaccountability in China, but they suggest that China is not the outlier often suggested.

'*the sacrifice imposed on one for the benefit of many*'. This is commonly known as 'utilitarianism' and informs many aspects of socio-economic decision-making in the West, such as the regular use of cost-benefit analysis, for instance in determining the allocation of health treatment and resources. Some form of consequentialism is prevalent across all societies.

'*some ethical safeguards, constraints and desiderata are universal and are universally accepted and cherished, such as the nature and scope of human rights*'. This statement appears unchallengeable, partly because there is a missing word, the universality claimed attaches to '(individual) human rights'. However, 'collective rights' are equally, if not more deserving, of protection and advancement. Indeed, the Chinese do favour collective rights. Though we have become used to the notion of rights being a 'possession' of the individual, collective rights may equally be asserted. This issue, and its wider implications, was comprehensively discussed in Chapter 5.

As the above brief commentary and discussions in earlier chapters have attempted to demonstrate, the universality of Western liberal individualism cannot be accepted in the absence of philosophical justifications which are either absent or often inadequate. This fundamental philosophical disagreement, morphed into an ideological political struggle in geopolitical terms will be explored in this latter context in the remaining chapters.

The other ethical challenge to China from the West is the one concerning a lack of democracy. Democracy, aside from problems agreeing to a definition, is in fact an issue of essential modes of decision-making in collectivities of various sizes, namely an issue of the modes of citizens' participation in governance. As was indicated in Chapter 5, all governance systems involve a balance of authoritarianism and democracy in terms of the effective political participation in decision-making by the people, for instance, direct democracy. Only in the smallest collectivity in a decentralised governance system can genuine direct democracy prevail, including in villages, communes, and parishes. In all other levels of regional political governance, some form of technocratic, elite leadership is essential. The issue is to ensure that these elitist governance structures are responsive to the requirements of the people. The issue, whether in China or elsewhere, is the achieving the best balance between meritocracy and citizens participation in governance.

The above discussion manifests the weakness of much of the West's criticism of China, which is based either on ideological values — which are no more or less valid than China's values — or hypocritical, imprecise thinking, and a low level of knowledge and understanding. As indicated in Chapter 1, in relation to the suppression of the Tiananmen Square student protests — or for that matter accurate and proportionate criticism of the current treatment of the Uyghur population — this does not mean the West is unable to condemn specific reprehensible actions by China. However, the obverse ability for China to criticise the West for its transgressions is equally valid. In general, however, China's stance is not to criticise other countries in relation to domestic matters.

Moreover, in geoeconomic and geopolitical terms, there should be attempts to understand the motivations of China in both its internal and external behaviour, which we will explore in the remaining chapters. For China these motivations are inextricably linked. They are important in recognising and responding to the role of China in a new global era.

A willingness to suspend 'Cold War' antagonism during the current phase of China's emergence — especially if the Cold War is based on either misconceived ideological judgements or a belief that there is a single universal set of political, economic, and societal structures and values — is crucial to the ability of the major global actors, including China and the US, to cooperate to resolve common and substantial global problems. Three of these global challenges are discussed in the next chapter.

Concluding Comments

The chapter has attempted to reflect on the cultural and social, as well as political, dimensions of Chinese society as it developed through the twentieth century, especially the changing nature of the influences on it over the past 30 years. The turmoil in the middle part of the twentieth century has given way gradually to a China emerging internally as a strong and dynamic middle-income country, alongside the social changes which come with greater prosperity for many if not all.

The twenty-first century has seen the emergence of NGOs, formal and informal, operating at all levels of governance and attempting to draw attention to issues that need remedial action, such as various environmental issues. China's attitudes towards and politico-legal treatment of NGOs lacks clarity and the CCP has not yet developed a *modus operandi* to handle the societal challenges posed by some NGO activism.

At the same time as the CCP emphasises the country as being committed to 'socialism with Chinese characteristics', Xi stresses the importance of Confucian ideals and links Confucianism with Marxism. The link is moral as well as nationalistic and political, and is linked with familial, clan, and collectivist societal characteristics. These social values may also be observed in Chinese populations living outside China, the so-called 'Bamboo Network'. The familial and financial roles of this external network in supporting the development of China during its early decades of outstanding economic growth should not be underestimated.

Finally, in terms of the ethical criticism often levelled at China by Western commentators, it is noted that problems arise from an unwillingness of these sources to understand that their own liberal individualist democratic position is not universally shared, not only by China but also some other East Asian countries. The validity or otherwise of the underlying different philosophical positions is a matter for debate and understanding, not the adoption of the unequivocal superiority of the Western position. How this antagonism plays out in geopolitical terms will be the subject of the remainder of the book.

PART 2

Global Insights

Chapter 7

Twenty-First Century Challenges: Climate Change, COVID-19 and Others

Introduction

There are three major challenges the world faces in the twenty-first century. They are a) climate change, accompanied by a loss of biodiversity and population movement; b) the maldistribution and misutilisation of natural resources, accompanied by severe environmental damage and unconstrained population growth; and c) the threat of pandemics and associated health and economic crises, such as COVID-19.

These three challenges are linked, and in relation to all of them, China has a significant role to play at a national level, and importantly, in achieving the essential global consensus for the action which is required. It can readily be seen that the above challenges require global solutions. The problem is that we do not have effective and genuinely global institutions. This absence is compounded by the rise of strong nationalisms across the world. It is argued that there is a distinctive, constructive role for China, in collaboration with other global actors, in resolving these global problems. China's activity in this respect is already evident as the remainder of the chapter will illustrate.

Moreover, there is a burgeoning conflict between the two major global economic powers, the US and China. Each has conflicting ideologies in the areas of the management of capitalism and institutional governance and in the projection of economic power. In the case of the US, this is often accompanied by the aggressive projection of political, financial, and military power. In respect of the three global problems, we need to examine: how China is already addressing these problems; what lessons China may be offering other countries; and the role China will attempt to establish in relation to the international agreements which already exist. (The precise nature of the US participation in the generation and execution of a global consensus for action is a separate question for resolution).

We will first define the problems involved under each of the headings and then outline the role China is already playing and could continue to play in resolving the various dimensions of the three challenges to humankind. Clearly, in one short chapter, it will not be possible to provide a comprehensive picture, either of the complex nature of the problems or the role China can play in their resolution. However, it will be possible to sketch out the nature of China's contribution to resolving these three global problems of modernity, all arising from the unplanned expansion of global human settlements and the uneven distribution of resource endowments.

Climate Change

The interrelationship of natural factors and substantial human pressures which is causing global warming — and the consequential alterations in global and regional weather patterns that are all contributing to a decline in global biodiversity — have been identified. The evidence to support the increase in global warming and its potential influence on global weather patterns is incontrovertible. Human action has played, and is still playing, a substantial part in driving global warming. The contribution of human actions, over the past 250 years and increasingly during the last 100 years, has meant global economic development has reached a number of crucial natural global constraints. The development has been driven by a variety of interlinked global factors. These are: a vast increase in global population, doubling to 7.5 billion over the last 100 years; vastly increased land use, especially for agricultural and industrial usage; substantial overuse of physically limited resources of sequestered carbon; overuse of available global water; unsustainable economic consumption in rich countries, especially in the West; and a dangerous increase in pollutants, harmful to human and other organic life forms on land and in the sea and air.

Many see this array of intensely damaging factors as an immediate global emergency and, potentially, an almost irreversible catastrophe emerging over the next 30 years or so. However, one need not share this apocalyptic vision to recognise the need for substantial, ongoing remedial actions to be taken at global level to significantly relax the pressure on all the above constraints. These remedies will involve a variety of specific actions.

They will include, *inter alia*, building resilience where communities shelter and livelihoods are threatened, specifically in coastal areas; targeting developing countries where impacts may be most severe; decreasing further expansion of land use; reducing the consumption of animal protein; rewilding of areas on land and in the sea; continuing to reduce the use of hydrocarbons to produce energy; and developing and utilising technology globally to provide solutions to ease the pressure on the above-listed constraints.

Starting from the policies towards climate change that China is adopting nationally, the commitment to action is clear. It is worth noting that in looking at China, we are looking at 20% of the world population, and the impact of, and on, that significant proportion of humankind.

China's vulnerability to sea-level rise is especially acute (Liu 2016). More than 550 million people live in China's coastal provinces — one of the most densely populated regions on Earth. Tens of millions of people live or work in low-lying areas in major Chinese cities, including Shanghai, Qingdao, and Xiamen. However, China is also the world's largest emitter of GHGs (greenhouse gases). Hence, there is no solution to global climate change without the active participation of China, and it has a strong vested interest in being strongly involved.

China's first five-year Climate Change Plan was published in 2014 (Hu 2016). Since the publication of that Plan, the Chinese government has adopted various measures. These have included adjusting its industrial structure, saving energy, increasing energy efficiency, optimising energy structure, controlling GHG emissions from non-energy activities, and increasing carbon sinks. Significant headways have therefore been made in mitigating climate change.

The aim, during the 2014 to 2020 period, was to ensure the achievement of the GHG emissions targets by 2020, so as to provide a solid foundation for achieving an emission peak before, at least, 2030. In addition, another objective has been to actively advance international negotiations on climate change, and to continue to promote multilateral and bilateral dialogues and exchanges as well as pragmatic cooperation on climate change with other countries.

In November 2014, in line with this aim of international collaboration, the Chinese government under Xi signed a concordat with the Obama administration to accelerate the reduction in US carbon emissions by 2025 (White House 2014). It also required China to increase the share of non-fossil fuels energy by 20% by 2030, and to start cutting carbon emissions, substantially, by the same date.

Progress towards these broad goals and the specific five-year plan commitments have been made by China. The US, under Trump, had withdrawn from the Paris Accord on Climate Change. However, Biden has promised to re-engage on this agreement. This lacuna, resulting from the US withdrawal, has provided an opportunity for China to be the leading player in stimulating the global effort to tackle climate change and to provide lessons for others to emulate.

China has reduced the role of coal in its economy. Chinese coal consumption is roughly 3% lower than its peak in 2013 (Henderson *et al.* 2017), which is achieved by various measures, including closing inefficient coal power plants, introducing coal power-efficiency standards, phasing out coal heating in northern China, and introducing market-based reforms to reduce the role of coal in the power generation fuel mix.

Structural shifts towards services in the economy and a cyclical downturn in some industries contributed to the decline, but Chinese government policies have been a key factor. For instance, the impending removal of the solar and wind power subsidy scheme at the end of 2020 has led to a race to connect renewable energy projects to the grid. Hence, the growth in solar and wind installations has kept up with — and even surpassed — the installation rate in 2019, despite COVID-19 setbacks for grid connections.

Despite the above successes, severe environmental problems still exist. For instance, CO_2 emissions rose in 2018 and 2019 (Climate Action Tracker 2020). In the context of the Paris Accords, China's Nationally Determined Contributions (NDCs) and the implementing national actions are not yet consistent with limiting warming to below 2°C, let alone 1.5°C. Failure to achieve these targets would entail other countries making much deeper reductions and comparably greater efforts than China.

Despite a more centralised system of governance, as has been observed elsewhere, the actions required involve numerous other state actors such as various state-owned energy companies, and energy tariff-setting spreading across different ministries, agencies, and local authorities.

Democratic contestation, in connection with climate change policies having a variety of economic impacts, is present in China, as in the West. This contestation was evident in relation to the removal of discrimination against migrant workers, as indicated in Chapter 3. The outcomes of nationally announced and authorised policies still have to be implemented through various ministries, private industrial companies, provinces, cities, towns, and villages. Nevertheless, China has an excellent record of delivering early against key targets in five-year plans. Moreover, climate change policies are being driven by national necessity as well as aiming to contribute to global objectives. The prospect of China making headway in achieving these targets still appears to be positive, as illustrated below.

The current emphasis on the extension of China's influence through its massive infrastructure investment projects outside of China must be considered as well. China's role in global energy finance, its investments in Arctic countries (Lino 2020), and the BRI initiative might be more influential in achieving global low-carbon transformations than various other interventions identified as fostering climate mitigation.

For the world to achieve its climate goals, significant action to reduce emissions will be required after 2030. Indeed, the Paris Agreement (UN 2015) calls for 'rapid reductions' in emissions after a global peak and net zero emissions during the second half of this century. For all these reasons, it is clear the world will need to do much more to meet its climate goals. It is also clear that China must play an important role in these efforts, for several reasons.

First, China has enormous potential to contribute to solutions to climate change. In the past decade, it has played a central role in dramatic cost reductions for solar power. This technology has the potential to significantly reduce power sector emissions around the world in the decades ahead.

China's current investments in electric vehicles and the use of hydrogen power could play a transformational role for those technologies, helping to reduce transport sector emissions around the world as well as in China (Power Technology 2021). The Chinese government's focus on innovation and commitment to clean energy could help generate further important technological discoveries and advances, with global impacts in the decades ahead.

Second, many countries look to China's development model with enormous interest. Countless countries would like to emulate China's economic miracle. The way China integrates climate change with economic development in the future has the potential to be a model for many countries around the world.

Third, China's activities abroad have considerable emissions impacts. The extent to which Chinese financial institutions and companies support low-carbon infrastructure, as opposed to high-carbon infrastructure, under the BRI will make an enormous difference in global emissions in the decades ahead.

There is huge potential for China's BRI renewable energy cooperation with other countries. This cooperation has been focused on the China-Pakistan Economic Corridor, the Bangladesh-China-India-Myanmar Economic Corridor, the China-Indochina Peninsula Economic Corridor, the China-Central Asia-West Asia Economic Corridor, the New Eurasian Land Bridge, the China-Russia-Mongolia Economic Corridor, and China-Africa Cooperation.

Renewable energy investments are profitable, economically viable, and have the utmost importance for reaching our climate goals. It is in China's own interest to focus on green development in BRI countries. The issue is to convince the countries involved that it is in their interests, as well as the world's, to invest in renewable projects which will remain profitable, rather than coal which may result in stranded assets and ecological damage. Luckily, in Africa the attraction of solar energy is obvious, which has been aided by the previous investment of China, resulting in the cost of solar panels to fall so substantially.

China is playing an ever-important role in Africa's energy transition, mainly in the form of massive investments and loans for various energy infrastructure projects. These range from extractive activities in oil and gas industries, to power generation facilities including both traditional and renewable energy sources, and transmission and distribution networks.

Hydropower projects are still the preferred projects for Chinese contractors in Africa; they are involved in 52% of all hydropower projects in the region (in terms of capacity), followed by 29.3% involvement in coal projects and 10.7% in gas projects (Global Data 2019).

Among other renewable energy sectors, China's Shanghai Electric and Dongfang Electric have won a bid to build a 6GW clean coal power plant on the Red Sea. Dongfang Electric has also been awarded a contract to develop and construct a 120MW wind park in the Ethiopian state of Somali.

Other major projects involving Chinese contractors include a 200MW solar farm that will be built by Sinohydro Group in Bui,

Ghana; a 100 MW Gwanda Solar Power Plant in Zimbabwe by CHINT Electrics; and the Benban solar farm in Egypt, the world's largest solar park, which became fully operational by August 2019 (Power Technology 2019).

China's domestic climate change agenda and its willingness to take a global lead on the issue are leading to an important set of initiatives. The major speech by Xi Jinping on September 29th, 2020 (Frangoul 2020) outlined a commitment to a set of extraordinary goals to be set out in the next five-year plan, representing a sea-change in moving the climate change agenda forward.

In his speech, Xi indicated that China would strive to become carbon neutral by 2060 and CO_2 emissions would peak before 2030. This commitment means that China would use clean energy sources and either capture or offset any remaining emissions. By removing the same amount of carbon emitted into the atmosphere, China would achieve 'net-zero' carbon emissions. The commitment to CO_2 emissions peaking before 2030 was a reiteration of the earlier target. In any case, it seems likely that the peak will be reached earlier, perhaps between 2022 and 2025. China frequently delivers on targets earlier than promised.

There was not much detail in the speech of the mechanisms to achieve the targets, but Xi's speech was followed some days later by the publication of a study. It suggests how China will reach its peak emissions in the next decade and then decrease them rapidly to reach carbon neutrality by 2060.

The lead author of the study, He Jiankun indicated that carbon neutrality is referring to all GHGs (Myllyvirta 2020). The 2060 target will mean replacing almost all fossil fuels from energy generation, leaving coal with a share of 5%, representing a massive 70% drop from current levels. Removing coal from other industrial sectors is even more problematic. It would entail cutting these emissions from a projected peak of 10.5 billion tons to 1.7 billion tons by 2060. This would probably require substantial use of carbon sinks and other carbon capture techniques.

A draft law, published in April 2020 (Wang 2020), accommodated the need for China to cut GHG emissions in its energy system, and in scenarios consistent with Paris Agreement climate goals, required major reductions in coal-fired power generation. The law would establish guaranteed minimum levels of renewables in each province, giving renewables priority access to the electricity grid. The government is also promoting ultra-high voltage (UHV) power transmission. This would take renewable electricity to where demand is greatest and reduce renewables 'curtailment', as part of its 'neo-infrastructure' COVID-19 economic recovery package.

One thing is clear from the above discussion, as the world meets the climate challenge in the decades ahead, China's role will be central. Moreover, the solution will be global and cooperative, not simply national. China will play an important role in climate diplomacy in the next several years and beyond. As the world considers the next steps under the Paris Agreement, the Chinese government's position and views will be key to shaping a global consensus.

COVID-19 and Future Pandemics

It has been a hundred years — in the aftermath of the First World War and the Spanish Flu pandemic in 1918/1919 — since the world has been faced with such a contagious and deadly viral pandemic. The world in 2020 — more than five times larger in population and vastly more connected, though, happily, also more advanced in medical science — is a completely different environment. Yet the situation is just as frightening, and in social and economic terms more disruptive than a century ago.

The SARS-CoV-2 virus, leading to the COVID-19 disease and pandemic, was detected in China's Hebei province in November/December 2019. At first, it was believed to be a respiratory virus, probably pneumonia. In some patients admitted to hospitals in Wuhan in late December, the disease appeared to be presenting as such and treated accordingly. However, some symptoms did not match with standard viral pneumonia, nor did the infections appear to resemble SARS-CoV-1 which shed virus particles after infection symptoms. This virus appeared to be infectious by shedding its virus before symptoms appeared.

The regional World Health Organisation (WHO) representative in China was notified on December 31st, 2019 of the unknown disease which was circulating in December in Wuhan city. The causal virus was rapidly identified and its genome produced by January 8th, 2020. The virus was beginning to circulate globally by then. The virus was a corona virus, named SARS-CoV-2 as it resembles SARS 1 in being an RNA virus. There was some delay, until January 25th, in confirming human transmission and in reporting this confirmation nationally in China. Later in January, with cases in Wuhan increasing rapidly, actions were taken on

January 23rd to lockdown the city of 11 million people. Investigation of the outbreak is continuing in 2021 (World Health Organisation 2021).

After declaring COVID-19 a major health emergency, the WHO subsequently stated it to be a pandemic as substantial numbers of cases started appearing in other countries. In some of these countries (in Europe and the US), unlike in China and South Korea, actions in the form of national lockdowns were significantly delayed. Lockdown happened in the UK on March 23rd, 2020. Policies in the UK, and elsewhere, were principally based on flawed epidemiological models, rather than looking at what was already happening in China. In the US, the virus was called 'China Virus' by former President Trump, and only minimal national action was authorised.

In fact, just as in the case of the Spanish Flu, viruses do not have a nationality. Their origin is irrelevant once they are transmitted between humans. Subsequently, Trump withdrew support for the WHO, arguing that it was dominated by China, even though this charge had little validity. This denigration of the one effective global organisation, among others which are essentially international, indicates clearly the problem of the inadequacy of truly global responses to genuine global problems. Currently, though the WHO provides advice on treating COVID-19, the developed countries have conducted national policies with little or no coherence or cooperation, save in the areas of vaccine development and treatment protocols. The cooperation has been mainly between scientists and doctors rather than governments. Given that the pandemic has spread to the majority of developing countries and emerging economies, global cooperation is even more imperative.

China's approach to tackling the impact of the outbreak of the COVID-19 disease, after an inevitably hesitant start, demonstrated its ability to deploy a strong public health response to slowing and containing the spread of the virus in China. This was supported by a collective response from the public to an extremely strict lockdown. Wuhan, where the initial multiple outbreaks of COVID-19 had occurred, was open and back to normal after around three months.

Western commentators insisted that in Wuhan and elsewhere in China, people were simply ordered to isolate. They were instructed not to leave the specific local area and to close all strictly non-essential activity. This explanation ignores the collectivist culture of the Chinese people who trusted and readily accepted the scientific advice provided by their central government. This cultural attitude — which has been explored in previous chapters — is not confined to China. As we have earlier alluded to, it is widely prevalent across East Asia. Also, the previous experience of SARS-CoV-1 led to these countries being well-prepared for the pandemic, including efficient test, trace, and isolate systems and procedures (China Briefing 2020a).

China has also been working collaboratively with the WHO and the world on testing, treatments, and vaccines, after it had assisted in the early release of the corona virus genome in January 2020. Future global collaboration will be crucial, including on vaccines, as the virus spreads around the world and shows no sign yet of its severe effects diminishing. In China, four main vaccine producers are involved: CanSino, CNBG, Sinovac, and ZFLongkema (China Briefing 2020b; Ng 2020). Notwithstanding some concerns about efficacy and delayed reporting of trial results, as in the West, Sinovac has signed deals to provide 46 million doses of its COVID-19 vaccine to Brazil and 50 million doses to Turkey. The company will also supply 40 million doses of vaccine bulk — the vaccine concentrate before it is divided into small vials — to Indonesia for local production. CanSino will deliver 35 million doses of its vaccine to Mexico, while CNBG is looking at markets in the Middle East and South America. The UAE is to jointly produce with CNBG about 100 million doses in 2021. CNBG has stated it can produce more than 1 billion doses in 2021. China has also joined the international COVID-19 Vaccines Global Access (COVAX) alliance led by the WHO. It has also joined the Coalition for Epidemic Preparedness Innovations (CEPI) scheme to make sure any proven safe and effective medicines are available globally. China's leadership will, therefore, have a crucial and powerful role to play in delivering vaccines to other countries around the world, to the mutual benefit of those countries and to China.

Aside from the direct public health lessons being derived from the pandemic, there are environmental changes which could assist with managing future pandemics, some of which have been initiated during the pandemic. The more creative and improved use of urban space: for instance, staggering rush hours to reduce congestion and crowding on public transport; further reducing air pollution in cities; looking at new business models attuned to remote working and remote learning; delivery of virtual public health care; the retrofitting of large cities to render them more liveable: strengthening the previously fractured community living in some countries that the pandemic has shown needs to be altered. These are all areas where China has an interest in, as indicated in Chapter 2, and where it is pursuing initiatives which could be of benefit to other countries.

China's underlying preparedness for the major epidemic which hit them in January 2020 — derived from their experience of SARS-CoV-1 — has lessons for the world, as it has for China as well (Zhong and Zeng 2006). The WHO investigation in 2021 will add to this knowledge (World Health Organisation 2021). It will be vital to ensure that all countries prepare for the next pandemic, which will surely come whether it is 20 years away or 100 years away. The world needs clear leadership in the post-COVID 19 world. China's actions should act as signposts. Inside countries, actions should be aimed at pandemic preparedness; the influencing of personal hygiene behaviour to reduce risks of the spread of infectious diseases; and the development of treatments and vaccines. Externally, China's actions will no doubt further support its already extensive investments in Africa in disease prevention, improved sanitation, etc., besides its environmental and ecological agendas.

Part of this endeavour should be to increase the funding and the public guidance weight of the WHO, ensuring that it becomes a genuine global organisation. China's sometimes rejection of what it considers to be overly Western-influenced international organisations may be countered when the WHO is able to play a strong and constructive role. For instance, in 2017, China proposed the establishment of a Health Silk Road as part of its BRI (Glueck and Gu 2020). The initiative was endorsed by representatives of participating nations and international bodies such as the WHO and OECD at a high-level meeting in Beijing. As a Chinese contribution to resolving the COVID-19 pandemic, the Health Silk Road (HSR) could be used as a conduit for the delivery of vaccination.

Maldistribution of Resources

The problematic issues surveyed — global warming/climate change and human pandemics — present serious challenges going forward, and solutions to which are neither obvious nor easy. However, they are essentially part of the more general problem of the global maldistribution of resources. This wider issue is linked to both global warming and the potential for more pandemics. They all raise ecological and resource utilisation challenges and are also linked to each other directly.

It is obvious that the key barrier to balanced, global economic development is the constraints on resources. Some of the constraints are simply that the over-developed West has consumed, and continues to consume (and control), the majority of the key natural resources, while at the same time damaging the earth's environment and ecologies. To an extent, the sheer volume and pace of China's own development has further added to these problems. This is the root cause of the unsustainable framework of global economic development that is presented at the beginning of the twenty-first century.

The connections between the specific ecological and environmental problems, including global warming, are increasingly part of our consciousness and conscience. They require an integrated approach to the underlying maldistribution of resources and their extensive and over-intensive use in the developed countries of the world (Lloyd 2017). Such an approach may mean more radical solutions than are currently envisaged. It may well be that one of the elements in a comprehensive solution will involve a moratorium on increasing aggregate consumption in the developed world. We need to tackle in imaginative ways the maldistribution of income both between and within countries via a genuinely global approach.

The roles that China may be able to play in addressing these sets of issues are likely to be significant. China's roles range from the experience of uneven resource distribution in China itself to the issues relating to China's involvement with other countries, such as its partnership investments along the routes of the BRI, especially in Africa. Various issues related to the overall global problem of the maldistribution of resources are covered in the below sections, indicating the differing roles that China may be able to play. One key issue where China's experience will be invaluable is the problem of inadequate water supplies (Lloyd 2017).

Scarce Water Supplies

There is a major global problem of inadequate water supplies and the provision of clean water and sanitation, one that requires both global and regional solutions (Lloyd 2017). A number of the less-developed regions of the world have a problem with the lack of safe drinking water and the frequent occurrence of droughts. In developed countries in the West, the problem is one of the overuse of water supplies by industry, commerce, and households. This issue of water scarcity is also an underlying factor in some of the existing regional political conflicts and their resolution, including the Palestine/Israel conflict.

Global industrial development has hitherto required, especially in the first stages of industrial and urban growth, substantial water use. Ways of economising on water usage as well as energy usage are going to become crucial during the next decades, in Africa especially. The cement industry, as well as being a problem because of its use of coal, also requires a considerable use of water (Miller *et al.* 2018). China is very much involved in Africa, and its deployment of expertise on the continent will be a considerable boon.

It should be noted that water is used, not only by households, but also substantially in industrial processes including modern intensive agriculture. It is estimated that globally, around 70% of freshwater supplies are used for irrigation purposes. As industrialisation spreads, we can expect the demands on water to increase. If this occurs in areas with already scarce water supplies, then the need of households particularly where populations are still growing rapidly (using 15% of global freshwater supplies) is likely, *inter alia,* to hamper industrial development (also using 15% globally). In the US, almost 80% of water supplies are used in agriculture (US Department of Agriculture 2019).

Over the last four decades, China has become the second-largest economy in the world and successfully supported nearly 20% of the global population with 9% of the world's arable land and only 6% of the world's total freshwater resources. By sharing its experiences and lessons in water resources management, economic development, and ecological protection, China can contribute greatly to the UN Sustainable Development Goals.

China's Own Water Shortage Issues and Remedial Action

China's own water utilisation problems have preoccupied its government for decades. There is a specific problem in the grain and vegetable growing areas in the North.

> 'China's per capita availability of water is 1/3 the world's average, and in the dry north where most of the grain and vegetables are grown, per capita availability is only 1/4 of that in the south. Over 300 million people in rural areas have no access to safe drinking water and 54% of China's main rivers contain water unfit for human consumption' (Cho 2011).

To deal with this problem, China has invested more than US$60 billion in the South-to-North Water Diversion Project, the largest of its kind ever undertaken in the world. The project involves drawing water from southern rivers and supplying it to the dry north. It is important to note that the areas fed by the project produce 1/3 of China's GDP.

The project consists of three lines — western, central, and eastern. Construction began in 2002. The eastern line was put into operation in 2013 and the central line in 2014. The western line is still in the planning stage. The water in the central route traverses more than 1,400 kilometres, starting from Danjiangkou Reservoir in Hubei province and arriving in Beijing and Tianjin. The eastern route traverses from Yangzhou in Jiangsu province to Shandong province and Tianjin.

Up to 120 million people have benefited from the project, and more than 40 major cities now rely on water transferred from the south. For example, three-quarters of Beijing's water supply come from the south, and 100% of the water used by the population of Tianjin comes from the south.

But the Chinese leadership is also committed to spending US$612.23 billion on water conservation over the next 10 years (China.Org 2019). Since 1998, China has taken 21 million acres of farmland out of production and required farmers to use more water-conserving irrigation practices, hence reducing the water consumption of agriculture from 83% in 1990 to 60% in 2010. Moreover, proposed industrial plants must prove there is enough water available for them to operate before construction begins, and once approved, they must recycle their water. New buildings in big cities like Beijing are outfitted with plumbing systems that recycle water for washing clothes and flushing toilets. Given the water resource problems of China, addressing these issues is imperative.

Sharing China's Experiences with the World

The success of China in managing its own scarce water resources has lessons for others. Victoria Kwakwa, World Bank Vice President for East Asia and the Pacific, stated in 2018 that:

> 'The Chinese experience in managing the development of water resources also has important lessons for other transitioning economies and informing efforts to address global risks to economic progress, poverty eradication, peace and security, and sustainable development' (Kwakwa 2018).

Since the third Ministerial Conference of the Forum on China-Africa Cooperation (FOCAC) held in Beijing in November 2006, China has accelerated agricultural investment in Africa and built new partnerships. Chinese companies operating in Africa established a China African Development (CAD) Fund in 2007 with an initial size of US$5 billion. By 2018, the CAD Fund had grown to US$10 billion and had invested more than US$4.6 billion in over 90 projects in 36 African countries. CAD Fund projects are expected to boost local exports by US$5.8 billion and create local tax revenue of US$1 billion (*Deloitte Insights* 2019).

For instance, CAD launched a US$20 million project for cotton cultivation and processing in Malawi in 2009. This project involved over 50,000 farming households to grow 17,000 tonnes of seed cotton and process the seed cotton into 6,800 tonnes of lint (Sun 2011).

The emphasis on China-Africa investment is connectivity. For instance, the Addis Ababa-Djibouti railway, estimated to cost US$4.5 billion, has cut the journey of more than 759 km from three days by road to 12 hours by rail. The project eases logistical bottlenecks in the region, giving Ethiopia's manufactured goods greater access to global export markets.

In January 2018, the Chinese Ambassador to Ethiopia Tan Jian said that the project is 'the first trans-boundary and longest electrified railway on the African continent. We [...] see this as an early harvest project of the Belt and Road Initiative. It is regarded by many as a lifeline project for both countries, for Ethiopia and for Djibouti' (*Deloitte Insights* 2019).

Another specific example of Chinese action is, for instance, Chinese experts (Li 2018) who started working with Nairobi water engineers seven years ago. In 2013, they developed efficient water purification chemical coagulants to cope with large fluctuations of raw water surges in the rainy season. The project reduced water treatment costs by 20%, improved water flow, and ensured that water quality met WHO standards. This not only solved the problems, but also transferred expertise to Nairobi's own local staff.

Global Food Shortages

The problem of an aggregate global food shortage by 2050 is as serious as any of the other problems considered in this chapter (Lloyd 2017). It is likely that by that time, medicine (both curative and preventative) will have advanced so far that diseases will not prove to be the major threat they currently are in poorer countries. Moreover, economic development in those countries should have proceeded far enough to represent a major public health advance through ensuring adequate sanitation. Providing that adequate supplies of potable water can be delivered, then the remaining major problem will be food production (and distribution).

It is already the case that there is considerable acute pressure on forests and other essential natural habitats arising from global population growth, and the global pressure on fish stocks caused by overfishing is one of the contributory factors to global warming. It is equally the case that the increase in epidemics and pandemics is related to the far closer relationship between urban areas and natural wildlife habitats.

China's investment in projects to improve African agricultural production is substantial. An early example may be given. In Guinea-Bissau, Chinese experts established 11 rice production demonstration areas covering a total of 2,000 hectares (Sun 2011). Yields per hectare reached 8–9 tonnes. There were 530 tonnes of fine varieties yielded and subsequent expansion of the plantation area amounted to 3,530 hectares. The yields for many new varieties were over three times higher than the varieties currently used.

Notwithstanding these types of projects, if the increasing global food shortage is to be tackled then newer technology solutions will be required, such as a new green revolution as the downsides of the first one emerge, such as its intensive energy and water usage. It is estimated that, as already indicated, almost 80% of fresh water supplies in the US are consumed by the agricultural sector (US Department of Agriculture 2019). This indicates one of the side-effects of the current technology introduced by the green revolution. Another is the use of pesticides. China is a leader in developing biotechnologies (as indicated in Chapter 2). Application of these technologies is one of the measures that can be taken to resolve the constraints of food production.

Biotechnology Solutions

Notwithstanding its many critics, particularly among the environmental movement, it seems self-evident that genetically modified (GM) foods are part of the answer to the problem of how to increase aggregate global food production to feed the still increasing global population in this century. The state, on behalf of society, should conduct scientific research and drive the implementation of GM crops, with satisfactory safeguards.

In 2017, the state-owned company ChemChina bought the Swiss-based company Syngenta — one of the four largest global agri-businesses — for US$43 billion (Shields 2017). Syngenta has a large R&D team working with the gene-editing technology CRISPR.

CRISPR could allow Syngenta to quickly modify the corn genomes to introduce insect resistance or other traits, bolstering China's food supply while transforming agribusiness there. The country's seed marketplace has some 3,000 companies, and none has more than a 10% share of corn.

China may one day need CRISPR plants to provide enough food for its massive population, says rice researcher Li Jiayang, former president of the Chinese Academy of Agricultural Sciences in Beijing and vice minister of agriculture. 'We have to feed 1.4 billion people with very limited natural resources' (Cohen 2019).

In January 2020, it was announced by Chinese officials that GM corn and soybean species have passed biosafety evaluations (The Pig Site 2020), moving the world's most populous country closer to the commercialisation of those two GM crops. However, there are two major regulatory frameworks concerning the clearance of GM food ingredients in China — the Agricultural GMO Regulation and the New Food Ingredient Regulation. It is likely that China will be careful about approving food products, despite importing soybeans from Brazil and US, both of which are from GM crops.

Global Population Growth

We cannot ignore the global population issue. It has been suggested that the rapidly expanding global population is the 'elephant in the room'. If the current rate of increase continues, then all of the global ecological problems that we face will be substantially more difficult to handle. The current global population was 6.2 billion in 2000; the UN estimates that by 2050, the population may have risen by 3.5 billion (1.7 billion in Asia), a more than 50% increase to around 9.7 billion (UN 2020).

The now abandoned one-child policy in China was a misguided policy which has led to a distortion of the balance of men and women. China, in common with many developed countries and middle-income countries, has a declining birth rate currently.

There is no evidence of any Chinese family planning advice being provided directly in Africa. Insofar as family planning in China has any lessons for African countries, then China and the US both provide evidence of the use of female contraception via intra-uterine devices and tubal ligation (sterilisation). In the US, female sterilisation is used by 13.7% of married couples; in China, the figure is 14.1%. The figure across Africa is around 2% (UN 2019a). Accepting the existence of religious constraints on birth control, the issue is how the use of this extreme method or preferably more benign methods can be encouraged in Africa.

China, especially in rural areas, has a deeply ingrained patriarchal culture, thus the responsibility of contraception falls primarily on women. Regulations encouraged women with one child to use IUDs, and those with two children to undergo tubal ligation. Registration with the local public security bureau is essential for the child to have access to health care and public education. This registration system could perhaps be emulated in equally patriarchal cultures in many African countries.

Concluding Comments

The connections between the various specific ecological and environmental problems, including global warming, are increasingly part of our consciousness and our collective conscience. They require an integrated approach to the ultimate causes: the underlying maldistribution of resources and their extensive and over-intensive use in the developed countries of the world. Such an approach may mean adopting more radical solutions than are currently envisaged. We have shown the role that China is already playing and can play in the future, in helping to tackle the three global challenges facing the world in the twenty-first century. The overall contribution that China can make to tackle these linked global problems is already considerable. The actual experience of China in water resource management and its development of renewables and the commitment to a substantial reduction of the use of coal, mean that China has been able to export this knowledge to the rest of the world to the global benefit of all.

China can contribute to resolving the problems which are immediately present in our world, but more is required. Close cooperation involves China, together with a more enlightened US administration and the EU, to be committed to ameliorating climate change. This would be a 'game-changer' for future global sustainable development, and could also bring an enhanced ability to resolve all three sets of interlinked problems discussed in this chapter.

Chapter 8

China's Emerging New Global Diplomacy

China's Strategic Partnerships

China's partnership diplomacy originates from the policy perspective that alliance formations or blocs no longer accord with the twenty-first century's changing global economic and political order (Liu and Liu 2016). Beijing has chosen to transcend its political and ideological differences with sovereign countries (Chen 2015). Instead, it has been establishing a network of partnerships by seeking common grounds with other states while reserving differences (Sun 2020). The nature of this policy is also consistent with China's diplomatic philosophy of non-alignment (Ministry of Foreign Affairs 2020).

The country's partnerships have evolved over time, having graduated from the more static bilateral relations of the 1990s (Strüver 2017). In the twenty-first century, Beijing's bilateral ties have become more flexible in according with changing circumstances and levels of economic and political development. Partnerships can also be upgraded on the basis of improvements in bilateral relations or the development of new convergences of interests. Beijing increasingly identifies such changes as the basis to justify a revamp of existing partnerships.

Through fashioning an international network of partnerships, China's bilateral diplomacy offers strategic reassurance to its partners (Medeiros 2009). It promises regional neighbouring countries, subjected to a history of disputes and geopolitical tensions with Beijing, the prospect of long term and constructive bilateral relations with mutual economic benefits.

Arguably, Beijing's focus on international bilateral partnership formation draws important inspiration from various aspects of China's long-standing civilisation (Goldstein 2001). The concept of *guanxi,* meaning relationships, is a Chinese social philosophy borne out of Confucianism. It stresses the importance of mutual reciprocity, obligations, and trust. China advocates *guanxi* with states around the world in the form of bilateral diplomatic relations. At the same time, the concept of 'partnership' is a form of *guanxi* that goes beyond standard diplomacy by promoting more complicated forms of country-to-country interaction (Kong 2019).

A couple of decades into the twenty-first century and the nature of China's partnership diplomacy has been systematically transforming. This became apparent from a marked rise in Beijing's policy of engaging in partnerships involving multilateral groups of countries (d'Hooghe 2007). Bilateral partnerships with sovereign states, therefore, increasingly co-exist with regional and global organisations. In recent decades, Beijing has placed a greater focus on relationship-building with the European Union (EU), African Union (AU), Association of Southeast Asian Nations (ASEAN), Arab Union, Community of Latin American and Caribbean States (CELAC), the Shanghai Cooperation Organisation (SCO), the Group of 20 economies (G20), various United Nations (UN) bodies, including the UN Human Rights Council, the World Trade Organisation (WTO), the Conference on the Parties (COP) on climate change, among many other such bodies.

China's motivations for engaging in various partnerships can also be driven by sector-specific concerns. Some country partnerships involve China's neighbouring regional states with whom China has always aspired to have good relations (Feng and Huang 2014). In other cases, Beijing seeks partnerships to access energy and mineral resources of numerous developing and several developed countries to secure its future development (Benoit and Tu 2020). For instance, China's energy needs are increasingly dependent on relations with natural resource-rich countries, such as Russia, Brazil, Saudi Arabia, Australia and various African, Central Asian, and South American economies. They are all considered essential to meeting the growing demands of China's rapid modernisation.

Some partner countries are geographically-aligned with China's international development initiatives (China Power 2017). These include states located along the BRI, a transcontinental programme which facilitates land and maritime transport access to empower China's vision of cross-border infrastructure connectivity. Some countries are less directly strategically-connected to China. These and other states are categorised in accordance with their partnership labels (see 'China's Bilateral Country Partnerships' section).

In some cases, multilateral regional partners support Beijing in securing and building relations with an entire region (Yu 2018). These forms of partnerships extend China's influence through a single channel in deepening cooperation involving the participation of multiple member states. Such partnerships also reflect Beijing's ambitions to advance its broader agenda of establishing a multi-polar international order (Leverett and Wu 2017).

China is one of only a few major global powers that claims to operate a non-formal alliance or non-bloc policy (Wu 2000). Beijing has not sought to enter into any existing alliances or create new ones which guarantee a mutual military defence obligation should one or more of the states become subject to aggression from a third state. China's partnership diplomacy therefore lacks the basis for substantive commitment arising from formal alliances such as multilateral or bilateral treaty arrangements.

Even so, informal China's partnership diplomacy is a significant factor in constructive engagements with countries around the world, rather than it being a function of Cold War-driven factionalism (Yue 2018). It can also result from China's objective of avoiding clashes with the existing international security apparatus founded and led by the US. From a historical perspective, China's participation in a formal alliance with the Soviet Union from 1950 to 1979 also contributed to its unwillingness in becoming embroiled in an obligatory alliance with a significant security component (Jersild 2015). China's policy of building partnerships without alignment can be therefore be best attributed to it being path-dependent on meeting certain objectives and goals covering a diverse range of policy areas (Li and Ye 2019).

China's partnerships also denote a shared commitment to managing unavoidable conflicts so that partner nations can continue to work together on other vital areas of common interest (*SCMP* 2016). Beijing's official view of partnerships encompasses somewhat broad and vague terrain, in the sense it neither expects partner countries to be wholly cooperative nor does it anticipate that no competition or sporadic tensions would arise in their relations. To the contrary, Beijing seems to accept that divergences in multiple areas of policy and political ideologies are likely to be a feature of many partnerships.

China's partnership diplomacy can also be regarded as a means by which to bridge disagreements about differences in partner countries' domestic politics. Such differences are subordinated to a shared purpose of cooperating on issues of international diplomacy. At the same time, China's partnerships have not been characterised by high levels of institutionalisation. Consequently, should one of the parties terminate or suspend the arrangement, its departure would not prove to be irreparably costly, other than any damage that is more symbolic in nature rather than material.

China's construct of a comprehensive system of partnerships spanning the globe is essentially driven by three principal elements. These include the requirement to defend against political and military pressure from the US, facilitate largely stable and peaceful relations with countries sharing its borders, and secure the objective of a domestic reform agenda enabling full-scale economic modernisation. China is not, however, the sole global power in promoting partnerships as a means of advancing its national interests. Rather, Beijing has focused on placing partnership diplomacy at the heart of its foreign policy strategy (Ferchen 2020).

To this extent, Beijing has been shaping the formation of a multidimensional global partnership network which spans major world powers, large and small neighbouring states, a plethora of emerging economies, and regional organisations. Arguably, as other countries and multilateral organisations have stepped up their efforts in similar pursuits, this was only after China was first to set up this form of partnership networking as a model for others to emulate.

By 2019, China had over 100 partnerships with various countries and regional organisations worldwide. Prospectively, Beijing's focus on the development of partnership diplomacy, whether on a bilateral or on an increasingly multilateral basis as evident in recent government attempts in stepping up international relations with global and regional bodies amid the coronavirus pandemic, could result in partnerships playing a more pivotal role in future foreign policy and for many years into the future.

Over the duration of China's partnership diplomacy, about 40 have been upgraded and several have been renewed more than once. Moreover, Beijing has become more open to establishing partnerships with smaller and medium-sized states and developing and lesser developed ones, all of whom are benefiting from China's principle of equality of nations in its mutual dealings. There are no formal or detailed definitions applicable to describing China's partnerships. During an address to the EU in 2004, then-Chinese Premier Wen Jiabao defined certain aspects of a 'comprehensive strategic partnership' (Men 2007).

Accordingly, the usage of 'comprehensive' can refer to a bilateral partnership being characterised as 'all-dimensional, wide-ranging, and multilayered'. Typically, it involves bilateral exchanges in political, economic, cultural, scientific, and technological areas. It also includes interactions at both bilateral and multilateral levels, irrespective of whether conducted by multiple governments or non-governmental organisations or people-to-people networks.

The term 'strategic' can refer to bilateral ties as manifesting stable and long-term cooperation with a view to building a broader dimension of relations and goes beyond any variations in political praxis or ideological dogma. Perhaps most strikingly, the references to 'partnership' gives rise to an ideal scenario of bilateral ties operating in accordance with several key principles of international cooperation enshrined under international law in the form of 'mutual respect', 'mutual trust', and 'equality'. In other words, each of the sides concerned should seek to establish 'win-win' relations that are mutually beneficial. These sets of principles were first articulated in 1999 by then-President Jiang Zemin who proposed they be enshrined into the practice of international relations and for the purposes of confrontation and conflict avoidance (Yu 2011).

Since 2013, China has launched a series of international cooperation initiatives spearheaded by the BRI and the AIIB. Propelled by this, China's partnership network has expanded with most BRI-related countries and AIIB members having established certain types of partnerships with China (Dollar 2015).

Chinese President Xi Jinping has frequently said that China strongly values its friendships with other countries and will continue to expand its partnerships. The final goal is to shape a global partnership network, while developing itself into a modern high upper income country by 2049. During the CCP's 19th National Party Congress, the 'partnership' concept was officially incorporated as a major instrument of China's international relations strategy (Scammacca and Dai 2017). Some of the principal and most common partnerships in place — ranked in order of importance to China — are detailed in the following section.

China's Bilateral Country Partnerships

i. Comprehensive Strategic Partnership of Coordination: Russia.
ii. Comprehensive Strategic Cooperative Partnership: Thailand, Vietnam, Myanmar, Cambodia and Laos, Pakistan (All-Weather Strategic Cooperative Partnership), Mozambique, Sierra Leone, Senegal, Ethiopia, Namibia, Zimbabwe, Belarus, the Democratic Republic of Congo, and Chile.
iii. Strategic Cooperative Partnership: India, South Korea, Bangladesh, Sri Lanka, and Afghanistan.
iv. Comprehensive Strategic Partnership: Germany (All Round Strategic Partnership), UK (Global Comprehensive Strategic Partnership for the 21st Century), Indonesia, Malaysia, Philippines Iran, Kazakhstan, Australia, New Zealand, South Africa, Hungary, Denmark, Saudi Arabia, France, Poland, Mexico, Serbia, Spain, Brazil, Italy, Greece, Peru, Ecuador, Portugal, Algeria, Venezuela, Egypt, Argentina, Mongolia, Uzbekistan, UAE, European Union, African Union, and ASEAN.
v. Strategic Partnership: Nigeria, Angola, Sudan, Iraq, Jordan, Sudan, Kazakhstan, Kyrgyzstan, Turkmenistan, Tajikistan, Canada, Czech Republic, Uruguay, Ireland (Strategic Partnership of Mutual Benefit), Ukraine, Switzerland (Innovative Strategic Partnership), Costa Rica, Qatar, Austria (Friendly Strategic Partnership), Morocco, Djibouti, Tonga, Fiji, and Pacific Islands.
vi. Strategic Cooperative Relations: Turkey, Brunei, and League of Arab States.
vii. All Round Friendly Cooperative Partnership: Bulgaria, Maldives, and Romania (Comprehensive Friendly Cooperative Partnership).
viii. Comprehensive Cooperative Partnership: Singapore (All Round Cooperative Partnership), Israel (Innovative Comprehensive Cooperative Partnership), the Netherlands, Nepal, Sao Tome and Principe, Croatia, East Timor-Leste, Ethiopia, Tanzania, Madagascar and Gabon, and CELAC.
ix. Cooperative/Friendly Partnership: Finland (Cooperative Partnership), Trinidad and Tobago, Antigua and Barbuda, and Jamaica (Friendly Partnership).
x. Friendly Cooperative Partnership: Uganda, Macedonia, Colombia, Gabon, Azerbaijan, Togo, Kuwait, and Montenegro.
xi. Traditional Friendly Relationship: Albania, Samoa, and Georgia.
xii. Strategic Relationship of Mutual Benefit: Japan (Feng and Huang 2014).

China's Ministry of Foreign Affairs provides no guidance on whether a partnership should start at a lower level, such as a Cooperative Partnership where both sides can gradually widen their scope of ties, before proceeding to a higher partnership status. Nonetheless, each partnership type is not without meaning. At a minimum, they suggest varying degrees of substantive development in ties involving China and its expanding line up of partners.

China's first strategic partnership was agreed with Brazil in 1993. From 1993 to 2003, China concluded 23 more partnerships. From 2005 to 2012 and 2013 to 2019, this rose by 43 and 26 additional countries respectively (Ren 2019). Given that these 10-year periods coincided with different Chinese leaderships, it is evident that each Chinese administration has maintained a consistent approach in building partnerships.

Changes in the portfolio of China's partnerships illustrate an important aspect of Beijing's partnership diplomacy. Many of the strategic arrangements began as a Friendly Cooperative Partnership and later evolved into a Strategic Partnership or Comprehensive Strategic Partnership.

The main consistent themes proposed by China in their upgrading of bilateral partnerships include: securing stable bilateral ties (often involving regular exchanges between high-level officials as representatives from each government); broad and detailed economic cooperation; non-interference in each partner's respective internal matters; emphasis on developing common interests; foreign policy coordination on a global and regional basis; and equality in practising international relations.

Each of these partnerships also differ in terms of substantive areas of cooperation. This can be broken down into cooperation on global and regional issues and sector-specific issues such as economy, security, military, space, culture, science, education, people exchanges, and various other core interests.

Russia and Pakistan are the two partner countries which include all these areas of cooperation (Lim 2016). Other countries have most or some of these constituent factors depending on the level of their partnerships.

Beijing typically attaches a greater degree of importance to a partnership when elevating it to a comprehensive strategic one. In so doing, it requires that revised and upgraded bilateral arrangements involve more and broader aspects of cooperation between the partners.

In general, Cooperative Partnerships are marked by comparatively fewer areas of cooperation. These forms of arrangements are normally established with a view to promoting bilateral ties on a stable platform for development. By contrast, a Strategic Partnership and Comprehensive Strategic Partnership both accord with wider agendas. These involve detailed plans for greater coordination. They also facilitate setting up more extensive means of regular interaction involving national leaders and heads of government ministries.

The conclusion of a Comprehensive Strategic Partnership can be determined by a partner country's general economic ties with China. Beijing will increase government-to-government linkages in cases which demonstrate a partner country's clear orientation in building economic relations with China. Certain countries already exercising a high degree of trading activities and other economic relations with China may also be more willing to enter into a higher-level partnership at the outset of forging such links.

Economic interests often play a major role in encouraging China to proceed with seeking partnerships with developed countries (Strüver 2016). Although significant economic factors can contribute to a strategic partner's provision of greater access to its domestic markets and higher supplies of its natural resources, China has also partnered with countries which have an important regional role and which may also act as openers to other key players in a region where Beijing has an interest in establishing a greater economic and political presence.

Political imperatives involving the development of policies which have a bearing on the evolution of the global order assume a more significant aspect of China's interplay with its developing world strategic partners and their ascendance within the ranking of partnerships. China has often exhibited a particular interest in forging relations with key emerging market economies and various other powers on the basis of their political synergies (Shullman 2019).

Certainly, the advantages of having strong political ties with global or regional partners will likely serve to enable China to expand its influence in multilateral institutions at each of these international levels. The end result could also enable greater legitimacy for China to advance its foreign policy interests around the world as well as becoming conducive in elevating China's status as a global superpower. In such case, this may seem to mainly advance Beijing's interests in building political ties with emerging economies and developing regions of the world, rather than with advanced countries.

As China accelerated its partnership expansion in recent years, the concept of a Comprehensive Strategic Partnership has become somewhat undermined and the thrust of its impact could be at risk of being devalued. It also imparts a misleading signal to those countries that are strategically important.

As more countries become China's strategic partners, their strategic value to China inevitably suffers a comparative decline. From this point of view, Beijing's rapid partnership network expansion may not serve its long-term international development. China may need to review its existing sets of partnerships and ensure that declared goals and objectives are matched by actions.

Another challenge for China's partnership diplomacy is that of increasing tensions with the United States. Those countries maintaining both a partnership with China and a formal alliance with the US may place legal treaty relations above those of a non-legally binding partnership. An increasing line-up of China's partners may fall into dual and conflicting situations. This may require a partner country to adopt a balancing strategy. For instance, a Chinese partner state may have to engage with the US in its treaty commitments including fulfilment of military and security cooperation. At the same time, it may want to shift the focus of its economic ties towards Beijing, particularly as China's economy catches up and eventually overtakes that of the US. Without a differentiation between these two sets of interactions with the global powers, it may lead to a disruption of Beijing's ability to effectively conduct its partnership programme.

Lastly, despite China having adapted certain commitments and principles for most of its partnerships, many features of these partnerships remain vaguely referenced and barely defined. Indeed, most countries having a partnership with China are still confused about what 'strategic' even means. In the absence of practical actions, more strictly defined criteria, and legal effect, many partnerships may become merely symbolic, carrying little or no weight when relations are challenged by a third power.

China and the European Union (EU)

The China-EU partnership heralds relations between a developing country which has attained superpower status and a formal group of advanced countries seeking to effectively manage their relations with this superpower's rise (Barysch *et al.* 2005).

The EU's approach towards China was set out in 2016 in the guise of the EU-China 2020 Strategic Agenda for Cooperation (EU-China 2020a). Alongside this agreement, the two sides committed to promoting the EU-China Comprehensive Strategic Partnership which would be fully implemented through their annual Summit. This format was designed to provide strategic guidance in their relationship essentially through three pillars annually underpinning the summit — the High-Level Strategic Dialogue, the High Level Economic and Trade Dialogue, and the bi-annual People-to-People Dialogue. Each of these would be achieved through regular meetings of counterparts and their broader range of sectoral dialogues. China and the EU also committed to enhancing dialogue at various regional and global levels (China Mission 2020).

In terms of their agreed ambitions to promote economic prosperity, both sides agreed to negotiate and conclude a comprehensive China-EU Investment Agreement which covers such areas as investment protection and market access. The EU and China 2020 Agenda also included sustainable development addressing climate change and environmental protection, among various socially inclusive and low carbon development policies.

This relationship was updated in 2019 as the EU perceived that the balance of challenges and opportunities had shifted over time. In this regard, China is concomitantly viewed as being a partner for cooperation and negotiation as well as an economic competitor and systemic rival.

While the EU has stated that 'the 2016 Strategy on China remains the cornerstone of EU engagement', the balance of challenges and opportunities presented by China have shifted to new levels. This coincides with the country's economic power and political influence having grown with 'unprecedented scale and speed', and in response, the EU has sought to strengthen its domestic policies and industrial base.

China has responded to the EU's positive and negative references of the country. In 2020, Beijing stated it is a partner, not a rival of the EU (Wintle 2020). It has pledged to continue efforts in deepening reform and opening its economy to provide the EU with a new round of cooperation and development opportunities.

At the 22nd China-EU leaders' meeting in 2020, China reiterated its desire to stabilise and improve its relations with the EU (Xinhuanet 2020a). This was a particularly significant gesture in the wake of the economic and health consequences spreading rapidly across Europe arising from the global coronavirus pandemic.

The principal political rifts between China and the EU remain in the spheres of human rights and its impact in Tibet and Xinjiang, but also the treatment of China's human rights lawyers (Berkofsky 2019). The EU addresses the issues under a regular human rights dialogue with China, alongside encouraging the rule of law and support for civil society.

A major and more recent split dividing the two sides has been that of Hong Kong's 'One Country, Two Systems'. This was designed to guarantee the territory a high degree of autonomy over the first 50 years of its handover by the British to China. The EU has expressed strong sentiments against the passing of China's tailor-made National Security Law for Hong Kong, stating that 'this law risks seriously undermining the high degree of autonomy of Hong Kong' (Burchard and Barigazzi 2020).

The European Parliament has pressed for the European Commission (EC), as the EU's executive body, to submit the case to the International Court of Justice in the Hague. The EC has said that it will look into taking possible measures with international partners against China on the matter.

Despite these emerging policy differences, China and the EU continue to engage in dialogue, including at the 2020 China-EU leaders' summit. The long-term course of China-EU relations remains fundamentally unchanged as both sides appear committed to resolving their disagreements by dialogue and negotiation. At the same time, they are converging substantively on a range of other policy areas, including climate change, international trade, global peace, and security.

China has increasingly shifted its approach towards greater cooperation with the EU on regional and global matters and to an increasingly lesser extent in its bilateral relations with various EU member countries. Some of this may be due to Beijing's growing awareness and support of the global trend towards regional multilateralism involving the EU's influential member states.

In the main, Beijing has come to recognise the EU as the world's most economically-advanced and politically influential regional grouping. The EU, as a set of supranational institutions, has therefore taken on the status of a major developed-world partner for China in the expansion of its international relations policy in spite of lingering mutual suspicions (*The Straits Times* 2019b).

China and Germany

The China-Germany All Round Strategic Partnership is considered one of China's most important partnerships with a European country.

It ranks alongside China's partnership with the EU in terms of the status falling within the framework of a Comprehensive Strategic Partnership (Xinhuanet 2017).

The China-Germany partnership was established in 2014, following a state visit by President Xi to Germany. In a joint statement on the new partnership, both countries presented their aims to hold regular consultations on regional and global political and security policy issues (German Federal Government 2014). They also agreed that a more detailed and comprehensive cooperation not only serve their common interests but also that of Europe and Asia.

Both countries view their relations as representing key opportunities for mutually beneficial cooperation (Schnellbach and Man 2015). This is deepened by the introduction of multiple dialogue and cooperation platforms at intergovernmental levels. In parallel with the EU, their partnership has engaged in detailed exchanges in relation to international crises including conflicts in Afghanistan, Syria, and Ukraine.

These have also included discussions on global challenges including climate change, environment, energy and resources security, food security, and international development cooperation (CGTN 2019). In relation to such matters, they have worked closely in international bodies such as the UN and the G20.

China and Germany have also been fostering the expansion and deepening of regional integration in Europe (Federal Foreign Office of Germany 2020) and regional cooperation in Asia. They have reaffirmed their recognition for the diplomatic concepts of sovereignty and territorial integrity, as Germany declared its support for peaceful development between both sides of the Taiwan Strait amid Berlin's reaffirmation of a 'One-China' policy.

Moreover, both sides have emphasised the importance of intensifying their dialogues on human rights and rule of law. All these forms of cooperation parallel aspects of the EU-China Comprehensive Strategic Partnership.

Above all, Germany has supported China's intensification of cooperation with the EU (Kundnani and Parello-Plesner 2012). To this end, Berlin has been cooperating more closely with Beijing at both bilateral and EU levels over the half-decade up to 2020. In doing so, they committed themselves to the EU-China 2020 Strategic Agenda and to successfully conclude the China-EU Investment Agreement which was agreed in principle by both sides at the end of 2020.

The latter agreement has been the centrepiece of fostering critical investment protection and market access for both countries. In that vein, they have agreed to further develop their bilateral economic relations in harmony with the principles of reciprocity and equality. This has included granting non-discriminatory treatment to Chinese and German companies which have been established in their host partner states in relation to access to public procurement. Both governments are also committed to securing equal market access and intellectual property protection as major areas for sustainable growth for both their investment communities (Federation of German Industries 2020).

On trade, while China and Germany have stated their support for strict adherence with WTO rules and a multilateral trade system, they have also pushed forward with bilateral coordination in relation to product standardisation, safety, and certification to further enable growth in their bilateral trade.

In 2019, both countries agreed to strengthen their All-Round Strategic Partnership through setting up dialogue arrangements at different levels. These are expected to play a more effective role in enhancing strategic communication on bilateral relations, in addition to expanding coordination on major international and regional issues (Federal Foreign Office of Germany 2021).

Also in 2019, China and Germany committed to deepening their partnership through working together in a wide range of sectors including smart manufacturing, internet technologies, fintech, green energy, sustainable development, and finance, and in expanding their cooperation in opening third markets. The bilateral relationship has been further enhanced by strategically synergising their respective national programmes — Beijing's 'Made in China 2025' and Berlin's 'Industry 4.0'.

In a more multilateral framework, China and Germany have also stepped up cooperation within the context of the BRI and jointly contributed to its development in several countries along the route. On a broader societal level, the partnership has been extended to sectors involving education, technology, science, tourism, health, culture, media, sport, and research, alongside expansion of people to people exchanges.

Germany is one of the five largest EU states (including France, Italy, Spain, and Poland) and among several smaller ones to have a Comprehensive Strategic Partnership with China. At times, this parallel set of bilateral relations has created tensions and even duplications of the EU's own strategic partnership with China. Over time, as the EU's relations with China have grown to the extent of designing cooperation agendas and negotiations for an investment agreement, this has helped resolve many problematic overlaps of competence. In essence, nowadays, EU member states and most especially Germany look to develop business transactions with China. On the other hand, the EU institutions deal mostly with the more complex features of China relations, whether they are human rights, rule of law, or broader issues concerning investment and trade.

During the period of its EU membership, Germany has increasingly conceded authority in its bilateral relations with China to policymaking at the EU level. To this extent, Berlin has favoured an approach whereby the EU's High Representative of the European External Actions Service (EEAS) orchestrates the defining role in policymaking on major political issues such as climate change, the overall economic circumstances surrounding investment and trade, among other broader aspects of international development with China.

China and Italy

The Italian republic has maintained a Comprehensive Strategic Partnership with China since 2004 (China.org 2004). Italy's ties with China are of particular interest, since it was the first, and thus far the largest western European state to officially join the BRI.

This was finalised in 2019 during a state visit to Italy by Xi in promoting the BRI (Amante 2020). This suggests that more developed European countries can be expected to give full recognition to the BRI as a major Chinese-led multilateral body in the promotion of global development. As a result, the Italian government has sought to play a leading role in China-EU cooperation through the BRI framework by establishing a special task force for the programme. The initiative is anticipated to become an engine of growth for their bilateral cooperation by enabling them to tap into third party markets via the BRI framework.

Besides this historic tying of the knot, the establishment of bilateral interfacing government committees and dialogue mechanisms, amid regular high-level interactions in recent years, have also bolstered their ties. Moreover, Beijing and Rome have stepped up their bilateral macroeconomic policy coordination under the auspices of the G20, World Bank, Asian Development Bank, Asian Infrastructure Investment Bank, and other multilateral mechanisms.

Since Italy's official signing up to the BRI, both sides have re-launched their strategic partnership from economic and industrial perspectives. This has included stepping up cooperation in aerospace, Artificial Intelligence, scientific research, environmental protection, sustainable development, and healthcare, and planning to deepen ties in other areas of technology and innovation (Xinhuanet 2019g). In that regard, Italy has been more restrained than other western European countries in imposing restrictions on Huawei (Rosca 2019). Some of the differences in Rome's policy orientation towards the embattled Chinese technology company, in contrast to that of other European countries, may be due to its official participation in the BRI.

China and Central & Eastern Europe '17+1'

A regional network of central and eastern European (CEE) countries was set up as a collective forum in 2012 in association with China. This included 11 EU member states and 5 non-member Western Balkan countries. At its inception, the regional forum was officially referred to as the '16+1'. More recently, Greece's formal joining of the association resulted in it being renamed to the '17+1' (Ciurtin 2019).

Although it was framed as a form of multilateralism, the format has remained in substance a mainly bilateral set of ties between China and the CEE states. In other words, the simultaneous promotion of individual bilateral channels by the Chinese government has encouraged CEE governments to compete for Beijing's involvement in funding and building infrastructure in their respective countries.

From a financial perspective, about 10% of China's European investments are in CEE, amounting to US$15 billion in 2019 (Matura 2019). The main part of the initiative has involved China developing the CEE region into a logistics hub. This includes the transportation of Chinese goods from the Greek port of Piraeus to markets across western Europe. The addition of Greece to the regional grouping was therefore a natural extension of China's CEE cooperation strategy.

Overall, the 17+1 format follows a China-developed and creative approach to regional cooperation. It shares common features with other multilateral regional cooperation platforms created by China to introduce non-Western 'south-south' multilateralism.

On the other hand, given CEE's more advanced development status relative to most emerging market economies and regions, the 17+1 grouping — covering trade and investment, economic sectors such as finance, connectivity, agriculture, science, and technology, and social areas including health, education, and culture — has progressed somewhat at variance with other China-led 'south-south' regional associations. For instance, there is a larger number of leaders' summits in addition to regular lower-level official gatherings between China and regional CEE forum members than in China's other multilateral arrangements with developing countries.

Moreover, CEE sub-regions and Chinese cities and provinces have been increasingly collaborating on exchanges and sharing ideas on co-development as a means of rebalancing the asymmetry in economic size relating to the two sets of players. The institutionalisation of sectoral coordination is not only skewed in favour of China's interests. Every format for cooperation and exchange encapsulates a particular policy area often being captained by CEE states on a unilateral actioned basis. Prospectively, this provides greater capacity for genuine interconnections of multilateralism, as opposed to nominal or superficial exchanges. The 17+1 grouping has also served as a key platform in advancing China's BRI programme across the region, given that CEE states' participation in the BRI is based on their respective areas of economic, trade, and financial specialisation.

The Dubrovnik Guidelines for Cooperation between China and CEE put strong emphasis on the platform's successes so far while signalling a more hands-on approach from China. Another notable point of the 2019 Dubrovnik summit is for the initiative to be opened up to new entrants; countries such as Austria, Belarus, and Moldova have expressed interest.

The EU attends 17+1 summits in its capacity as an observer institution. In 2016, it consented to the forum becoming a part of the EU's overall China strategy. This strategy outlines the programmes and agreements that embody the EU's engagement with China. These embrace principles that are very close to the EU's integrative policies with third countries, including establishing a level playing field of standards, transparency in public tenders, and reciprocity, which each of the various EU member states such as those in the 17+1 grouping have endorsed.

A European Parliament initiative in 2018 stressed, among other things, that member states' participation in the 17+1 format must enable the EU to speak with one voice in its relationship with China (European Parliament 2018). To this extent, Beijing's co-relationship with the EU and 17+1 may be the first instance of Chinese multilateralism based on parallel constructs of cooperation at both regional and sub-regional levels with another part of the world.

China and the African Union

In its engagement with Africa, China has promoted its relations with the continent as an innovative and equality-driven international power. In contrast to the colonialism of European powers and the neo-colonialist practices of American-led global institutions, Beijing identifies itself to be a developing country with similar ambitions and concerns to those of Africa. In particular, it claims to have no interest in meddling with the internal affairs of individual African states in the pursuit of its objectives with the region (Harshe 2019).

Instead, China's government has emphasised the principle of non-interference and mutual benefit in its relations with respective African states (Debelo 2017). Beijing has offered to cooperate even with the smallest of the continent's states on equal terms, while affirming every African government's sovereign right to develop and coordinate their own domestic agendas free of influence or control from external powers. This policy orientation has found wide appeal and support with all African governments as well as the general public across the continent in spite of certain inconsistencies (Mumuni 2017).

China's Africa partnership diplomacy is particularly poignant when considered in relation to the memories of the 1980s World Bank and IMF structural adjustment policies. These were heavily criticised for the unfairness in dismantling many countries' public sectors and associated displacements of workers. For decades since that period, virtually all African countries have consequently seized the opportunity to avail of China's model of economic support which has crucially excluded anti-public ownership conditionality (Arbab 2007).

African countries have concluded that in contrast to the strings-attached provision of Western-backed institutional lending programmes, Beijing undertakes large scale capital projects and infrastructure investments without insisting upon political and economic reform. This non-conditioned approach has supported China into becoming Africa's second largest source of infrastructure funding and capital projects, only behind African governments themselves (Labuschagne and Marais 2019).

In recent years, China's trade and investment with Africa has been driven by various layers of bilateral and multilateral institutional relations. These have increasingly turned towards combining financial programmes and new infrastructure initiatives to develop China's and Africa's co-development interests (African Union 2019).

Accordingly, from the mid-2000s up to 2019, China's investment in infrastructure and associated construction projects across sub-Saharan Africa totalled in excess of US$300 billion. A further US$190 billion has flowed into the Arab countries, including North Africa and nearby parts of the Middle East.

A newly added dimension in China-Africa relations has been Beijing's BRI strategy. This views the Africa Union (AU) as a critical market for China's direct outbound investment and technology applications. In this context, China's BRI and the African Continental Free Trade Area (AfCFTA) which encompasses the region's economy of US$3 trillion, are key global and continental frameworks (Phiri and Mungomba 2019).

The two strategies are being geared to address infrastructural under-development and bottlenecks in international trade. Interlinked with the AU's flagship project 'Agenda 2063', BRI-infrastructure related projects are anticipated to boost intra-Africa trade, the African Peace and Security Architecture, and intra-continental people-to-people exchanges (Zhang and Tesfaye 2018). Chinese and AU leaders have also called for innovation-led development and the upgrade of industries through big data, cloud computing, and AI to connect African and Chinese markets in furthering the free movement of goods, capital, and technologies (Kartik *et al.* 2017).

Although Africa can be described as a geographically-diverse and politically-heterogeneous region which transposes itself into various sub-regions, China's relations with the AU have been increasingly conducted as a coherent form of relationship-building. This is spearheaded by China's Comprehensive Strategic Partnership with the 55-nation AU since 2000.

In 2006, the Forum on China-Africa Cooperation (FOCAC) was created at Chinese and AU ministerial levels with the objective of achieving collective consultation and dialogue. It was also designed as an institution that would become a powerfully symbolic cooperation mechanism dedicated to conveying the interests of developing countries. According to FOCAC, the AU-China 'partnership has delivered concrete outcomes that are beneficial to Africa, although Africa needs to utilise the partnership to its fullest in terms of the potential of the available market and the business opportunities. There is also a need to align the partnership to the strategic objectives of the African Union'.

Certainly, as a multilateral institution, the FOCAC has grown into a major platform. During the 2018 FOCAC summit in Beijing, both sides agreed to build a closer China-Africa community with a shared future, by charting a course of future development in bilateral and multilateral relations (African Union 2019).

In 2020, Chinese President Xi Jinping and Senegal President Macky Sall, as FOCAC's respective co-chairs, pledged to work alongside other FOCAC members in accordance with the principles of extensive consultation so that FOCAC can play a leading role in China-Africa relations. The two leaders also called for concerted efforts to synergise China's two centenary goals and the AU's Agenda 2063 at the Extraordinary China Africa Summit on Solidarity to tackle the COVID-19 pandemic.

The efforts are anticipated to enable both sides to expand and develop the China-Africa Comprehensive Strategic Partnership. In light of this growing relationship, the AU set up a permanent representation in Beijing. Its purpose is to support the work of the African Group of Ambassadors in Beijing to consolidate alignment with AU policy positions.

Further major co-development initiatives are anticipated to arise from a FOCAC meeting held in Senegal in 2021. This should uphold the AU as the region's dominant intergovernmental organisation whose closest external relations are currently in association with China. The Chinese government's comprehensive pan-African approach is therefore mirrored across multiple levels, including FOCAC and related mechanisms such as the China-Africa Joint Business Council and other regional bodies.

Pan-African security commitments have also been formally set up under the China-Africa Comprehensive Strategic Partnership. The China-Africa Defence and Security Forum may therefore become a platform for China to build a new regional security infrastructure in Africa. In 2019, China and the AU forged a closer partnership in food security. The AU's Commissioner for Social Affairs referred to the agreement as another dimension of the multifaceted partnership between China and the AU (CGTN Africa 2019). These China-participant multilateral organisations have taken on a transcontinental approach to cooperation in development and security matters.

Further joint efforts include China's provision of technical advice to African governments on maritime security, anti-corruption training, cybersecurity, intelligence-sharing, police collaboration, and the enabling of energy security. The effects of these collaborations have been to position China as a pan-African security provider at both continental and national levels with strong political and commercial interests underpinning a growing network of military-to-military relationships (UN 2019b).

In conclusion, the expanding partnership between China and the AU has been generally welcomed by the African community. Its long-term success will depend on China's continued multilayered engagement not only with the AU but also African regional communities and national governments. Indeed, given the intensity of activities arising out of Beijing's partnerships across Africa, the continent may serve to become the model of how China will operate at similar expansive multilayered structures in other regions across the world.

China's Bilateral Partnerships with Angola and Congo

Africa has been a vital source of China's oil supply. Angola is China's third principal source of imported crude and Congo the 12th biggest crude supplier. The latter is also fast expanding its oil exports to China. This is in addition to being the principal supplier of cobalt, a metal essentially used for electric vehicle (EV) batteries, and of huge significance to China's burgeoning electric motor vehicle industry.

Following the end of Angola's decades-long civil war in 2002, its relations with China blossomed as Beijing forged extensive economic collaboration. There was a particular focus on the African state's reconstruction and development programme, including the underdeveloped oil sector at the time.

China has since actively engaged in large-scale economic cooperation with Angola, such as on energy-related infrastructure projects, in exchange for purchases of its substantial oil exports (Begu *et al.* 2015).

China's relations with Angola have been officially designated as a mid-ranking Cooperative Partnership, despite China's multiple offers to upgrade the relationship (Xinhuanet 2018a). The two countries' political ties have therefore remained relatively subdued in contrast to China's more active diplomatic ties with numerous other African states. In some cases, China-Angola relations have been described as a strategic partnership of necessity, rather than one of genuine ties (Corkin 2011). This ongoing state of affairs sits alongside Angola being one of China's two largest African trading partners since 2007. Yet, the other large trading partner, South Africa, closely cooperates with China in various political and institutional guises, including at the multilateral level of the Brazil, Russia, India, China, South Africa (BRICS) forum.

The China Export Import Bank, a key financier of Angolan infrastructure, has provided up to US$20 billion in oil-backed credit lines to Luanda since the early 2000s. The bulk of financing has been channelled into infrastructure to fund the activities of Chinese construction companies. In contrast, China's state oil majors active in Angola have received relatively little in such financial support. This was partly because several oil blocks that came up for competitive tenders were never granted to the Chinese energy giants. The predominant winners tended to be the Western oil majors.

In all likelihood, the relative inactivity of China's oil majors in Angola can be attributed to Luanda's policy preference of avoiding dependence on any one major international player, including China, in managing its energy assets. This was despite the fact China has been the country's largest export market by a long stretch.

Even so, in 2004, Angola's government eschewed an IMF structural loan in favour of China's less conditional financing for economic development. This also indicated that while Luanda viewed Chinese financing as important and accessible, they were still wary of opening their key oil sector to Chinese state enterprises.

Hence, while bilateral diplomatic relations were generally constructive, the Angolan side purposely limited their commitment to a more diverse and deeper strategic partnership with China. This meant that broader socio-political relations including security, defence, culture, technology, or people-to-people exchanges, even though increasingly evident at the China-AU level, were not so much a feature of bilateral China-Angola engagement. Nevertheless, given their extensive energy, trade, and infrastructural commitments amid still positive and friendly political ties, the bilateral relationship will likely endure for the foreseeable future (Chen 2012).

At the other end of the spectrum of China's bilateral relations with individual African states is Beijing's dealings with the Democratic Republic of Congo (Congo). These ties count among the most valued of Beijing's partnerships with any single African state.

Their Comprehensive Strategic Cooperative Partnership ranks their relations within the second highest category of Beijing's international ties. The two countries' burgeoning trade and economic ties emanate from this partnership. Other than trade and investment in general, the ties also focus on engineering projects covering various sectors including infrastructure, agriculture, health, mining, logistics, and telecommunications.

By 2020, China's direct investment in Congo exceeded US$10 billion — a sum which has more than doubled since 2015 (Feng 2020b). The country hosts nearly half of the world's cobalt reserves — a key component of China's EV production ambitions. It also has other substantial raw materials which China has developed a voracious appetite for. These reserves, including copper, gold, and other industrial metals, are estimated to be as much as US$24 trillion in value. Given this attractive line-up of commodities which are much in demand in China's public investments into domestic infrastructure in 2020, Congo has turned into China's fifth largest investment destination in Africa in recent years.

The two countries have also concluded some of the largest single trade and investment contracts in Africa. Typically, these have involved some kind of joint venture involving the Congolese government and Chinese state-owned enterprises. Most of the tie-ups were formed out of guaranteed reimbursements by the Congolese government for public infrastructure projects to be financed by Chinese loans.

The country's lack of infrastructure, of course, has been one of the main obstacles to Congo's development. Of the 53 engineering projects being carried out by Chinese contractors in 2020, over half have involved the building of roads, drinking water, electricity, and other infrastructure development.

About 30 Chinese-funded engineering companies have been involved in a series of major remote infrastructure developments. These have involved the construction of large-scale hospitals, schools, hydroelectric power plants, and telecoms networks for over 10,000 villages and rural communities, in addition to water conservancy projects and agricultural training centres. Many of these Chinese-backed activities are found in parts of Congo involving complex production settings and inhospitable living conditions that most Western commercial infrastructure companies would likely not engage in due to the high levels of associated risks.

Other more high-profile Chinese-funded projects have included the construction of prestigious national landmarks including the People's Palace and the Stade des Martyrs in the Congolese capital, Kinshasa.

As the coronavirus pandemic began to strike Congo, the two governments' bilateral partnership has ventured into new areas of cooperation. This has ranged from projects on epidemic prevention including Chinese-funded medicine supplies and infectious disease prevention to the building of new healthcare facilities. Beijing has also doubled-up on efforts to stabilise bilateral trade involving the ongoing development of industrial supply chains, e-commerce, and modern infrastructure construction.

At a time of crisis revolving around the worldwide coronavirus pandemic, China and Congo's high-level partnership has fuelled a new dimension to their relations. Such an outcome would not likely have materialised if their relations are limited only to certain areas or sectors of common interest. A key factor in the elevation of their bilateral partnership followed on from the Congolese former Prime Minister Bruno Tshibala's vocal support for China's multilateral BRI programme for Africa at the 2018 FOCAC summit in Beijing. Accordingly, Tshibala stated that the summit 'fully reflected the importance China attaches to Africa and came as evidence that Africa and China can build a community with a shared future'.

In conclusion, contrary to the widely held notion that China's main focus in Africa is that of essentially exploiting its leverage as a superpower over individual African states, Beijing's policy is more of growing its influence on a pan-continental scale. This has been undertaken as part of a multilayered strategy, including at continental multilateral institutional levels and on a country-by-country partnership basis. Alongside Xi's pledges of up to US$60 billion in financial support for Africa in 2019, maybe of even greater importance has been the plethora of smaller scale projects in Africa's villages, communities, and major cities at bilateral levels of cooperation.

China has thus, either by design or default or maybe both, woven a web of intricate relations across the African continent with various pivotal regional multilateral institutions and African governments. While Beijing has scored numerous successes in its bilateral relations with African states, it has also experienced several failures. Regardless of the setbacks it encountered, China has persisted in furthering its engagement with Africa by formulating parallel high-profile strategies at both regional multilateral and bilateral levels.

Perhaps this dual strategy was initially invoked as an insurance policy against the risks or limitations Beijing faced in solely developing certain bilateral ties such as with Angola in the early days of its African involvement. Over time, Beijing has understood the need to diversify its relations by supplementing country bilateral arrangements with increased engagement with regional African organisations.

China's policymakers have been clearly aligning themselves to a world where multilateralism at regional levels has evolved into a means of empowering Africa's 55, being members of the African Union, generally small to mid-sized states, rather than relying exclusively on China's largesse to leverage from benefits in a solely bilateral country context.

Chapter 9

ASEAN and Wider East Asia: The Cradle of China's Global Re-Emergence

Introduction

China's relations with East Asia date back to the Shang dynasty (circa 1600 BCE) when Chinese traders began establishing trade links and early settlements, principally in Southeast Asia. As Imperial China's power expanded, particularly during the Han period (circa 200 BCE–220 CE), it absorbed parts of nearby IndoChina (Frederic *et al.* 2011).

The Han dynasty until and including the Qing dynasty (circa 1640–1912) saw further military conquests and expanding trading routes. These stretched across the Southeast Asian archipelago, the Korean peninsula and Japan, bringing these regions within China's growing overseas informal networks of 'tributary' states (Kang 2012). For East Asian countries desirous of a relationship (either in the form of economic, political, or other ties) with China as the regional hegemonic power, this entailed the provision of tributes. Even so, the term 'tributary system' was not, strictly speaking, part of the Chinese lexicon. As an expression, it was derived from European descriptions of Chinese pre-colonial era relations with foreign states. Otherwise, it can be more appropriately described as a system of relations which incorporated China's surrounding East Asian societies into the common construct of a Chinese-founded Confucian philosophy and Chinese-propagated Buddhist regional societal order with powerful trade linkages.

The height of China's so-called tributary system was during the Ming dynasty (circa 1340–1640) (Lee 2016). The East Asian societies which formed part of the tributary order in this period included what are now Brunei, Cambodia, Laos, parts of Burma, provinces of Sumatra and Java in Indonesia, areas of Malaysia, parts of the Philippines, and Japan. Of all the tributary states, Thailand was considered the most loyal. This was particularly because some of its royal elites, such as King Rama I of the Rama dynasty and King Taksin of the preceding Thonburi Kingdom, were of partly Chinese origin (Chin 1993), with King Rama IV even openly describing himself as both Thai and Chinese.

Another factor in their close relations entailed the Thai Kingdom becoming one of China's major trading partners. Thailand also accepted the largest waves of Chinese migrations over several centuries (Wade 2009).

Korea and Vietnam were considered by the Chinese court as having the highest-level status of all surrounding tributary states. Unlike most other tributary states where China practised non-interference in their affairs, both Korea and Vietnam fell more directly under China's suzerainty and control. In fact, Chinese rule over Korea followed separate invasions during the Han and Qing dynasties. China exercised an especially powerful influence over Korea from the early seventeenth century to the end of the nineteenth century. Meanwhile, Vietnam had been subject to direct Chinese domination arising out of four separate invasions and ensuing occupations from 111 BCE to 938 CE as well as during the fourteenth century, although it otherwise remained a tributary state of China's until French colonial rule near the turn of the twentieth century (Zhang 2015).

Needless to say, China's influences across East Asia go far beyond its conquests, occupations, and system of tributary states. They are also vested in the region's relatively common social and political structures. To this extent, China's cultural and linguistic influences have been evident across the region. Prior to the European colonial era, Chinese characters formed the scripts of both Vietnam and Korea, and in even earlier periods, those of Thailand, Laos, and other parts of Southeast Asia. Chinese characters still constitute a major script of written Japanese, in the form of Kanji which literally means 'Han characters' (Liu 1969). Being historically derived from Chinese culture, the East Asian cultural sphere, as it is sometimes referred to, also shares features such as literature, art, cuisine, science, medicine, architecture, laws, rituals, and superstitious practices among other socio-cultural foundations.

China's ties with East Asia significantly expanded during the first half of the Qing era, and reached its highpoint of influence at the end of the eighteenth century. However, the Qing's defeat to the British Empire in the first Opium War of 1842 signalled a turning point in China's history and its interactions with East Asia (Smith 2015).

For about 100 years leading up to the Second World War, China descended into a fragmented state largely controlled by warlords. Throughout this period, its ties with the surrounding region dwindled, first under the yoke of expanding European and Russian empires across East Asia which also grabbed and occupied large swathes of China's territory, and followed by Japanese domination over much of China and Northeast Asia from the early twentieth century onwards (Bickers 2012).

Perhaps the most significant interaction between China and the region during this tumultuous period were the large numbers of Chinese migrants seeking refuge in Southeast Asia to escape political and economic turmoil back home. The enduring and powerful legacy originating from these waves of mass migrations out of China into Southeast Asia are discussed in the section on 'The Bamboo Network: Overseas Chinese Role in China's Development' in Chapter 6.

China's era of 'humiliation' under Western powers and its occupation by Japan, before and during the Second World War, pushed China into a psychology of nationalism and quasi-isolation. During the period of the Republic of China (RoC) from 1912 to 1949, China evidenced the rise of nationalism under the umbrella of the Kuomintang (KMT, Chinese Nationalist Party). The Chinese nationalists fought wars on all fronts, including with both internal and external enemies. Chief among these were the Japanese Imperial Army, Chinese warlords, and various other insurgent groups. Eventually, the KMT were ousted from power by the Chinese Communist Party (CCP) in the civil war from 1945 to 1949 (Chan 2019).

It was perhaps inevitable that China's relations with the region during the RoC era were either minimal or non-existent, as it was embroiled in these various conflicts. In fact, rather than reigniting ties with the region, the KMT leaned purposely towards developing relations with powers outside of East Asia for the first time in China's history. These ties were particularly oriented towards the United States. During the interwar years, KMT's first leader and RoC President Sun Yat-sen favoured a Western democratic model of government. His successor Chiang Kai-shek allied with the US, during the war with Japan and in repelling the threat of an invasion by the Soviet Union (USSR) after the end of the war (Lary 2015).

However, with the defeat of the nationalists in 1949, Mao Zedong's victorious CCP turned towards quasi-isolationism at the advent of the Cold War, maintaining relations only with the Soviet bloc. China's interactions with most of its East Asian neighbours irrevocably soured through its involvement in the Korean War from 1950 to 1953. Throughout the conflict, Beijing actively backed the Communist regime of North Korea against the south's UN-led forces. Although the largest contingent was supplied by South Korea, there were also much smaller contingents from several Asian countries formally allied to the US, including the Philippines, Thailand, and Japan (Shu 1995).

As a consequence of the war and the heavy casualties suffered by Chinese and allied North Korean forces, Beijing's relations with the East Asian region fell into a deep freeze throughout much of the Cold War era. If anything, China's ties with regional countries, which were either allied with the US or part of the non-aligned movement or had closer relations with the USSR, often verged on outright hostility. In what can be best described as a 'pressure-cooker' regional geopolitical environment over the 1950s to early 1970s, Mao's foreign policy was fundamentally aimed at exporting revolution into surrounding countries.

This typically meant supporting guerrilla insurgencies across Southeast Asia, often involving sizeable ethnic Chinese communities living in those countries. As such, Chinese-inspired revolutionary movements ranged across Burma, Thailand, Malaysia, Indonesia, and the Philippines. In turn, governments of the region often turned to anti-Chinese counter-insurgencies and even genocidal pogroms, in at least one case. Although the region's governments aimed to quell unrest among the Chinese diaspora — dissension that was partly driven by support from China and the USSR in the earlier years — much of the unrest also reflected real economic and political grievances among ethnic Chinese. This also included a legacy of resistance from wartime and independence struggles (Chen 2001).

However, by the time of the Sino-US rapprochement in 1972 and Mao's death in 1976, Beijing's policy of fomenting revolution across the region changed rapidly. Mao embraced an alternative position aimed at supporting the role of ethnic Chinese as citizens of their respective East Asian host states. This policy outlook was particularly embraced under Deng Xiaoping's leadership of China from 1978. Still, even in the early years of Deng's governance, China continued a volatile relationship with several of the region's countries. Not the least of these was China's tensions with neighbouring Vietnam. The two countries fought a short and bloody war in 1979, largely in response to Hanoi's invasion of Beijing-friendly Cambodia that swept away the Chinese-sponsored Pol Pot's Khmer Rouge (Chen 2019).

Arguably, East Asia had become the violent conflict epicentre of the Cold War between the three principal powers of the US, the USSR, and China. For Beijing, that conflict exploded into direct outright military confrontation with South Korea as an American ally in the early-1950s, and with Vietnam as key Soviet ally in the late 1970s. The legacy of conflict at the height of the Cold War remained bitterly embedded in China's political relations with many countries around the region, including, albeit to a lesser extent, after the Cold War's end in 1990 (Ali 2012).

The violent Cold War legacy was on top of the deep grievance that China had held over Japan's unwillingness to officially apologise for the atrocities it committed during its occupation from 1937 to 1945. Yet, in spite of many un-reconciled differences, China and its neighbouring states have also pushed forward on various fronts, from expanding trade and investment in the 1990s to the development of improved bilateral political relations, and more recently, towards the founding of regional multilateral institutions.

China's 'Open Door' Era

Modern-day China's ties with East Asia essentially started at the time of Deng Xiaoping's open door reform policy in 1978. Even so, Deng's principal focus of overseas relations was oriented towards the West and the US in particular.

In the wake of the Tiananmen protests in 1989, that policy changed as the US and other Western states invoked wide-scale military and limited commercial and financial sanctions against China. Notably, though, US Congress-approved commercial and financial sanctions were revoked by then-US President George HW Bush's subsequent executive orders.

Nevertheless, Deng's response to Western sanctions was to revive relations with East Asia, particularly as many of those states held a different outlook on economic and political engagement with China from the West (Cormier 2013). As regional countries shared similar and longstanding social and cultural traditions with China given their common historical links, they exercised a different approach to human rights and political freedoms from the US and Western Europe. Indeed, much of the region's political governance tended more towards illiberal management of democracy or even outright authoritarian one-party control in the early 1990s (Gilley 2014).

In that context and somewhat ironically, Beijing's first improving bilateral relationship in the wake of Tiananmen was with its former domestic political arch-rivals — the KMT in Taiwan. Both the island's government and its powerful business sector were keen to exploit economic linkages with Beijing as it opened trading and investment opportunities with the world (Goldstein 2015).

In the space of only a few years, their bilateral relations visibly warmed. Taiwan's export-oriented businesses began voraciously investing across southern China. Their principal target investments were in low-cost industries such as clothing, textiles, footwear, toys, and low-value electronics. As these investment and trade ties expanded, both governments set up unofficial dialogue channels for the first time since the CCP's ascendancy to power in 1949.

Also, during that period, China's relations with Japan began to improve. In 1991, Japan's then-Prime Minister Toshiki Kaifu made an official visit to China. It was the first visit by a major international leader to the country since the Tiananmen protests. As such, it marked Japan's interest in preferring not to exclude China from the post-Cold War international order (Kokobun *et al.* 2017).

In 1992, China launched diplomatic relations with South Korea, after eschewing its veto on Seoul gaining membership in the United Nations. It became evident that while the West downgraded their relations with China as a reaction to the controversial Tiananmen events, East Asian governments looked to upgrade their economic ties with Beijing. Concurrently, regional leaders began extending the hand of prospective political relations, reminiscent of their centuries-old interactions (Wade and Chin 2018).

As the 1990s rolled on, bilateral economic ties flourished. Over the space of a decade from 1990 to 2000, China's trade with Malaysia surged by a multiple of eleven; trade with South Korea rose by seven-fold; and trade linkages with Taiwan and Indonesia increased up to five-fold in each case. As their economic ties took on greater interdependence, the so-called Asian Tigers (i.e., Taiwan, Hong Kong, Singapore, and South Korea) and Asian Cubs (i.e., Malaysia, Thailand, and Indonesia) set about shifting capital into China's higher value-added production centres in the southern and eastern coastal provinces (Suehiro 2017).

China's Double-Edged Bilateral Diplomacy

On a political level, since becoming China's President in 2013, Xi Jinping has been steering China toward peaceful development with its East Asian neighbours. This policy dynamic is a key part of Xi's strategy in building a 'peaceful and stable international environment', and 'that peaceful development is the right path' (Ministry of Foreign Affairs 2015a). Moreover, one of Xi's first steps has been to reverse some of the fragmented East Asian-directed policies of the preceding Hu Jintao-led administration. This culminated in the setting up of a foreign policy coordinating body having a special emphasis on East Asia.

Yet Beijing has also been sending out somewhat mixed signals in its political intentions in sometimes fraught bilateral relations with various regional countries. Certainly, during the Hu Jintao era, China became more assertive in various territorial disputes. These ranged from conflicts with Japan in the East China Sea over the Diaoyu (Senkaku) islands, to disputes with Vietnam and the Philippines in the South China Sea (SCS) over the Paracel and Spratly islands. While major confrontations have not arisen during Xi's term in office, minor incidents in the form of frequent combative naval manoeuvres are nonetheless still commonplace.

Still, in its formal pronouncements, the Chinese leadership has softened its rhetoric over territorial sovereignty issues in the SCS since 2018. Meantime, Beijing has increasingly articulated the objectives of building a new peaceful and secure international order while further embracing regional economic integration.

The roots of this new international order were originally set out during a foreign policy address at the CCP's Sixteenth National Party Congress in 2002. Then-President Jiang Zemin elaborated on China's 'periphery diplomacy' with a view to upholding the principles of treating neighbouring countries as partners and strengthening regional cooperation. The new policy course also advocated for upgrading cooperation with China's neighbouring states to a new level. This regional security strategy was, a decade or so later, more effectively put into practice by President Xi, who has emphasised improving working relations and cooperation with regional powers while simultaneously downplaying territorial disputes and other aspects of contention (Xue 2020).

Furthermore, in recent years and during the coronavirus pandemic, China has expanded its diplomacy outreach with Southeast Asian nations by pursuing the concept of 'win-win' cooperation. In practical terms, this has involved not only a 'reset' of previous Chinese foreign policy missteps in the SCS, but also the development of closer bilateral ties with other SCS claimants, including greater economic integration through trade and investment amid joint development projects of SCS energy reserves.

Examples of how Beijing's evolving foreign policy strategy has played out in bilateral diplomacy across the region are provided in the country-by-country analyses listed below. It should be noted that these are East Asian countries (except for Brunei) which make up the regional multilateral ASEAN + 3 grouping. It also takes into account country rankings, in descending order of importance, ascribed by Beijing according to levels of strategic partnerships,

The period of coverage is from 2016 to 2020, largely in parallel with Donald Trump's term in office as US president. From the perspective of East Asia's geopolitical context, the main feature of this period is Trump's 'America First' policy. Amid his generally unpredictable diplomacy across the region, it is argued that this signature policy began a process of incrementally distancing America's traditional East Asian allies and partners — away from US influence and towards China.

At the same time, Washington's intense trade dispute with China, the significant ramping up of geopolitical tensions with Beijing over its national security law for Hong Kong, and various sanctions on Chinese companies, all combined to motivate Beijing to cooperate more closely with each of its East Asian neighbours.

Cambodia

Of all the Southeast Asian states, Cambodia stands out as having developed very close ties with China (*SCMP* 2018b), given its offers of significant infrastructure investments and loans. China's investments in Cambodia have been increasing substantially, with about US$690 million of direct investment in 2019 on top of a US$350 million cumulative sum previously invested. There are several BRI-related projects, including the Phnom Penh-Sihanoukville expressway and the second phase of the Sihanoukville Special Economic Zone which plans to host Chinese companies. Bilateral trade has also been increasing rapidly, hitting nearly US$10 billion in 2019, well ahead of the agreed 2023 target date.

Political ties between the two governments drew ever closer in 2016 when President Xi made a state visit to Cambodia to hold in-depth talks with Prime Minister Hun Sen, who referred to China as the Southeast Asian state's 'closest friend'. The strength of their ties was most controversially evident when Phnom Penh de-facto vetoed an ASEAN consensus-requiring statement referring to the Hague's Permanent Court of Arbitration (PCA) ruling against China's claims with the Philippines in the South China Sea. Cambodia's government denied that it was under any undue influence from Beijing in taking that position.

In turn, China's government committed to providing economic and donor support to Cambodia, as the country's relations with the US and the EU were severely strained after Phnom Penh engaged in suppression of political opposition to the government, leading to the imposition of trade sanctions by EU in mid-2020. Subsequently, by end-2020, China agreed to a free trade agreement with Phnom Penh that would upgrade their economic partnership in the form of a higher degree of market access and liberalised flows of investment, goods, and services. Perhaps most alarmingly for US interests in the region have been rumours of an agreement for Cambodia to host the Chinese navy at its Ream Naval Base, although the two countries publicly denied such an accord is in place.

Laos

The government of Laos strongly affirmed its close ties with China in early 2016 (*Vientiane Times* 2020). A principal component of this policy was the Laos government's eagerness to attract Chinese infrastructure projects under the BRI programme, including the Laos-China high-speed railway project that cost about US$6 billion and was scheduled for completion in 2021. Meanwhile, a major expressway connecting Vientiane and Vang Vieng was finalised end-2020.

China's actual investment in the country has amounted to over US$8 billion, as Beijing became Laos' largest foreign direct investor and second-largest trade partner behind its closest neighbour, Vietnam. Somewhat controversially, China has been funding a number of bridges and dams across the Mekong River, the largest of which is the Xayaburi Dam. The hydroelectric dams threaten to reduce water levels for about 50 million people, mostly living downriver in Vietnam. Even so, Laos and

Vietnam have constructively engaged to deal with these issues, as both sides prefer to neither estrange their relations with each other nor with China.

China and Laos have also agreed to a number of bilateral accords for joint economic development by Chinese companies in Laos' agricultural and financial sectors. In early 2020, Beijing agreed to a revamped China-Laos Comprehensive Strategic Partnership as an action plan to develop greater cooperation in defence, public security, and regional and international affairs — a sign that Beijing views Vientiane not only as an important bilateral partner, but also as a key ASEAN member which can help advance its multilateralist regional agenda through 'ASEAN centrality'.

Myanmar

The electoral success of Aung San Suu Kyi in April 2016 in becoming Myanmar's State Counsellor, or otherwise its Premier, seemed to augur a major transformation of the country's military past towards a fledgling democracy. In particular, it heralded a seismic shift away from the military's longstanding ties with China in favour of improved connections with the West, although a military-led *coup d'etat* and Suu Kyi's detention in February 2021 may have eviscerated any real long-term return to democracy.

In spite of Suu Kyi's seeming swing towards Western-inspired liberalism and democracy, her first official international meeting after coming to power took place in Beijing with President Xi, followed by a visit to Washington DC. Her talks with the Chinese leadership were perhaps in recognition of the crucial role Beijing has played in Myanmar's economy (*Myanmar Times* 2020).

That pivotal economic relationship gradually evolved into a closer political tie-up with Beijing following Western governments' criticisms of Suu Kyi's handling of the Rohingya refugee crisis. On that matter, China played a low-profile but key role in ameliorating the crisis which involved Myanmar and Bangladesh by mediating an agreement between both sides. China successfully leveraged its economic clout through the BRI to achieve this resolution, as both countries received substantial Chinese funding for cross-border infrastructure projects.

In response to concerns over EU trade sanctions which could prove damaging to Myanmar's economy, Suu Kyi hosted President Xi in early

2020 with a state visit — the first such visit to the country by a Chinese leader in 20 years. On the agenda of the meeting were several stalled BRI projects, including investments into a Chinese-funded deep-sea port located on the Bay of Bengal and several special economic zones, both of which would serve as crucial hubs for China's east-west shipping routes while enabling it to access the Indian Ocean.

With these large-scale investments, China currently accounts for a quarter of total foreign investment into Myanmar. Although Singapore remains the country's top investor, second-place China is catching up fast and is expected to overtake once some of the proposed BRI projects materialise. China is also Myanmar's largest trade partner, accounting for US$11 billion in trade revenue in 2018.

While Myanmar's post-COVID-19 economic growth was expected to return to robust levels in 2022, the military coup in early 2021 has dampened those expectations with projected growth of −8.9% in 2021 and 1.4% in 2022 according to the IMF.

Thailand

In the wake of the military's seizure of power in 2014, Thailand's longstanding political ties with the West have existed on somewhat shaky ground. The military's rewrite of the country's constitution in 2015 permanently restructured the political institutions such that election outcomes would be tilted towards more Bangkok-centric and authoritarian styles of government. Hence, even after the 2019 undeniably democratic elections, a high degree of political power continues to be vested in the military, especially as a result of its presence in the unelected upper house of parliament.

As the West pulls away from its formerly close ties with Thailand, the military-backed Thai Prime Minister Prayuth Chan-ocha has been fostering steadily stronger relations with China (*Bangkok Post* 2020). This is especially evident in a series of arms deals as Beijing ventures to become the kingdom's largest weapons supplier, and more generally in trade where China has established itself as Thailand's largest trade partner. This has remained the case ever since 2013 when China stepped ahead of Japan, which had for several decades been Thailand's main regional economic partner.

Bilateral trade volumes between China and Thailand reached US$92 billion in 2019, and look set to continue rising as China facilitates greater domestic market access to Thailand's producers. China also claimed prime slot in becoming Thailand's largest foreign direct investor in 2019.

A number of Chinese-funded large-scale infrastructure projects are underway, such as the Thailand-China high-speed railway. In particular, the Thailand-China Rayong Industrial Park has turned out to be a showcase for bilateral economic relations, attracting realised investments from over 100 Chinese enterprises. On the services front, Chinese tourism accounted for the largest group of foreign visitors for nearly a decade, reaching in excess of 10 million visitors in 2018 and 2019.

Both countries have promoted each other's major economic programmes by complementing China's BRI with Thailand's 4.0 and Eastern Economic Corridor projects. Thailand's 'future industries' policy has been substantially supported by large Chinese technology companies, including Huawei, Alibaba, JD.com, and several others. The end result has been a significant expansion of Chinese investment into developing Thailand's digital economy in the form of funding Artificial Intelligence, 5G communications, as well as modern logistics.

In meetings between the two countries' leaderships in 2020, China reiterated its support of Thailand's development path in accordance with the latter's national conditions, but also importantly of Thailand's maintaining of 'social stability' (*Bangkok Post* 2020). China's reference to this aspect of development is likely recognition by Beijing that democracy is not necessarily the only means by which a country's stability is secured, especially given the preceding decades of polarised political violence which punctuated Thailand's transition towards democracy.

On the economic front, China has proposed advancing their already strong bilateral relation into post-COVID-19 cooperation including vaccine cooperation and joint pandemic control. Beijing has also offered to synergise its grand Guangdong-Hong Kong-Macau Greater Bay Area reconstruction with Thailand's Eastern Economic Corridor in the form of a vast region-to-region integration. Moreover, China has floated the idea of developing new connectivity platforms where Beijing would encourage its enterprises to invest in Thailand through the BRI and in the country's digital infrastructure.

Equally importantly, China has reiterated its views that Thailand is an important regional multilateral player, and is supporting Bangkok in its role of working to chart a post-2020 vision for building an Asia-Pacific multilateral community through the Asia-Pacific Economic Community

(APEC). Given Thailand's ambitions for such a broad regional platform, beyond its role of advancing ASEAN centrality, Beijing is keen to harness the new opportunities presented by Thailand's government in supporting the expansion of regional multilateralism.

Vietnam

Vietnam is probably the main Southeast Asian state which has consistently and stridently stood up to China's interventionist actions in the SCS (Huong 2020). This is particularly in light of ongoing clashes over several islands, which are claimed by both countries and currently occupied by various Chinese military structures supported by naval vessels. There was continuous reporting of Chinese naval ships undertaking intimidation tactics off the coast of Vietnam throughout 2020, including the sinking of a Vietnamese fishing vessel near disputed waters off the Paracel Islands.

As a counterbalance to a string of naval skirmishes with China in the SCS, Hanoi became more constructively engaged with the United States involving certain areas of naval cooperation and military training. Their improving ties were further bolstered following a Vietnamese naval skirmish with China in 2015, when a Chinese oil rig that was transferred to Vietnam's exclusive economic zone led to unprecedented nationalist protests and rioting across the country. Alarmingly, for Hanoi, the protestors targeted Chinese companies and workers, after which the government quickly clamped down on further nationalist sentiments. While the disturbances did cause a major temporary rift between the two countries' Communist Party leaderships, both sides stepped back from further clashes in order not to derail their long-term economic cooperation.

In line with mending relations, China's Foreign Minister Wang Yi held virtual talks with his Vietnamese counterpart Pham Binh Minh in 2020. Wang raised the SCS dispute during the meeting to affirm that both countries should engage in bilateral dialogue in accordance with the agreements reached by the leaderships of the two countries and their respective ruling parties. The Chinese government also praised Vietnam for its control of the coronavirus epidemic, stating that both countries made effective use of their respective institutional apparatus in controlling its domestic spread.

Further efforts in building economic relations saw China's government proactively supporting the relocation of manufacturing operations into

Vietnam's lower-cost production base. From mid-2018 to mid-2019 alone, a total of 56 major Chinese companies shifted production out of China into Vietnam. These included producers from a broad range of sectors such as textiles, transport and logistics, big data, internet applications, and business consulting.

At the outset of the country's assuming the chairmanship of ASEAN for 2020, Vietnam's President Nguyen Xuan Phuc stated his desire to improve economic relations with China. However, while China-Vietnam trade exceeded US$100 billion in 2019, trade flows favoured China by a surplus of around US$20 billion that year. This gave rise to stepped-up efforts, including political reconciliation, by Vietnam's leadership to improve the country's access to Chinese growth and its large domestic market.

Still, Vietnam's dependency on Chinese inputs for production has been rising over the last 10 years, while other Southeast Asian economies have seen a decline in their trade deficits with China. Over the short term, this trend will likely continue as Chinese producers target Vietnam's relatively open trading arrangements and investment conditions. In addition, Chinese investors have been looking to take advantage of Vietnam's fast-growing list of free trade agreements (FTAs) with large trading partners such as the EU, the Eurasian Economic Community (EEC), and the UK. Vietnam's FTA with the EU was launched in 2020 — an outcome which has eluded China ever since its trade agreement negotiations began with the EU in 2013.

One ongoing negative economic consequence of their antagonistic bilateral relations concerning their SCS territorial disputes has been the Vietnamese government's reticence in officially signing up to China's BRI. Clearly, Vietnam's strategic position in the SCS would doubtless make it an invaluable partner in China's maritime BRI ambitions. Yet the extent in which more favourable relations will emerge between China and Vietnam remains an open-ended issue given their ongoing SCS tensions.

In all likelihood, over the longer term, Vietnam will follow the policy course seemingly being adopted by other Southeast Asian states through collective diplomatic ASEAN-centred actions with China. That would mean all parties concluding a mandatory Code of Conduct (CoC) to assure peaceful cooperation in the intensely disputed region.

Indonesia

Indonesia marked the 70th anniversary of bilateral relations with China in 2020. In 1950, Jakarta was one of the initial few countries to agree to diplomatic relations with Mao's Communist China. In 2005, the two countries agreed to a strategic partnership which was elevated into a comprehensive strategic partnership in 2013.

Since 2016, Xi has visited Indonesia on two occasions, while Indonesia's President Joko Widodo 'Jokowi' has made five trips to China. In total, the leaders have held eight bilateral summits with a view to promoting future relations, which have been gaining greater momentum in each passing year as their countries' developmental positions converge.

At the beginning of Jokowi's re-elected term in office in 2019, Xi conveyed the message that both countries share extensive common bilateral, multilateral, and regional interests. In 2020, Jokowi reciprocated by calling for stronger ties between the two East Asian nations (*The Jakarta Post* 2020), by advancing the interests of developing countries and promoting multilateralism.

Partly as a result of these political interactions, China has recently become Indonesia's main economic partner amid fast-expanding, large-scale Chinese investment. This development was expected to transpire ever since Xi first announced the sea and ocean route role of the BRI — the 21st Century Maritime Silk Road — on a visit to Indonesia's capital, Jakarta in 2013. Accordingly, in 2018, both governments agreed to jointly harmonise efforts in building the BRI and Indonesia's 'Global Maritime Fulcrum'.

One of China's flagship large-scale infrastructure investments in Indonesia is the US$6 billion Jakarta-Bandung high-speed railway. The project is scheduled for completion in 2021 as one of the first Chinese-built city connection rail links in Southeast Asia. Other significant Chinese-financed infrastructure projects are the Surabaya-Madura Bridge — the country's longest cross-sea connection; the Jatigede dam — Indonesia's second-largest hydropower project; and the US$1.8 billion Banten province coal-fired plant — to be completed by a Chinese state energy provider.

The two states have also launched intergovernmental cooperation in regional economic corridors, with a view of China facilitating Indonesia's industrialisation programmes. In 2019, Indonesia reportedly proposed 28 major projects to Chinese investors amounting to US$91 billion in value.

As Chinese investors are increasingly willing to fund projects in Indonesia largely due to the encouragement of Beijing, China has risen from being Indonesia's ninth-largest foreign investor to its second-largest after Singapore since 2016. Given the island state often serves as a platform through which state-owned and private Chinese enterprises invest into Indonesia, China-origin investments may well account for the largest share of foreign inward investment in Indonesia since 2018.

In 2019 alone, Chinese direct investment reached US$4.7 billion, involving over 2,100 commercial projects and accounting for 17% of total investments into the country. The significant role of private Chinese corporate investment is also evident from Alibaba's US$1.1 billion and Tencent's US$150 million equity stakes in two of Indonesia's largest tech unicorns, Tokopedia and Gojek, respectively (Wu and Zhu 2017).

Bilateral trade has also seen equally high levels of growth. Total two-way trade reached US$80 billion in 2019, representing an increase of 1000% since 2000.

While China is aiming to become a high-income economy by 2030 and thereby making it the world's largest (World Bank 2020), Indonesia is on track towards achieving the highly-prized status of calling itself one of the world's top five economies by 2024 (World Economic Forum 2020). In achieving this goal, Indonesia's ambassador to China said that Jakarta could be in a position to expand its digital economy to US$100 billion in annual value through close cooperation with China.

There are also political rifts in the China-Indonesia relationship. In 2019, Chinese fishing boats were found off the coast of Indonesia's Natuna Islands in the South China Sea. The incident prompted Jakarta to issue a diplomatic protest with Beijing. Indonesia warned that the island group lies within its exclusive economic zone, whereas China claimed that the group of islands falls within its territorial nine-dash-line.

Other political minefields include controversies over enduring anti-Chinese sentiments among the Indonesian public, given the dramatic economic inequalities apparent between indigenous Malay-Indonesians and ethnic Chinese-Indonesians. As a result of simmering racial tensions, relatively small issues may easily erupt. One example was the 2018 protests concerning large numbers of Chinese expatriate workers hired as labour for BRI-related infrastructure projects amid growing accusations of corruption.

With the delicate political issues in mind, Indonesia's minister for maritime affairs and investment, Luhut Pandjaitan stated at a regional forum in 2018 that ASEAN should adopt a balanced line between China and the US. The rationale is based on the regional bloc being a key economic and strategic partner with which both superpowers would want to maintain good relations.

All the same, Xi and Jokowi have been careful to maintain their strengthening relations. Wary of the prospect of growing US influence in Jakarta, Xi highlighted in a meeting at end-2020 the level of Beijing's close bilateral ties with Indonesia. He stated that 'China values Indonesia's status and role in regional and international affairs ... and is ready to work with Indonesia to uphold the UN-centred international system'. Furthermore, Xi stated his interest to work with Indonesia in enhancing regional integration initiatives, including the BRI, the Global Maritime Fulcrum and the Regional Comprehensive Economic Partnership that would fast track regional economic opening and people movement.

Given Indonesia's fast-expanding economy valued at over US$1 trillion, a large and youthful population that is still growing, there is a heightened sense in Beijing that the Southeast Asian nation is emerging into a pivotal player in both regional and global multilateral contexts. As such, China's leaders are likely to seek a greater level of strategic international cooperation with Jakarta going forward.

Malaysia

Shortly after the Philippines' newly elected President Rodrigo Duterte's controversial swing towards China in 2016, Malaysia's then-Prime Minister Najib Razak ascribed to a similar international policy by forging closer security relations with Beijing, albeit with less fanfare than Duterte. Malaysia concluded its first-ever defence procurement from China, which involved several naval vessels alongside Chinese investment deals worth up to US$34 billion.

However, a globally reverberating money-laundering scandal connected to Malaysian state-controlled investment firm 1 Malaysia Development Berhad (1MDB), which was set up by Razak, contributed to his election defeat just over a year later. The firm was accused of laundering money for Razak by paying three Chinese construction firms large sums, two of which were for pipeline projects costing US$2.3 billion with allegedly little evidence of any work having been performed.

When 92-year-old Mahathir Mohammad won Malaysia's premiership in a surprise election victory in 2018, he stated in his hallmark boldness that China was engaged in a 'new version of colonialism' by engaging in unbalanced deals with less-powerful countries. Mahathir also committed to reviewing so-called 'unequal treaties' which included large-scale Chinese-funded infrastructure projects clinched during the Razak years.

After re-negotiations with China, Mahathir managed to upgrade several deals in Malaysia's favour, essentially by pressing down on the projects' building costs. The China-Malaysia Kuantan Industrial Park and Bandar Malaysia were among the notable high-profile and expensive BRI-related infrastructure projects that successfully benefited from the cost reductions, under his administration. These outcomes may have opened opportunities for other regional countries to push for the lowering of their China-owed debts by renegotiating the terms surrounding Chinese-funded infrastructure projects.

Indeed, the Singapore-based Institute of Southeast Asian Studies (ISEAS) pointed out that many of the region's economies should be in a better position to negotiate more advantageously over the costs and financing of large-scale infrastructure projects in future. Nevertheless, such re-negotiations by Southeast Asian governments have been in the context of maintaining strong ties with Beijing, much as what Mahathir had engaged in during his term in office, in spite of his criticisms of China at the outset of his recent premiership.

Although Mahathir only served two out of his five mandated years in office, Malaysia's bilateral trade with China nevertheless continued to hit annual record highs during those years — US$103 billion in 2018 and US$111 billion in 2019. China has been Malaysia's largest trade partner for the last 10 consecutive years and its largest inward direct investor from 2017 to 2019, inching out the US.

Since Mahathir's removal from office in early 2020, the current Prime Minister Muhyiddin Yassin has adopted a more cordial approach in relations towards China (*The Straits Times* 2020a). While the country has voiced concerns over China's SCS interventions, Muhyiddin's coalition government has maintained a low profile and non-confrontational approach towards the various disputes while consistently acting through ASEAN in resolving SCS issues with China.

By and large, China has viewed Muhyiddin's similarly shortlived premiership, following his resignation after 18 months in office, as an opportunity to strengthen bilateral ties, including upgrading their Strategic Partnership. At a meeting between Muhyiddin and China's Foreign Minister Wang Yi near end-2020, Beijing offered setting up a high-level intergovernmental committee to explore bilateral cooperation in the post-COVID-19 era. Some of the economic proposals involved expanding joint

BRI cooperation, in which Beijing would actively encourage Chinese companies to invest in Malaysia; working on key projects, including developing the digital economy, 5G roll-out, and satellite navigation, although a China-financed Malaysia-Singapore high-speed rail link was cancelled in early 2021.

China has also pushed for notable proposals on the political front, including a greater role for Malaysia to promote regional multilateralism. In this area, Beijing has highlighted Malaysia's important role in regional coordination, such as Kuala Lumpur guiding East Asian leaders to promote East Asian cooperation. China-Malaysia improved bilateral relations have also involved focusing on ASEAN centrality, regional stability, and further development of China-ASEAN ties. Beijing reiterated its support for Malaysia to host the 2020 Asia-Pacific Economic Cooperation (APEC) summit.

From these perspectives, China has worked to enhance cooperation with Malaysia as a key partner in advancing greater East Asian multilateralism, with Kuala Lumpur acting as a key mover within the framework of ASEAN centrality. In other words, Beijing has taken the long-term view that Malaysia is likely to be a leader in the cause of regional multilateralism, irrespective of the country's ongoing volatile political scene.

The Philippines

Arguably, East Asia's first major post-Cold War political shock came in 2016, when a newly-elected Philippines President Rodrigo Duterte announced his country's swing away from its over century-long alliance and relationship with the US towards uplifting political and economic ties with China (Valente 2020). Often referred to as the Trump of Asia, Duterte's highly-populist form of politicking, particularly the alleged government-sanctioned extra-judicial killings of suspects involved in his war on drugs, was subjected to heavy criticisms from Western governments, especially that of then-US President Barak Obama. As an alternative to Washington, Duterte found common ground with China's policy of non-interference in sovereign countries' internal affairs.

At the forefront of Duterte's shift towards closer ties with Beijing was an appreciation of the reality of China as a globally ascendant military, political, and economic superpower and the repercussions for neighbouring, smaller countries such as the Philippines. Evidence of this asymmetry in power relations lays in China's ignoring the 2016 PCA decision in favour of the Philippines' claims to sovereignty overlapping with those of China's in the SCS.

Another reason for Duterte's olive branch to Beijing was economic pragmatism. Several of the Philippines' biggest family-run conglomerates had been gradually strengthening business linkages with China some years before Duterte took office. These powerful corporate holdings are held by privileged elites in wealthy families, many of whom are of ethnic-Chinese descent.

In line with this decades-long trend of Filipino-Chinese commercial connections building, Duterte's first official visit to Beijing in 2017 was dedicated to raising up to US$24 billion of infrastructure-related and other investment commitments from Chinese public and private sources, albeit with the blessing of China's President Xi. These funds included US$15 billion in high-profile developments of railways, power, telecoms, international airport, and smart-city projects in the country. Each commitment has been incrementally activated, by China since 2017. Additionally, the Philippines' energy sector received a strong boost in 2020 when Duterte lifted a moratorium on oil and gas development in the West Philippines Sea following negotiations with China on the area's joint cooperation.

While several large-scale infrastructure and energy cooperation projects have been announced by Duterte's administration, the Philippines' president has been persistently dogged by domestic anti-China pressure throughout his term in office. Most prominently, the public has called for the president to take a tougher stance against China after the downing of Philippine fishing boats and ongoing clashes with Chinese naval vessels on its SCS-claimed atolls. Indeed, Filipinos' public trust in China has also fallen to its lowest levels on record following a series of these incidents. Partly as a result, Duterte has on occasion wavered in his pro-Beijing stance. Yet he has also flipped in his relations with Washington, threatening to terminate a historical military agreement for visiting US forces at one point, and then soon after suspending that threat.

Even so, China has also played its part in revitalising relations with the Philippines, including the provision of growing investment in the country's infrastructure-deficient economy. According to the Philippine Central Bank, Chinese foreign direct investment rose to nearly US$1.75 billion in 2019. This was up from only a half million dollars in 2015, the year before Duterte's election to office. Over 2019 and

2020, China has also become the country's second-largest foreign direct investor behind Singapore, although many Chinese investments are also routed through Singapore and identified as originating from this hub, thereby understating a significant level of investment likely to be of Chinese origin. On the trade front, China has become the Philippines' largest export market and main source of imports.

President Xi paid his first state visit to the Philippines in 2018, during which he and Duterte raised the status of their bilateral partnership to that of a Comprehensive Strategic Partnership. Both also agreed to handle their SCS disputes under a peaceful and cooperative framework. In that regard, both leaders committed to work alongside ASEAN countries in developing the consensus-based CoC, within a three-year period, for the region's stability.

According to Xi, given that both countries have similar developmental challenges in transforming themselves into higher-income states, this has made them 'natural partners with a common destiny'. As a result, the Chinese leader has pledged to seek greater cooperation between China's BRI and the Philippines' 'Build, Build, Build', and 'the Golden Age of Infrastructure' development programmes. Beijing has also promised to work with Manila on bilateral security and people-to-people exchanges. Overall, relations between the two governments have been significantly improving. The two leaders have even discussed SCS marine resource development as separate projects from the oil and gas sector.

Nevertheless, caution is still exercised by both sides. Beijing remains wary of the ongoing US military presence in the Philippines, while Manila maintains an account of persistently unfavourable public opinion towards China, particularly their distrust of what may be Beijing's agenda in the South China Sea.

Singapore

Singapore has maintained long and close multifaceted relations with China since the early years of Beijing's opening to the world for business. This can be essentially credited to Deng's and modern Singapore's founder Lee Kuan Yew's close relations, both being reportedly of Hakka ethnic Chinese origin.

However, in the twenty-first century, China's ties with Singapore have not been as close as in past decades. Strategically, Beijing has plans to redirect East Asia's mainly sea-based trade flows through its maritime and land-based BRI programmes. This could have long-term ramifications for Singapore, which has traditionally acted as a pivotal node for Chinese goods shipments between East Asia, the Middle East, and Europe.

Yet another challenge to Singapore's relations with China may be Beijing's 'Made in China 2025' industrial policy. This has sought to coordinate government subsidies and information technology to boost China into becoming the world's high-tech production leader, potentially sidelining Singapore's still sizeable and important electronics manufacturing sector.

Despite some downsides to their relations, there are also plenty of reasons to believe their traditionally constructive relations will endure. This is particularly evident in their economic ties. For instance, China has been Singapore's largest trade partner from 2013 to 2020. In turn, Singapore has been China's largest source of inward foreign direct investment for seven consecutive years. Singapore also became the first ASEAN state to agree an 'express channel' with China in response to the coronavirus pandemic. The purpose of the scheme is to speed along exchanges of people and products between the two countries.

Over a longer-term horizon, Singapore has engaged in and will continue launching numerous bilateral intergovernment-based infrastructure projects in China. These have included the Suzhou Industrial Park, the Tianjin Eco-City, and strategic interconnection projects in central China's city of Chongqing. Future coordination on other mega-projects includes a new 'international land-sea corridor', a Smart City in Shenzhen, and a Singapore-Shanghai cooperative city venture.

Singapore has otherwise been actively involved in jointly building the BRI with China. As a result, their bilateral relations have been enhanced given the island state's capacity to inject substantial levels of investment capital, debt finance, and technology-related investments into BRI-related projects.

At a meeting between Xi and Singapore Prime Minister Lee Hsien Loong in 2019, the Chinese side proposed greater synergy between the BRI and the Master Plan on ASEAN Connectivity 2025. It will be an initiative in which Singapore takes a leading role in promoting economic integration across East Asia. In turn, Lee put forward his interest to cooperate more intensively on investment and connectivity under the BRI framework (*The Straits Times* 2020b).

On a few occasions, Singapore has conveyed criticisms over Beijing's claims and actions in the South China Sea. In spite of some rifts in relations, however, Singapore has been a major backer of China's efforts to promote regional economic integration and overall development of China-ASEAN relations.

Today, China views Singapore's sophistication in more of a regional context than a single country it once looked at, partly emulating the Deng-Lee era. To that extent, China appears most keen to involve Singapore as a partner in fostering overall East Asian economic integration and further development of the BRI.

South Korea

Some of the principal political tremors across East Asia in recent years have been events unfolding on the Korean peninsula. While much attention was given to Trump's rapprochement with North Korea leader Kim Jong-un, perhaps the real geopolitical game-changer has been Seoul's below-the-radar drift towards Beijing (Bernal 2020). Events on this front, however, have managed to avoid any fundamental destabilisation of Seoul's security ties with the US.

In 2016, then-South Korea President Park Geun-hye undertook a high-stakes programme of setting up the US Terminal High Altitude Air Defence (THAAD) anti-missile system in the country. This decision was prompted by a North Korean nuclear test earlier in that year and what Park reportedly saw as a lack of any supportive response from President Xi in reining in Kim.

Initially, most of South Korea's public supported the deployment of THAAD, believing it to be a prudent policy of countering the possibility of an attack arising out of North Korea's rapidly escalating nuclear weapons arsenal.

However, the THAAD placement was fiercely opposed and criticised by China's leadership, especially in relation to the ability of the system's radar to track China's own weapons movements. Progressively, Beijing flagged various warning signs against the deployment, intimating that it could give rise to a regionally destabilising arms race.

Since China's increasingly assertive criticisms of the THAAD deployment in South Korea, which ran concurrently with escalating domestic political scandals embroiling Park, the principal left-of-centre mainstream political opposition became increasingly forceful in campaigning for the removal of THAAD during the 2017 presidential elections. It shook the ground of Korean politics, marking the first time a major Korean political party had campaigned to renege on a US defence deployment in the country.

Moreover, the opposition party's electoral success in 2017 — resulting in the first loss of parliamentary majority for the conservative ruling party in nearly two decades — laid the groundwork for further upheavals in Korean politics. Over time, President Moon Jae-in's administration has fostered a policy of incrementally withdrawing from its close-knit cooperation with US leadership over defence and security policies and inching towards a more amenable position in relations with Beijing.

Almost immediately upon coming to power, Moon called for a new era of ties with China and quickly sought to reassure Beijing over the deployment of THAAD in South Korea. When invited by Xi to China, Moon declared in his opening remarks at the Great Hall of the People: 'It is hoped that South Korea's dream becomes as helpful for China as China's dream becomes an opportunity for South Korea' (Lee 2020).

This shared ambition, in its broadest economic context, has taken shape in the form of the China-South Korean Free Trade Agreement (FTA). This accord accounts for the largest trade flows of any bilateral FTA in the world and contributes towards China subsequently becoming Seoul's largest trade partner. Two-way trade reached US$285 billion in 2019 with a US$75 billion trade surplus favouring South Korea. Investment by South Korean companies in China has also been gaining ground. In 2019, there were 34 investment projects in China, ranking only behind South Korea's investments in the US which numbered 46. China's investment into South Korea still lags most other countries with less than US$1 billion.

On the political front, while Moon has improved ties with China, THAAD has not been removed. To some degree, China's trade war with the US, tensions in the SCS, a range of other geopolitical flashpoints, and the coronavirus pandemic have likely persuaded Xi to shelve the THAAD dispute with Seoul for the time being. Of equal importance, over the last couple of years since the beginning of Moon's presidency, trilateral political relations between China, South Korea, and Japan have been on the mend. Noticeably more cordial relations gave rise to the first annual trilateral summit of the three nations in Chengdu, China at end-2019, breaking its suspension since 2016. Also, at the end of 2019, South Korea and China agreed to fully normalise relations by announcing a plan to expand cultural and diplomatic ties. Xi also planned to visit South Korea by end-2020 as his first overseas official visit since the coronavirus outbreak — a major sign of the importance Beijing attaches in elevating its relations with Seoul.

To a large extent, Beijing has actively moved to improve ties with Moon's administration. China's strategic detente with Seoul may also have been encouraged by the souring of relations between South Korea and the US on both economic and political fronts. In the latter case, this arose when Trump side-lined Moon and other regional leaders by dealing directly with North Korea leader Kim Jong-un in negotiating a ballistic missile test moratorium and nuclear disarmament programme, both of which have since completely failed to materialise. In the international policy paralysis which arose following the failed second Trump-Kim summit in 2019, Moon shifted the focus of his foreign policy from dealing with Pyongyang's nuclear and conventional military threat to Beijing.

What has become clear, since the placement of the US THAAD missile defence system in South Korea, is that Seoul is opened to pursuing both warmer bilateral ties and increasingly multilateral relations with Beijing with regards to the wider region. As a result, mutual support and policy alignment between the two nations have become increasingly the norm, especially as the US under Trump stepped away not only from its traditional regional security and defence roles but also as South Korea's main economic partner.

Japan

The lack of any tangible outcome arising from the first meeting between Japan's former Prime Minister Shinzo Abe and Donald Trump very shortly after his surprise election win was reflected a couple of days later during Abe's trip to the 2016 APEC summit in Peru. At the sidelines of the gathering of regional leaders, Abe reportedly expressed to Xi his desire to improve their bilateral ties, stating that he would 'like to forge a stable and good relationship' (*The Japan Times* 2019).

Abe also added that he was looking forward to jointly marking the 40th anniversary of the China-Japan peace and friendship treaty and the 45th anniversary of the normalisation of diplomatic relations.

This rapprochement was a far cry from Abe's controversial visits and regular offerings at the Yasukuni Shrine in Japan — an act many in Asia took offence as a memorial to Japanese militarism. Abe's olive branch to Xi also further distanced him from proposals in the early years of his administration — rewriting the key Article 9 of Japan's post-war pacifist constitution.

More significantly, Abe's reaching out to Xi essentially pointed to an end in his efforts in side-lining China regionally, which was particularly apparent through his combined efforts with former US President Barak Obama in their design of the Trans-Pacific Partnership free trade accord that excluded China's participation — regarded by many observers to be as much as a geopolitical strategy of China containment as an international trade policy.

In subsequent years, a somewhat gradualist approach emerged towards improving political relations with China. The highlights of this tentative building of diplomatic ties included Abe's visit to China in 2018. This was reciprocated by Xi's trip to Japan in 2019 — the first by a Chinese leader in 10 years. During these visits, the leaders jointly announced their aspirations in elevating their bilateral ties to new levels. In concrete terms, the visits prompted the start of people-to-people exchanges between their respective political parties, national legislatures, and cultural representatives, as well as greater economic cooperation.

The real pull factor in their bilateral coordination is the converging of powerful economic forces. China was Japan's second-largest export market, with export volumes of US$135 billion, in 2018. Overall, Beijing has been Tokyo's largest trade partner in recent years, while China's and Japan's successful efforts in concluding the Regional Comprehensive Economic Partnership (RCEP) at end-2020 will probably propel bilateral trade to even higher levels in the next few years.

Wherever there are 'ups' in China-Japan ties, there are also accompanying 'downs'. As tensions with China arose in disputed areas of the SCS and East China Sea (ECS), Abe signed up with Washington, New Delhi, and Canberra to re-form the 2007-founded Quadrilateral Security Dialogue or 'the Quad'.

The stated aim of the grouping is to uphold a so-called rules-based, free and open Indo-Pacific (FOIP), including freedom of sea navigation. Although the grouping did not officially name China as a rival to their collaboration — other than former US Secretary of State Mike Pompeo's direct negative reference to China at a Quad summit in 2020 — it has been largely aimed at containing Beijing in the disputed SCS and ECS, and competing with China's maritime version of the BRI.

Shortly after the onset of the coronavirus pandemic, Abe instituted a policy of diversifying international trade supply chains by encouraging Japanese companies to shift out of China, back to Japan, or to set up in Southeast Asia. Up to US$600 million in Japanese government funding for corporations that chose to relocate was ploughed into the scheme. By end-2020, about a hundred Japanese enterprises had taken advantage of the relocation offers. Yet, over time, the number of Japanese companies exiting China has been relatively small. Ultimately, few Japanese corporations have been willing to forgo opportunities in China's expanding giant consumer market, modern infrastructure, and highly-trained yet still relatively inexpensive workforce (Dooley and Inoue 2020).

In the wake of Abe's sudden resignation as Prime Minister in mid-2020 before the end of his full term, Yoshihide Suga — his successor — has continued to some extent the policies set in place by Abe. These include a primary focus on Japan's defence and security relations with the US and other Western nations such as Australia. At the same time, Suga has stepped up building economic relations, including signing up to RCEP, amid people-to-people exchanges with China. Suga has also spoken with both Chinese and US leaders directly — a sign of the carefully balanced relations Tokyo is likely to follow, albeit one where the emphasis will be on steadily improving relations with China. As a result, any notion of an economic decoupling from China — a policy gradually sought and activated by the Trump administration — will likely be a non-starter for both Japanese policymakers and companies alike, in both short and longer time horizons.

ASEAN

Besides its bilateral relations with all 10 Southeast Asian countries, China also maintains a separate Comprehensive Strategic Partnership with the Association of Southeast Asian Nations (ASEAN). The dual level partnership is a reflection of how Southeast Asia's linkages with China have become more complex, as they adopt a more multilateral focus over solely bilateral ties from 2000 onwards. The first major manifestation was China's 2002 FTA with the formal country grouping (Ministry of Commerce 2020).

In the context of this FTA, China proceeded to revise its Foreign Trade Law, in 2004. The new version incorporated China's Five Principles of Peaceful Coexistence, including equality and mutual benefit. The revised law highlighted an emphasis on 'entering into or participating in regional economic trade agreements as customs unions, free trade agreements, and regional economic organisations'.

At the 17th National Party Congress in 2007, then-President Hu Jintao affirmed that China would 'implement a free trade strategy, strengthen bilateral and multilateral economic and trade cooperation'. This declaration, amid the preceding pivotal law changes, was a manifestation of China's newly defined and upgraded regionalism strategy in diplomatic and economic terms, following its pivotally symbolic trade agreement with ASEAN as a multilateral regional institution.

The Rise of China-ASEAN + 3 Trade Relations

Beijing has concluded bilateral FTAs with several ASEAN states and South Korea. The latter FTA has become the world's largest FTA-based bilateral trading relationship where more than US$280 billion in goods and services were traded in 2019 (Huo 2020). More recently, both countries agreed to develop a joint economic cooperation development plan from 2021 to 2025. This involves coordinated promotion of China's Belt and Road Initiative (BRI) alongside Korea's Northern and Southern Policy. Although the latter is designed to build economic relations with ASEAN and India, it will also foster economic ties with China, Japan, the US, and other major economies.

China has also been negotiating several regional trade agreements. This includes the China-Japan-Korea FTA. All parties have agreed to push for further negotiations towards concluding an agreement by 2021.

China's and East Asian countries' most ambitious trading accord has been the RCEP. This was signed into effect on November 2020 by ASEAN member states, China, Japan, and South Korea, otherwise known as the 'ASEAN + 3' (Xinhuanet 2020c). Australia and New Zealand were the other signatories, otherwise referred to as 'ASEAN + 5'. India was a negotiating partner since RCEP's negotiations were launched in 2013. However, it withdrew its involvement at end-2019. Even so, the remaining 15 signatories reiterated their intention of welcoming New Delhi as a member whenever it chooses to come on board.

The ASEAN + 3 grouping has been meeting regularly in this format since 1997. China and other Northeast Asian states, namely Japan and South Korea, have all openly endorsed ASEAN as the principal regional organisation, which by having a deep experience of consensus-building can play a special role towards nurturing the region's community spirit. In practical terms, the bloc's main goal has been to create an East Asian economic community, the pinnacle of which has become the regional 15-member-signed RCEP. RCEP is discussed in greater detail in the analysis below.

China and ASEAN + 3: Responses to the Asian and Global Financial Crises

The Asian Financial Crisis (AFC) of 1997–98 fundamentally impacted East Asia's view of itself (Lai 2012). Until that time, most of its individual states were confident in their respective abilities to continue expanding rapidly, and almost considered themselves as impregnable economies within the paradigm of 'globalisation'. In the early-to-mid 1990s, this view was enhanced by several regional governments' promotion of 'Asian values'.

This sub-paradigm to globalisation touted unique Asian economic qualities enabling the region to avoid the deep economic recessions of the early 1990s, which mainly afflicted Anglo-Saxon Western economies. Some regional governments also believed their adherence to economic principles inherent within the conceptual framework of 'Asian values' enabled them to weather several currency and financial crises during the period, including the so-called 'Tequila Crisis' which mainly impacted Mexico and several Latin American developing economies in the early 1990s.

However, the collapse of many regional currencies and connected asset markets in 1996/97, along with ensuing economic and financial chaos, fundamentally altered the region's perception that 'Asian values' were a guarantor of economic success. Instead, the economic devastation that arose redirected regional governments towards undertaking a more collectivist, rather than previously individual, 'external trade-driven' approach.

That is not to understate the role played by the harsh structural adjustment programmes required by the IMF in the post-crisis period.

The economic reforms meted out by the IMF brought home the notion that the privileged position East Asian countries held during the Cold War, in terms of their relations with the US, had ended. Washington now considered the so-called 'Asian Tiger' and 'Asian Cub' economies to be rivals as much as allies.

Without any regional solution to ameliorate the economic crisis — despite an attempt by Japan to establish a regional currency institution, which was vetoed by the US — the region's economies persisted in looking to develop home-grown alternatives to Washington's Bretton Woods institutions. In particular, the 10 nations of ASEAN began to develop collusive mechanisms of economic integration, the idea of which was 'together is stronger'. Ultimately, this gave birth to the ASEAN Economic Community (AEC) in 2015 (Inamo 2015).

Given the vacuum of initial collective responses to the AFC, China's role in maintaining the value of the Chinese Yuan to the US dollar played a major role in underwriting regional financial and economic stability. The purpose of the measure was to avoid a damaging competitive devaluation of the region's still export-oriented economies and to enable its battered economies some breathing space in reaching out for an economic recovery. In effect, by the early 2000s, China's policy of currency stability had worked, and a new era of regional financial cooperation begun to develop a slowly evolving consciousness. China also gained significant credit for its actions which, in the longer run, offset the negative spill over from its policy of not supporting Japan's proposed regional monetary fund in the late-1990s.

A decade later, the 2008 Global Financial Crisis further tested China's and East Asian countries' abilities in working together. This time around, the region had to survive a devastating blow to the entire global economy and its financial markets. China led the way by tilting away from export-focused growth towards domestic investment-driven expansion. The historic policy stimulus was driven by one of the largest credit booms ever, as bank lending of up to CNY9.6 billion (over US$1 trillion) for 2009 alone reached nearly half of China's GDP that year (Li *et al.* 2012).

The World Bank saw this stimulus measure as the single-most important factor in the longer-term recovery of the region from the earlier AFC and further consolidated China's role as integral to the region's economic cohesion. Indeed, the economic expansion it directly spawned, from 2010 to 2014, gave birth to the creation of a vast market for East Asian manufactured and commodity exports, for which China has developed a ravenous appetite ever since.

On a more institutional regional level, China began to support various multilateral initiatives. The first such arrangement was the Chiang Mai Initiative Multilateralisation (CMIM) launched in 2000 as a bilateral currency swap involving the ASEAN + 3 (Institute for International Economies 2002) countries and was designed to deal with liquidity crises without recourse to the IMF. Following the GFC, the bilateral swap facility was upgraded in 2010 into a multicurrency arrangement with foreign exchange reserves of US$120 billion and then beefed up to US$240 billion in 2012. As a follow-on to the CMIM, China also played a significant role in the establishment of the ASEAN + 3 Macroeconomic Research Office (AMRO) and shared the first Chair of the organisation with Japan.

The currency facility has been playing a prominent role in strengthening and stabilising ASEAN currencies during periods of global emerging market turmoil since 2012. Further development, which is to become embedded in the region's financial architecture, will also likely play an important role during the coming decade. As a further sign of China's multilateral engagement in the region, the Lancang-Mekong cooperation strategy was initiated in 2016. Under this newly-created sub-regional format involving China, Thailand, Vietnam, Myanmar, Laos, and Cambodia, the six countries have been building physical and social infrastructure across IndoChina to promote economic and social development.

The world has been experiencing an unprecedented pandemic-driven global economic slowdown since 2020. At the same time, geopolitical tensions and rising economic nationalism across the globe are adding to the COVID-19 pandemic's devastating effects on international trade flows, not dissimilar in many respects to the 30% drop in global trade during the 1930s Great Depression (World Trade Organisation 2020).

In response to staggering economic contractions the world over, China has been looking to launch another massive economic stimulus. This time, it has shifted from its post-Global Financial Crisis and decade-long public investment-led growth strategy towards invigorating domestic household consumption and fostering a high-tech services sector (Bloomberg 2020b).

Under this emerging new paradigm, East Asia has risen in importance to China as a means of facilitating its restructuring agenda. To this extent, imports of higher-end industrial, technology, and consumer goods have been flooding in from across the region. According to official Chinese trade data, China's imports were hitting all-time high monthly levels in September 2020, such that nearly every regional country was exporting record amounts of goods and services to China following China's return to growth in the second half of 2020. This trend is set to continue as China pivots regionally and as Beijing steadily beefs up its domestic demand as a proportion of GDP.

On the COVID-19 front, the Chinese government has made a priority of providing assistance to East Asian countries. This was set out through the ASEAN + 3 format as the principal platform for regional pandemic shared assistance. Accordingly, Beijing has supplied large quantities of masks and personal protective equipment throughout the region, amid its overall international plan for financial pandemic support of US$2 billion coordinated through the United Nations.

Unsurprisingly, Beijing's efforts in providing pandemic support across East Asia were cynically dubbed 'mask diplomacy' by Western media and think tanks. However, this should not belittle the expansive and concerted efforts undertaken by China and the health ministries of the ASEAN + 3 in sharing technical and material supplies and financial support in assisting the strained health services of the region as a whole. More specifically, China has assisted the lesser developed Southeast Asian economies, including the provision of medical training to healthcare workers in these countries. This has involved not only the provision of Chinese civilian health teams to these countries, but in some instances, Beijing has also provided its higher-end military healthcare professionals to key neighbouring states such as Cambodia — the first country in the world to receive Chinese assistance of this kind. Other countries in the region, including Philippines, Myanmar and Malaysia, have received large amounts of Chinese medical supplies and training.

Concurrently, China has offered the countries of IndoChina priority in Chinese-produced vaccines and post clinical trials. The Chinese government has referred to the vaccines it will produce as a 'global public good' that should be readily accessible and affordable especially for developing countries once it is rolled out in China. Perhaps more substantively, China's state-owned Sinovac has partnered with a company in Indonesia and the Philippine government to produce and distribute its vaccines, respectively, in those countries. Overall, the ASEAN + 3 arrangements in coordinating the needed measures in supporting healthcare systems across East Asia, especially in lesser developed Southeast Asia, will provide one of the key platforms for strategic guidance on regional cooperation during and after the COVID-19 pandemic.

In the midst of the global pandemic, the signing of RCEP in November 2020 has taken on elevated significance. This is especially the case given the ongoing and heightened need for the integration of East Asia's supply chains with China's in dealing with the current and probable future pandemics. RCEP is more than just the world's largest free trade arrangement. It is the culmination of multiple '10 + 1' FTAs between ASEAN and China, Japan, South Korea, Australia, and New Zealand. It also consolidates other existing pairs of free trade partnerships between the latter five. RCEP is also a platform for enhancing a stalled trilateral trade arrangement between China, Japan and South Korea.

After RCEP takes effect, which could be in 2021 or early 2022, more than 90% of goods traded in the region will benefit from zero tariff rates within 20 years. According to some estimates, RCEP is expected to drive a regional net increase of US$519 billion in exports and contribute to a net increase of US$186 billion each year in global GDP by 2030 (Savic 2020a). For East Asia's policymakers, RCEP promises a new era of regional multilateralism through the establishment of a new pattern of open economic integration and significant expansion of intra-region economic dependency.

More specifically, RCEP will deepen the value chain of industrial output in the region by adopting common regional rules of origin. It will use new technologies to promote customs facilitation, promote the development of new cross-border logistics, and apply negative lists to advance investment liberalisation, foreign ownership, and investment policy transparency.

Beyond trade integration, RCEP will also act as a magnet for expanding regional countries' multilateral investment programmes. These include China's over US$2 trillion BRI, Japan's US$200 billion 'Asia Dream' and South Korea's 'North and South Initiative'. All these government-inspired cross-border economic development programmes focus on prioritising regional interconnection through building modern infrastructure and transport linkages. They also share similar objectives in developing inclusion-based models of economic development.

As such, they incorporate the dynamism of Asian SMEs, training and education for highly-skilled human resources, while supporting sustainable development through the adoption of environmental technologies and roll-out of renewable energy. Up until 2020, these various state-driven international programmes were largely insulated from each other. RCEP promises to establish both the economic groundwork and accommodative political will for constructing multilateral institutional platforms by which these various initiatives can build bridges to operate increasingly seamlessly over the medium to long term.

RCEP's importance to the region, given the intensification of China's role in supporting East Asia's economic prospects or even the very survival of some of the region's stagnating economies, is no less significant in the face of the conclusion of a former US-led rival regional trade agreement, the Comprehensive and Progressive Agreement for Trans-Pacific Partnership (CPTPP) in 2018 (Tobin 2019). Its member countries include Japan, Singapore, Malaysia, Vietnam, Brunei, Australia, New Zealand, Canada, Mexico, Chile, and Peru.

Yet, without the membership of an economy such as China's and acting as the principal demand engine for other member economies' exports, the CPTPP is unlikely to have the significant punch in kick-starting economic growth post COVID-19 induced recessions that a successfully-concluded RCEP would otherwise more likely provide for its member countries.

Even so, given China's political and economic philosophy of openness to international institutions and economic groupings, Beijing has put forward its interest in future membership of the CPTPP. Given this expanding trade multilateralism, both trade agreements will no doubt be an invaluable boon for reviving East Asia's economy to become the engine for future economic growth (Tait 2020).

China's Expansive BRI Diplomacy in ASEAN

In advancing strategic partnership diplomacy, Xi has since 2013 placed great weight on outbound and state-directed investment policies, including his signature Belt and Road Initiative (BRI). The BRI has underscored the importance of providing preferential loans in financing large-scale infrastructure and energy projects, particularly across Southeast Asia, in China's regional diplomacy (Oxford Business Group 2020).

The US-China trade war of 2018 and 2019, amid severe and ongoing trade frictions between the US and other East Asian countries, also prompted China to transfer increased financial resources into Southeast Asia under the BRI programme. By the end of 2019, four out of the top five recipients of Chinese funding among over 100 countries now affiliated to the BRI were Indonesia, Singapore, Malaysia, and Laos.

Other Chinese-founded and co-led financial institutions have also played key roles in the provision of funding to regional economies. These have included the US$100 billion-capitalised AIIB, the US$50 billion BRICS New Development Bank (NDB) and the US$40 billion Silk Road Fund (SRF). Increasingly, these and other sources of Chinese funding have become major alternatives to more traditional lenders into the region, including the US-led International Monetary Fund, the World Bank, and the US-Japan co-managed Asian Development Bank.

Thus, East Asia has seen the coordinated development of alternative arrangements in which China has come to play a major regional role. In that regard, Southeast Asia has been especially welcoming of China's non-conditional ideological financial support for countries' infrastructure and other important economic sectors. This is in spite of the doubts and criticisms surfacing in other parts of the world over China's so-called 'debt-trap diplomacy' (Rana and Ji 2020).

Whether these countries' governments will be able to repay the substantial increases in debt owing to China is another matter. Nonetheless, since Chinese debt financing is mainly committed to much-needed infrastructure which should improve economic efficiency and growth, the likelihood will be that as East Asian countries' income levels rise thanks in part to the new infrastructure, the vast majority of debt owing should become accommodatively repayable. One should also take into account that Chinese policy banks, such as the China Development Bank and China Export Import Bank which have provided about 85% of BRI funding, have done so at highly-concessional rates (Hurley *et al*. 2018).

China's Growing Focus on ASEAN Centrality

In the early 1990s, China was suspicious of various regional multilateral institutions, perceiving them as mainly being political tools of the United States. Even ASEAN was regarded as a partially anti-China grouping. For instance, when the ASEAN Regional Forum (ARF) was about to be launched in 1993, China was hesitant to join the multilateral grouping. There was a concern among the Chinese leadership that China might either be subjected to heavy criticism or come under some form of pressure within the organisation. China ultimately participated after deciding that it would be better off influencing the forum from within than not being involved (Haacke 2009).

Also, in that decade, China became progressively involved in sub-regional multilateral economic cooperation projects. In Northeast Asia this included the Tumen River Development Programme (Asia Dialogue 2017) and the Bohai economic circle. In Southeast Asia, it was engaged in the Greater Mekong Sub-region Cooperation Programme (Asia Dialogue 2019) and the Pan-Beibu (Tonkin) Gulf regional economic zone.

After several years of cautious participation in various regional multilateral forums, Beijing realised in the latter half of the 1990s that its previous perceptions of East Asian regional institutions were not as they had thought. Chinese officials began to understand that China's participation in those multilateral activities was helpful in reducing the 'China threat' rhetoric in its neighbourhood and creating a more benign China image.

Moreover, Beijing discovered that it could use these regional institutions to better protect its own national security interests. For example, at the ARF, China found that many smaller states in East Asia shared its views in opposing the set up of formal preventative diplomacy mechanisms in regional cross-border crisis management (Liu and Tsai 2014). ARF had thereby set the stage for China to diffuse the political pressures from active proponents of preventative diplomacy, primarily the United States.

By 2001, when the SCO was formed, Chinese leaders were fully convinced that multilateral regional organisations were significant mechanisms for China to articulate its interests, project influence, cultivate soft power, and promote multilateralism. Since that time, China has been transformed into an active organiser and user of multilateral projects.

However, before engaging in more high-level multilateral institution building, Beijing participated in a number of smaller-scale regional initiatives, where it began to accumulate invaluable experience in this context. Bilaterally with ASEAN in 2000, China participated in the Chiang Mai Initiative for Multilateralisation with a view to East Asian cooperation on financial security (Asian Regional Integration Center 2021).

In 2001, China along with Laos, Myanmar, and Thailand held a ministerial-level meeting on drug trafficking that was publicised under the Beijing Declaration. In 2002, China and ASEAN signed a joint declaration of cooperation in non-traditional security areas, which specified issues of cooperation between the two sides, including drugs, arms and human trafficking, piracy, terrorism, money laundering, and internet crime (Ministry of Foreign Affairs 2002). In the Declaration on the Conduct of Parties in the South China Sea signed between China and ASEAN in 2002, Beijing pledged to cooperate with various parties concerned with marine environmental protection, sea search and rescue operations, and anti-piracy (China.org 2012).

The AFC in 1997–1998 also offered an important opportunity for China to cut its teeth in regional multilateralism. Criticism of World Bank and IMF initiatives to support the region in the wake of the AFC facilitated the establishment of the ASEAN + 3 grouping. Partly in this context, China's commitment not to devalue its currency elevated Beijing in the views of most ASEAN countries, which increasingly regarded China as a responsible major power that respected their interests (Cheng 2013). The ASEAN + 3 grouping and the later developed East Asia Summit (EAS) demonstrated that China's active participation in regional economic cooperation contributed to a strengthening of regional identification and common interests.

In more recent years, as a rising superpower, China has upgraded its efforts in providing positive input towards East Asian political and economic cohesion and progress. Chief among these initiatives has been the launch of China's BRI which has served as an important showcase in helping countries understand what kind of multilateral role China intends to play. To explore China's new model of 'win-win' cooperation, the BRI's doctrine has been to welcome collective inputs from other regional countries' joint initiatives and existing multilateral institutions (Soong 2019).

Furthermore, Beijing has recognised that BRI should serve as only one among other East Asian cooperative agendas. As such, China's government has not intended for it to dominate or replace other initiatives and efforts, other than constructively promoting connections with other such policy measures. By this means, China has begun to accord with the collective actions of Southeast Asian countries in bringing the AEC to fruition in 2015. Beijing has also increasingly supported ASEAN to play a leading role in East Asia networking activities (such as the annual EAS, ARF and the bi-annual Asia-Europe Meeting).

As for the development of China-ASEAN relations, one indication of significant multilateralism has been their cooperation in initiatives in accordance with the 'ASEAN Way' approach (Hernandez 2008). For instance, China and ASEAN agreed to negotiate their FTA in 2000 and completed the full agreement in 2010, which contributed substantially to boosting their economic relations. China and ASEAN have also worked together in handling many SCS incidents in a gradualist and cooperative fashion.

As a result, China has taken a markedly different approach to SCS disputes from 2000 onwards, in contrast to its more belligerent and unilateralist measures in the mid-1990s. In the 2002 Declaration on the CoC, China has committed to resolve disputes peacefully while pushing for joint exploitation of oil and gas reserves in the SCS without abandoning sovereignty claims to the region. These changes are reflected in several joint resource exploration programmes China has since conducted with Vietnam and the Philippines. A final CoC that would assume a mandatory reference in SCS disputes has been targeted for 2021 (The Geopolitics 2020).

Similar constructive levels of engagement have also been applied to China's disputes with Japan in the ECS. With this in mind, the two governments signed an in-principle agreement to jointly exploit the resources in the disputed maritime region.

China was also the first of ASEAN's dialogue partners in agreeing to a Treaty of Amity and Cooperation (TAC) with Southeast Asia (Embassy of China in US 2003), alongside forging a framework agreement for comprehensive economic cooperation with ASEAN (ASEAN 2015) and a Protocol to the Treaty on a Southeast Asian Nuclear Weapons Free Zone.

For Beijing, important elements of its regional geostrategic and security goals are focused on the issues of how to cope with Washington's attempts at dominance in the region and of hedging against US efforts at containment using China's neighbours. China has responded to the challenges by adopting a policy of actively supporting and participating in mainly ASEAN-centred regional institutions and groupings, in addition to its own regionally-developmental multilateral initiatives such as the BRI and East Asian co-founded institutions such as the CMIM.

From an economic perspective, and one which is no less strategically important for Beijing, has been its interest in developing regional financial stability and economic integration. Again, ASEAN-centrality has been key in this regard — its latest manifestation being the RCEP, a free trade agreement which began largely as an ASEAN initiative but becoming an increasingly China-sponsored multilateral agreement.

As China's economic and political relations have steered towards ASEAN, and the same in reverse, other regional countries, including

Japan, South Korea, Australia, and New Zealand, have begun to increasingly gravitate towards this powerful emerging economic grouping. The next step may well be for China to secure even broader regional economic and geostrategic multilateral roles by pivoting to ASEAN-centrality, and based on its strong bilateral relations with some of these countries, to advance its interests in the greater Asia-Pacific region through forums such as CPTPP, APEC, and others.

The Significance of ASEAN + 3 in Shaping China's Future Multilateralism

In a 2019 report issued by the Washington-based think tank the Centre for Strategic and International Studies (CSIS), its survey of nearly 200 non-government experts in international relations across Southeast Asia found an overwhelmingly ascendant Chinese political influence in the region. In pursuing a stable and cooperative regional order, China and its East Asian neighbours will need to concentrate on working together within the framework of the ASEAN + 3 as a means of comprehensively and effectively handling their ongoing disputes and burgeoning cooperation agendas.

The most problematic issue in achieving this involves the US as a major power in the region allied with many countries there, particularly as Washington policymakers now view China as a global strategic rival and the greatest threat to democracy since the Second World War. Japan, as an ally of the US, also appears reluctant to accept China's role as a principal security player in a regional multilateral setting.

Moving from a security order dominated by traditional global powers to a new order based on regional collective leadership and equal participation will therefore likely be a long process of seismic transformation. There is neither complete consensus nor a ready model for this new security architecture.

In this context, Beijing is well aware of ASEAN's importance to its strategy of building a new type of security order for a shared future based on collective efforts. As an invaluable support, China's perspective on ASEAN has not been affected by the differences and disputes that have arisen with some of its member states concerning the SCS. To face the challenges that are emerging, it is especially important for China and ASEAN relations to strengthen further. Only then can East Asia flourish as China and ASEAN constitute core elements in the collective leadership of East Asia.

Also from this perspective, if there is a greater shift towards stabilising influences in China's relations with East Asia, the prime mover will probably be ASEAN + 3 as a consensus-driven bloc. Indeed, the idea of ASEAN-centrality is strongly backed by several important powers outside of East Asia, including India, Russia, and Australia. Even some elements in US policymaking circles have begun to recognise the significance of ASEAN-centrality, albeit from the point of view of lessening China's regional role, such as in attributing the principal role into ASEAN in finalising the RCEP negotiations.

Many developments further indicate that China intends to continue adhering to an ASEAN + 3 regional policy framework in the foreseeable future. These include improved bilateral relationships with all China's neighbouring states, growing support for new forms of regional economic cooperation, and more active participation in multilateral security and economic arrangements.

At some stage, the key to China's future relations with East Asia will be tested in how Beijing handles the issue of Taiwan. By treating Taiwan as a solely internal matter, Beijing has precluded the possibility of turning towards a region-specific multilateral-based resolution of the situation.

On an issue as sensitive as this, it may at the very least serve Beijing well to direct its future approach to one that guarantees a peaceful resolution of Taiwan's position based on the tenets of multilateral codes of conduct China is aiming to successfully conclude with ASEAN by 2021.

How these negotiations play out to relieve the region of decades-long SCS disputes may set the platform by which other regional simmering tensions are resolved. Should such a collectivist balance of interests materialise, then China's concurrent bilateral and multilateral policy endeavours through the ASEAN + 3 grouping will have evolved into a global force, let alone a regional one.

Chapter 10

Russia and India: China's Eurasian Dream and Indo-Pacific Nightmare?

China and Russia: Common Interests Revitalise a Former Friendship

Throughout much of the Cold War era, China was a key ally of the Soviet Union. During this period, a Sino-Soviet policy was engineered to expand the economic ideology of state socialism and the political dominance of their respective communist parties.

Ultimately, the Sino-Soviet alliance fell apart. It became evident that China's then-leader Mao Zedong grew disenchanted with his junior role in the relationship as then-Soviet Premier Nikita Khrushchev was unwilling to acknowledge China to be a power of equal status with the Soviets (Li and Xia 2018).

In the twenty-first century, China and Russia's leaders have reformulated their relations. Their ties are no longer based on a formal alliance of the Cold War era, but an ever closer and strategically important partnership founded on multiple levels of cooperation (Savic 2016). The key driver of this reinvigorated relationship between these once bitterly-divided rivals has been their increasingly shared interests in reshaping the US-centric global order that came into being at the end of the Cold War in the early 1990s (Bolt 2018).

Since that time, the US military and its network of alliances have sprawled across Asia and Europe as constant reminders of Washington's encroachment into Beijing's and Moscow's respective backyards. For China, the uncomfortable US military presence is most evident in the South China Sea, Japan, and the Korean peninsula which is not too distant from Beijing. For Russia, the US threat is in Ukraine, the Black Sea region, and the Baltic States, an even closer distance to the country's second city of St Petersburg.

There is general consensus among geopolitical observers that Chinese President Xi Jinping and Russian President Vladimir Putin view America's foreign policy as actively seeking to undermine their systems of political and economic governance, and ultimately desirous of 'regime change' (O'Keefe and Mauldin 2020; Burns 2017).

Indeed, both leaders, who regularly meet in person or converse by phone, reportedly compare notes on how Washington plots to undermine their regimes.

The growing East-West divide became the subject of an official US national security document issued in 2018. Then-Defence Secretary James 'Mad Dog' Mattiss of the Trump administration authored a re-designed US national defence strategy for the twenty-first century. In a publicly-released, summarised version of a much longer classified document, it announced a switch in policy focus from America's near two-decade 'War on Terror' to one of great power rivalry. The new policy officially designated China and Russia as America's 'strategic competitors' and 'revisionist powers' (US Department of Defense 2018).

Both Xi and Putin came to power within six months of each other in early 2013. For Xi, his term in office was the beginning of a maximum two five-year leadership of the nation — a formal time limit instituted since the end of the Mao era. In 2018, this was constitutionally amended when Xi was proclaimed as China's President-for-life. For Putin, late-2012 marked his second consecutive two-terms in office. This followed a four-year break from his elected back-to-back administrations over 2000 to 2008. But Putin amended the Russian constitution through a referendum in 2020. This enabled him to serve more consecutive terms in office, and potentially up until 2036.

These unprecedented constitutional changes that extended the governance of both countries' incumbent leaders (Litinova and Moritsugu 2020) are unlikely to be a mere coincidence. The constitutional revisions are reflective of a coordinated approach. Both these leaders aspire to preside over the emergence of a newly evolving multi-polar world order.

Their version of a re-sculptured global system will be one where the two countries' twenty-first century partnership is at the centre of reformed global institutions and re-defined sets of international relations. At the heart of the two countries' relations are the two leaders' personal ties — a growing magnetic attraction which cannot be underplayed in how the story of China and Russia's partnership unfolds. As Putin once famously noted, the only leader in the world with whom he had celebrated his birthday is Xi (Gan 2018). In reciprocating, Xi awarded Putin with China's 'Medal of Friendship', calling the Russian president his 'best, most intimate friend' (Lemon 2018).

The two leaders' bonhomie has been fuelled by their regular visits to one another's home cities. Xi has visited Moscow more than any other capital city since he assumed power. Xi and Putin have met on about 30 separate occasions in the six years leading to 2019 (Xinhuanet 2019e). They coordinate their positions on almost every major international issue. For example, when voting in the United Nations Security Council, they accord about four-fifths of the time (European Parliament 2013), more than any other pairing of permanent Security Council members.

Both heads of state have also worked together to strengthen the UN, through which they coordinate their principal foreign policy interests. At the same time, they have created new multilateral institutions as alternatives or complements to US-led international organisations. The most notable ones include the SCO and BRICS.

In terms of foreign trade, Russia is quickly pivoting eastwards to China. Moscow's main source of global project finance is China, which has displaced the US and Europe since the West's imposition of sanctions in 2014 and following years (Hong Kong TDC 2018). Direct investment flows could indeed be even greater since China tends to direct finance through financial entrepots such as Hong Kong, the Caribbean, and other offshore hubs.

Since 2014, China has also become the top buyer of Russian crude oil. A decade ago, all oil and gas pipelines flowed westwards across Russia into Europe. Since the completion of the eastwards-oriented Power of Siberia pipeline in 2019, China has become the second largest market for Russian gas behind Germany. As their economic and institutional linkages grow, Chinese and Russian national security documents refer to their relationship as a 'Comprehensive Strategic Partnership'. According to Xi, 'we share a high degree of consensus on the strategic significance of the China-Russia relationship'.

Russia's Foreign Ministry describes their relations as one based on 'comprehensive, equal, and trust-based partnership and strategic cooperation'. Moreover, Putin has characterised Russia's role in this partnership as one where 'they [China] are vying for global leadership and Russia is not going to race China on this' — a far cry from the Sino-Soviet split of the 1960s. Both countries' ever closer international cooperation since 2013 has not only been generally complementary in their range of activities, but also been increasingly about bolstering each other's shared interests on regional and global stages.

The New Era of Strategic Partnership

Beijing and Moscow have largely formulated their economic and political relations based on an evolving series of strategic partnerships. While neither country has a 'model' strategic partnership, both China and Russia employ several core principles which underpin their formal relations.

Since the Cold War's end, China and Russia's relations began to gradually mend. New relations were marked by ongoing bilateral diplomacy including partnership accords in 1994 and 1996 followed by the 2001 Treaty of Friendship and Cooperation. The Comprehensive Strategic Partnership of Cooperation in 2012, 'the 2012 Strategic Partnership', was a further landmark. It was underpinned by China's five main principles of peaceful coexistence, including mutual respect for sovereignty and territorial integrity, mutual non-aggression, mutual benefit, and equality. The document also specified several key economic targets in their bilateral development.

The 2012 Strategic Partnership was ratified by China's then-President Hu Jintao and Putin. It was intended to serve as the basis of their relations over a 10-year period (China Embassy 2012). Notably, it was superseded by a 2014 bilateral agreement, 'the 2014 Strategic Partnership', calling for a new stage in relations. The 2014 Strategic Partnership was the brainchild of Xi who used it to quickly signal his desire for an intensification of bilateral relations involving economic, political, and security ties (Ministry of Foreign Affairs 2015b). It was also symbolically poignant given the 2014 Strategic Partnership was set up almost immediately after Russia had annexed Crimea and its consequent strained relations with the West.

Mega-Project Diplomacy

Some of the numerous much vaunted commercial transactions arising from the 2014 Strategic Partnership involved a long-term US$400 billion gas supply agreement (Anishchuk 2014). The so-called 'eastern route' was agreed between the countries' two main energy giants, Russia's state-owned domestic gas production monopoly Gazprom and state-controlled China National Petroleum Corporation (CNPC), one of China's big three oil companies. Another pivotal deal agreed between both sides was for Russia to build the 'Power of Siberia' pipeline; a project which was alluded to in the 2014 Strategic Partnership as a means of consolidating the newfound dynamic Sino-Russian energy relationship.

One other mammoth energy agreement between CNPC and Russia's largest state-owned oil company, Rosneft, also came into existence around the same time. This deal involved Russia's supplying oil worth up to US$270 billion and would prospectively enable Russia to become China's largest international supplier of oil. Shortly after in 2016, Russia displaced Saudi Arabia as China's number one source for oil imports. Russia also fast became one of China's largest providers of natural gas accounting for nearly half of China's demand for overseas gas supplies mainly through its Power of Siberia pipeline. In 2020, Russia also announced plans to begin working on a second eastward pipeline, the 'Power of Siberia 2' (Reuters 2020b).

There is little sign of giant China-Russian projects abating any time in the near future. Both sides continue to convey greater interest in fusing their economies through more mega-projects. If anything, China's appetite appears to be growing for more financial risk burden-sharing over future projects across Russia. This is in stark contrast to their initial mega-deals where Russia took on the bulk of financing risks, particularly in building energy infrastructure to connect with China. One example is the start of construction for an US$11 billion polymer facility in the Amur region of the Russian Far East (Kantchev 2020).

Branded as one of the largest polymer plants in the world, the mega-project aims to manufacture plastic components destined for China's growing consumer-related market. Politically, the project has been showcased as a display of expanding bilateral trade relations and involves another one of China's main three state-owned oil companies, Sinopec. The Chinese entity will hold a 40% stake in the joint venture, alongside Russia's Sibur Holding, being the country's largest petrochemicals concern. The plant will be scheduled to begin production in 2024. It is also part of the countries' growing trend of setting up new industry-related initiatives to deepen ties amid the growing coronavirus pandemic and escalating global geopolitical tensions.

Financial and Trade Cooperation

The People's Bank of China (PBOC) and the Central Bank of Russia (CBR) agreed to substantial currency swap arrangements to facilitate settlements in their national currencies (Bank of Russia 2016). This swap was the first to be set up with a country outside of the Asian region where the idea was to boost bilateral trade and reduce reliance on the US dollar for international transactions.

Although setbacks have cropped up in their attempts to diversify away from the dollar, the two countries have pushed forward in conducting more of their trade in their own currencies. CBR data indicates the dollar's share of bilateral trade fell below 50% in 2020 for the first time on record. This is in contrast to more than 90% of trade in 2014. In spite of the dollar's decline, the Chinese and Russian currencies still only account for a relatively small proportion of their bilateral trade as the Euro has become the main alternative currency to the dollar in their transactions.

Bilateral trade also grew from US$70 billion in 2016 to over US$110 billion in 2019 in spite of a slowing global economy. Xi and Putin have also committed to a new target of US$200 billion in trade flows by 2024 (Keegan 2019). There are signs that as trade volumes grow so does Russia's variety of exports to China. Energy has historically accounted for 70% of Russia's export, although the portfolio is diversifying into nuclear power systems, aviation, agricultural commodities, food products, and other sectors increasingly tapping into China's domestic consumer market.

Russia's Role in China's Belt and Road Initiative

Over the years 2014 to 2020, Russia was one of the top five destinations for Chinese foreign direct investment, especially in the energy infrastructure and petrochemicals sectors. Some of this was channelled under the umbrella of the BRI. Intergovernmental cooperation through official BRI channels has been instrumental in funding China's largest investments in Russia, including the earlier mentioned petrochemicals plant in Russia's Far East.

China's funding of this venture has been partially provided through the US$40 billion SRF, another BRI vehicle. The SRF has also supplied funding for the giant Yamal LNG project in the Russian Arctic. This was at a crucial time when Western sanctions severely crimped long-term debt finance to several major Russian energy companies involved in giant power projects.

China and Russia's economic relations have also been driven by various bilateral intergovernmental commissions and numerous sprouting sub-commissions as their ties have prospered. According to Putin, in spite of often slow progress in reaching agreements, both sides have invariably maintained a common goal of cooperation on a wide range of complex issues to eventually find a solution and bridge each other's culture gaps (Savic 2016).

Consumer and Technology Cooperation

On the joint consumer economy front, both sides have been expanding their bilateral interests. This has included cooperation on digital payment systems. In 2019, one of Russia's largest technology and social media companies, Yandex was the first online retailer to utilise China's WeChat Pay (East West Digital News 2018). China's AliPay also set up a joint venture operation with Russia's Mail.ru (*SCMP* 2019), offering digital payment services to Russian customers. If implemented by Russia, they would likely have to apply the same protocols as existing in China and provide Chinese officials with control of their mutual digital currency.

Russian banks are also the world's second largest users of China's Cross-Border Interbank Payment System (CIPS) (Russia Briefing 2019). The CIPS is widely used as an alternative to the Brussels-based SWIFT network. Advances in consumer technology and payments should also facilitate broader services interaction, particularly in facilitating tourism from China. In 2019, over 2 million Chinese visited Russia spending over US$1 billion in the country (OZY 2020).

In the telecommunications sector, China and Russia have also been deepening their cooperation. This is in spite of their governments' regulatory regimes being relatively similar in respect of limiting cross border data flows. Moreover, both governments have been pushing ahead with cooperation in digital infrastructure, just as Western governments led by the US are shunning Huawei. Undeterred by Western suspicions over the Chinese tech company, Russia has selected Huawei equipment in supporting its roll out of a 5G network (Doffman 2019) — an outcome celebrated with great fanfare in a ceremony timed with Xi's last visit to Moscow.

The two countries have been closely cooperating on alternative global navigation satellite systems to those of the West by having both commercial and military applications. China's BeiDou and Russia's GLONASS satellite networks launched an agreement in 2018 to test equipment along BRI hubs by hosting one another's base stations (Cozzens 2019). However, both governments' adherence to internet sovereignty and protection of personal data will not likely facilitate their jointly becoming broader regional communications hubs beyond their borders.

Harmonising the BRI with Russia's EAEU and Beyond

As a result of the 2014 Strategic Partnership and as personal ties between Xi and Putin have significantly strengthened, the two leaders have engaged upon a historic expansion of bilateral ties which have been progressing in fields outside of economic relations. Much of their coordinated efforts have focused on developing essential 'core interests' involving often complex areas of foreign policy. Most notably was the announcement at the annual parade commemorating the 'Great Patriotic War in defeating European and Japanese fascism' in May 2015, which called for the harmonisation of the Chinese-led BRI with Russia's Eurasian Economic Union (EAEU) (Inozemtsev 2019).

Beijing's policy of integrating the BRI — across Central Asia, the Caucasus, and other parts of the former Soviet Union — with Moscow's EAEU at the time presented a picture of China-Russia relations where the objective was adaptation to the needs' of each partner. This was a policy approach starkly at variance with the EU's Eastern Partnership programme which required a revocation of former Soviet states' formal trade and economic affiliations with Russia. Not only did this necessitate signing up to an economic association with the EU but also a political association which further pushed former Soviet states transitioning into the EU programme away from their traditional diplomatic and political ties with Russia.

Xi and Putin further consolidated their carefully manicured and intensifying bilateral ties at several global and regional summits in 2015, including at the BRICS development summit in Goa, India in October 2015. They put forward their plans to enhance cooperation at various other regional and global fora over a pivotal couple of years as they cemented their newfound partnership coordination within various multilateral organisations.

For instance, at the G20 Hangzhou Summit in 2016, the China-Russia dialogue was treated as the highest of priorities by both Xi and Putin. The interactions focused on carving out various sets of principles, including the rule of law that would regulate and govern two-way investment between the two nations. This involved other significant commercial structural issues such as state-backed funding of cross border infrastructure and other projects, and also investments in privatised state companies, general investment, and intellectual property protections.

China and Russia's coordinated integration of the BRI and EAEU has also facilitated the development of the SCO. While the SCO is an institution founded and managed separately to the BRI and EAEU, it has nevertheless gained global and regional prestige as an influential intergovernmental organisation which embodies the rise of the transcontinental concept and territorial space increasingly referred to as Eurasia.

Within that context, India and Pakistan took on full membership of the organisation in 2017. In 2019, the integration of China and Russia's signature international development programmes led to the first stage of their 'Greater Eurasia Partnership' as both the EAEU and China agreed to implement a free trade area between them in the near future. The idea is for this economic integration to be mirrored further afield across Eurasia to eventually conjoin with Southeast Asia, South Asia, the Middle East, and Africa.

Increasingly, various other co-development formats have marked pivotal changes in China-Russia relations which continue to expand outside of exclusively economic and political spheres. These have included bilateral promotion of socio-cultural integration. For instance, in 2017's China-Russia Media Exchange Year, both countries' mainly state-run media have been earmarked to become indispensable platforms of conveying information and communications to each other countries' publics about their government's coordinated efforts at strategic partnership.

In that vein, China's National People's Congress and the two chambers of the Russian Parliament have undertaken in-depth and focused campaigns to actively build an understanding of their respective institutions and how they function. This has involved various supervisory and legislative initiatives setting up programmes and policies for exchanges of guidance and information in both countries' municipal, provincial, and national level development policies, particularly for advancing their higher-end industrial, technology, and resource sectors (Russia State Duma 2020).

Expanding Security and Military Ties

Another aspect of China and Russia's growing cooperation has recently involved a significant upgrade of their mutual defence and geostrategic interests. One of the most prominent outcomes in their joint approach to international security has been their opposition to the deployment of the THAAD missile defence system in South Korea. In warning that THAAD risked provoking an Asia-Pacific nuclear and anti-ballistic missile free for all, they accelerated their coordinated exercises in warfare including joint naval manoeuvres that were held in the SCS for the first time in their respective nations' histories. In 2019, both sides also began joint air patrols of the SCS and the ECS (Gady 2017).

China and Russia's military cooperation has expanded to geographic theatres outside of East Asia. In 2017, their navies conducted joint exercises in the Baltic Sea for the first time. In 2018, China participated in Russia's annual Vostok 'Eastward' military exercises. China's People's Liberation Army (PLA) also took part in Russia's giant Tsentr 'Centre' military drills in 2019 which took place across the entire country (Ellyat 2019). In 2020, the PLA participated in the Kavkaz 'Caucasus' strategic military manoeuvres involving joint strike and battlefield control exercises near the central Asian region of Russia's Astrakhan (Clark 2020).

All these jointly-held exercises have been held on the basis of what both sides' security institutions — China's Central Military Commission (CMC) and Russia's Defence Ministry — have publicly stated, which is that the existence of a complex international security picture has required ever closer cooperation and interaction between their respective militaries. In the development of their military forces, China and Russia have largely complementary operational needs.

As a result, they have been working together in developing new military capabilities. These have included space, missile technologies, unmanned systems, and training data for artificial intelligence. They have also looked to fill mutual capability gaps in their respective defence sectors and to accelerate the development of innovative technologies. Their militaries have begun to cooperate in more sensitive domains such as theatre hypersonic weapons, submarine technology, and space-based and undersea sensor technology. As their cooperation has expanded into higher tech sectors, they have begun supporting one another in mitigating the increasing line-up of US sanctions and restrictions on technology exports.

Russia has also furnished China with advanced weapons systems, including its S-400 surface-to-air missile system with China being the first country to receive this ground-breaking state-of-the-art Russian defence system (Tass 2019). Russia's Su-35 fighter jets have also enabled China to more effectively mobilise forces around its coastal provinces and near-shore areas, including Taiwan (*The National Interest* 2020).

Through combined military exercises and training which have grown in frequency, geographic reach, and overall coverage, Russia has provided China with operational training being designed to offset the Chinese military's lack of practical experience. As bilateral relations deepen further, their cooperation has begun to increasingly take place off reported channels. The announcement that Russia was providing China with its advanced early warning missile detection system was not expected in Western circles — underscoring the increasingly discreet nature of their intensifying cooperation.

The Russian government has also indirectly backed China's SCS claims (Tass 2016), such as supporting Beijing's stance in opposing interference from non-region powers such as the US and UK. In parallel, China voiced sympathetic and understanding views in relation to Russia's annexation of Crimea (European Council on Foreign Relations 2015). Beijing also supported in principle Russian military involvement during the Syrian conflict while sending arms to the Syrian government and reiterated its position for the war to be settled through political negotiation. In Venezuela, for instance, Russia provided arms transfers on credit and supplied Venezuela's government with updated armoured and air capabilities. Meanwhile, China transferred some weapons alongside surveillance technology and funding for military support to the country.

A Growing Partnership of Unequals?

The yawning economic gap between China and Russia could see a faltering of their relations at some point in the future. At the end of the Cold War, China's economy was about two and a half times the size of Russia's. This was mainly attributable to a precipitous drop in GDP as the Soviet economy literally collapsed. Yet, by end 2019 that gap was even greater as China's economy was worth US$14.3 trillion or roughly 16% of the global economy (Visual Capitalist 2019). Russia's GDP was only US$1.7 trillion, having also shrunk in nominal terms due to the steep fall of the Russian currency over 2014 to 2015.

The divergent economic growth trends have also exacerbated differences in their economic performance. China's growth rates exceed those of Russia's by more than four times. These yawning gaps in economic conditions may accentuate an imbalance in their capacity to project power and potentially leading to rifts in their respective global ambitions. On the other hand, as long as Xi and Putin stay in power for the foreseeable future, these two leaders will have little incentive to disturb the trajectory of their seemingly close and mutually beneficial partnership.

The initial stages of the coronavirus pandemic may also have been a source of friction between the two sides in early 2020. Russia abruptly closed its 4,200-kilometre border with China while disagreements over Moscow government's controversial pandemic measures targeting Chinese residents in the Russian capital could also have damaged relations for a brief period of time (*The Moscow Times* 2020).

Top-Down Is Turning to Bottom-Up

It is not just the leaderships of these countries which have an affinity for each other. Improving perceptions of China are becoming evident among the Russian public. In a 2019 international poll of peoples' attitudes towards other countries, over two-thirds of Russians held a positive view of China (Pew Research Center 2019). This is in contrast to less than a fifth who held a negative opinion.

While China received the most favourable view from Russian citizens than any other country, it also recorded the lowest unfavourable ratings from the Russian public. Meantime, China's government constantly portrays a highly-positive message of Russia to their population, especially through their state-run media and its endorsement of mass tourism to the country.

What may undermine the China-Russia relationship may arise more from its successes than its failures. As economic integration accelerates giving rise to greater volumes of cross border worker migration, there have been more reported instances of public protests in opposition to the increased presence of Chinese workers and businesses in Russia.

The regions most affected have been the sparsely-populated Russian Far East and parts of southern Siberia. Widespread demonstrations across these regions erupted when a locally-elected governor representing Russia's nationalist party and the main opposition to Putin's ruling

United Russia party was removed from office by the Kremlin in 2019. There have also been reported demonstrations over Chinese investments on Lake Baikal in the Russian Far East and logging projects in Siberia's forests (*The Straits Times* 2019a).

COVID-19 and US Tensions Shift China Closer to Russia

Both countries have announced joint scientific cooperation geared toward testing vaccines for COVID-19. It is a further sign of the long-term trend of fusing each country's rising economic importance to each other. At China's annual National People's Congress meeting of legislators in 2020, Chinese Foreign Minister Wang Yi stated that the two countries would stand 'shoulder to shoulder' (Xinhuanet 2020b) against US attempts to lay the blame of responsibility on China for the pandemic's consequences. In response, both sides established the years 2020 and 2021 to become the China-Russia Year of Scientific and Technological Innovation. The initiative was designed to fast-track exchanges in advanced technology, research and development of vaccines and drugs, and fostering bio-security.

While the pandemic has made China an even more invaluable economic lifeline for Moscow, the latter has become a more needed security partner for Beijing. This is particularly as China came under pressure throughout President Trump's administration on multiple fronts, including over trade, technology, Hong Kong, Taiwan, and the SCS.

Both sides have exhibited quiet support for one another with regards to geopolitical flashpoints throughout 2020. In particular, Moscow stressed that China's efforts to safeguard national security in Hong Kong was a purely internal matter. Meanwhile, China's PLA attended the 75th year of the Victory Parade in Moscow despite it being initially cancelled due to the pandemic. Clearly, the recent new dynamics in their relationship are somewhat of a turnaround following Russia's annexation of Crimea in 2014, when Moscow essentially fell back on Beijing for financial, economic, and political support. In 2020, it was China rather than Russia which openly exhibited more enthusiasm in forging ahead with closer ties.

Yet, there is little sign that Washington's policies targeting either of these states — since 2014 for Russia and 2016 for China — are likely to be reversed by forthcoming US administrations. As long as the US national defence strategy is set on identifying both countries as national security threats and 'strategic competitors', China and Russia will likely continue to seek closer relations in order to fend off US provocations in nearby and neighbouring states and regions, in addition to disparaging their state-oriented systems of governance.

China and India: Intensifying Turbulence Amid Ongoing Mutual Interests and Dialogue

Historical Connections

China-India cultural exchanges date back to around 1500 BCE during their respective Shang-Zhou and Vedic civilisations (Tan and Geng 2005). In the first three centuries CE, numerous Buddhist scholars and pilgrims visited China along the ancient Silk Route. Renowned religious scholars from India, including Dharmakshema, Kumarajiva, and Bodhidharma, spread Buddhist teachings across China.

Chinese pilgrims also travelled to India; some of the most celebrated were Fa Zian and Xuan Zang. Indeed, the ancient civilisational connections between China and India are represented by a Buddhist temple in China's Henan province. The White Horse Monastery there is often referred to as the 'cradle of Buddhism in China', being the abode of Indian monks during the third century BCE.

Their modern-day relations began in 1950 with India becoming the first non-aligned country outside of the Communist bloc to forge official diplomatic ties with China. In 1954, India's then-Prime Minister Jawaharlal Nehru was the country's first premier to visit China. In the same year, China's Premier Zhou Enlai visited India (Keith 1989). Under their respective leaderships, both countries committed to the Five Principles of Peaceful Coexistence which emphasises equality, mutual benefit, mutual trust, and respect for sovereignty and territoriality.

In 1955, Zhou and Nehru participated in the Asian-African Conference in Bandung, Indonesia. This event advocated the Bandung Spirit of friendship, cooperation, and solidarity among the essentially developing countries of these continents. Several years later in 1962, the two countries' border conflict set back bilateral ties (Verma 2016). However, by 1976, China and India re-established diplomatic ties leading to gradually better relations. Then-Indian Prime Minister Rajiv Gandhi's historic visit in 1988 to China signalled the onset of a new era in normalised bilateral ties. At the same time, the two countries negotiated a solution to their territorial dispute.

In 1993 during then-Indian Prime Minister Narasimha Rao's travel to China, both countries' assent to the Agreement on the Maintenance of Peace and Tranquillity along the Line of Actual Control supported the increasing stability in their mutual relations. In 1996, then-Chinese President Jiang Zemin visited India and they agreed to engage in a constructive partnership of cooperation for the twenty-first century. In support of this, they agreed on setting up Confidence Building Measures in the Military Field along the Line of Actual Control.

During then-Indian Prime Minister Atal Bihari Vajpayee's 2003 visit to China, both sides settled on the Declaration on Principles for Relations and Comprehensive Cooperation and appointed Special Representatives to explore the framework of a boundary agreement. In its wake, over 20 rounds of talks were held. Altogether, both countries have developed over 50 dialogue platforms covering economic, political, and consular issues, in addition to dialogues on regional and global issues. Within this detailed framework, both countries' foreign ministers meet on a regular basis (Nation 2018).

Recent Bilateral Diplomacy

China's Foreign Minister Wang Yi visited India in 2018 to attend the first high-level gathering on people-to-people and cultural exchanges (Xinhuanet 2018c). Then-Indian External Affairs Minister Sushma Swaraj also visited China in that year. In so doing, she participated at the SCO's Council of Foreign Ministers meetings while holding bilateral discussions with Wang Yi and China's Vice President Wang Qishan.

When China's President Xi Jinping visited India in 2014, bilateral ties were elevated to a Closer Development Partnership. Also arising from that official trip were more than 16 agreements. These covered a range of areas such as trade, commerce, space cooperation, railways, pharmaceuticals, the establishment of industrial parks, and city twinning projects. A Memorandum of Understanding (MoU) also looked to open the Nathula route for an ancient Indian pilgrimage (Indian Ministry of External Affairs 2014). Indian Prime Minister Narendra Modi visited China in 2015 and addressed the opening session of the First State and Provincial Leaders' Forum in Beijing.

Accordingly, two dozen inter-government agreements were signed. These included accords on tackling climate change alongside 26 business sector agreements; Modi announced the extension of an e-visa facility for Chinese tourists travelling to India (Ministry of Foreign Affairs 2016). This was on top of, during then-Indian President Pranab Mukherjee's state visit to China in 2016 including Guangdong province and Beijing, where up to 10 MoUs in the fields of research and education were agreed (Ministry of Foreign Affairs 2016).

Xi and Modi's Strained Relationship-Building

Since coming to power in their respective countries, both Xi and Modi have often taken their bilateral relationship-building to positive new levels, albeit punctuated with tensions over military-to-military border clashes in areas that are legacies of historical disputes carried over from the British Empire's arbitrary delineations of international borders.

For the most part, Xi and Modi have exercised cordial and constructive ties, including hosting 16 bilateral meetings for one another since 2014. They have met on five separate occasions at the sidelines of multilateral gatherings, including Modi's visit to China in 2018 to participate in the Hangzhou G20 Summit. At the time, Xi and Modi reaffirmed their respective countries' development ambitions as opportunities rather than threats. Also in that year, Xi attended the BRICS summit in Goa, India where similar reassurances were exchanged (Hawkins 2018).

Perhaps the most eye-catching series of diplomatic events between Xi and Modi was their so-called 'hometown diplomacy'. The two leaders agreed to significantly enhance efforts in their bilateral convergence by holding informal summits at distinctive venues in their home states.

The first informal summit — held at Wuhan, China in 2018 — enabled both sides to reach broad consensus on long term and strategic issues. These included matters of global and bilateral significance and each leader's respective vision for national development (Indian Ministry of External Affairs 2018). The informal meeting also included dialogue on policy coordination, environmental protection, healthcare and medicine, energy conservation, infrastructure, technology, and energy resource development.

Various dialogue mechanisms were set up including joint groups on economic relations, science and technology; a strategic economic dialogue on macroeconomic cooperation including infrastructure, environment, energy, technology, and policy coordination; China's State Council Development Research Centre on global economic cooperation; the India-China Financial Dialogue; and a series of other institutional arrangements including on information and communications technology, industrial park cooperation, agriculture, skills development, and vocational education.

At the last informal summit — held at Mamallapuram, Chennai in 2019 — Xi and Modi reaffirmed the Wuhan consensus and concluded in working towards a closer partnership in their joint development efforts. They also agreed to promote mutually beneficial cooperation in various fields, enhance in-depth strategic communication, and advance the process of mutual learning and exchanges between two 'ancient civilisations' (Indian Ministry of External Affairs 2018). In practical terms, this involved setting up a high-level mechanism on trade and economic cooperation. Subsequently in that year, several dialogues were held in both New Delhi and Beijing on skills development, pharmaceuticals, finance, and trade in services.

The last dialogue at the Development Research Centre in Wuhan, China was held towards the end of 2019. Here, the two sides reached agreements on striving for high quality and sustainable industrial development. This included seeking measures to reform global governance mechanisms, upholding multilateral trade institutions and measures, amid securing the means of safeguarding against global financial and economic instability (Xinhuanet 2019f).

Intergovernmental and Political Exchanges

In spite of the international media's portrayal of heightened mistrust and intensive frictions between both countries' political administrations, the reality of relations is somewhat more complex than this media depiction. Each country's government ministries, political parties, and legislatures actively engage in ongoing high-level exchanges and shared governance experiences. For instance, inter-parliamentary friendship groups maintain regular contacts and meetings between leading and specialised working groups of both national parliaments. As a result, numerous members of parliament from China and India have engaged in official visits to each other's government institutions over the last decade.

The International Department of the Central Committee of the CCP and India's Ministry of External Affairs continue to set up new visits, although they are suspended during the COVID-19 pandemic. These below-the-radar exchange mechanisms have evolved into a groundbreaking format by which to secure long term bilateral political mutual trust, foster interaction between both countries' provincial and state-level apparatus, amid enhancing various means of working together in a range of policy areas. They also serve as an insurance policy against headline-grabbing and highly-emotive disputes which might derail their vital long-term relationship building.

As examples of this discreet — some say 'behind-the-scenes' — diplomacy, the two countries have held several 'hand-in-hand' collaborations in tackling international terrorism amid promoting ongoing mutual trust in jointly improving their anti-terrorism capabilities (Gady 2015). China's and India's bilateral defence cooperation has also been growing steadily. There have been regular high-level exchanges between Defence Ministers and Service Chiefs, amid functional and military educational exchanges. Both countries have also held annual defence and security dialogues, although the last such dialogue was held in 2015.

For the most part — since a border clash in 2014 and the Doklam standoff in 2017 (*The Guardian* 2017) — peace along the border areas was maintained under the Working Mechanism for Consultations and Coordination of China-India Border Affairs in addition to a 2013 Border Defence Cooperation Agreement (Indian Ministry of External Affairs 2013). Generally peaceful and constructive border relations have been punctuated by bursts of rising levels of violence between the two sides' militaries. The last incident was the Galwan Valley clash in 2020 which reportedly left many dead on both sides, although the number of casualties was undisclosed by the Chinese (Duhalde *et al.* 2020).

Given the suspension of military dialogue on these border areas since 2015, it may not come as a surprise that such violence is likely to arise at some point in time. Perhaps there is no substitute to detailed bilateral discussions between the armed forces in averting their regular border clashes, in spite of seemingly improving ties at higher political levels?

Engagement in High-Level Multilateralism

On the international front, China and India are members of various multilateral institutions, including the Russia-India-China trilateral arrangement, BRICS, SCO, and the G20. Both countries also participate in a number of major Asian multilateral lending institutions. For instance, India became one of the first co-founding members of the China-launched AIIB in 2015. India is the AIIB's second largest shareholder behind China having an 8% shareholding in the bank, is a single member constituency on the board of directors, and has hosted the bank's third annual general meeting in Mumbai in 2018.

In 2020, India became the AIIB's top borrower receiving US$4.5 billion in funds; about one-third of the bank's approved loans was allocated to India (Krishnan 2020b). A further US$1 billion of borrowing was also in the pipeline during 2020; the funds were earmarked for mass metro rail systems in Delhi, Mumbai, and Chennai. India has been the main beneficiary of AIIB's COVID-19 related relief funding, receiving up to US$1.25 billion. The second tranche of the loan, amounting to US$750 million, was approved only two days after the Galwan Valley clash between Chinese and Indian troops (Asia Infrastructure Investment Bank 2020).

In what was the most serious physical conflict between the two sides since their brief war in the 1962, China's government was quick not to let the border tensions damage their relations more broadly. According to Sun Weidong, China's Ambassador to India, 'The boundary question is only part of China-India relations. We need to keep it in the larger picture of China-India relations and not let the boundary dispute affect the normal development of bilateral relations' (Haidar 2020).

China and India also co-founded the multilateral NDB of the BRICS countries. While the bank is headquartered in Shanghai, its first serving president, KV Kamath, was from India.

Burgeoning Economic Ties

India is China's 12th largest trade partner and 7th biggest export destination. China is India's second largest trade partner and third largest export market. The two countries' bilateral trade has been rapidly increasing since the early 1990s, when it was less than US$3 billion a year. In 2019, overall trade reached US$93 billion, although heavily in favour of China. In fact, two-thirds of India's overall trade deficit of US$57 billion was attributable to China as New Delhi's imports from China rose by 45 times over 20 years to 2019 (PTI Beijing 2019).

Just over half the value of India's imports from China arises from three sectors, namely electrical machinery, mechanical equipment for nuclear reactors, and organic chemicals. Otherwise, India's imports from China are typically manufactured goods including chemicals, mineral fuels and metals, electronics, furniture, mattresses, toys, watches, musical instruments, sporting goods, iron and steel products, and fertilisers.

India's top exports to China are organic chemicals, iron ore, unfinished diamonds, seafood, cotton, and granite stone. In recent years, India's exports of coffee, tea, and spices have experienced a steep increase, making it the largest exporter of these commodities to China. Other focused agricultural products have also been rising, such as sugar, rice, various fruits, and fish oil.

The endless trend in favour of China may be coming to an end though. In 2020, India's exports to China rose for most of that year relative to 2019. Meanwhile, China's exports to India correspondingly shrunk by a wide margin. It is also the second year in a row that India's trade deficit has declined since 2005.

Bilateral foreign direct investment (FDI) in the non-financial sector has been small relative to cross-border trade. According to China's Ministry of Commerce, the country's accumulated FDI in India stood at just over US$30 billion since 2005 amid a presence of over 1,000 companies. Even so, Chinese investment in India has been somewhat volatile on a year-to-year basis. It did advance quite strongly in 2018 and 2019, reaching US$3.8 billion and US$4.1 billion respectively (Kapoor 2020).

Most Chinese companies in India are invested in electrical equipment manufacturing, metallurgy, chemicals, renewable energy, automotive, smartphones, optical fibre, and construction equipment. The bulk of enterprises in these sectors tend to be state-owned holdings such as Sino Hydro, Sinosteel, Baoshan Iron & Steel, Chongqing Lifan Industry, Dongfang, Shougang, and Sany Heavy Industry. In 2020, mounting concerns arose over slowing FDI from China, due to a tightening of India's inward investment policy in that year following the Galwan Valley clash. Officially, investment restrictions were imposed to specifically control FDI from countries that share land borders with India through a designated government screening route.

Although no country was singled out as a major target for screening, the process by its very nature has implicitly made China the principal concern. The restrictive new rules may only end up being a temporary measure. Significant bilateral investment relations will continue to be realised over the longer term, particularly in areas of infrastructure and manufacturing that are of paramount interest to India's value-added economic upgrading. The drawback in restricting Chinese direct investment in India would be lacking in sufficient alternatives in compensating for its loss from other international sources.

China's Tech-Rush into India Stalls

China's investment in the Indian technology sector has been mainly led by private Chinese interests. These companies include some of China's most powerful tech giants, such as Huawei, ZTE, Haier, TCL, Oppo, Vivo, and Midea. Chinese investments involved in India's technology and public infrastructure sectors have come under the most scrutiny of any Chinese investor sources (Mankotia 2020).

Various mobile Chinese apps including WeChat, Vigo Video, ShareIt, UC Browser, Cam Scanner, PUBG, and popular short video app TikTok were banned in 2020 on account of threats to India's national security over their alleged connections to the Chinese government (Bhargava 2020). Half the country's app downloads were from Chinese owned-developers which saw a triple-digit increase in downloads from 2016 to 2018. India's government has also been targeting fintech startups for closure where they are considered to have connections with Chinese nationals or companies.

Chinese investments in Indian startups are otherwise booming, rising close to US$4 billion in 2019 from US$381 million in 2016 (Global Data 2020). The scale of these investments could have been higher, since Chinese funds are often routed through international hubs such as Singapore, Hong Kong, and Mauritius.

The majority of Indian startups worth over US$1 billion (referred to as 'unicorns') are supported by China's largest e-commerce tech companies such as Bytedance, Alibaba, and Tencent. Alibaba's giant affiliate, Ant Financial, has invested over US$2.6 billion in four Indian unicorns (Technology for You 2020). Its main Chinese rival, Tencent, has funded five unicorns in India up to US$2.4 billion. Several other high-profile Chinese investment houses have featured as investors in Indian tech companies, including Fosun, Didi Chuxing, Meituan-Dianping, Steadview Capital, SAIF Partners, China Lodging Group, Hillhouse Capital, and Sailing Capital.

Chinese smartphones such as Xiaomi, Vivo, and Oppo have penetrated the Indian mobile phone market with an accumulated national market share exceeding 72% (Counterpoint 2020). As a further sign of China's growing tech presence in India, several Chinese telecoms companies, alongside Huawei, have set up processing assemblies in major Indian industrial zones, including Andhra Pradesh, Noide, and Tamil Nadu (Kannan 2015). India's government has even given Huawei permission to conduct 5G initial operations in India, as the country's optical fibre sector sees rising investments from Chinese companies such as Hengtong, ZIT, and Fiberhome (Kazmin and Findlay 2020).

Even so, as the Indian government cuts contracts with numerous Chinese IT vendors, eventual restrictions on Huawei cannot be completely excluded. Outside the world of tech, major China automakers, such as YAPP autos, BYD auto, and MG motors, have been setting up manufacturing facilities in India (Chauhan 2020).

India's FDI into China, although comparatively much smaller at around US$1 billion in total, has been annually declining from US$26 million in 2018 to US$21 million in 2019. Most Indian companies are mainly located in Chinese tier one cities, namely Guangzhou, Shenzhen, Shanghai, and Beijing. The bulk of their operations are in manufacturing, such as pharmaceuticals, tubing, auto-parts, and renewable energy. Some of the more high-profile companies include Infosys, Mahindra & Mahindra, Adani Global, Tata, Binani Cement, Sundaram Fasteners, Essel Packaging, Jindal Steel, Bharat Heavy Electricals, Godrej & Boyce, Reliance Industries, Wipro, Bharat Forge, Suzlon Energy, Aurobindo Pharma, Matrix Pharma, TCS and Dr Reddy's Laboratories (Krishnan 2020a).

Simmering Economic Tensions

From another economic standpoint, India's backing away from the RCEP at end-2019 was largely driven by its unwillingness to open the country's manufacturing to lower-cost competitors such as China. The constantly ballooning trade deficit with China had become a major source of concern in bilateral ties, given it was India's largest trade deficit with any single country. To alleviate the politically-sensitive deficit, India has been ratcheting up its economic defences. This has included imposition of anti-dumping duties on various Chinese goods with a view to protecting domestic producers from cheap imports.

As a part of this process, nearly 400 Indian products have been subjected to new technical regulations of which about 150 measures are worth up to US$47 billion of imports from China (Bloomberg 2020a). This is on top of a raft of quality control orders which have been raised on sets of goods ranging from toys to air conditioners to chemicals. How China responds to these new trade and non-tariff barriers remains open to question, particularly in light of Beijing's support for ongoing free trade while benefiting from persistently sizeable trade surpluses with India.

CPEC and Quad: A Geopolitical Chessboard

On the geopolitical front, China-India bilateral tensions have been nervously simmering since 2015. The tensions are especially evident after Beijing announced its financial sponsorship of the US$46 billion China-Pakistan Economic Corridor (CPEC). Geographically, CPEC connects China to the Indian Ocean through Pakistan's southern port of Gwadar on the Arabian Sea. Prior to CPEC's entry into Pakistan, it passes through Gilgit-Baltistan, an area of Kashmir that is administered by Islamabad but also claimed by India. Currently, New Delhi administers the other part of Kashmir which is split into Ladakh and Jammu and Kashmir.

In 2019, Modi abolished the regions' autonomous status and left them directly under the control of the federal government, as New Delhi began to fret over regional instability amid China's increased backing of Pakistan's economy and its military. To allay India's concerns over CPEC crossing over Pakistan-controlled Kashmir, Beijing offered for New Delhi to join CPEC (PTI 2016). It has kept the offer open since 2016 while the Indian government remains unresponsive. Even so, the offer has not made India any more predisposed to CPEC.

India also sees Pakistan's Gwadar as a part of China's 'string of pearls' bases which extend from its eastern coast to the Arabian Sea (Holmes 2013). Modi's government is concerned the port, which has been leased to China for 40 years, could become a Chinese naval station. Should this transpire, it would be perceived as a direct threat to India's energy and economic security, since more than two-thirds of Indian energy imports flow through this region.

To counter China's strategic positioning in the Indian Ocean and its access to the Middle East, India has elevated its involvement with the US-led Quadrilateral Initiative (Quad). The grouping is also made up of the so-called Indo-Pacific region's democracies, including Australia and Japan.

The Galwan Valley clash was also a contributing factor in persuading Indian policymakers to step up their involvement in the Quad. The bloc is essentially a China containment strategy, even though such a geopolitical position is somewhat contrary to India's traditional non-aligned status in superpower rivalry.

At the Quad's second-ever ministerial meeting held at the foreign affairs level in Japan in 2020, India refrained from calling out China directly as a country which the US, in its declarations, would like to contain (Johnson and Sugiyama 2020). What one may surmise from India's policy variant at the Quad meeting is a part-continuation of New Delhi's approach in essentially dealing with differences with China bilaterally rather than within a confrontational bloc of countries.

Two Steps Forward, One Step Back

Various tensions have come to the fore in China-India ties since 2020, exacerbating and reinforcing the hitherto existing rifts in their relations. Some of the new sources of tension can be mainly attributed to sudden violent border incidents. China's strategic positioning in the region, such as in the case of CPEC, is gradually sapping the two countries' already thinning levels of mutual trust. In turn, India's more active involvement in the Quad may further erode trust, should this grouping become more than a mere talk-shop and actively take measures in disputed areas of the SCS, for instance.

At the same time, as both countries emerge to become the new superpowers of the twenty-first century, they are also aware of sharing common goals in their respective development paths. These include numerous interdependent linkages, especially India's need for Chinese capital to finance the country's serious infrastructure deficit. New Delhi also requires China's know-how in building manufacturing and technology clusters throughout the country as part of Modi's 'Make in India' campaign.

While their disputes may often rule the headlines, by contrast their ongoing and numerous low-key, multilayered, and institution-driven dialogues will likely be more determinative of their future path. Alternatively, should China's growing influence across the sub-continent feel like a form of encirclement, New Delhi may become more prone towards involvement in US-led China-containment initiatives such as the Quad.

The China-India bilateral relationship will likely face various cliff-edge moments reminiscent of their violent clashes in the Himalayas. The Western media will certainly grab whatever tensions that arise and happily promote an end to their sometimes rocky relationship. The reality will probably be somewhat more complicated. China's and India's leaders recognise that the twenty-first century will be theirs as the world gravitates towards Asia economically, politically, and culturally. Ultimately, neither Beijing nor New Delhi will want to jeopardise the prospect of their respective destinies as once great civilisations whose re-emergence are long overdue and flourishing as the new world leaders of the future.

Chapter 11

A New International Order

Introduction

The above four chapters have explored the interactions of China within an emerging international world order; the extension of China's increasing economic power and political influence across the world, and the need for, and the ability of, China to contribute to the challenging global problems. It is not yet appropriate to use the term global or supranational order in institutional terms. Currently, all the organisations at the world level are intergovernmental and depend on the agreements of member states, including of course the United Nations and its various agencies.

The one organisation which one might have hoped would be closest in practical operation — the WHO — has proved just as exposed to a lack of solidarity as the others. Its lack of cohesion and enforcement has been particularly laid bare over the course of the coronavirus pandemic.

What is emerging, along with greater hopes for solidarity, are a variety of active regional organisations across the world, with which China is notably either a member or otherwise engaged in cooperation. Independently, as other chapters have indicated, China has followed a path based on two broad principles. The first is a partnership model with other countries in areas of economics, trade, and finance, using its growing technological development to support policies in all these areas. The second is a political approach towards other countries based on the principle of political non-interference in their internal affairs.

Despite these paths to peaceful international coexistence and cooperation and its own foreswearing of interference in the internal affairs of other countries, China has been challenged in areas of external policy and increasingly in various internal issues by the US-led West.

Yet, it is not clear that there is a unanimous position being taken on China by all the countries within the 'Western sphere of influence'. For instance, on 'banning' Huawei, Hungary is deploying its equipment and Germany is not imposing a full ban (*Global Times* 2020). The EU is also not willing to join the US in imposing trade sanctions on China (Politico 2020). Indeed, there is an emerging consensus within the EU that it should play the role of 'honest broker' between the US and China and not take sides (Centre for European Reform 2020). Moreover, the growing economic, trade, financial, and technological partnerships, which are continuing to develop in East Asia within ASEAN and notably the recent RCEP trade agreement, have to an extent weakened the impact of the US sanctions on China and diluted the impact of some of the 'hyperbolic' ideological attacks by the US on China.

Another related aspect of overall Western political positioning on the economic model adopted by China is the attitude of Western-dominated international institutions such as the World Bank, IMF, WTO, and Bank for International Settlements (BIS). The perspective of these institutions, and any advice that they offer, tends still to be based on a neoliberal market model and the Washington Consensus (Williamson 2004).

In current circumstances — with the dominance of state-led market economies especially in most East Asian countries and their increasing global weight in terms of GDP and international trade — these institutions do not appear fit for purpose. Moreover, there are new, embryonic financial challengers to the existing international institutions, which are supported by China, Russia, and other major emerging market countries. These institutions include: the BRICS, AIIB, NDB, Eurasian Development Bank. There are also economic, trade, financial, and political regional groupings which are emerging around the world; they are partly modelled on the EU but have their own characteristics. Although the recently signed RCEP trade agreement — including China, Japan, South Korea, and 12 other Asia-Pacific regional countries 10 of which are also members of ASEAN — is currently operating as a free trade agreement, it is an example of such an emerging powerful grouping, accounting for almost one-third of the global trading economy.

This chapter will argue that there needs to be a sufficiently wide recognition across the globe that a new international order is emerging. Moreover, it is one which will not, and should not, be dominated by a

US-led Western alliance. It will suggest that this increasing transformation should be recognised, not by conflict between alternative sets of opposing economic approaches, but by reconciliation between differing models in the interests of global advance, equity, and ecological equilibrium.

To the extent possible, this reconciliation should enable an agreed framework of institutions, operating under a unified system of governance, which according to the ILO Global Commission (2019), should be one that:

> 'Is genuinely supportive of and conducive to national development strategies ('there can be no successful globalisation without a successful localisation'), where powerful actors are held accountable, and where efforts to achieve coherence between economic and social objectives would place the needs and aspirations of ordinary people at the centre of rules and policies'.

We will first examine the current position of China, specifically how it perceives its future role in the world and its intended development over the next 30 years up to 2050, given the various global problems discussed in Chapter 7.

We will then examine the position of the US, especially how it views the evolution of relations with China and how it appears to view the development of its current hegemonic international position going forward. This section will include a brief critique of the current set of international institutions which are heavily weighted in favour of the US Washington Consensus model of global political economy.

The likely interactions and attitudes manifested between the two superpowers and the other major powers and regional groupings will then be explored. The aim will be to suggest how the development of regional 'clusters of countries', with ties covering trade, economics, finance, technological cooperation, and politics, indicates an interest in avoiding polarisation between the US and China. This prognosis would be particularly relevant within the context of a modernising world which should be leaving behind nineteenth century models of 'great power' rivalries.

One issue between the US and China which appears to be redolent with echoes of nineteenth century military conflicts is the territorial disputes in the South China Sea. This will be the penultimate issue to be examined to discover the basis of the problems involved and the potential for resolution.

Finally, we will explore the prospects of a reconciliation of differences between the US and China. These prospects should be sufficient to enable an agreement on peaceful coexistence, to develop a plan for the reform of the current inadequate set of international organisations, and to move them towards a more global pattern of intervention on an agreed basis. There should also be an enhanced recognition, going beyond observer status at the UN, of the various regional organisations in global bodies (e.g., ASEAN from 2007).

China at a Crossroads

China is a middle-income country, so it still has some way to go in terms of prospectively increasing its per capita income. Its socio-economic growth path is targeted on a continued increase in real wage growth to benefit all its citizens. China also wishes to continue being integrated into overall global trading patterns, and also through its own independent but collaborative partnership approach, to work closely with both developed and developing countries.

The West, especially among the strongly liberal individualist, neoliberal market economies such as the US, is still in thrall to 'New Keynesian' economics (Gordon 2020). This theory of economics actually has little to do with the still valuable insights of Keynes, but New Keynesian economics was especially prevalent in the 1990s up to the 2008 Global Financial Crisis. After briefly being challenged, it has reasserted itself as a mainstream theory. Given this ideological absorption, Washington and its main allies seem incapable of fully appreciating the innovative nature of the political economy of China.

Insofar as this is the case, then the following recommendations of the World Bank, culled from a 2019 joint exercise between Chinese authorities and the World Bank (World Bank 2019c), might be judged accordingly:

> 'Global trade and investments can continue to be an important source of growth for China. Facing new challenges and a new global environment, China will have to continue to improve its international competitiveness and raise the quality and innovativeness of its exports. It will need to continue to pursue policy and institutional reforms to open its economy further and integrate with the global economy'.

> 'These actions would provide critical new drivers of growth for China's economy by promoting market competition, access to global frontier technologies, collaboration with globally leading firms, and integration into and upgrading within GVCs. China could continue to encourage pilot programmes and pioneering regions to test new policy and institutional reforms. The resulting successes could be replicated and disseminated more quickly. Special economic zones and other platforms are likely to further open up the economy'.

The above advice was certainly followed during the period between 1990 and 2010, as the post-Deng approach of what has been called state-capitalism was gradually pursued in China. Subsequently, China has followed a more tailored path to securing its own internal and external strategic economic interests in its pursuit of industrial development.

Internally, this has been in the form of a) pursuance of agricultural productivity improvement allied to a shift of rural populations to urban industrial centres, and b) a socialist market and planning approach, including with resident Western companies, as indicated in Chapters 2 and 3.

Externally, it has been by engaging with the world's trading arrangements and collaborating with companies and governments around the world, including through the BRI. However, the past decade — intensifying over the past four years — has witnessed rising hostility by the US towards China in trade and economic arenas. More recently, there has been an added ideological dimension to the hostility. This hostility, perhaps exacerbated by the spreading coronavirus pandemic, has ironically led to the US taking extreme actions that have damaged the global trade and interconnected investment environment (Steinbeck 2018).

Ironically, it is the US that is challenging the policy of further integrating China into the world economy, against the advice of the World Bank. Having faced this hostility and preparing for more to come, China is extending its own economic growth development pattern to other countries, through the expansion of trade and investment linkages with the countries and regions of East Asia, Eurasia, Africa, the Caribbean and Latin America, and the EU. The major initiative has been to develop combined domestic and external projects, in the form of transcontinental interconnections of the BRI, based on a partnership investment model.

China's External 'Tributary Growth' Patterns

As indicated in Chapter 3 and subsequently, we argue that China's expected returns on the BRI are fourfold: addressing the perception of the 'China threat'; achieving long-term economic and strategic benefits; assuaging China's concern over the US maritime threat to China's trade and energy communication lifelines through the South China Sea; and rebuilding a cooperative international order which may then become more aligned with China's political and economic interests.

The approach of the BRI may therefore be characterised as defensive rather than expansionary; concerned principally to enhance the connectivity of China internationally. Nonetheless, it would be naïve not to recognise the advantages that the BRI brings to many Chinese companies, including major state-owned infrastructure companies and private technology companies.

However, this pattern of economic development and trade is not accompanied by any hegemonic approach in terms of a political strategy. China aims to ensure the BRI provides mutually beneficial results for all countries involved, including China itself, as discussed in earlier chapters.

The BRI also provides China with an opportunity, in the form of the DSR to complement the hard infrastructure investments of the BRI. This will be facilitated by the adoption of international communications and data-transfer standards, rules on trade and investment, and environmental requirements via China's active participation in international institutions and regional organisations. The essential aim is to vastly extend China's connectivity with major areas of the developing and developed world, while at the same time developing its own economy and the welfare of its citizens further.

As indicated in Chapter 2 and elsewhere, digitisation is a key technology area being pursued by China and demonstrated in relation to the DSR. A specific example of China's international cooperative approach in the technological area is provided in the next section to illustrate the nature and aims of one DSR project in the context of the overall BRI infrastructure and transport development.

The PEACE Project

The Pakistan East Asia Africa Cable Express (PEACE), spanning 12,000 km, is being deployed by Huawei Marine (Huawei 2017) and is set to come online in 2020/21. The project will be partly funded by the state-owned China Construction Bank.

The PEACE network is a submarine cable system. The undersea cable will connect Pakistan's Gwadar Port to a landing point near Mombasa in Kenya. It is one of many undersea cable links being built by Chinese companies like Huawei Marine. The network aims to reduce network latency (i.e., speeding connectivity) by adopting the shortest direct route connectivity and enhancing route diversity between Asia, Africa, and Europe. On its completion, PEACE will become the shortest route of high-speed information traffic between Asia and Africa. Moreover, it will provide higher capacity and increased stability compared to the pre-existing networks which are challenged by low traffic and constant blackouts.

However, the significance of the PEACE system is not limited to its technological and commercial benefits. It has strategic importance in that its starting point, the Gwadar Port, is a key part of the CPEC (USCC 2019). The network is a collection of geographical linkages in the domains of road, rail, and air transportation systems between China and Pakistan. It also extends its network into Iran, Afghanistan, India, and Central Asia. Moreover, the PEACE system leads to East Africa, where China carries out a great number of its flagship infrastructure projects, with an additional connecting point in Marseilles, France, which has long been a hub for submarine networks in Europe.

In participating, French telecommunications companies hope to seize the opportunities presented by the rapid African technological development and the Sino-African economic exchanges. The cable system also encompasses Djibouti, where China has constructed its very first overseas small military base, which is focused on affording protection to its logistics investments in East Africa, and the increasing numbers of Chinese citizens working in the region.

The scale of the enterprise is astounding (PEACE 2019). It is an attempt to connect large swathes of Africa, the Middle East, Southeast Asia, and even Europe, to a technological network dominated by the Chinese state or by one of its corporations. It is likely to advance China to become an indispensable and even dominant actor in the age of global digitalisation. PEACE will also connect China's BRI regional focal points within China and around the globe.

The extensive technological network will compensate for the limitations of the physical land-based projects. Thus, we can clearly see the complementary functions of the DSR and the new land-based and maritime-based Silk Road. Moreover, PEACE has already brought together communications companies from various continents, including Chinese, French, and African telecommunications companies.

PEACE and other similar DSR networks have transformative impacts on the connectivity and technological advancement of developing nations. According to Connecting Africa (2019), international connectivity is an important element in the maturing communications market for Africa. This is not to ignore the contribution the project is adding to China's geo-political goals of enhancing mutual benefits and mutual trust with countries around the world.

One of the major obstacles for these technological connectivity projects is the concern for information security. According to the Centre for Strategic and International Studies (Kitson and Liew 2019), the deployment of infrastructure along the BRI largely excludes US technology, evoking US concerns about data traffic surveillance and wider strategic concerns.

Currently, many countries in Europe are formulating plans and taking steps to increase their control over domestic technological infrastructures. These initiatives will gradually become more plausible with technological maturation. Potentially, this development will allow cooperation with China. The issue — as evidenced by Washington's 'persuasion' of the UK to abandon Huawei on bogus security grounds — is that the US is currently opposed to any such collaboration.

Ironically, the use of Chinese equipment in 5G networks is unlikely to lead to a fragmentation of the global technological ecosystem, given that 5G standards are dictated by internationally established telecoms associations, namely the 3rd Generation Partnership Project (3GPP) of the International Telecommunications Union (ITU).[1]

The use of Chinese equipment will largely be a question of effectiveness and cost, rather than a preference for a specific standard. In December 2017, China's National Standards Committee further issued a 'One Belt One Road' Action Plan (2018–2020), proposing to deepen the standardisation of infrastructure networks and increase the level of compatibility between Chinese and international standards. In fact, in July 2020, the ITU Radio communication sector (ITU-R) approved 3GPP 5G technology as the International Mobile Telecommunications-2020 (IMT-2020) 5G standard.

[1] International Telecommunication Union (ITU): www.itu.int/en/about/Pages/default.aspx

Over the past 20 years, the ITU has approved 3G, 4G, and now the current 5G standards. Huawei is represented as one of the technology companies on the ITU's Standards Working Party.

It is clear that whatever the problems are with China's BRI soft power 'propaganda' approach in convincing Western countries of its good intentions, the BRI has been notably successful and China via Huawei and others are fully participating in setting international standards.

Propaganda: China and the West

In terms of conventional propaganda, as indicated in Chapter 4, China has a limited ability to counter Western 'influence projection'. China's attempts to achieve a deeper appreciation in the West of the cultural and philosophical underpinning of Chinese internal and external policies have hitherto not been successful. The reasons, as explained in Chapter 4, appear to be the combination of a naïve, relatively crude, promotional-style approach by China's government, amid a correspondingly successful anti-China prosecution by Western governmental and media criticism.

One of the most prolific commentators and writers analysing Chinese self-promotional activities in Western countries, and in countries via the Chinese diaspora, is the influential New Zealand academic Anne-Marie Brady. Her articles, briefings, and books demonstrate a penetrating insight into the activities of China's 'United Front', in New Zealand, Australia, and more widely, in Beijing's application of conventional 'soft power'.

The problem is that her contributions are written from the standpoint of the Western trope of liberal individualist democracy. To take such a position is perfectly acceptable, whatever its validity, but it does distort one's perspective. As has been portrayed throughout this book, a substantial majority of Western commentators, including academics, find it almost impossible to be other than judgemental when writing about China.

Clearly, understanding another culture, let alone one which has a political philosophy which appears diametrically-opposed to the prevailing Western model, is profoundly difficult. For China, with its socialist collectivist political approach, one can only expect there to be attacks from right-of-centre politicians and academics.

However, there is a further problem for China. Many left-of-centre politicians and academics are less than sympathetic to China. Many of the Western world's intellectual and political elites tend to display a general reluctance to analyse modern twenty-first century China. The reluctance arises principally because of cultural factors and a lack of tangible experience of China. In the case of the Western political left, it is also seeking to avoid the mistakes made in its initial strong endorsement of and support for the Soviet Union's Communist Party. This position is not helped by the Western media's incessant and overwhelming portrayal of China's governance system, albeit erroneously, as bearing a resemblance to the Stalinist Soviet Communist Party governance system. China is not the Soviet Union. This portrayal of China as an almost mirror image of the most autocratic period of the Soviet Union has become even more apparent since the advent of Xi Jinping as leader.

Well-informed in terms of their empirical research, writers such as Brady and Klimes as well as other Western commentators have a strong influence on US and other English-speaking countries' political opinion and positioning regarding China. Retaining an objective, non-judgemental view is difficult, even where there is detailed empirical research, as these two writers and others display. It is too easy to allow an ideological framework to distort not the empirical data presented, but certainly its interpretation.

Our concern, to which the remainder of this chapter is devoted, is that the achievement of a *modus vivendi* between the West and China is the most urgent task to be undertaken. The danger is that an increasingly intense Cold War is looming and it needs to be avoided. Constructive dialogue is imperative. As indicated in Chapter 5 in Part I, there are qualitative differences in political philosophy to be explored. Moreover, in some areas these differences relate not only to China, but to other East Asian countries. However, it will be useful first to consider the issues of political economy: trade, competition, and technology.

The US: From Isolationism to Global Hegemony

The attacks on Huawei and other Chinese technology companies (see Chapter 2) are clear examples of seriously distorting global supply chains and global trading patterns, while also damaging US companies in relation to the collateral damage done. The US hostility to Japan in the 1980s provides China — and the rest of the world — with a salutary reminder of how challenges to the global status quo are met by the US.

Once a 'statist' economic development path moves a country to a position of being able to rival substantially the dominant technology and trade position of the US hegemonic leadership of the neoliberal economic international order, then that country is likely to be subjected to dislocative trade, financial, and economic sanctions. The history of the attacks on Japan in the 1980s has repeated itself during the recent past, though with the added dimension of a more fundamental ideological challenge in the case of China.

Leaving aside the underlying political motivation of the US in launching a trade war on China and its blatant attempt to damage Huawei by whatever means possible, it seems evident that the commitment of the US to capitalism does not extend to international trade competition. Maybe except for its relatively brief period of global trade dominance, it never did. Any student of the latter quarter of the nineteenth century will recognise the protectionist instincts of the US (Lloyd 2021). Moreover, the addition of an ideological dimension to US foreign intervention in the Second World War following the earlier moralising fervour of US President Woodrow Wilson after the First World War, has seen Washington become increasingly dominant on the global scene.

However good the intentions of successive twentieth and twenty-first century American governments, it has become increasingly clear that the US global leadership position is allied with a wholesale commitment to an ideological position supporting the US version of liberal individualist democracy and neoliberal market economics.

The US position seemed perfectly tenable in earlier opposition to a despotic, Stalinist communist regime in Russia, allied to an understandable concern about the Maoist revolutionary movement in China. Even so, there were concerns arising in the 1960s and 1970s about the ideological stance behind US military intervention in Vietnam and their frequent involvement in defeating anti-colonial revolutionary movements, not to mention certain wholly democratic governments, in Latin America and elsewhere.

Following the collapse of the Soviet Union and a rapprochement of sorts with both Maoist and post-Mao governments in China, the US entered the twenty-first century believing that the 'end of history' (Fukuyama 1992) had seen the unchallengeable dominance of the neoliberal consensus and the Western liberal-individualist world order. This monumental assumption was maintained only up to the 2008 Global Financial Crisis.

During the period of the 'ascendancy', US confidence was perhaps dented only by extremist Islamic terrorist attacks and by subsequent failures to achieve nation-state rebuilding across the world. Indeed, for a period in the first decade of this century, notably under the presidency of George W Bush, it regarded its 'indirect rebuilding' of China as a success in terms of China's growing integration into the world economic order (White House 2020).

The shock of the Global Financial Crisis in 2008 caused some reflection about the efficacy and certitude of US economic ideology. This was accompanied by a growing concern over China's success in elevating its economy into becoming the world's second largest after the crisis in terms of a statist approach to economic development.

At the same time, inside the US security establishment, concerns were also being raised about the leading role played by the CCP in the governance of China. This is reflected in the majority view of the US-China Economic and Security Review Commission Report to Congress (US-China Economic and Security Review Commission 2005), with one dissenting voice who took the view that the report judged China too harshly. The concerns appeared to relate to various issues: China's growing strategic economic importance, coupled with its burgeoning national defence capabilities; its increasing influence over the geopolitical environment; and, in the longer term, the cultural and ideological uniqueness of China that may pose a specific political threat to US influence.

Avoiding a New Cold War

Notwithstanding some recent countermeasures by Beijing in response to US actions on trade, technology, human rights, and interference in domestic affairs, the global polity requires, from both President Xi and the new US administration, a return to a bilateral policy of 'constructive engagement'. At a minimum, the trade and technology war initiated by Trump — which enveloped Huawei and other Chinese companies, accompanied by strong political attacks on China and collateral damage to non-Chinese companies and US allies — needs a truce.

Measures should at a minimum aim to protect the global community of trading nations from economic damage. It needs to ensure that the progress of global innovation in technological and environmental areas should not be hampered by unfair trade and technological restrictions from either side. Priority should be given to engaging in worldwide concerted efforts in tackling the economically and health-debilitating effects of the coronavirus pandemic and in collaborative efforts to mitigate the impacts of climate change and associated global problems.

This request for constructive engagement appears likely to be rebuffed in the short-term by the US. The ideological tone of the White House May 2020 paper, and the subsequent ideological rhetoric from then-US Secretary Pompeo in 2020 (Pompeo 2020), have exacerbated the tensions surrounding the trade and industrial policy disputes with China. The new Biden administration appears to be adopting a softer tone, while the ideological undertones are still present. Though cloaked in security concerns, the various industrial and trade protectionist actions can be remedied. More serious is the propaganda being deployed by various US interests and enthusiastically endorsed by some US allies, which are motivated by ideological concerns.

However sincerely held are these concerns, China is not the Islamic State, nor is it the Soviet Union. It is essential to appreciate the significant differing political and philosophical perspectives between the Western, and especially the US, world view, to those of China and other East Asian countries. Hard though it may be to accept, these differing philosophical/cultural positions should be regarded, by both sides, as equally valid. This should not prevent pressure being put on China, based on an understanding of its cultural positioning, to accept more diversity than maintaining a Han dominance allows. As the majority group, a greater tolerance might be expected of the group while not disturbing social harmony (Mukherjee 2010).

We have attempted to argue in this book: rather than 'dusting off' old Cold War manuals developed in the Soviet era, a new understanding is required of the re-emergence of China as a global power and the consequential need for a new international order based on collaboration and mutual respect.

Promoting a Greater Interchange of Ideas

The differences between China and the US, and more widely, differences between East and West, are sometimes narrowly portrayed as individualism versus collectivism (this portrayal and the underlying political philosophies were discussed in Chapters 5 and 6). The tendency at a geopolitical level is for the profound nature of the approaches to be subsumed under simplistic rhetoric and emotively-charged exchanges of propaganda messaging.

From a Western perspective — though informed by an acquaintance with China and East Asia and by analytical research — the authors are distinctly aware of the one-sided propaganda meted out by politicians and amplified by a Western mainstream media which uncritically supports and further accentuates these views. Some of the responses from China fall into the same trap.

In this environment, it is imperative for a balanced and objective view to be promoted among the academic community, not just in the West, but through cultural and scientific exchanges with Chinese and other East Asian academic communities. Think-tanks tend to take up positions generally aligned with either the right or the left, but even here one requires objectivity.

One problem in relation to the US elites lies in their hegemonic approach, not simply in promoting the prevailing Western-oriented international world order, but also in their adamantine defence of the liberal-individualist philosophy and neoliberal market view of political economy. To be fair, as has been remarked about China in Chapters 5 and 6, there are cultural and political philosophical values which are embedded. In the contexts of contemporary political issues and conflicts, it is perhaps too much to expect either politicians or the populace to embrace a balanced political and philosophical discourse, however devoutly we may wish it could be so.

In our view, it is only through an objective academic discourse that an understanding can be appreciated of the different political, cultural, and philosophical approaches to economic, political, social, and cultural activities and policies. We are optimistic about longer term outcomes. Nonetheless, there are also reasons to be hopeful, even in the medium term, that the current US ideological position, supported by other Western-oriented countries, will be demonstrated to be counter-productive. If so, this could permit a return to constructive engagement, abandoning ideological confrontation.

The US sense of empowerment comes from its financial, trade, and technology dominance since the Second World War, supported by a massive lead in military power. The sense of empowerment is linked to the apparent ascendancy of Western liberal individualist democracy and a free market economy, remarked on by Fukuyama (1992). The coalescence of these factors is unfortunate, and potentially damaging. There is a need for peaceful coexistence and intensive global cooperation by US and China, whether on COVID-19, its economic aftermath, or climate change.

Third Country and Regional Grouping Reactions to the US/China Conflict and Potential Interventions

There are other geopolitical participants with an interest in ameliorating the conflict between the US and China. This is especially so in relation to the substantial challenges faced by the world over the next half-century. Some of these challenges have been discussed in Chapters 8, 9, and 10, which examine the various relationships between China and other principal countries and regional groupings of the world.

In what follows, it will be suggested that rather than focusing simply on a narrow set of alliances clustered around the two principal protagonists, a less rigid identification with either the US or China is possible. This may be divined in the attitudes of a wide and growing variety of countries involved in global regional groupings. Some of these regional groupings are now considered on the basis of their positioning regarding the US and China. Each of them has varying degrees of potential for intervening; perhaps assisting in reducing tensions and perhaps even resolving problems between China and the US.

Certainly, it is the self-interests of individual countries and regional groupings of countries to avoid becoming embroiled in US-China confrontations. This is an increasingly multi-polar world, which is also becoming interwoven via economic, trade, technology, and communications interconnections (Morgan Stanley 2020). Chapters 8, 9, and 10 have indicated the complexity of China's regional and international connections. This new global environment places a premium on the need for the establishment of effective diplomatic dialogues involving the US and China. We may now explore the possibilities.

EU Attitudes and Positioning for Mediation

The eighth EU-China High-Level Trade and Economic Dialogue (EU-China 2020b), held in June 2020 under the theme 'Post-COVID-19 China-EU Cooperation, Promote Steady Recovery and Growth for Global Economy', has produced fruitful outcomes and consensus. The investment agreement between the two parties has been initialled, though it still has to be ratified.

Both sides appreciated the progress made in the China-EU Comprehensive Agreement on Investment negotiations, albeit over a long seven-year period. They agreed to strengthen supervision and guidance to complete negotiations and reach agreement on a high-level investment treaty within the year. China has signed bilateral investment agreements with 26 out of 27 EU member states, laying a solid foundation for a deeper investment agreement between both sides.

Finally, at the end of the six-month German Presidency of the European Council in late December 2020, the Comprehensive Agreement on Investment (CAI) was agreed at a high-level video conference that included, among others, the participation of Angela Merkel, the German Chancellor; Charles Michel, President of the European Council; Ursula von der Leyen, President of the European Commission; and President Xi Jinping of China. However, the ratification procedure was subsequently indefinitely stalled, in May 2021, following EU sanctions on China and Chinese countersanctions.

Of itself, the agreement is relatively modest; it is not a full trade agreement, but it does allow for far easier involvement of EU companies already operating in China and wishing to expand in various areas of economic activities. The agreement provides better balance in terms of reciprocal market access in China and the EU. Perhaps more importantly, the CAI represents an independent geopolitical route for an economic partnership between the EU and China, and a potent global signal of the joint desire of the EU and of China to promote multilateral interregional solidarity and coordination (Konstantinidis 2021). In the future, this should lead to intensified collaboration on climate change and the environment, and to managed, fair economic competition in pursuit of technological development.

Nonetheless, the EU will still regard China as a 'systemic rival' promoting a model of governance at variance with that of the EU. In this respect, the US has expressed concern about the CAI. The EU is likely to be engaged with the US on issues of governance in China, including on human rights and on the demonstration of an open society. Indeed, these issues are likely to be high on the agenda of future sessions of the bilateral Dialogue between the European External Action Service and the US Department of State on China. The EU-US Dialogue on China (US Mission to the European Union 2020) was launched on October 23rd, 2020.

Given the apparent 'midway' positioning of the EU between the US and China, it might in theory be presumed to be able to act as 'honest broker' between the US and China. Despite the potential political problems involved, EU intervention could bring together the two sides in the context of establishing an ad hoc trilateral forum to tackle specific problem areas affecting the interests of all three parties.

Such a forum that provides an informal, multilateral route to conflict resolution between the US and China in areas of broad economic and trade conflicts could be valuable. However, this potential for conflict resolution would be unlikely to stretch to cover discussion of alternative models of governance, even though the EU itself offers a variety of models, not all of which are wholly aligned with the specific US model (Treib *et al.* 2007).

Indo-Pacific Forum

The Indo-Pacific forum, usually referred to by the US as the 'Quad', was initiated as a security dialogue in 2007 by then-Prime Minister Shinzo Abe of Japan, with the support of then-Vice President Dick Cheney of the US, then-Prime Minister John Howard of Australia, and then-Prime Minister Manmohan Singh of India. It fell into desuetude after the Australian withdrawal in 2008. However, it was resuscitated in 2017, with a broader remit covering infrastructure, telecommunications, and cybersecurity, though the US still regards it as a potential military security organisation and one geared to opposing China. For instance, at the May 2020 meeting in Japan, then-US Secretary of State Mike Pompeo called for the four democracies to collaborate 'to protect our people and partners from the Communist Party of China's exploitation, corruption, and coercion'. It is to be hoped that the tone of such rhetorical interventions will be softened under the new US administration (Grossman 2020).

India has a broader geopolitical perspective, as suggested in a speech to the Shangri-La Dialogue that was hosted by the International Institute of Strategic Studies in 2018 (IISS 2018). Indian Prime Minister Narendra Modi emphasised that in the Indian vision, the Indo-Pacific extended 'from the shores of Africa to that of the Americas' where India would promote a 'democratic and rules-based order, in which all nations, small and large, thrive'.

The drawback to the Indo-Pacific Forum (Quad) is its constrained resources in being able to go much further in political terms than discussion and rhetoric. However, bringing about any substantive real change in the designated 'Indo-Pacific' seems remote without the full participation of the various groupings of ASEAN countries which include China: notably the EAS, ARF, and the ASEAN Defence Ministers Meeting Plus where China is also a member. In 2018, the official communique noted that various regional country leaders, including India's Modi and Japan's Abe, had 'reaffirmed their strong support for ASEAN's unity and centrality' for East Asian development (The Wire 2018).

Despite the current attempts by the US, with a degree of equivocation by India, for the Quad to take an aggressive, oppositional stance towards China, it could gradually become a context in which the ideological belligerence of the US towards China could be ameliorated and a more constructive dialogue to begin. The East Asian countries involved (and others who may be recruited, such as South Korea and Vietnam) all have substantial and growing, trade, economic, and financial linkages with China. This was more recently enshrined, when 15 East Asian nations including Australia and New Zealand signed up to the world's largest trading bloc, the RCEP, in November 2020. In short, they have a vested interest in avoiding turmoil in various areas of integration. Current US policy may be an inhibiting factor in preventing such a fruitful dialogue, but policies change, as will the rise of China's economy and its importance for these countries.

Russia

Russia is an increasingly close strategic partner of China, as Chapter 10 demonstrates, and its relations with the US are equally as fraught as those between US and China. It seems unlikely they will be in a position to act as any type of broker or interlocutor in terms of initiating a dialogue between the US and China. In any continuing ideological battle between the US and China, Russia would essentially support China.

India

In the time when India was ruled by the Congress Party and Nehru was the Prime Minister, his foreign policy position was clearly defined in terms of the then Cold War between the US and the Soviet Union. India and a group of 120 other 'Third World' countries were the 'Non-Aligned Movement' in the 1950s and 1960s.

If this is the position of India now under the current leadership of Modi, then it would be appropriate to consider New Delhi as a possible interlocutor between China and the US. The issue currently is whether the practical economic and trade linkages between India and China, as discussed in Chapter 10, amid the volatile political disputes between them on the one hand — and the loose ties with the US on the other — would provide any relationship which might approximate to a potential interlocutor role. Nonetheless, as two major emerging economies, there are coincidence of interests between India and China. However, on balance, an intermediary role seems doubtful (Narayanan 2021).

Africa

Africa is a politically-contested continent between the US and China, though China has strong and growing investment partnerships with a number of key African states along the BRI. Moreover, the US fears,

> 'Africa, therefore, is fast becoming a battleground for competing ideologies and models of domestic and international governance. The more African states accept China's model of governance and abandon liberal norms and multiparty democracy, the easier it will be for Beijing to enlist African support for other geopolitical objectives. This trend is not only injurious to US interests on the continent but will also have adverse implications for the United States' position globally' (US-China Economic and Security Review Commission 2020).

One strategic aim of the BRI is to establish a zone of shared development encompassing Central and Western Asia and the whole of Africa. African states from north to south, which are continuing to develop close links with China and probably supporting China's geoeconomic and geopolitical positioning, are not likely to intervene publicly in any attempt to provide a forum for the resolution of US-China ideological conflict.

Given the concerns raised in the above quotation, it appears that the African states themselves are likely to become caught up in the US-China economic and political rivalries. Insofar as the African Union is able to voice any concerns on behalf of African states collectively, it is likely to adopt a neutral position, as will many of the individual states. It is doubtful if this route offers much hope of effective interlocution between the two behemoths.

Political Rhetoric and Realpolitik

Irrespective of whether an interlocutor can be found to provide a forum for a road to peaceful coexistence, it is worth looking beyond the surface of the political rhetoric. Whatever may appear to be irreconcilable differences between the two sides, there are always some cool heads in governments amid vital communication back-channels.

The modern media-dominated world presents a major problem for political leaders. Hungry for conflict situations to be hyped and a 24-hours news agenda, it is ever easier for missteps to be made. Social media is waiting to further exaggerate and polarise any issue and debate.

Ideally, the US and China should resolve their differences bilaterally. Normally, diplomatic back channels between countries remain open, however severe the dislocation. If progress is to be made, then extreme care is required from leaderships of the main participants — the US, China, and perhaps other key national actors. The process of unwinding both the rhetoric and the more aggressive and damaging actions would probably need to be established. As in past conflicts, including that of the original Cold War, this could be initiated by a summit meeting between the two presidents of the US and China, forming a commitment to return to constructive engagement.

Given the apparent gulf between the US and China, other channels including academic, business, as well as diplomatic might be used, but how influential these may be is uncertain. It is going to be important that a better-informed electorate in Western countries is developed over a longish period. However, if any kind of constructive engagement by the elites is going to be accepted, then China needs also to be prepared to respond to any overtures, without fearing that dialogue is actually going to threaten its governance system.

In this situation, reconciliation should not be seen as calling on either the US or China to abandon their differing ideological positions. The intention is to achieve sufficient political trust in order to establish a genuine dialogue involving also support from various sections of civil society. The intention must be to promote a deeper understanding of the apparently 'opposing' value systems (Bell 2017).

To reach such a level of constructive engagement would entail a diplomatic course of action over a period of 5–10 years: this is the minimum length of time which is likely to be required. The reconciliation will have to accept, from both sides, a recognition of differing values, political systems, and societal structures, and that neither system is ethically or politically superior. These are the difficult conditions that both sides will have to accept before gradual progress can be made. This acceptance may be harder for the US, and some other Western countries, than for China.

Unfortunately, one arena where political rhetoric and military 'sabre-rattling' are leading to fears of actual conflict directly involving the US and China are the disputes around the South China Sea. This is heightened by the substantial US force deployment around China's seaboard. It is worth exploring how this disputation has occurred, its complex modalities, and how it might be resolved.

Potential Military Conflict around China's Shores

South China Sea Disputes

The South China Sea disputes are complex and historically longstanding, a point on which China bases its claims in the various maritime economic zones. The issues are complicated and involve various protagonists: Japan, Brunei, Malaysia, the Philippines, Indonesia, Taiwan, Vietnam, as well as China. Each has overlapping territorial claims to parts of the maritime zones. For instance, Indonesia's exclusive economic zone around the Natuna Islands also overlaps with China's claims. The disputes cover issues such as territorial integrity, sovereignty, resources, and freedom of navigation.

China's contemporary economic diplomacy has its roots in the Han dynasty tributary system, which is renewed as an approach under the BRI. Ultimately, the tributary system proved unsustainable for Han China (Chua 2017). Regardless, it seems unlikely this historic memory will interfere with China's pursuance of a policy which is principally concerned with maintaining open access to the seas around its coastal areas.

In January 2017, China published a White Paper entitled 'China's Policies on Asia-Pacific Security Cooperation' (ISEAS 2017). The White Paper emphasises peaceful development in the region and friendly cooperation with all countries, and reinforced the Five Principles of Peaceful Coexistence. The White Paper also states that 'small and medium-sized countries need not and should not take sides among big countries' but should 'build an Asia-Pacific partnership featuring mutual trust, inclusiveness, and mutually beneficial cooperation'.

On the South China Sea disputes, the White Paper stresses China's commitment to a peaceful resolution through cooperation. Nevertheless, the White Paper states that China has 'indisputable sovereignty over the Nansha Islands and their adjacent waters'. It also mentions momentum towards establishing a Code of Conduct in the region. China urges external parties not to 'internationalise and judicialise the South China Sea issue'. Under the topic of common security, the paper states: 'We should respect and accommodate the legitimate security concerns of all parties. To beef up a military alliance targeted at a third party is not conducive to maintaining common security'. This is a clear reference to the US but also to Japan and Australia, on their mutual agreement concluded in November 2020 for military cooperation involving an ongoing presence of Australian troops in Japan and joint exercises in the South China Sea (Graham and Koshino 2020).

Clearly, China is not prepared to compromise on some of its key claims over the East and South China Seas, especially as it perceives a growing antagonistic military threat close to its shores. However, China appears willing to take some form of leadership in writing the rules for Asia-Pacific trade, and even the security agenda. Despite displeasure towards American involvement and alliances in the region, China does not appear to be planning to take strong military actions. Arguably, its main motivation emanates from China's need to secure guaranteed navigation rights in the seas around its coastline and beyond in the (contested) economic zone. Beijing sees security, perhaps not unreasonably, as being threatened by the massive US military existence and accumulating presence of other countries' naval forces in the area (Duchatel 2020).

In terms of resolving the multifarious and complex South China Sea disputes, China appears willing to offer cooperation to resolve issues via joint bilateral organisations (Qi 2019b), while also accepting a mediating role from ASEAN. The problem is that some of the disputes appear to be more intractable than others, and on some of these, namely with the Philippines, Beijing is extremely reluctant to accept the international legal ruling under the UNCLOS (it should be noted that the US is not a party to UNCLOS).

China's need to exert a measure of unilateral sovereignty in the South China Sea is predicated on its need to coordinate its defence capability to protect its eastern seaboard. This endeavour cannot be isolated from its motivation to respond to US forward defence positioning in the Pacific and Asia. The US defence position cannot also be separated from its promulgation of trade, economic, and industrial interests in the pursuance of the global political hegemony which it seeks to maintain. However, in practice, US policy responses to China's attempts to maintain its coastal security — even where it is making legal territorial claims — tend to elicit a strong reaction on the US side (Congressional Research Service 2021). Often, these take the form of 'freedom of navigation operations' (FONOP). In the Pacific area, and especially in East Asia, the US minimum political objective is the containment of China.

The United States refuses to be constrained by multilateral treaties and organisations set up to achieve collective security. This was exemplified, as the US Congressional Research Service observed in 2016, when Washington did not look kindly at the ARF because a 'problem would arise if East Asian governments used the ARF or other future consultative organisations in attempts to restrain the United States from acting on certain security issues' (Niksch 2016). Ironically, ASEAN is currently working to provide solutions to the South China Sea disputes and to avoid any military action by any of the nations involved, including China.

At an ASEAN Ministerial meeting in September 2020 (ASEAN 2020), the issues involved were discussed, though not resolved. The communique indicated that there was an exchange of views on:

> 'Regional and international issues of common interest and concern, including terrorism and violent extremism, cybersecurity, and the South China Sea. The Meeting discussed the situation in the South China Sea, during which concerns were expressed by some countries over recent developments in the South China Sea and underscored the importance of promoting and maintaining peace and stability, a rules-based order, freedom of navigation in and overflight above the South China Sea, and ensuring unimpeded lawful commerce in the South China Sea'.
>
> 'The Ministers noted the positive progress in the negotiations on the Code of Conduct in the South China Sea (CoC) despite the challenging COVID-19 situation and looked forward to the early conclusion of an effective and substantive CoC that is consistent with international law, including the 1982 UNCLOS and does not prejudice the legitimate rights and interests of all nations including those not party to these negotiations'.

US 'Forward Defence' Strategy

It is important to recognise that the unilateral US 'forward defence' strategy, in what the US terms the Indo-Pacific region, represents a US bi-partisan agreement on Asia-Pacific policy. The suggestion that the Democrats prefer multilateralism while Republicans are unilateralists is irrelevant. There is a bi-partisan approach to Asia-Pacific policy.

It should be recalled that the massive intervention in Vietnam in the 1960s and 1970s was a unilateral initiative of the US, which took place mainly under two Democratic administrations of John F. Kennedy and Lyndon Johnson. The Biden presidency is unlikely to depart from the bi-partisan approach. Moreover, it was under the Obama administration that the US increased naval destroyer transits through the Taiwan Strait; there were 12 in 2016 (Power 2019).

More generally, and in line with the combined trade, economic, and ideological hegemonic approach of the US, Trump's declaration of trade war against China inflicted some economic damage on a number of China's Southeast Asian neighbouring economies. These economies are linked in the already substantially integrated and regionally networked economy. This economic situation is defined as a 'Sinocentric regional division of labour' (Hung 2017). In fact, the whole cross border, interwoven economy is threatened by the 7.5% penalty tariff Washington imposed on US$300 billion worth of Chinese exports to the US.

Notwithstanding this collateral economic damage imposed on other East Asian countries via the US trade sanctions, far more damage would be inflicted on these countries by US military action against China in the area. If we add the US, probably unreasonable, concern that China may attempt to invade Taiwan and the separate risk of an accidental triggering of minor naval actions in the South China Sea, then the potential for military conflict in the region is real.

The underlying motivation for the US 'forward defence strategy' is attributable not to aggressive military moves by China — even the Pentagon admits that China's military posture is one of 'strategic defence' — but to the US wish of dominating and controlling the East Pacific. This desire is despite the fact that the territory concerned is 6,000 miles from Hawaii, the headquarters of US Indo-Pacific Command (US Indo-Pacific Command 2021). This Command (Bello 2020) can deploy 5 aircraft carrier strike groups, over 1,000 missile carrying aircraft, almost 200 other ships, plus 2 large Marine Expeditionary Forces. This deployment includes two island chains — an inner and an outer chain of military bases — essentially shadowing China's Southern and Eastern seaboards. This deployment can hardly be described as a defence of US territory, except by US military intelligence defence strategists, and the deployment of 'forward defence'.

According to the US National Security Strategy (2017) paper:

> 'The United States must retain overmatch — the combination of capabilities in sufficient scale to prevent enemy success and to ensure that America's sons and daughters will never be in a fair fight'.

If one needs confirmation of the intention of the US to exert not only hegemony but domination across the world, this must surely be it. Whatever the motivation, good or bad, then this statement of intent leaves little reason to doubt US defence policy objectives.

China's Defence Strategy

By contrast, China has responded to the threat of misadventure being translated into an attack on its strategic eastern seaboard by attempting to nullify any potential attack using its defence strategy of Anti-Access/Area Denial (A2/AD).

China is thus engaged in 'strategic defence' and seeks a limited, modern, and technologically advanced defence force, sufficient only to defend its territorial interests from attack by another power. There are over 63,000 US air, sea, and land forces personnel stationed in immediate reach of China's eastern region, including cities around the coast, such as Shanghai, which represent the key prosperous Chinese economic zones and trading ports and are critical given China's still high absolute level of foreign trade. Moreover, these eastern seaboard ports have no open access to the Pacific.

China's national prosperity currently depends crucially upon an arc of cities around its Eastern seaboard. Movement of imports and exports to sustain China's economic growth-poles in this area is critical. China has to maintain access to the South China Sea. It is the inexorable logic which influences China's desire to manage, if not control, the South China Sea.

Defending its eastern and southeastern seaboard, installing air and sea strategic installations, and attempting to seek a wider control over the South China Sea are not a choice for China. Rather it is a strategic defence necessity. Its ability to concentrate on these specific defensive capabilities is just that; unlike the US deploying 'Pax Americana', it does not seek a role in patrolling the high seas of the world.

The extent of US military concern about China is captured in a US military graduate paper (Reed 2015), which reads 'China is, without question, America's conceptual foe'. The document even goes as far as portraying Chinese actions in the Pacific as akin 'to Nazi Germany's unchecked rise prior to World War II. The scenarios presented ironically patterned Chinese perceived aggression along the lines of Imperial Japan in the 1930s'. This is obviously not a formal US defence position paper, but it is indicative of the thinking of some in the US military.

Reconciliation and the Way Forward

Since early 2020, the world has been tackling the COVID-19 pandemic. Globally, this battle is set to continue into 2022, even with hopefully safe and effective vaccines made available to all across the world who require them. Temporarily, the pandemic has drawn attention to the pressing need by the international community to deal with the other substantial, and potentially divisive, major problem of global warming and the associated climate change.

Unfortunately, the immediate problem of the pandemic has not yet been fully addressed as a clear global problem, which would require governments to work together under the auspices of the WHO. Scientists have, fortunately, worked together intensively across national boundaries, with strong inputs from China's own scientific community. Moreover, the international COVAX initiative is starting in February 2021 to deliver vaccines around the world.

These issues and other associated global problems, discussed in Chapter 7, demonstrate the need for intensive global cooperation among countries to work in partnership with one another. The problem is not global scientific cooperation and collaborations such as the Intergovernmental Panel on Climate Change in relation to environmental risks. The problem is a lack of sufficient and effective global cooperation at international political levels to take sufficient coordinated action.

Happily, the new Biden administration has immediately recognised the need for global collaboration on climate change (NPR 2020) in light of the pressures and motivations from the empirical facts on the ground.

Moreover, the need for further expert scientific cooperation has been growing due to pressures arising from actual climate-related events. These include the increasing prevalence of severe weather events. Moreover, the likelihood of further pandemics will drive that collaboration, spreading eventually to politicians concerned over adverse public reactions in their countries.

Other economic pressures are likely to arise from energy markets, given that 80% reduction in the costs of renewables, such as solar panels (driven by the sheer scale of production by China), is likely to lead to reductions in the viability of the production of fossil fuels, especially of fracking in the US (GlobeNewswire 2020).

Is Constructive Political Engagement Ultimately Possible?

Ignoring the likelihood of any fortuitous turn of events over other pressing global issues leading to collaboration between the US and China: the key issue that remains is whether any resolution of the apparently fundamental ideological differences is possible?

At present, the signs are not propitious. However, this does not entail that a gradual easing of the current antagonistic situation is not possible. It simply means that such an easing of the US-China relationship will take time to be reached. This is likely to depend on when the ideological attitude of the US administration become self-defeating and injurious to US business interests, and hampers the ability of the US to work closely with China on global problems. Then, pressure for change may materialise. It would also be good if more intensive academic as well as political contacts can support a rapprochement.

Tension around the disputed territorial rights in the South China Sea is a potential flashpoint which could lead to unwanted military clashes. Ideally, and in the absence of US provocative interventions, the disputes could be resolved through negotiations within the ASEAN framework, while respecting earlier UNCLOS rulings. China's principal aim is twofold: a) to ensure free navigation rights in the South China Sea, and b) in terms of its construction of artificial islands to secure its defence capability.

The first objective of China is capable of being resolved by negotiations within ASEAN (Tuan 2020), providing China is willing to be flexible and to offer appropriate compensation where necessary. ASEAN discussions on the issue will continue.

The second objective is part of China's strategic A2/AD defence approach aimed at nullifying the US 'forward defence' strategy. Ultimately this specific issue could be resolved by a US-China Peace Accord in which the US abandons its hegemonic military Indo-Pacific 'overmatch' strategy. Currently, given existing US policy towards China (especially, but not exclusively, its ideological component), there seems little chance of this overarching issue being resolved. The complexity of the issues involved and the US strategic position are set out in the latest Congressional Research Service document on the subject (Congressional Research Service 2021). The document's conclusions suggest that the strategic great power competition actively pursued by the US is under-resourced. This conclusion and the inevitable Chinese response, in relation to the wrongly named US 'forward defence' approach indicates the constraints on any meaningful dialogue, especially from the US side.

The issues of how to resolve deeper ideological conflicts between the US and China, of which the issues in the South China Sea are but one extreme manifestation, are problematic but not irresolvable in principle. However, even with potential mediation, such as via the EU, the resolution requires goodwill and careful long-term preparation on both sides. It should be possible to achieve peaceful coexistence, if only to resolve major global challenges such as climate change and to develop a mutual respect for divergent views on fundamental political philosophy.

Concluding Comments

There are clear signs of a new international order emerging, in which China will be playing a major role. The institutions and framework of the existing order are failing and need reformation. The outlines of what is required are also beginning to appear.

China is pursuing a successful development strategy internally and externally, but one which is aimed essentially at global connectivity rather than any attempt to construct any new world order. It seeks partnership not dominance, though clearly it seeks economic benefits from its investments along the BRI. It also, through the DSR, seeks telecommunications and digital leadership, and to influence, though not to determine international standards. China is also deploying its technological strengths in relation to tackling crucial global challenges, including the area of climate change.

The US also seeks to maintain its strong position in relation to technology and in trade. It is evidently reluctant to surrender leadership in these multilateral areas, to China, as it was in relation to Japan in the 1980s. Unfortunately, the US also wishes to maintain its current ideological hegemony in the Western world and sees China as an (inferior) ideological competitor. This is despite China's abjuring from proselytising its model of political economy and governance.

The US aims to use its current global financial power and defence capability to support its hegemonic approach, while also deploy effective propaganda tools to support its political philosophical model.

The growing ideological confrontation is concerning for areas of the world which have some degree of independence from either the US or China, though there may be economic, trade, technology, and political linkages to either or both of the main protagonists.

We have suggested ASEAN, the Indo-Pacific Dialogue, and the European Union as possible candidates in attempting to create forums for dialogue. These should provide for reconciliation in various areas of contention and the stimulation of a meaningful dialogue. The objective should be to achieve a position where the two sides' apparently opposing political philosophical positions can be ameliorated through peaceful coexistence and constructive engagement.

It is also the responsibility of the two main protagonists to engage gradually over a period to reach an accepted understanding of each other's position. This should involve a range of contacts — political, academic, and civil society organisations — to achieve the understanding required. Such an accommodation would also then provide the space to tackle cooperatively and constructively the other urgent and major global problems confronting the world, while accepting that resolving differences in political philosophy is likely to take far longer.

Yet, in seeking a roadmap for constructive engagement between Washington and Beijing, one should be mindful that China's rise on the world stage, particularly in the wake of the 2008 Global Financial Crisis and whatever transpires in the aftermath of the coronavirus pandemic, is reverberating powerfully across the world. For the first time since Western European powers launched global empires from the fifteenth to the nineteenth centuries to America's global dominance since the onset of the twentieth century, we are witnessing the emergence of a new China-driven paradigm influencing multiple spheres of society, whether that be economic, technological, political, or even cultural. These nascent civilisational influences are shifting from what is collectively known as 'the West', mainly constituted of North America and Europe, towards East Asia, being centred on the now fast-expanding re-emergence of China as a global superpower.

At the same time, Beijing's ascendancy to superpower status has neither passed unnoticed nor unchallenged. Since Donald Trump's election as US President in 2016, the US and followed somewhat reluctantly by other Western nations, has adopted a blatantly more distrustful and increasingly invective tone in their relations with China. From the EU's labelling of China in 2019 as an 'economic competitor in pursuit of technological leadership and a systemic rival promoting alternative models of governance' to the then-US Director of National Intelligence John Ratcliffe's assertion in 2020 that 'China poses the greatest threat to democracy and freedom worldwide since World War Two', there are ominous signs of an emerging new Cold War as Trump's combative approach towards China has been similarly set into motion by the Biden administration, albeit with new sets of strategies and agendas.

That being said, Washington's fiery political rhetoric has yet to be fully matched in terms of actual belligerent policy actions. For example, throughout pandemic-stricken 2020, China's exports to the world had been booming, while its global trade surplus and inward foreign direct investments hit all-time highs in spite of many countries' highly-selective measures in narrowing economic ties with China. This was no less the case for American consumers whose surging demand for Chinese goods culminated in the US succumbing to yet another record trade deficit with China, in spite of American-imposed tariffs hurting hundreds of billions of dollars in two-way trade. Even the Trump administration's phase one trade deal, requiring China to purchase US$200 billion of energy, agriculture, and manufactured products over 2020–21, barely counteracted the ballooning trade deficit.

Perhaps of greater concern for China has been the intensifying line up of US sanctions on a fast-growing number of Chinese technology companies. This includes, from the earliest — Washington's blacklisting of Huawei for allegedly breaking US sanctions on Iran, to the latest — restrictions in the supply of US-designed technology to Chinese companies allegedly involved in the country's military-industrial complex (US Treasury 2020).

In the latter case, the sanctions, which arose on November 17th, 2020, were related to Chinese companies owned or controlled by China's military (India Blooms 2020). This more recent sanctions regime targeted even larger Chinese entities than previous technology-related sanctions, including China's main chipmaker, Semiconductor Manufacturing International Corporation (SMIC) and the fourth largest state-owned oil giant, China National Overseas Oil Corporation (CNOOC). Altogether, these military-connected sanctions impacted around 35 Chinese companies by end-2020. Moreover, there have been ongoing threats by various American regulators to delist over 200 Chinese companies, having a total market valuation of roughly US$2.2 trillion, from US stock exchanges in early 2021.

Given this mounting pressure from trade tariffs and sanctions of technology and energy companies amid a cacophony of criticism over China's domestic policies and regional ambitions right across the US political spectrum, it was perhaps only inevitable that Beijing would begin to eye retaliatory responses. At end 2020, this arose in the guise of China's own versions of Western sanctions legislation, including its Unreliable Entity List Law and Export Control Law. The latter, in particular, exercises an extraterritorial authority to penalise overseas-based organisations and individuals who are posing a risk to China's national security and national interests. It also empowers China to sanction foreign governments where they apply 'abusive' export controls on Chinese goods. Moreover, the former law could sanction foreign companies which restrict supplies of technology to Chinese enterprises. Since these laws came into place, several large US defence contractors have been threatened with Chinese sanctions following their supply of high-tech military weapons to Taiwan. Despite these threats, China has not launched sanctions by the first quarter of 2021 against any specific US or other Western company.

Along with these fast-changing sanctions regimes and ever deepening political rifts between China and the US, Chinese leaders have been signalling an incremental modification in their approach towards championing globalisation and multilateralism. At the forefront has been Beijing's accelerating policy momentum towards securing closer economic relations with its East Asian neighbours (Savic 2020a). This was partly evident in the November 2020 signing of the RCEP. Billed as the world's largest free trade agreement, the largely China-influenced and otherwise ASEAN-driven trade pact that brings together 10 ASEAN states, China, Japan, South Korea, Australia, and New Zealand was Beijing's response to the previous US-led TPP, a strategy largely designed to contain China's growing economic influence in the Asia-Pacific.

This policy orientation in furtherance of East Asian integration was also manifested shortly after RCEP was signed, when Xi expressed an interest in joining the mainly Japan-sponsored CPTPP, even though its standards on industrial subsidies, state enterprises, labour, and the environment were not historically viewed by China as 'trade issues' for negotiation in such economic pacts. Still, it may be a forerunner of China's willingness to abandon certain key principles, which it has historically considered to be matters of non-negotiable 'sovereignty', in favour of an implied flexibility in concluding regional multilateral economic agreements. Indeed, there are increased signs of such an approach in China's negotiations with other regional multilateral grouping such as the EU, AU, EEC, etc.

Even so, while China is extending olive branches to these and other regional centres of power, it should be stressed that for now, Beijing lays a particular focus on 'ASEAN centrality' as the beating heart of its integrative ambitions with East Asia. During a speech reported by Xinhua in November 2020 at the 17th China-ASEAN Expo, Xi stated: 'The world is facing increasing instability and uncertainty ... and the international order and global governance system are being affected ... Under this new situation, China regards ASEAN as the *priority* [our italics] direction of neighbouring diplomacy. China supports ASEAN's central position in East Asian cooperation and supports ASEAN's role in building an open and inclusive regional structure'.

From another perspective, China's policymakers appear to be increasingly aligning themselves with regional multilateral institutions in tandem with the evolving realities that the broader sweep of globalisation is fragmenting as America and other Western nations raise protective barriers against China's political and economic brinkmanship outside of its borders. In response, Beijing appears to be adopting regionally-defined integrative strategies which are inclined towards an increasing 'South-South' approach of closer cooperation between developing nations.

For instance, China and Russia have begun the process of realising the 'Greater Eurasia Partnership'. This was an idea first put forward by Putin in 2015, and which Xi committed to advancing in practical terms in 2020. This envisages co-developing China's BRI with Russia's EAEU, a process which was kicked off in 2019 with an in-principle free trade agreement in effectively conjoining the two international cross border initiatives. The launching of Greater Eurasian projects and joint international initiatives was then set out at a meeting between the Chinese and

Russian premiers in December 2020. This involved plans for enhancing and harmonising their global strategies under various multilateral frameworks including the BRICS, SCO, EAS, Asia-Europe Meeting, APEC and other regionally-centred bodies.

Beyond the Eurasian space, China plans to replicate the concept of region-based integration on a broader international stage. Hence, Beijing is promoting linkages with regional associations of countries across the developing world, including the Middle East, South Asia, Africa, and Latin America. As an example, China's ongoing negotiation of an economic pact with the Gulf Cooperation Council (GCC) may eventually mirror its trade agreement with ASEAN. To this extent, just as the China-ASEAN trade treaty was the fulcrum for a broader regional multilateral arrangement in the form of RCEP, so too could a prospective China-GCC economic agreement expand into a tie-up involving the wider Middle East.

China's initial tentative pivot towards an increasingly region-centric form of globalisation is not a wholly new enterprise. It is, in many ways, a natural evolution of Beijing's ongoing multilateral institutional relationship-building. Ever since the 2008 Global Financial Crisis, this has involved Chinese leaders increasingly striving for cooperation and joint development with regional blocs of countries and their associated multilateralist institutions, as explored in Chapters 8, 9, and 10. However, since the advent of Xi to China's presidency, this regional institutional focus has crystallised into a more defined and prioritised policy outcome. At the same time, global political and economic multilateral institutions such as the UN, the G20 and the WTO remain equally pivotal as China pursues a multi-regional institutional development strategy.

President Xi's upgrading of the importance of regional multilateral institutions to China's international diplomacy and development strategy is, in part, a counterweight to the intensifying pushback it is facing from the US and some of its Western allies. Even so, China stresses that this form of regional institutional diplomacy will not result in the exclusion of other countries, from whatever part of the world or stage of development, in its inter- or intra-regional initiatives — whether that be the open-ended invitation for India to rejoin RCEP, Japan to participate in the BRI, or for that matter, the US to become a member of the AIIB.

For China, therefore, its three-decade old system of bilateral strategic partnerships with governments of various countries still remains a key tool of its international diplomacy. Nonetheless, it is a strategy which is increasingly being less prioritised as Beijing's intensifies its focus on building ties and expanding influence within fast-evolving regional multilateral institutions and existing global organisations. By fashioning such a triple strategy approach to international relations, Beijing is set to promote and support initiatives designed to integrate its ties with institutionalised groupings of countries into broader pan-regional structures, just as formalised ASEAN + China economic linkages are the basis for the more expansive RCEP. Eventually, the end game would probably be to form shared transcontinental economic and political frameworks, starting with an emphasis on regional institutions essentially constituted of developing world countries, backed up by vast cross border logistical and financing infrastructure mechanisms evident in the expanding nature of Xi's signature BRI programme. From this perspective, China's re-emergence in the modern world over the course of the remaining twenty-first century would not only be evidenced by a shift of global economic and political power from West to East, but also from North to South heralding a truly global era.

Bibliography

Adcock, A. and Ordish, R. (2008) *China Intellectual Property Challenges and Solutions: An Essential Business Guide,* John Wiley & Sons (Asia)

African Union (2019) *AUC to Explore Stronger and Mutually Beneficial Partnership Opportunities with China to Strengthen Investments and Unleash Africa's Potential*, press release

Albert, E. and Maizland, L. (2020) *Religion in China* https://www.cfr.org/backgrounder/religion-china

Ali, S.M. (2012) *US-China Cold War Collaboration, 1971–1989*, Routledge

Alibaba (2019) *E-Commerce Development: Experience from China (Vol 2)*, World Bank Report

Althusser, L. (1971) *Ideology and Ideological State Apparatuses (Notes Towards an Investigation)*, In L. Althusser (ed.), *Lenin and Philosophy and Other Essays*, London: Verso

Amante, A. (2020) *Italy Says China a key Strategic Partner, Despite US Concerns* https://www.reuters.com/article/us-china-italy-idUSKBN25L1LR

Anderlini, J. (2019) *How China's Smart-city Tech Focuses on Its Own Citizens* https://www.ft.com/content/46bc137a-5d27-11e9-840c-530737425559

Andreas, J. and Zhan, S. (2016) *Hukou and Land: Market Reform and Rural Displacement in China*, The Journal of Peasant Studies, Vol. 43, pp. 798–827

Angle, S.C. (2011) *Mou Zongsan and his Nineteen Lectures on Chinese Philosophy* https://digitalcollections.wesleyan.edu/object/ceasfp-37

Anishchuk, A. (2014) *As Putin Looks East, China and Russia Sign $400-billion Gas Deal*, Reuters

Arbab, F. (2007) *China-Africa Interaction: Prospects for a Strategic Partnership*? Cornell International Affairs Review, Vol. 1, No 1, pp. 1–2

Artuc, E., Bastos, P. and Rijkers, B. (2018) *'Robots', Tasks and Trade Development*, Economics Development Research Group, World Bank Policy Research Working Paper 8674

ASEAN (2015) *Framework Agreement on Comprehensive Economic Co-Operation Between the Association of South East Asian Nations and the People's Republic of China* https://arc-agreement.asean.org/file/doc/2015/03/framework-agreement-on-comprehensive-economic-co-operation-between-asean-and-the-people-s-republic-of-china.pdf

ASEAN (2020) *Joint Communique of the 53rd ASEAN Foreign Ministers' Meeting* https://asean.org/joint-communique-of-the-53rd-asean-foreign-ministers-meeting/

ASEAN Secretariat (2018) *Overview of ASEAN Plus Three Cooperation* https://asean.org/wp-content/uploads/2016/01/Overview-of-APT-Cooperation-Jul-2018.pdf

Asia Dialogue (2017) *Economic Integration in the Tumen River Region* https://theasiadialogue.com/2017/04/12/economic-integration-in-the-tumen-river-region/

Asia Dialogue (2019) *China's Embrace of the Greater Mekong Subregion* https://theasiadialogue.com/2019/04/11/chinas-embrace-of-the-greater-mekong-subregion/

Asia Infrastructure Investment Bank (2020) *AIIB Approves USD750-M Loan to India for COVID-19 Response* https://www.aiib.org/en/news-events/news/2020/AIIB-Approves-USD750-M-Loan-to-India-for-COVID-19-Response.html

Asian Regional Integration Center (2021) *Chiang Mai Initiative [Multilateralization]* https://aric.adb.org/initiative/chiang-mai-initiative

Atha, K. *et al.* (2020) *China's Smart Cities Development,* https://www.uscc.gov/sites/default/files/2020-04/China_Smart_Cities_Development.pdf

Awai, Y. (2015) *Li Ka-shing Restructures Business to Hedge Against China Risk*, Nikkei Asia

Backer, L.C. (2014) *Crafting a Theory of Socialist Democracy for China in the 21st Century: Considering Hu Angang's* (胡鞍钢) *Theory of Collective Presidency in the Context of the of the Emerging Chinese Constitutional State* https://ssrn.com/abstract=2432393

Bader, J. (2019) *June 4, 1989: A Personal Recollection* https://www.brookings.edu/blog/order-from-chaos/2019/05/29/june-4-1989-a-personal-recollection/

Balding, C. (2018) *Why Democracies Are Turning Against Belt and Road: Corruption, Debt, and Backlash* https://www.foreignaffairs.com/articles/china/2018-10-24/why-democracies-are-turning-against-belt-and-road

Bangkok Post (2020) *Engagement Key to Sino-Thai Ties* https://www.bangkokpost.com/opinion/opinion/1947028/engagement-key-to-sino-thai-ties

Bank of Russia (2016) *The Central Bank of the Russian Federation and People's Bank of China Successfully Launched Bilateral Currency Swap Arrangement* https://www.cbr.ru/eng/press/PR/?file=02032016_100000eng2016-03-02T09_19_55.htm

Barmé, G. (2012) *Telling Chinese Stories* https://soundcloud.com/sydney-ideas/professor-geremie-r-barme-telling-chinese-stories

Barysch, K., Grant, C. and Leonard, M. (2005) *EU-China Relations Factsheet* https://eeas.europa.eu/headquarters/headquarters-Homepage/34728/eu-china-relations-factsheet_en

Begu, L.S., Berghezan, R.I. and Paiu, M. (2015) *China and Angola: The Risks of a Strategic Partnership*, Journal of Social and Economic Statistics, Vol. 4, No. 1, pp. 65–75

Beidou (2020) *The 11th China Satellite Navigation Conference Will Be Held from November 23rd to 25th in Chengdu* https://www.beidou.org/ennewsdetail_1102.html

Bell, D.A. (2017) *Comparing Political Values in China and the West: What Can Be Learned and Why It Matters* https://www.annualreviews.org/doi/pdf/10.1146/annurev-polisci-051215-031821

Bello, W. (2020) *Trump and the Asia-Pacific: The Persistence of American Unilateralism,* Focus on the Global South

Benoit, P. and Tu, K.J. (2020) *Is China Still a Developing Country, and Why it Matters for Energy and Climate*, Columbia University Centre on Global Energy Policy

Berkofsky, A. (2019) *China and the EU: 'Strategic Partners' No More*, Institute for Security and Development Policy, Issue and Policy Briefs

Bernal, G. (2020) *South Korea Seeks to Boost China Ties, With an eye Toward North Korea*, The Diplomat

Bhargava, Y. (2020) *Government Bans 59 Apps including China-Based Tik Tok, WeChat*, The Hindu

Bickers, R. (2012) *The Scramble for China: Foreign Devils in the Qing Empire, 1832–1914*, Penguin Books

BIS (2018) *Committee on Payments and Market Infrastructures* https://www.bis.org/list/cpmi_all/sdt_1/index.htm

Bloomberg (2020a) *India Plans to Impose Strict Rules and Tariffs on Chinese Imports* https://www.bloombergquint.com/economy-finance/india-is-said-to-weigh-strict-rules-tariffs-on-chinese-imports

Bloomberg (2020b) *China's New Growth Plan May Push Economy Past US Within Decade* https://www.bloomberg.com/news/articles/2020-10-25/china-s-new-growth-plan-may-push-economy-past-u-s-within-decade

Bloomberg (2020c) *China's Liu Urges More Solid Capital Market Reform* https://www.bloomberg.com/news/articles/2020-10-31/china-s-liu-urges-more-solid-capital-market-reform

BNP Paribas (2019) Chi Lo. Investing 25/01/2019 https://investors-corner.bnpparibas-am.com/investing/china-policy-opening-inward/

Bolt, P.J. (2018) *China, Russia and Twenty-First Century Global Geopolitics*, Oxford University Press

Brady, A.M. (2012) *China's Thought Management*, Routledge

Brady, A.M. (2018) China in Xi's 'New Era': New Zealand and the CCP'S 'Magic Weapons'. Journal of Democracy, 2018 muse.jhu.edu

Breslin, S. (1998) '*"Made in China": The Growth of Chinese Trade*', CSGR Working Paper No. 19

Brown, K. and Bērziņa-Čerenkova, U.A. (2018) *Ideology in the Era of Xi Jinping*, Journal of Chinese Political Science, Vol. 23, pp. 323–339

Bruzdzinski, J.E. (2005), *Demystifying Shashoujian: China's 'Assassin's Mace' Concept*, The MITRE Corporation

Buhai, S. cf. Herrlee G. Creel (1974) *Shen Pu-hai: A Chinese Political Philosopher of the Fourth Century B.C.*, Chicago: University of Chicago Press

Burchard, H.V.D. and Barigazzi, J. (2020) *EU Policymakers Propose Taking China to Court Over Hong Kong Security Law*, Politico

Burns, R. (2017) *Intelligence Report: The Kremlin Believes the US Wants Regime Change in Russia*, Business Insider

Bush, G.H.W. (1989) *Press Conference, June 5, 1989* https://www.c-span.org/video/?7909-1/president-george-hw-bush-tiananmen-square-crackdown

Business Wire (2017) *Alibaba Launches Global Research Programme for Cutting-Edge Technology Development* https://www.businesswire.com/news/home/20171010006804/en/Alibaba-Launches-Global-Research-Program-for-Cutting-Edge-Technology-Development

Calinoff, J. and Gordon, D. (2020) *Port Investments in the Belt and Road Initiative: Is Beijing Grabbing Strategic Assets?* Survival, Vol. 62, No. 4, pp. 59–80

Campden Wealth (2020) *Up Close and Personal: Perspectives On Asian Family Offices* http://www.campdenfb.com/article/close-and-personal-perspectives-asian-family-offices

Cartwright, M. (2017) *The Mandate of Heaven*, Ancient History Encyclopedia https://www.ancient.eu/Mandate_of_Heaven/

CDRF (2018) *China Development Research Foundation 2018 Annual Report* https://cdrf-en.cdrf.org.cn/ndbg/5106.jhtml

CEIC (2020) *China* https://www.ceicdata.com/en/country/china

Centre for European Reform (2020) *Europe, The US and China: A Love-Hate Triangle* https://www.cer.eu/publications/archive/policy-brief/2020/europe-us-and-china-love-hate-triangle

CGTN Africa (2019) *China and African Union Sign MoU on Food Security* https://africa.cgtn.com/2019/09/05/china-and-african-union-sign-mou-on-food-security/

CGTN (2019) *China Keen to Build on Comprehensive Strategic Partnership with Germany* https://news.cgtn.com/news/3d3d774e7859444d35457a6333566d54/index.html

Chan, F.G. (2019) *China at the Crossroads: Nationalists and Communists, 1927–1949*, Taylor & Francis

Chang, W. and Madison, N. (2013) *Inside China's Legal System*, Chandos Publishing

Chauhan, C.P. (2020) *Will China Fade Away on the Indian Automobile Turf?* The Economic Times

Chen, J. (2001) *Mao's China and the Cold War*, The University of North Carolina Press

Chen, C.K.A. (2009) *Development of The Sage-King Narratives: Idealized Concepts of Rulership in Warring States Chinese Thought* https://open.library.ubc.ca/cIRcle/collections/ubctheses/24/items/1.0073403

Chen, M. (2012) *Energy Ties and the China-Angola Strategic Partnership*, The Newsletter 62 Winter

Chen, M. (2015) *Transcend Left and Right* https://www.rujiazg.com/article/4939

Chen, J. (2019) *From Mao to Deng: China's Changing Relations with the United States*, CWIHP Working Paper 92

Cheng, J. (2013) *China's Regional Strategy and Challenges in East Asia*, Centre d'étude français sur la Chine contemporaire, China Perspectives 2

Cheng, S. and Shen, T. (2019) *Residency Restrictions to Be Scrapped in Many of China's Cities* https://www.caixinglobal.com/2019-04-08/residency-restrictions-to-be-scrapped-in-many-of-chinas-cities-101401792.html

Chin, J.K. (1993) *King Taksin and China: Siam-Chinese Relations During the Thonburi Period as Seen From Chinese Sources,* University of London

China Banking News (2019) *China's Mobile Payments Penetration Rate, Highest in the World* https://www.chinabankingnews.com/2019/04/15/chinas-mobile-payments-penetration-rate-highest-in-the-world-at-86-pwc-report/

China Briefing (2018) *The Beijing-Tianjin-Hebei Integration Plan* https://www.china-briefing.com/news/the-beijing-tianjin-hebei-integration-plan/

China Briefing (2019) *33 million Businesses Given A Social Credit Score* https://www.china-briefing.com/news/chinas-corporate-social-credit-system-how-it-works/

China Briefing (2020a) *China Corona Virus Updates* https://www.china-briefing.com/news/china-coronavirus-updates-latest-developments-business-advisory-part-2/

China Briefing (2020b) *Vaccine Development* https://www.china-briefing.com/news/chinas-covid-19-vaccine-development-and-availability/

China Briefing (2020c) *China's Cybersecurity Law* https://www.china-briefing.com/news/chinas-cybersecurity-law-an-introduction-for-foreign-businesspeople/

China Briefing (2020d) *China's Incentives for Integrated Circuit, Software Enterprises* https://www.china-briefing.com/news/china-integrated-circuit-software-enterprises-tax-incentives/

China Cadre Learning Network (2016) *Xi Jinping's Cultural Security Concept*

China Daily (2014) *China to Expand Yangtze Transport Capacity* http://www.chinadaily.com.cn/business/2014-06/12/content_17581907.htm

China Daily (2016) *New Five-Year Plan Brings Hope to China's West* http://europe.chinadaily.com.cn/business/2016-12/27/content_27786295.htm

China Daily (2018) *Guangzhou Mino Automotive Equipment Inks Deal with Siemens* http://www.chinadaily.com.cn/a/201812/12/WS5c110670a310eff303290aa5.html

China Daily (2020) *Synergy of Yangtze Delta Region Stressed* https://www.chinadaily.com.cn/regional/2020-08/24/content_37538956.htm

China Embassy (2012) *China, Russia Agree to Enhance Strategic Partnership* http://www.china-embassy.org/eng/zgyw/t938783.htm

China Embassy UK (2020) *White Paper--Freedom of Religious Belief in China* http://www.china-embassy.org/eng/zt/zjxy/t36492.htm

China Labour Bulletin (2019) *The State of Labour Relations in China* https://clb.org.hk/content/state-labour-relations-china-2019

China Mission (2020) *Key Documents on China-EU Relations* http://www.chinamission.be/eng/zywj/zywd/

China.Org (2004) *China, Italy to Establish Comprehensive Strategic Partnership* http://www.china.org.cn/english/2004/May/94711.htm

China.Org (2010) *Brief History of the Communist Party of China* https://cpcchina.chinadaily.com.cn/2010-09/07/content_13901594_7.htm

China.org (2012) *ASEAN Joint Statement on DOC in South China Sea* https://China.org.cn/world/2012-11/20/content_27167423.htm

China.Org (2019) *New Plan Puts Greater Water Efficiency on Tap* http://www.china.org.cn/china/2019-04/25/content_74720155.htm

China.Org (2020) *Chinese People's Political Consultative Conference* http://www.china.org.cn/english/27750.htm

China Power (2017) *How Will the Belt and Road Initiative Advance China's Interests?* http://chinapower.csis.org/china-belt-and-road-initiative

China Power (2019) *Is China Ready for Intelligent Automation?* https://chinapower.csis.org/china-intelligent-automation/

China Science and Technology Newsletter (2017) *Next Generation Artificial Intelligence Development Plan*, No. 17. http://fi.china-embassy.org/eng/kxjs/P020171025789108009001.pdf

Chinafile (2015) *Does Xi Jinping Represent a Return to the Mao Era?* https://www.chinafile.com/reporting-opinion/features/does-xi-jinping-represent-return-mao-era

Chiu, C., Ip, C. and Silverman, A. (2012) *Understanding Social Media in China*, McKinsey Quarterly (1)

Cho, R. (2011) *How China is Dealing with Its Water Crisis,* Columbia University

Choukroune, L. (2015) *The Language of Rights and the Politics of Law: Perspectives on China's Last Legal Ditch Struggle*, International Journal for the Semiotics of Law, Vol. 29, pp. 779–803

Chua, D. (2017) *Troubled Waters: China Seeks Return to Vassal States in the South China Sea* https://international.thenewslens.com/article/63032

Ciurtin, H. (2019) *The '16+1' Becomes the '17+1': Greece Joins China's Dwindling Cooperation Framework in Central and Eastern Europe*, The Jamestown Foundation China Brief, Vol. 19, No. 10

Clark, R. (2020) *Kavkaz 2020 and Turkey — A Lesson for the West and NATO*, UK Defence Journal

Climate Action Tracker (2020) https://climateactiontracker.org/

CNBC (2020) *China Is Ramping Up Its Own Chip Industry Amid a Brewing Tech War. That Could Hurt US Firms* https://www.cnbc.com/2019/06/04/china-ramps-up-own-semiconductor-industry-amid-the-trade-war.html

Cohen, J. (2019) *China's CRISPR revolution*, Science, Vol. 365, No. 6452, pp. 420–421

Connecting Africa (2019) *Bringing PEACE to Africa's Comms Ecosystem* http://www.connectingafrica.com/document.asp?doc_id=749886

Congressional Research Service (2011) *China's Currency Policy: An Analysis of the Economic Issues* https://www.everycrsreport.com/reports/RS21625.html

Congressional Research Service (2021) *U.S.-China Strategic Competition in South and East China Seas: Background and Issues for Congress* https://fas.org/sgp/crs/row/R42784.pdf

Cormier, M. (2013) *The Legacy of Tiananmen Square*, Goose Lane Editions

Corkin, L. (2011) *Uneasy allies: China's evolving relations with Angola*, Routledge, Journal of Contemporary African Studies, Vol. 29, No. 2, pp. 169–180

Counterpoint (2020) *India Smartphone Market Share: By Quarter* https://www.counterpointresearch.com/india-smartphone-share/

Covington (2019) *China Enacts Encryption Law* https://www.cov.com/en/news-and-insights/insights/2019/10/china-enacts-encryption-law

Cozzens, T. (2019) *Russia Passes Law on GLONASS-Beidou Cooperation*, GPS World

Creel, H.G. (1974) *Shen Pu-hai: A Chinese Political Philosopher of the Fourth Century B.C.*, University of Chicago Press

Cyranoski, D. (2019) *The CRISPR-baby Scandal: What's Next for Human Gene-editing*, Nature, Vol. 566, No. 7745, pp. 440–442

Dace, H. (2020) *China's Tech Landscape: A Primer* https://institute.global/policy/chinas-tech-landscape-primer

Debelo, A.R. (2017) *The African Union's Peace and Security Partnership with China*, African Peacebuilding Network Briefing Note No. 12

Deloitte (2019) *Future in The Balance? How Countries Are Pursuing an AI Advantage* https://www2.deloitte.com/us/en/insights/focus/cognitive-technologies/ai-investment-by-country.html

Deloitte (2020a) *Smart City* https://www2.deloitte.com/cn/en/pages/public-sector/topics/smart-city.html

Deloitte (2020b) *Rise of the 'Big 4': The semiconductor industry in Asia Pacific* https://www2.deloitte.com/content/dam/Deloitte/cn/Documents/technology-media-telecommunications/cn-tmt-rise-of-the-big-4-en-082820.pdf

Deloitte Insights (2019) *China's Role in African Infrastructure and Capital Projects* https://www2.deloitte.com/us/en/insights/industry/public-sector/china-investment-africa-infrastructure-development.html

Deutsche Gessellschaft fur Internationale Zussammenarbeit (2020) *Standardisation of Key Areas of Work* https://gib-foundation.org/wp-content/uploads/2020/05/International_Standards_for_Sustainable_Infrastructure-2.pdf

d'Hooghe, I. (2007) *The Rise of China's Public Diplomacy*, Netherlands Institute of Public Relations Clingendael Diplomacy Papers No 12

d'Hooghe, I. (2014) *China's Public Diplomacy*, Brill

Dictionary of World History (2020) *May Fourth Movement,* Oxford University Press

Digital Electronic Money Association (2020) *Libra Link to Dollar* https://www.diem.com/en-us/white-paper/#cover-letter

Dillon, M. (2001) *Religious Minorities and China*, Minority Rights Group International

Doffman, Z. (2019) *Huawei Just Launched 5G In Russia with Putin's Support: 'Hello Splinternet'* https://www.forbes.com/sites/zakdoffman/2019/09/01/hello-splinternet-huawei-deploys-5g-in-russia-with-putins-support/

Dollar, D. (2015) *China's Rise as a Regional and Global Power — The AIIB and the 'One Belt, One Road'*, Centre for International Relations and Sustainable Development, Horizons Summer No. 4

Dooley, B. and Inoue, M. (2020) *Japan is Paying Firms to Make Things at Home. But China's Pull is Still Strong*, New York Times

Drezner, D.W. (2013) *The Political Economy of Document Number Nine* https://foreignpolicy.com/2013/08/20/the-political-economy-of-document-number-nine/

Duchatel, M. (2020) *Generally Stable? Facing US Pushback in the South China Sea* https://www.institutmontaigne.org/en/blog/china-trends-6-generally-stable-facing-us-pushback-south-china-sea

Dudarenok, A.G. and Zakkour, M. (2019) *New Retail Born in China Going Global: How Chinese Tech are Changing Global Commerce*, Independently Published

Dueck, A. and Han, B. (2012) *Psychology of Religion in China*, Pastoral Psychology, Vol. 61, pp. 605–622

Duhalde, M., Wong, D. and Lee, K. (2020) *India-China Border Clash Explained*, South China Morning Post

Dunford, M. and Bonschab, T. (2013) *Chinese Regional Development and Policy*, Regions Magazine, Vol. 289, No. 1, pp. 10–13

East West Digital News (2018) *Chinese WeChat Pay Comes to Russia, Russian Mir Goes Global* https://www.ewdn.com/2018/11/15/chinese-wechat-pay-comes-to-russia-russian-mir-goes-global/

Eberstadt, N. (2019) *China's Demographic Outlook to 2040 and Its Implications* https://globalcoalitiononaging.com/wp-content/uploads/2019/01/China%E2%80%99s-Demographic-Outlook.pdf

Ebrey, P.B. (2010) *The Cambridge Illustrated History of China*, Cambridge University Press

ECNS (2013) *Xi Promises Opportunities for Overseas Chinese Investment* http://www.ecns.cn/business/2013/09-26/82359.shtml

Economic Intelligence Unit (2018) *Automation Readiness Index* https://www.automationreadiness.eiu.com/

Edquist, C. (2001) *The Systems of Innovation Approach and Innovation Policy: An Account of the State of the Art,* DRUID Conference, Aalborg, Denmark

Ellyat, H. (2019) *Russia Conducts Massive Military Drills with China, Sending a Message to the West*, CNBC

Embassy of China in US (2003) *China Accedes to the Treaty of Amity and Cooperation in Southeast Asia* https://china-embassy.org/eng/xw/t34707.htm

Ericsson (2020) *Ericsson Selected as China Mobile 5G RAN and Core Network Vendor; China Telecom and China Unicom Select Ericsson 5G* https://www.ericsson.com/en/news/2020/4/china-mobile-5g-network https://www.ericsson.com/en/news/2020/5/china-telecom-and-china-unicom-select-ericsson-5g

EU-China (2020a) *EU-China 2020 Strategic Agenda for Cooperation* https://eeas.europa.eu/archives/docs/china/docs/eu-china_2020_strategic_agenda_en.pdf

EU-China (2020b) *EU and China Discuss Trade and Economic Relations* https://ec.europa.eu/commission/presscorner/detail/en/ip_20_1419

European Commission (2016) *Growth & Innovation Smart Specialisation Platform* https://s3platform.jrc.ec.europa.eu/

European Commission (2017) *R & D Expenditure* https://ec.europa.eu/eurostat/statistics-explained/index.php?title=Main_Page

European Commission (2020) *Comparison within G20* https://ec.europa.eu/eurostat/documents/2995521/10928892/1-02062020-AP-EN.pdf/c3253596-bbda-491e-6f59-62a7e5f5c965

European Council on Foreign Relations (2015) *Relations with China on Russia/Ukraine* https://ecfr.eu/scorecard/2015/china/48

European Parliament (2013) *The Positions of Russia and China at the UN Security Council in the Light of Recent Crises* https://www.europarl.europa.eu/RegData/etudes/note/join/2013/433800/EXPO-SEDE_NT(2013)433800_EN.pdf

European Parliament (2018) *European Parliament Resolution of 12 September 2018 on The State Of EU-China Relations* https://www.europarl.europa.eu/doceo/document/TA-8-2018-0343_EN.html

Ekman, A. and de Esperanza Picardo, C. (2020) *Towards Urban Decoupling? China's Smart City Ambitions at The Time of Covid-19* https://www.iss.europa.eu/content/towards-urban-decoupling-china%E2%80%99s-smart-city-ambitions-time-covid-19

FBIC Group (2020) *Social Commerce* https://web.archive.org/web/20201128125913/https://www.fbicgroup.com/sites/default/files/Social_commerce.pdf

Federal Foreign Office of Germany (2020) *Germany and China — Enhancing Dialogue, Deepening Cooperation* https://www.auswaertiges-amt.de/en/aussenpolitik/laenderinformationen/china-node/maas-meets-chinese-foreign-minister-wang/2306984

Federal Foreign Office of Germany (2021) *Germany and China: Bilateral Relations* https://www.auswaertiges-amt.de/en/aussenpolitik/laenderinformationen/china-node/china/228916

Federation of German Industries (2020) *The EU-China Investment Treaty* https://english.bdi.eu/article/news/the-eu-china-investment-treaty/

Feng, E. (2020a) *As US Views of China Grow More Negative, Chinese Support for Their Government Rises* https://www.npr.org/2020/09/23/913650298/

Feng, D. (2020b) *China and the DR Congo Strengthen Bilateral Ties*, Global Times

Feng, Z. and Huang, J. (2014) *China's Strategic Partnership Diplomacy: Engaging with a Changing World*, European Strategic Partnerships Observatory Working Paper No. 8

Ferchen, M. (2020) *How China is Reshaping International Development*, Carnegie Endowment for International Peace https://carnegieendowment.org/2020/01/08/how-china-is-reshaping-international-development-pub-80703

Fitch Solutions (2019) *Sustainability Trends: Influencers, Drivers and Implications by Industry* https://store.fitchsolutions.com/all-products/sustainability-trends-influencers-drivers-and-implications-by-industry

Fitch Solutions (2020) *China's New Infrastructure Investments to Underpin Economic Growth Over the Next Decade* https://www.fitchsolutions.com/information-technology/chinas-new-infrastructure-investments-underpin-economic-growth-over-next-decade-29-07-2020

Frangoul, A. (2020) *President Xi Tells UN That China Will Be 'Carbon Neutral' Within Four Decades* https://www.cnbc.com/2020/09/23/china-claims-it-will-be-carbon-neutral-by-the-year-2060.html

Frankel, J. (2015) *The Plaza Accord, 30 Years Later* https://www.nber.org/system/files/working_papers/w21813/w21813.pdf

Frederic, P.M., Vandome, A.F. and McBrewster, J. (2011) *Han Dynasty*, Alphascript Publishing

Fu, H. and Palmer, M. (2017) *Mediation in Contemporary China: Continuity and Change*, Wildy, Simmonds and Hill Publishing

Fukuyama, F. (1992) *The End of History and the Last Man*, Free Press

Gady, F.S. (2015) *China and India Hold Joint Military Exercise*, The Diplomat

Gady, F.S. (2017) *China, Russia Kick Off Anti-Ballistic Missile Defence Exercise*, The Diplomat

Gan, N. (2018) *Why Xi Jinping's the Man for Me ...*, South China Morning Post

Gao, M. (2008) *The Battle for China's Past: Mao and the Cultural Revolution*, Abebooks.co.uk

Garten, J.E. (2001) *China in the WTO: Let's Cut It Some Slack* https://www.bloomberg.com/news/articles/2001-10-07/china-in-the-wto-lets-cut-it-some-slack

German Federal Government (2014) *Joint Declaration between Germany and China*, Press Release No. 102

Gilley, B. (2014) *The Nature of Asian Politics*, Cambridge University Press

Global Data (2019) *China's NOCs to be Fourth Highest Upstream Investors in Africa Over Next Five Years, Says Global Data* https://www.globaldata.com/chinas-nocs-to-be-fourth-highest-upstream-investors-in-africa-over-next-five-years-says-globaldata/

Global Data (2020) *China's Investment Appetite for Indian Tech Startups Grows Stronger, Says Global Data* https://www.globaldata.com/chinas-investment-appetite-for-indian-tech-startups-grows-stronger-says-globaldata/

Global Market Insights (2016) *Electronic Design Automation (EDA) Market* https://www.gminsights.com/industry-analysis/electronic-design-automation-eda-market

Global Times (2020) *Germany's Huawei Stance Can Be Example for EU Countries: Analysts* https://www.globaltimes.cn/content/1201997.shtml

GlobeNewswire (2020) *Increasing-Environmental Concerns Expected to Restrain the Market* https://www.globenewswire.com/news-release/2020/09/11/2092351/0/en/Worldwide-Shale-Gas-Industry-to-2025-Increasing-Environmental-Concerns-Expected-to-Restrain-the-Market.html

Glueck, U. and Gu, D. (2020) *The Belt and Road Initiative The View from China 2020* https://cms.law/en/media/international/images/top-publication/bri/belt-and-road-initiative-china-english

Goldman, D. (2020) *How Huawei Can Work Around US Chip Ban*, Asia Times

Goldstein, A. (2001) *The diplomatic face of China's grand strategy: A rising power's emerging choice*. The China Quarterly, No. 168, pp. 835–864

Goldstein, S.M. (2015) *China and Taiwan*, Polity Press

Gordon, R.J. (2020) *What Is New-Keynesian Economics?* Journal of Economic Literature, Vol. 28, No. 3, pp. 1115–1171

Graham, E. and Koshino, Y. (2020) *Australia and Japan Inch Closer Towards Landmark Defence Agreement* https://www.iiss.org/blogs/analysis/2020/12/australia-japan-landmark-defence-agreement

Grossman, D. (2020) *The Quad Is Poised to Become Openly Anti-China Soon* https://www.rand.org/blog/2020/07/the-quad-is-poised-to-become-openly-anti-china-soon.html

Haacke, J. (2009) *The ASEAN Regional Forum: From Dialogue to Practical Security Cooperation?* Cambridge Review of International Affairs, Vol. 22, No. 3, pp. 427–429

Haidar, S. (2020) *India China Relations are of Global Significance: Chinese Envoy Sun Weidong*, The Hindu

Hallpike, C. (1995) *The Social Poison of Individual Rights*, Theme School of International Justice and Human Rights, McMaster University

Han, W. (2018) *Western Provinces Leading E-Commerce Growth, Alibaba Says*, Caixin

Harsha, D. (2020) *Ash Center Research Team Unveils Findings from Long-Term Public Opinion Survey* https://news.harvard.edu/gazette/story/2020/07/long-term-survey-reveals-chinese-government-satisfaction

Harshe, R. (2019) *China in Africa: Developmental Partnership or Imperial Dominance?* Observer Research Foundation

Hawkins, V. (2018) *Modi's Successful Diplomacy*, Alpha Edition

Hawkins, A. (2019) *How Elderly, Sickly Farmers Are Quenching China's Thirst for Data* https://www.wired.co.uk/article/china-ai-healthcare

He, H. (2015) *Governance, Social Organisation and Reform in Rural China,* Palgrave Macmillan, UK

Henderson, C., Song, R. and Joffe, P. (2017) *China's Decline in Coal Consumption Drives Global Slowdown in Emissions* https://www.wri.org/blog/2017/01/china-s-decline-coal-consumption-drives-global-slowdown-emissions

Hernandez, C.G. (2008) *ASEAN's China Strategy Towards a Regional Order: A Philippine View*, 3rd Berlin Conference on Asian Security

Hickert, C. and Ding, J. (2018) *What Top Chinese Officials Are Hearing About AI Competition and Policy* https://www.newamerica.org/cybersecurity-initiative/digichina/blog/read-what-top-chinese-officials-are-hearing-about-ai-competition-and-policy/

Higgins, S. (2016) *China's Central Bank Discusses Digital Currency Launch* https://www.coindesk.com/peoples-bank-of-china-discusses-plans-to-issue-digital-currency

Hobbes, T. (1651) *Leviathan*, Collins Fontana Library

Hoffman, S. (2019) *The Complicated Truth About China's Social Credit System* https://www.wired.co.uk/article/china-social-credit-system-explained

Holmes, L. (2009) *Communism: A Very Short Introduction*, Oxford University Press

Holmes, J.R. (2013) *Gwadar and the 'String of Pearls'*, The Diplomat

Hong Kong TDC (2018) *Russia: A Prime Belt and Road Investment Destination* https://hkmb.hktdc.com/en/1X0AEN03/hktdc-research/Russia-A-Prime-Belt-and-Road-Investment-Destination

Hsu, J.Y.J. (2014) *Chinese Non-Governmental Organisations and Civil Society: A Review of The Literature*, Geography Compass, Vol. 8, No. 2, pp. 98–110

Hu, A. (2016) *The Five-Year Plan: A New Tool for Energy Saving and Emissions Reduction in China,* Advances in Climate Change Research, Vol. 7, No. 4, pp. 222–228

Huang, C. (2014) *Integration of Beijing, Tianjin and Hebei Set to be Signature Project of Xi Jinping's Administration*, South China Morning Post

Huang, Y. and Smith, J, (2001) *China's Record on Intellectual Property Rights is Getting Better and Better*, Foreign Policy

Huang, W., Wei, Y., Guo, J. and Cao, J. (2017) *Next Generation Innovation and Development of Intelligent Transportation Systems in China,* Science China Information Sciences, Vol. 60, No. 11

Huawei (2017) *Huawei Marine and Tropical Science Commences Work on the Construction of the PEACE Submarine Cable Linking South Asia with East Africa* https://www.huawei.com/en/news/2017/11/PEACE-Submarine-Cable-SouthAsia-EastAfrica

Human Rights Watch (2003) *The July 1, 2003 Protest* https://www.hrw.org/legacy/backgrounder/asia/china/hk0904/2.htm

Hung, H.-F. (2017) *The China Boom*, New York: Columbia University Press

Hunter, A. and Chan, K.K. (2010) *Protestantism in Contemporary China,* Cambridge University Press

Huo, J. (2020) *Cooperation with China Crucial to South Korean Economy,* Global Times

Huong, L.T. (2020) *Rough Waters Ahead for Vietnam-China Relations* https://carnegieendowment.org/2020/09/30/rough-waters-ahead-for-vietnam-china-relations-pub-82826

Hurley, J., Morris, S. and Portelance, G. (2018) *Examining the Debt Implications of the Belt and Road Initiative from a Policy Perspective*, Centre for Global Development, CGD Policy Paper 121

IDC (2020) *Worldwide Smart Cities Spending Guide* https://www.idc.com/tracker/showproductinfo.jsp?containerId=IDC_P37477

IISS (2018) *IISS Shangri-La Dialogue 2018* https://www.iiss.org/events/shangri-la-dialogue/shangri-la-dialogue-2018

ILO Global Commission (2019) *Work for a Brighter Future* https://www.ilo.org/global/topics/future-of-work/publications/WCMS_662410/lang--en/index.htm

IMF (2021) *Country Data* https://www.imf.org/en/Countries/CHN#data

IMF (2019) *China's Productivity Convergence and Growth Potential — A Stocktaking and Sectoral Approach*, Working Paper WP 19/263

Inamo, S. (2015) *The Foundation of the ASEAN Economic Community,* Cambridge University Press

India Blooms (2020) *Washington Adds China's SMIC to Entity List, Restricting Access to Key Enabling U.S. Technology* https://www.indiablooms.com/

world-details/USN/27269/washington-adds-china-s-smic-to-entity-list-restricting-access-to-key-enabling-u-s-technology.html

Indian Ministry of External Affairs (2013) *Agreement between the Government of the Republic of India and the Government of the People's Republic of China on Border Defence Cooperation* https://www.mea.gov.in/bilateral-documents.htm?dtl/22366/Agreement+between+the+Government+of+the+Republic+of+India+and+the+Government+of+the+Peoples+Republic+of+China+on+Border+Defence+Cooperation

Indian Ministry of External Affairs (2014) *Joint Statement between the Republic of India and the People's Republic of China on Building a Closer Developmental Partnership* https://www.mea.gov.in/bilateral-documents.htm?dtl/24022/

Indian Ministry of External Affairs (2018) *India-China Informal Summit at Wuhan* https://mea.gov.in/press-releases.htm?dtl/29853/IndiaChina_Informal_Summit_at_Wuhan

Inozemtsev, V. (2019) *Integrating the Eurasian Union and China's Belt and Road: A Bridge Too Far*? https://www.timesca.com/index.php/news/26-opinion-head/21302-integrating-the-eurasian-union-and-china-s-belt-and-road-a-bridge-too-far

Institute for International Economies (2002) *The Chiang Mai Initiative* https://www.piie.com/publications/chapters_preview/345/3iie3381.pdf

Inui, T., Takahashi, W. and Ishida, M. (2020) *A Proposal for An Asian Digital Common Currency* https://voxeu.org/article/proposal-asian-digital-common-currency

Investopedia (2020) *China's GDP Examined: A Service-Sector Surge* https://www.investopedia.com/articles/investing/103114/chinas-gdp-examined-servicesector-surge.asp

Irwin, D.A. and Klenow, P.J. (1996) *Sematech: Purpose andPerformance,* PNAS, Vol. 93, No. 23, pp. 12739–12742

ISEAS (2017) *China's White Paper on Security Cooperation in the Asia-Pacific Region and Chinese Grand Strategy* https://www.iseas.edu.sg/images/pdf/ISEAS_Perspective_2017_22.pdf

Iwomoto, K. (2021) *China's New Year Digital Yuan Tests Hasten Asia E-Currency Race* https://asia.nikkei.com/Spotlight/Asia-Insight/China-s-New-Year-digital-yuan-tests-hasten-Asia-e-currency-race

Jencks, H.W. (1989) *The Losses in Tiananmen Square* https://www.airforcemag.com/PDF/MagazineArchive/Documents/1989/November%201989/1189losses.pdf

Jersild, A. (2015) *The Sino-Soviet Alliance: An International History*, Chapel Hill, University of North Carolina Press

Jiang, J. (2003) *The National People's Congress of China*, Foreign Languages Press

Jiang, Y. (2011) *The Mandate of Heaven and The Great Ming Code*, Asian Law Series No. 21, University of Washington Press

Jing, M. and Dai, S. (2017) *China Recruits Baidu, Alibaba and Tencent to AI 'National Team'* https://www.scmp.com/tech/china-tech/article/2120913/china-recruits-baidu-alibaba-and-tencent-ai-national-team

Jing, S. (2018) *Tianjin FTZ Pushes for Building of Free Port*, China Daily

Johnson, J. and Sugiyama, S. (2020) *Quad Meeting in Tokyo Prizes Symbolism Over Substance*, The Japan Times

Jones, L. and Hameiri, S. (2020) *Debunking the Myth of Debt-trap Diplomacy*, Chatham House

Kang, D. (2012) *East Asia Before the West*, Columbia University Press

Kannan, S. (2015) *The Chinese Firms Opening Factories in India*, BBC News

Kantchev, G. (2020) *Russia, China Deepen Ties with Construction of Massive Polymer Plant*, The Wall Street Journal

Kapoor, M. (2020) *Six Things to Know About India-China Economic Relations*, Bloomberg. https://www.bloombergquint.com/economy-finance/six-things-toknow-about-india-china-economic-relations

Kartik, J., Kassiri, O. and Sun, I.Y. (2017) *The Closest Look Yet a Chinese Economic Engagement in Africa,* McKinsey and Company Report

Kaufman, Alison Adcock (2010) *The 'Century of Humiliation', Then and Now: Chinese Perceptions of the International Order*, Pacific Focus, Inha Journal of International Studies, Vol. 25, No. 1, pp. 1–33

Kazmin, A. and Findlay, S. (2020) *India Moves to Cut Huawei Gear from Telecom Network*, Financial Times

Keegan, E. (2019) *China, Russia set to Double Trade to US$200 billion by 2024 With Help of Soybeans*, South China Morning Post

Keith, R.C. (1989) *Zhou Enlai, Jawaharlal Nehru and Estranged Afro–Asian Unity*, Palgrave Macmillan

Kemp, J. (2014) *Joint Resource Development in South China Sea* www.japantimes.co.jp/opinion/2014/09/02/commentary/world-commentary/joint-resource-development-south-china-sea/

Kendall, F. (2015) *A Case for Reform: Improving DOD's Ability to Respond to the Pace of Technological Change,* Testimony by Frank Kendall, Under Secretary of Defense (Acquisition, Technology, & Logistics), Before House Armed Services Committee Hearing, January 28, 2015

Keyong, D. and Donghyun, P. (2019) Reforming Pension Insurance in the People's Republic of China EAST ASIA Working Paper Series No. 19 December 2019 ADB

Kiely, J. and Jessup, J.B. (2016) *Recovering Buddhism in Modern China*, Columbia University Press

Kitson, A. and Liew, K. (2019) *China Doubles Down on Its Digital Silk Road* https://reconnectingasia.csis.org/analysis/entries/china-doubles-down-its-digital-silk-road/

Klimes, O. (2017) *China's Cultural Soft Power: The Central Concept in the Early Xi Jinping Era,* AUC Philologica, No. 4, pp. 127–150

Klimes, O. and Marinelli, M. (2018) *Introduction: Ideology, Propaganda, And Political Discourse in The Xi Jinping Era,* Journal of Chinese Political Science, Vol. 23, No. 3, pp. 313–322

Knight, N. J. (1982) *Mao and History: An Interpretive Essay on Some Problems in Mao Zedong's Philosophy of History,* Doctor of Philosophy Thesis, School of Oriental and African Studies, University of London https://eprints.soas.ac.uk/28782/1/10672950.pdf

Kobayashi, S., Jia, B. and Sano, J. (1999) *The 'Three Reforms' in China: Progress and Outlook*, Sakura Institute of Research, Inc. Paper No 45

Kokobun, R., Soeya, Y., Takahara, A. and Kawashima, S. (2017) *Japan-China Relations in the Modern Era*, Routledge

Koleski, K. (2017) *The 13th Five Year Plan* https://www.uscc.gov/sites/default/files/Research/The%2013th%20Five-Year%20Plan_Final_2.14.17_Updated%20(002).pdf

Kong, L. (2019) *Exploring China's Soft Power: Manifestations of the Chinese Dream in Contemporary Practices of Cultural Diplomacy,* PhD Thesis, University of York https://etheses.whiterose.ac.uk/27062/7/Kong_202046173_Final%20Thesis%20revised%20.pdf

Konstantinidis, M. (2021) *The EU-China Comprehensive Agreement on Investment: A Tale of Sound and Fury* https://www.ejiltalk.org/the-eu-china-comprehensive-agreement-on-investment-a-tale-of-sound-and-fury/

KPMG (2016) *Opportunities for Chinese and Foreign Businesses* https://home.kpmg/xx/en/home/insights/2016/10/the-13th-fyp-opportunity-analysis-for-chinese-and-foreign-business.html

Krishnan, A. (2020a) *Indian Companies in China Brace for Uncertainty Amid Outbreak*, The Hindu

Krishnan, A. (2020b) *One Third of Funding by AIIB Has Gone to India*, The Hindu

Kundnani, H. and Parello-Plesner, J. (2012) *China and Germany: Why the Emerging Special Relationship Matters for Europe*, European Council on Foreign Relations, Policy Brief 55

Kwakwa, V. (2018) *China: A Watershed Moment for Water Governance* https://www.worldbank.org/en/news/press-release/2018/11/07/china-a-watershed-moment-for-water-governance

Labuschagne, J.P. and Marais, H. (2019) *If You Want to Prosper, Consider Building Roads — China's Role in Infrastructure and Capital Projects*, Deloitte Insights

Lai, J. (2012) *Financial Crisis and Institutional Change in East Asia* (*Critical Studies of the Asia-Pacific*), Palgrave Macmillan

Langer, J. (2018) *Rapid Changes in The Chinese Legal System, An Increasingly Attractive Venue for IP Litigation* https://www.ipwatchdog.com/2018/05/07/rapid-changes-chinese-legal-system-attractive-venue-ip-litigation/id=96099/

Lapedus, M. (2020) *China Speeds up Advanced Chip Development,* Semi-conductor Engineering, January 2020 Edition

Lary, D. (2015) *China's Civil War: A Social History, 1945–1949*, Cambridge University Press

Lee, J. (2016) *China's Hegemony Four Hundred Years of East Asian Domination*, Columbia University Press

Lee, K. (2020) *Moon Invites President Xi to Visit Seoul in First Half of This Year for Peace in Korea, Asia, the World*, The Korea Post

Lei, X., Zhang, Y. and Li, J. (2016) *Review of China's Household Contract Responsibility System with Remuneration Linked to Output*, Advances in Economics, Business and Management Research, Vol. 20, pp. 88–90

Lemon, J. (2018) '*Vladimir Putin is My Best, Most Intimate Friend', Chinese President Xi Jinping Says*, Newsweek

Leverett, F. and Wu, B. (2017) *The New Silk Road and China's Evolving Grand Strategy*, The China Journal, Vol. 77, pp. 110–132

Lexis PSL (2020) *The Analects of Confucius* http://www.confucius-1.com/analects/

Li, F. (2018) *Prof. Li Fengting Speaks at 1st Scoping Meeting of UN Global Science-Policy-Business Forum* https://unep-iesd.tongji.edu.cn/iesden/35/4b/c13757a144715/page.htm

Li, L., Willett, T.D. and Zhang, N. (2012) *The Effects of the Global Financial Crisis on China's Financial Market and Macroeconomy*, Economics Research International

Li, D. and Xia, Y. (2018) *Mao and the Sino-Soviet Split, 1959–1973: A New History*, Lexington Books

Li, Q. and Ye, M. (2019) *China's Emerging Partnership Network: What, Who, Where, When and Why,* International Trade, Politics and Development, Vol. 3, No. 2, pp. 66–81

Liang, Z. and Ma, Z (2004) *China's Floating Population: New Evidence from the 2000 Census*, Population and Development Review, Wiley Online Library

Lim, T.W. (2016) *China's One Belt One Road Initiative*, World Scientific Publishing

Lin, C.-C. (2016) *The Judicialization of Politics in Taiwan*, Asian Journal of Law and Society, Vol. 3, No. 2

Linklaters (2020) *China Publishes Revised Personal Data Protection Guidelines* https://e.linklaters.com/67/1105/downloads/20200330-china-publishes-revised-personal-data-protection-guidelines.pdf

Lino, M.R. (2020) *Understanding China's Arctic Activities* https://www.iiss.org/blogs/analysis/2020/02/china-arctic

Litinova, D. and Moritsugu, K. (2020) *Putin's, Xi's Ruler-for-Life Moves Pose Challenges to West*, AP News

Liu, S. (1969) *Chinese Characters and Their Impact on Other Languages of East Asia*, Eurasia Book Co

Liu, J. (2011) *Picturing A Green Virtual Public Space for Social Change: A Study of Internet Activism and Web-Based Environmental Collective Actions in China*, Chinese Journal of Communication, Vol. 4, No. 2, pp. 137–166

Liu, H. (2012) *Transnational Chinese Sphere in Singapore: Dynamics, Transformations and Characteristics*, Journal of Current Chinese Affairs, Vol. 41, No. 2, pp. 37–60

Liu, L.C. (2014a) *Hakka Chinese Political Leadership in East and Southeast Asia, and South America* https://liamchingliu.wordpress.com/2014/09/20/hakka-chinese-political-leadership-in-east-and-southeast-asia-and-south-america/

Liu, C. (2014b) *In 'Reporting from Beijing' China Announces Modern Vocational Education Development Strategy 2014–2020*, Section of Science, Technology and Education. Embassy of Switzerland in China

Liu, Z. (2016) *Main Conclusions of China's 3rd National Assessment on Climate Change* https://web.archive.org/web/20200428054420/http://www.360doc.com/content/16/0113/00/27398134_527482646.shtml

Liu, R. (2019) *China's Criminal Legislation on Embezzlement and Bribery*, Springer Singapore

Liu, R. and Liu, F. (2016) *To Ally or Not to Ally?* The Griffith Tsinghua 'How China Sees the World' Working Paper Series No. 2

Liu, T. and Tsai, T. (2014) *Swords into Ploughshares? China's Soft Power Strategy in Southeast Asia and its Challenges*, Revista Brasileira de Politica Internacional, Vol. 57, p. 28

Lloyd, M. (2017) *The Revolution of Civil Society,* lulu.com

Lloyd, M. (2019) *The Federalist Revolution*, Forum Press

Lloyd, M. (2020) *GPI Website Blog on Huawei* https://gpilondon.com/

Lloyd, M. (2021) *British Business Banking*, Agenda Publications

Lo, K.D. and Waters, R.D. (2012) *New Technologies, New Cultural Traditions: The Impact of Facebook on Chinese Nongovernmental Organizations*, China Media Research, Vol. 8, No. 4, pp. 99–110

Locke, J. (1690) *Second Treatise on Government* https://english.hku.hk/staff/kjohnson/PDF/LockeJohnSECONDTREATISE1690.pdf

Long, S. (1998) *The Overseas Chinese*, Prospect Magazine

Macrotrends (2020) *China GDP Per Capita 1960–2021* https://www.macrotrends.net/countries/CHN/china/gdp-per-capita

Mankotia, A.S. (2020) *Chinese Tech Companies with Government Links Face Curbs*, The Economic Times

Marketing to China (2019) *The Ultimate Guide to Cross-Border E-Commerce* https://www.marketingtochina.com/cbec-cross-border-e-com

Matura, T. (2019) *China and CEE: 16+1 is Here to Stay*, Emerging Europe

McKinsey (2017) *Jobs Lost, Jobs Gained: What the Future of Work Will Mean for Jobs, Skills, And Wages* https://www.mckinsey.com/featured-insights/future-of-work/jobs-lost-jobs-gained-what-the-future-of-work-will-mean-for-jobs-skills-and-wages

Mead, M. (1964) *Continuities in Cultural Evolution*, Yale University Press

Medeiros, E.S. (2009) *China's International Behaviour: Activism, Opportunism and Diversification*, Rand Corporation

Melchers (2020) *China's New E-Commerce Law Improves Online Market Regulation* https://melchers-china.com/chinas-new-e-commerce-law-improves-online-market-regulation/

Men, J. (2007) *The EU-China Strategic Partnership: Achievements and Challenges,* European Studies Centre, University of Pittsburgh, Policy Paper No. 12

Mill, J.S. (1859) *On Liberty*, Amazon Books Kindle Edition

Miller, S.A., Horvath, A. and Monteiro, P.J.M. (2018) *Impacts of Booming Concrete Production On Water Resources Worldwide*, Nature Sustainability, Vol. 1, pp. 69–76

Ministry of Commerce, People's Republic of China Press Conference (2019) *Stabilizing Foreign Trade, Stabilizing Foreign Investment, and Promoting Consumption.* http://english.mofcom.gov.cn › newsrelease › press

Ministry of Commerce, People's Republic of China (2020) *China-ASEAN FTA* http://fta.mofcom.gov.cn/topic/chinaasean.shtml

Ministry of Foreign Affairs, People's Republic of China (2002) *Joint Declaration of ASEAN and China on Cooperation in the Field of Non-traditional Security Issues* https://www.fmprc.gov.cn/nanhai/eng/zcfg_1/t26290.htm

Ministry of Foreign Affairs, People's Republic of China (2015a) *Speech by H.E. Xi Jinping President of the People's Republic of China at the Welcoming Dinner Hosted by Local Governments and Friendly Organizations in the United States* https://www.fmprc.gov.cn/mfa_eng/topics_665678/xjpdmgjxgsfwbcxlhgcl70znxlfh/t1305429.shtml

Ministry of Foreign Affairs, People's Republic of China (2015b) *Xi Jinping Holds Talks with President Vladimir Putin of Russia* https://www.fmprc.gov.cn/mfa_eng/topics_665678/xjpcxelsjnwgzzsl70znqdbfelshskstbels/t1263258.shtml

Ministry of Foreign Affairs, People's Republic of China (2016) *Xi Jinping Holds Talks with President Pranab Mukherjee of India* https://www.fmprc.gov.cn/mfa_eng/zxxx_662805/t1367581.shtml

Ministry of Foreign Affairs, People's Republic of China (2020) *Study and Implement Xi Jinping Thought on Diplomacy ... Speech by Wang Yi* https://www.fmprc.gov.cn/mfa_eng/zxxx_662805/t1799305.shtml

Mohamad, M. (1999) *The Way Forward: Growth, Prosperity and Multiracial Harmony in Malaysia*, Weidenfeld and Nicholson

Morishima, M. (1982) *Why Has Japan Succeeded? Western Technology and the Japanese Ethos*, Cambridge University Press

Morgan Stanley (2020) *Five Reasons for the Trend Towards Multi-Polarity* https://www.morganstanley.com.au/ideas/five-reasons-for-the-trend-towards-multipolarity

Morris, I. (2020) *Ericsson, Huawei & Nokia's 5G 'wins' Are No Big Deal* https://www.lightreading.com/5g/ericsson-huawei-and-nokias-5g-wins-are-no-big-deal/a/d-id/757677

Morrison, W.M. and Labonte, M. (2009) *China's Currency: A Summary of the Economic Issues* https://www.everycrsreport.com/files/20111219_RS21625_dbbcbc4260c002d7e8e6e608b5abdd644d4f6c12.pdf

Mukherjee, K. (2010) *Is There a Distinct Style of Asian Democracy?* Journal of Asian and African Studies, Vol. 45, No. 6, pp. 684–694

Mumuni, S.M. (2017) *China's Non-intervention Policy in Africa: Principle versus Pragmatism*, African Journal of Political Science and International Relations, Research Paper

Myanmar Times (2020) *Why Must Myanmar Reshape its Relationship with China* https://www.mmtimes.com/news/why-must-myanmar-reshape-its-relationship-china.html

Myllyvirta, L. (2020) *Influential Academics Reveal How China Can Achieve Its 'Carbon Neutrality' Goal* https://www.carbonbrief.org/influential-academics-reveal-how-china-can-achieve-its-carbon-neutrality-goal

Narayanan, M.K. (2021) *Reframing India's Foreign Policy Priorities* https://www.thehindu.com/opinion/lead/reframing-indias-foreign-policy-priorities/article33552868.ece

Nation, J. (2018) *India-China Relations and the Reconstruction of Strategic Partnerships*, Alpha Edition

National Endowment for Democracy (2020) https://fundit.fr/en/institutions/national-endowment-democracy-ned and www.ned.org

National Security Law (2015) *China Law NPC*, Policy Papers, Article 77

Nature (2020) *Coronavirus: How Many Papers Have Been Published?* https://www.nature.com/articles/d41586-020-00253-8

Naughton, B. (2001) *Zhu Rongji: The Twilight of a Brilliant Career* https://www.hoover.org/sites/default/files/uploads/documents/clm1_BN.pdf

Naughton, B. (2007) *The Chinese Economy: Transitions and Growth*, MIT Press

NDRC (2019) *13th Five Year Plan* https://en.ndrc.gov.cn/policies/202105/P020210527785800103339.pdf

Nelson, C. (2013) *The Third Plenum* https://www.chinabusinessreview.com/the-third-plenum-of-the-18th-chinese-communist-party-congress-a-primer/

Ng, E. (2020) *In China's Covid-19 Vaccine Race, Five Stocks Are on Analysts' Watch List as Clinical Trials End, Production Anticipated* https://www.scmp.com/business/investor-relations/article/3115408/chinas-covid-19-vaccine-race-five-stocks-are-analysts

NH Global Partners (2019) *China's Social Security System Explained* https://nhglobalpartners.com/china-social-security-system-explained/

Niksch, L. (2016) *Regional Security Consultative Organizations in East Asia and Their Implications for the United States,* CRS Report for Congress

Nittas, V., Mütsch, M., Ehrler, F., Milo, A. and Puhan, E. (2018) *Electronic Patient-Generated Health Data to Facilitate Prevention and Health Promotion: A Scoping Review Protocol,* BMJ Open, Vol. 8, No. 8

NPC Observer (2019) *Foreign Investment Law* https://npcobserver.com/legislation/foreign-investment-law/

NPR (2020) *Biden Moves to Have U.S. Rejoin Climate Accord* https://www.npr.org/sections/inauguration-day-live-updates/2021/01/20/958923821/biden-moves-to-have-u-s-rejoin-climate-accord?t=1613228106033

Nokia (2020) *Nokia signs contract with Central China Holdings Co. Ltd in 'smarter real estate' infrastructure deal* https://www.nokia.com/about-us/news/releases/2020/04/27/nokia-signs-contract-with-central-china-holdings-co-ltd-in-smarter-real-estate-infrastructure-deal/

O'Brien, K. and Li, L. (2006) *Rightful Resistance in Rural China,* Cambridge University Press

OECD (2015) *Education Indicators in Focus* https://www.oecd.org/education/EDIF%2031%20(2015)--ENG--Final.pdf

OECD (2018) *World Management Survey* https://www.oecd.org/economy/surveys/Management-Practices-Workforce-Selection-and-productivity-Stefanie-Wolter.pdf

OECD (2019) *Economic Surveys China* https://www.oecd.org/economy/surveys/china-2019-OECD-economic-survey-overview.pdf

O'Keefe, K. and Mauldin, W. (2020) *Mike Pompeo Urges Chinese People to Change Communist Party*, The Wall Street Journal

Oxford Business Group (2020) *China's Belt and Road Initiative Reshaping South-east Asia* https://oxfordbusinessgroup.com/analysis/road-china%E2%80%99s-belt-and-road-initiative-reshaping-south-east-asia

Oxford Economics (2010) *The International Distribution of Household Wealth,* Deloitte

OZY (2020) *Chinese Tourists Are Flocking to Russia* https://www.ozy.com/the-new-and-the-next/why-chinese-tourists-are-flocking-to-russia/264589/

Pan, D. (2020a) *Chinese Government Advisers Propose Regional Stablecoin for 4 Asian Countries* https://www.coindesk.com/chinese-government-advisers-propose-regional-stablecoin-for-4-asian-countries

Pan, Y. (2020b) China's Central Bank Digital Currency DCEP Pilot Launches https://www.kapronasia.com/china-banking-research-category/china-s-central-bank-digital-currency-dcep-launches-in-pilot.html

Pang, Q. (2019) *State-Society Relations and Confucian Revivalism in Contemporary China*, Palgrave Macmillan

PEACE (2019) *Hengtong Bringing First Carrier Neutral Open Submarine Cable System to Pakistan* http://www.peacecable.net/news/Detail/16603

Perlez, J. (2015) *New China-Led Bank Pledges to Fend Off Graft* https://www.nytimes.com/2015/04/12/world/asia/new-china-led-bank-pledges-to-fend-off-graft.html

Perry, E.J. (2015) *The Populist Dream of Chinese Democracy*, The Journal of Asian Studies, Vol. 74, No. 4, pp. 903–915

Pew Research Center (2019) *Attitudes toward China* https://pewresearch.org/global/2019/12/05/attitudes-toward-china-2019

Phiri, M. and Mungomba, N. (2019) *Leveraging the BRI for Africa's Industrialization and Intra-Trade*, Zambia Institute for Policy Analysis and Research, Working Paper No. 38

Pisacane, G. Murphy, L. and Zhang, C (2016) *Arbitration in China: Rules and Perspectives*, SpringerLink

Pointe Bello (2019) *The Digital Silk Road Initiative: Wiring Global IT and Telecommunications to Advance Beijing's Global Ambitions* https://a.storyblok.com/f/58650/x/0c5c298009/pointe-bello-digital-silk-road-2019.pdf

Pompeo, M. (2020) *Communist China and the Free World's Future* https://2017-2021.state.gov/communist-china-and-the-free-worlds-future-2/index.html

Politico (2020) *EU Won't Follow Trump into A Trade War Over Hong Kong* https://www.politico.eu/article/eu-hong-kong-trade-china-agreement/

Poston, D.L. and Wong, J.H. (2016) *The Chinese Diaspora: The Current Distribution of the Overseas Chinese Population*, Chinese Journal of Sociology, Vol. 3, No. 2, pp. 348–373

Power, J. (2019) *US Warships Made 92 Trips Through the Taiwan Strait Since 2007* https://www.scmp.com/week-asia/geopolitics/article/3008621/us-warships-made-92-trips-through-taiwan-strait-2007

Power Technology (2019) *China Continues to Build Much-Needed Power Capacity in Africa* https://www.power-technology.com/comment/chinese-investment-in-africa-2019/

Power Technology (2021) *Will China Do for Hydrogen What It Did for Solar Power?* https://www.power-technology.com/features/will-china-do-for-hydrogen-what-it-did-for-solar-power/

PR Newswire (2020) *China ETC (Electronic Toll Collection) Industry Report, 2015–2019* https://www.prnewswire.com/news-releases/china-etc-electronic-toll-collection-industry-report-2015-2019-300205627.html

Preen, M. (2018) *The Beijing-Tianjin-Hebei Integration Plan* https://www.china-briefing.com/news/the-beijing-tianjin-hebei-integration-plan

PricewaterhouseCoopers (2017) *Sizing the Prize* https://www.pwc.com/gx/en/issues/analytics/assets/pwc-ai-analysis-sizing-the-prize-report.pdf

PricewaterhouseCoopers (2018) *What Will Be the Net Impact of AI and Related Technologies on Jobs in China?* https://www.pwc.com/gx/en/issues/artificial-intelligence/impact-of-ai-on-jobs-in-china.pdf

PricewaterhouseCoopers (2019) *China Economic Quarterly* https://www.pwccn.com/en/research-and-insights/china-economic-quarterly-q4-2019-2.pdf

PTI Beijing (2019) *India-China Trade Dips by Nearly $3billion in 2019*, The Hindu Business Line

PTI (2016) *Beijing Wants India, Others to Join CPEC Due to Pakistan's Appetite, Says Chinese Media*, The Economic Times

Public Broadcasting Service (2019) *Timeline: Tiananmen Square* https://www.pbs.org/wgbh/frontline/article/timeline-tiananmen-square/

Qi, H. (2019a) *The Power of the Supreme People's Court: Reconceptualizing Judicial Power in Contemporary China*, Routledge

Qi, H. (2019b) *Joint Development in The South China Sea: China's Incentives and Policy Choices*, Journal of Contemporary East Asia Studies, Vol. 8, No. 2, pp. 220–239

Rana, P.B. and Ji, X (2020) *Belt & Road Stakeholders Don't Believe China Uses 'Debt-Trap' Diplomacy*, The Diplomat

Randhawa, D. (2020) *China's Central Bank Digital Currency: Implications for ASEAN*, (pp. 6–9, Rep.). S. Rajaratnam School of International Studies. doi:10.2307/resrep28277.7

Red Digital China (2020) *2020 Chinese Digital Marketing Trend: Latest China Internet Report* https://www.reddigitalchina.com/blog/2020-chinese-digital-marketing-trend-latest-china-internet-report/

Redding, S.G. (1993) *The Spirit of Chinese Capitalism*, Walter de Gruyter

Reed, N. (2015) *Air Sea Battle to Joint Concept for Access and Maneouvres in the Global Commons: Imperatives for a Continuation of a Crucial Warfighting Concept*, MS thesis, Joint Advanced Warfighting School, National Defense University

Refworld (2015) *Hukou Reform Policy and its Local Implementation* https://www.refworld.org/docid/57551d0c4.html

Reid, A. (1995) *Sojourners and Settlers — Histories of Southeast Asia and the Chinese*, University of Hawaii Press

Reinbold, B. and Wen, Y. (2018) *Housing Costs and Regional Income Inequality in China and the U.S.*, Federal Reserve Bank of St Louis

Ren, H. (2019) *China Keeps Expanding Global Network of Partnerships* http://en.people.cn/n3/2019/0806/c90000-9603582.html

Reuters (2018) *China to Bar People with Bad 'Social Credit' From Planes, Trains* https://www.reuters.com/article/us-china-credit-idUSKCN1GS10S

Reuters (2020a) *China Tells Ant to Expect Scrutiny of Credit Business Ahead of Record Listing: Sources* https://www.reuters.com/article/us-ant-group-ipo-china-regulator/china-tells-ant-to-expect-scrutiny-of-credit-business-ahead-of-record-listing-sources-idUKKBN27J14I

Reuters (2020b) *Gazprom Starts Work on Power of Siberia-2 Pipeline* https://www.reuters.com/article/russia-china-gazprom-idUSR4N2CB012

Roberts, H. *et al.* (2020) *The Chinese Approach to Artificial Intelligence: An Analysis of Policy, Ethics, And Regulation*, AI & Society, Vol. 36, pp. 59–77

Rolfe, A. (2021) *SWIFT and PBoC Set Up JV for Internationalisation of Digital Yuan* https://www.paymentscardsandmobile.com/swift-and-pboc-set-up-jv-for-internationalisation-of-digital-yuan/

Rosca, M. (2019) *Italian Industry Minister Calls for Huawei Access to 5G Network*, Politico

Ross, R. and Feng, Z. (2015) *China's Ascent: Power, Security and the future of International Politics*, Cornell University Press, Goldstein, A., Chapter 3, Parsing's China Rise: International Circumstances and National Attributes

Russel, D.R. and Berger, B.H. (2020) *Weaponizing the Belt and Road Initiative* https://asiasociety.org/sites/default/files/2020-09/Weaponizing%20the%20Belt%20and%20Road%20Initiative_0.pdf

Russia Briefing (2019) *Russian & Chinese Alternatives for SWIFT Global Banking Network Coming Online* https://www.russia-briefing.com/news/russian-chinese-alternatives-swift-global-banking-network-coming-online.html/

Russia State Duma (2020) *Parliaments of Russia and China to Exchange Experience in Legal Regulation in Various Areas* http://duma.gov.ru/en/news/49910/

Sanghamitra, C. (2013) *Falun Gong in China: Responses and Reactions*, Lap Lambert Academic Publishing

Satake, M. (1999) *Trade Conflict between Japan and the United States over Automobiles and Automotive Parts*, Journal of the Graduate School of International Cultural Studies, Tohoku University

Savic, B. (2016) *Behind China and Russia's Special Relationship*, The Diplomat

Savic, B. (2020a) *Are China's Export Control Law and the RCEP Pulling in Different Directions?*, South China Morning Post

Savic, B. (2020b) *China's New Digital Industrial Transformation,* The Diplomat

Scammacca, P. and Dai, M. (2017) *The Implications of the 19th Chinese Communist Party Congress, Foundation for Law and International Affairs* https://flia.org/summary-implications-19th-chinese-communist-party-congress/

Schmidt, S. (2011) *Mou Zongsan, Hegel and Kant: The Quest for Confucian Modernity*, Philosophy East and West, Vol. 61, No. 2, pp. 260–302

Schnellbach, C. and Man, J. (2015) *Embracing a Different Kind of Partnership*, Centre for Applied Policy Research, Working Paper

Schurmann, F. (1966) *Ideology and Organization in Communist China*, University of California Press

ScienceDirect (2020) *Smart Cities* https://www.sciencedirect.com/topics/earth-and-planetary-sciences/smart-city

SCMP (2016) *Quick Guide to China's Diplomatic Levels* https://www.scmp.com/news/china/diplomacy-defence/article/1903455/quick-guide-chinas-diplomatic-levels

SCMP (2018a) *Tianjin City in China Eyes US$16 Billion Fund for AI Work, Dwarfing EU's Plan to Spend US$1.78 Billion* https://www.scmp.com/tech/innovation/article/2146428/tianjin-city-china-eyes-us16-billion-fund-ai-work-dwarfing-eus-plan

SCMP (2018b) *Cambodia Says Relations with China Are at 'Best Stage' Ever After Agreeing US$259m Loan to Build Road* https://www.scmp.com/news/china/diplomacy-defence/article/2156142/cambodia-says-relations-china-are-best-stage-ever-after

SCMP (2019) *Alipay Sets Sights on Digital Payments Outside Asia as it Teams up With Russia's Mail.ru* https://scmp.com/tech/enterprises/article/3032187/alipay-sets-sights-digital-payments-outside-asia-it-teams-russias

SCMP (2020) *Didi Partners with China's Central Bank on Digital Currency Research and Development* https://www.scmp.com/tech/apps-social/article/3092379/didi-partners-chinas-central-bank-digital-currency-research-and

Shaheed, A. and Richter, R.P. (2018) *Is 'Human Rights' a Western Concept?* https://theglobalobservatory.org/2018/10/are-human-rights-a-western-concept/

Shakya, T. (2009) *China's Religions (Re) Awakening and The Impact of Religion on Chinese Society* https://www.brookings.edu/wp-content/uploads/2012/04/20090406_china.pdf

Shambaugh, D. (2013) *China as a Global Power: Understanding Beijing's Competing Identities*, Sigur Center for Asian Studies, Elliot School of International Affairs, George Washington University

Sharma, B.P. and Singh, K.P. (2019) *The Politics of Soft Power: Belt and Road Initiative (BRI) as Charm Influence in South Asia*, China and the World, Vol. 2, No. 1

Shen, X. (2020) *Chinese ICT on the Digital Silk Road: A Case Study of Infrastructure Building in Pakistan*, Simon Fraser University

Shi, L., Chen, W., Xu, J. and Ling, L. (2020) *Trends and Characteristics of Inter-Provincial Migrants in Mainland China and Its Relation with Economic Factors: A Panel Data Analysis from 2011 to 2016*, *Sustainability*, Vol. 12, No. 2

Shields, M. (2017) *Chemchina Clinches Landmark $43 Billion Takeover of Syngenta* https://www.reuters.com/article/us-syngenta-ag-m-a-chemchina-idUSKBN1810CU

Shoham, Y., Perrault, R., Brynjolfsson, E. *et al.* (2018) *The AI Index 2018 Annual Report*, AI Index Steering Committee, Human-Centered AI Initiative, Stanford University

Shu, G.Z. (1995) *Mao's Military Romanticism: China and the Korean War, 1950–53*, University Press of Kansas

Shullman, D.O. (2019) *Protect the Party: China's Growing Influence in the Developing World*, The Brookings Institution

Sima, Y. (2011) *Grassroots Environmental Activism and the Internet: Constructing a Green Public Sphere in China*, Asian Studies Review, Vol. 35, pp. 477–497

Skidmore, D. (2020) *The 1989 Tiananmen Crackdown Was Not Inevitable*, The Diplomat

Skinner, C. (2020) *FS Club Jack Ma*

Smith, R. (2015) *Qing Dynasty and Traditional Chinese Culture*, Rowman & Littlefield

Song, Q. and Smith, J.P. (2019) *Hukou System, Mechanisms, and Health Stratification across the Life Course in Rural and Urban China*, Heath Place, Vol. 58

Soong, J.J. (2019) *China's One Belt and One Road Initiative Meets ASEAN Economic Community: Propelling and Deepening Regional Economic Integration?* The Chinese Economy, Vol. 51, No. 4, pp. 291–297

State Council (2020) *Policies of Promoting High-quality Development of Integrated Circuit Industry and Software Industry* (Guo Fa No.8 [2020])

Statista (2019) *Enrollment Rate in Tertiary Education in China 1990–2019* https://www.statista.com/statistics/1113954/china-tertiary-education-college-university-enrollment-rate/#

Statista (2020) *Ecommerce China* https://www.statista.com/outlook/243/117/ecommerce/china

Statista (2020) *Social Media Ad Revenue in China 2012–2022* https://www.statista.com/statistics/859367/china-social-media-advertising-revenue

Steinbeck, D. (2018) *U.S.-China Trade War and Its Global Impacts*, China Quarterly of International Strategic Studies, Vol. 4, No. 4, pp. 515–542

Strüver, G. (2016) *International Alignment between Interests and Ideology: The Case of China's Partnership Diplomacy*, GIGA Working Papers, No. 283, German Institute of Global and Area Studies

Strüver, G. (2017) *China's Partnership Diplomacy: International Alignments Based on Interests or Ideology*, The Chinese Journal of International Politics, Vol. 10, No. 2, pp. 31–65

Suehiro, A. (2017) *China's Offensive in Southeast Asia: Regional Architecture and the Process of Sinocization,* Journal of Contemporary East Asia Studies, Vol. 6, No. 2, pp. 107–131

Sullivan, J. and Xie, L. (2009) *Environmental Activism, Social Networks and The Internet*, The China Quarterly, Vol. 198, pp. 422–432

Sumption, J. (2019) *Lord Sumption's Reith Lectures and Responses* https://ukhumanrightsblog.com/2019/07/29/the-reith-lectures-2019-lord-sumptions-lecture-and-responses/

Sun, H.L. (2011) *Understanding China's Agricultural Investments in Africa* https://media.africaportal.org/documents/saia_OP_102.pdf

Sun, D. (2020) *China's Partnership Diplomacy in the Middle East* https://theasiadialogue.com/2020/03/24/chinas-partnership-diplomacy-in-the-middle-east/

Suryadinata, L. (2017) *The Rise of China and the Chinese Overseas: A Study of Beijing's Changing Policy in Southeast Asia and Beyond*, ISEAS — Yusof Ishak Institute

Tait, S. (2020) *Finalizing FTAs Will be a Boost for Southeast Asian Economy* https://www.thejakartapost.com/academia/2020/09/21/finalizing-ftas-will-be-a-boost-for-southeast-asian-economy.html

Tan, C. and Geng, Y. (2005) *India and China: Twenty Centuries of Civilisation: 3*, Centre for Studies in Civilisations

Tan, F. (1990) *The People's Daily: Politics and Popular Will-Journalistic Defiance in China During the Spring of 1989*, Pacific Affairs, Vol. 63, No. 2, pp. 151–169

Tass (2016) *Putin: Russia is Staying Out of South China Sea Dispute* https://tass.com/politics/898040

Tass (2019) *Russia Completes Delivery of Second S-400 Missile System Regimental Set to China* https://tass.com/world/1113113

Technology for You (2020) *China's Investment Appetite for Indian Tech Startups Grows Stronger, Says Globaldata* http://www.technologyforyou.org/chinas-investment-appetite-for-indian-tech-startups-grows-stronger-says-globaldata/

Theobald, U. (2013) *Huang Zongxi* http://www.chinaknowledge.de/History/Qing/personshuangzongxi.html

Theobald, U. (2016) *The Donglin Faction* http://www.chinaknowledge.de/History/Terms/donglindang.html

The Atlantic (2018) *China's Dystopian Tech Could be Contagious* https://www.theatlantic.com/technology/archive/2018/02/chinas-dangerous-dream-of-urban-control/553097/

The Basic Law of the Hong Kong Special Administrative Region of the People's Republic of China (2020) Published by the Constitutional and Mainland Affairs Bureau Hong Kong Special Administrative Region Government

The Geopolitics (2020) *A Storm Ahead for the ASEAN-China Code of Conduct Negotiations* https://thegeopolitics.com/a-storm-ahead-for-the-asean-china-code-of-conduct-negotiations/

The Guardian (2017) *Indian and Chinese Troops Clash in Disputed Himalayan Border Region* https://www.theguardian.com/world/2017/aug/16/indian-chinese-troops-clash-disputed-himalayan-border-region

The Guardian (2019) *China Bans 23m From Buying Travel Tickets as Part of 'Social Credit' System* https://www.theguardian.com/world/2019/mar/01/china-bans-23m-discredited-citizens-from-buying-travel-tickets-social-credit-system

The Jakarta Post (2020) *Jokowi Expresses Hope for Stronger, Mutually Beneficial Ties with China* https://www.thejakartapost.com/news/2020/09/01/jokowi-expresses-hope-for-stronger-mutually-beneficial-ties-with-china.html

The Japan Times (2019) *China to Host Trilateral Leaders' Summit* https://www.japantimes.co.jp/news/2019/12/11/national/politics-diplomacy/china-japan-south-korea-trilateral-summit/

The Moscow Times (2020) *Moscow Targets Chinese Nationals Amid Coronavirus Fears. And the Arctic Heats Up in Record Speed* https://www.themoscowtimes.com/2020/02/27/moscow-targets-chinese-nationals-amid-coronavirus-fears-and-the-arctic-heats-up-in-record-speed

The National Interest (2020) *Look Out America, China is Now Flying Russia's SU-35 Flanker-E Fighters* https://nationalinterest.org/blog/buzz/look-out-america-china-now-flying-russias-su-35-flanker-e-fighters-132567

The New York Times (1989) *2 US Officials Went to Beijing Secretly in July* https://www.nytimes.com/1989/12/19/world/2-us-officials-went-to-beijing-secretly-in-july.html

The Pig Site (2020) *China Announces Plans to Issue Bio-Safety Certificates to Domestic Soybean and Corn* https://www.thepigsite.com/news/2020/01/china-announces-plans-to-issue-biosafety-certificates-to-domestic-gm-soybean-and-corn

The Register (2020) *TSMC to Build New 5nm Chip Factory in Arizona with US Government Backing* https://www.theregister.com/2020/05/15/tsmc_to_build_new_5nm_fab_in_usa/

The Straits Times (2019a) *Fuelled by China Fears, Russians Protest Baikal Bottling Plant* https://www.straitstimes.com/world/europe/fuelled-by-china-fears-russians-protest-baikal-bottling-plant

The Straits Times (2019b) *Xi Jinping Says EU, China 'Advancing' Together Despite Suspicions* https://www.straitstimes.com/world/europe/xi-jinping-says-eu-china-advancing-together-despite-suspicions

The Straits Times (2020a) *Malaysian PM Muhyiddin Meets China's Defence Minister on Bilateral Cooperation* https://www.straitstimes.com/asia/se-asia/malaysian-pm-muhyiddin-meets-chinas-defence-minister-on-bilateral-cooperation

The Straits Times (2020b) *30 Years of S'pore-China Ties: Singapore Leaders Send Congratulatory Messages* https://www.straitstimes.com/singapore/singapore-leaders-send-congratulatory-messages

The Tribune (2020) *Chinese Communist Party's Membership Increases to 91.91 million* https://www.tribuneindia.com/news/world/chinese-communist-partys-membership-increases-to-91-91-million-107128

The Wire (2018) *Quad Meets Again, Discusses Rules-Based Order in 'Inclusive' Indo-Pacific* https://thewire.in/diplomacy/quad-meets-again-discusses-rules-based-order-and-inclusive-indo-pacific

Thomson Reuters (2018) *Thomson Reuters Names the World's Top 100 Technology Companies* https://www.thomsonreuters.com/en/press-releases/2018/january/thomson-reuters-names-the-worlds-top-100-technology-companies.html

Tobin, J. (1987) *Essays in Economics*, MIT Press

Tobin, M. (2019) *Explained the Difference Between the RCEP and the CPTPP*, South China Morning Post

Treib, O., Bähr, H. and Falkner, G. (2007) *Modes of Governance: A Note Towards Conceptual Clarification,* Journal of European Public Policy, Vol. 14, pp. 1–20

Tuan, L.A. (2020) *ASEAN Centrality and the Major Powers: South China Sea Case Study* http://unsworks.unsw.edu.au/fapi/datastream/unsworks:66163/SOURCE02?view=true

UN (2015) *The Paris Agreement* https://unfccc.int/process-and-meetings/the-paris-agreement/the-paris-agreement

UN (2018) *World Urbanization Prospects: The 2018 Revision* https://population.un.org/wup/Publications/Files/WUP2018-Report.pdf

UN (2019a) *Contraceptive Use by Method* https://www.un.org/development/desa/pd/sites/www.un.org.development.desa.pd/files/files/documents/2020/Jan/un_2019_contraceptiveusebymethod_databooklet.pdf

UN (2019b) *China-Africa Cooperation Boosts United Nations Partnership with African Union, Secretary-General Tells Security Council Ministerial Meeting* https://www.un.org/press/en/2019/sgsm19772.doc.htm

UN (2020) *Population Databases* https://www.un.org/en/development/desa/population/publications/database/index.asp

UNCITRAL (2019) *United Nations Convention on International Settlement Agreements Resulting from Mediation* (*New York, 2018*) (*the 'Singapore Convention on Mediation*') https://uncitral.un.org/en/texts/mediation/conventions/international_settlement_agreements

UNCTAD (2020) *Inclusive Growth and E-commerce: China's Experience* https://unctad.org/system/files/non-official-document/dtl_eWeek2017c11-aliresearch_en.pdf

USCC (2019) *China and The World* https://www.uscc.gov/sites/default/files/2019-09/Chapter%203%20Section%201-%20Belt%20and%20Road%20Initative_0.pdf

US-China Business Council (2017) *China's 2017 Communist Party Leadership Structure & Transition* https://www.uschina.org/sites/default/files/chinas_2017_communist_party_leadership_structure_transition_updated.pdf

US-China Economic and Security Review Commission (2005) *Report to Congress* https://www.uscc.gov/sites/default/files/annual_reports/2005-Report-to-Congress.pdf

US-China Economic and Security Review Commission (2020) *Smart Cities Development* https://www.uscc.gov/sites/default/files/2020-04/China_Smart_Cities_Development.pdf

US-China Economic and Security Review Commission (2020) *China's Engagement with Africa: Foundations for an Alternative Governance Regime* https://www.uscc.gov/research/chinas-engagement-africa-foundations-alternative-governance-regime

US Department of Agriculture (2019) *Irrigation and Water Use* https://www.ers.usda.gov/topics/farm-practices-management/irrigation-water-use/

US Department of Defense (2018) *Summary of the 2018 National Defense Strategy of the USA: Sharpening the American Military's Competitive Edge* https://dod.defense.gov/Portals/1/Documents/pubs/2018-National-Defense-Strategy-Summary.pdf

US Indo-Pacific Command (2021) *USPACOM Area of Responsibility* https://www.pacom.mil/About-USINDOPACOM/USPACOM-Area-of-Responsibility/

US Mission to the European Union (2020) *Launch of the U.S.-EU Dialogue on China* https://useu.usmission.gov/launch-of-the-u-s-eu-dialogue-on-china/

US National Security Strategy (2017) *National Security Strategy of the United States of America* https://trumpwhitehouse.archives.gov/wp-content/uploads/2017/12/NSS-Final-12-18-2017-0905.pdf

US Treasury (2020) *Addressing the Threat from Securities Investments That Finance Communist Chinese Military Companies* https://home.treasury.gov/system/files/126/13959.pdf

Valente, C.S. (2020) *Duterte Call for Further Strengthening of 'PH-China' Ties Amid Challenges*, The Manila Times

VanDyck, C.K. (2017) *Concept and Definition of Civil Society Sustainability* https://csis-website-prod.s3.amazonaws.com/s3fs-public/publication/170630_VanDyck_CivilSocietySustainability_Web.pdf

Verma, S.K. (2016) *1962: The War That Wasn't*, Aleph Book Company

Vientiane Times (2020) *Laos, China Enhance Relations, Broaden Cooperation* http://www.vientianetimes.org.la/freeContent/FreeConten_Laos05.php

Visual Capitalist (2019) *The $88 Trillion World Economy in One Chart* https://www.visualcapitalist.com/the-88-trillion-world-economy-in-one-chart/

Wade, G. (2009) *Southeast Asia-China Interactions,* NUS Press

Wade, G. and Chin, J.K. (2018) *China and Southeast Asia: Historical Interactions*, Routledge

Wagner, R. (2014) *Fate's Gift Money: The Chinese Case of Coping with The Asymmetry Between Man and Fate.* In Hagen, J. and Welker, M. (eds.), Money as God, Cambridge University Press, pp. 184–218

Walder, A.G. and Gong, X. (1993) *Workers in the Tiananmen Protests: The Politics of the Beijing Workers' Autonomous Federation,* The Australian Journal of Chinese Affairs, Vol. 29, pp. 1–29

Wang, J. (2015) *NGO and Social Media Praxis: Activist as Researcher*, Chinese Journal of Communication, Vol. 8, No. 1, pp. 18–41

Wang, S. (2017) *Criminal Law in China*, Wolters Kluwer

Wang, L. (2018) *Self-Determination and Minority Rights in China*, Brill

Wang, O. (2019a) *Hong Kong Remains Key Gateway as China's FDI Rises ... Despite Protests*, South China Morning Post

Wang, X.Y. (2019b) *China's Social Credit System: The Chinese Citizens' Perspective* https://blogs.ucl.ac.uk/assa/2019/12/09/chinas-social-credit-system-the-chinese-citizens-perspective/

Wang, B. (2020) *China Drafts New Energy Law in Opening-up Determination*, Global Times

Wang, H., Zhang, M. and Zhong, M. (2019) *Opportunities and Challenges for the Construction of a Smart City Geo-Spatial Framework in a Small Urban Area in Central China*, MDPI, Smart Cities, Vol. 2, pp. 245–258

Westmore, B. (2017) *An Immediate Chinese Challenge: Further Addressing Income Inequality*, OECD

White House (2014) *U.S.-China Joint Announcement on Climate Change and Clean Energy Cooperation* https://obamawhitehouse.archives.gov/the-press-office/2014/11/11/fact-sheet-us-china-joint-announcement-climate-change-and-clean-energy-c

White House (2020) *United States Strategic Approach to the People's Republic of China* https://china.usembassy-china.org.cn/wp-content/uploads/sites/252/U.S.-Strategic-Approach-to-The-Peoples-Republic-of-China-Report-5.24v1.pdf

Williamson, J. (2004) *Washington Consensus*, Peterson Institute for International Economics

Wilson Center (2016) *Xi Jinping's Cultural Reform Agenda* https://www.wilsoncenter.org/xi-jinpings-cultural-reform-agenda

Wintle, T. (2020) *China-EU Relations Need Not Be 'Knock-Out Match' Says Chinese Ambassador to EU* https://newseu.cgtn.com/news/2020-06-19/China-says-relations-with-EU-need-not-be-knock-out-match--RqGutSXT44/index.html

Wong, R. (2015) *Different Legal Traditions Keep Hong Kong and China Apart*, South China Morning Post

World Bank (2016a) *Digital Adoption Index* https://www.worldbank.org/en/publication/wdr2016/Digital-Adoption-Index

World Bank (2016b) *Hebei Air Pollution Control Programme (P54672)*, Environment and Social Systems Assessment (ESSA)

World Bank (2018) *World Development Report: Digital Dividends* https://www.worldbank.org/en/publication/wdr2018

World Bank (2019a) *Innovative China: New Drivers of Growth* https://openknowledge.worldbank.org/handle/10986/32351

World Bank (2019b) *China Trade Statistics* https://wits.worldbank.org/CountryProfile/en/CHN

World Bank (2019c) *China GDP Growth* https://data.worldbank.org/country/CN

World Bank (2020) *China 2030 Overview* https://www.worldbank.org/content/dam/Worldbank/document/China-2030-overview.pdf

World Economic Forum (2013) *The Future Role of Civil Society* http://www3.weforum.org/docs/WEF_FutureRoleCivilSociety_Report_2013.pdf

World Economic Forum (2020) *China Could Overtake the US as The World's Largest Economy By 2024* https://www.weforum.org/agenda/2020/07/largest-global-economies-1992-2008-2024/

World Education News + Reviews (2019) *Education in China* https://wenr.wes.org/2019/12/education-in-china-3

World Health Organisation (2021) *COVID-19 Virtual Press Conference Transcript — 9 February 2021* https://www.who.int/publications/m/item/covid-19-virtual-press-conference-transcript---9-february-2021

World Intellectual Property Organisation (2016) *World Intellectual Property Indicators* https://www.wipo.int/publications/en/details.jsp?id=4526

World Top Exports (2020) *China's Top Imports* https://www.worldstopexports.com/chinas-top-10-imports/

World Trade Organisation (2020) *Services Trade Drops 30% in Q2 as COVID-19 Ravages International Travel* https://www.wto.org/english/news_e/news20_e/serv_22oct20_e.htm

Wu, K. and Zhu, J. (2017) *China's Tencent Invests in Indonesia's Go-Jek Amid SE Asia Push,* Reuters https://www.reuters.com/article/us-gojek-m-a-tencent-idUSKBN19P17N

Wu, X. (2000) *US Security Policy in Asia: Implications for China-US Relations* https://www.brookings.edu/research/u-s-security-policy-in-asia-implications-for-china-u-s-relations

Xi, J. (2013) *CCP Speech to the Party's Elected Central Committee* (Translated text) https://palladiummag.com/2019/05/31/xi-jinping-in-translation-chinas-guiding-ideology/

Xi, J. (2016) *A New Starting Point for China's Development, A New Blueprint for Global Growth*, Qiushi Journal, Vol. 8, No. 4

Xiang, L. (2016) *Xi's Dream and China's Future,* Survival, Vol. 58, No. 3, pp. 53–62

Xiang, L. (2019) *The Quest for Legitimacy in Chinese Politics*, Routledge
Xie, L. (2012) *Environmental activism in China*, Routledge
Xinhuanet (2017) *Chinese President Proposes to Promote China-Germany Comprehensive Strategic Partnership* http://www.xinhuanet.com//english/2017-07/04/c_136416927.htm
Xinhuanet (2017) *Xi Jinping's report at the 19th CPC National Congress* http://www.xinhuanet.com/english/special/2017-11/03/c_136725942.htm
Xinhuanet (2018a) *China Hopes to Promote Ties with Angola to New Stage: FM* http://www.xinhuanet.com/english/2018-01/14/c_136894605.htm
Xinhuanet (2018b) *Police to Help 100 million Migrants Settle in Cities By 2020* http://www.xinhuanet.com/english/2018-01/26/c_136925024.htm
Xinhuanet (2018c) *China, India Hail High-Level People to People Exchanges Mechanism* www.xinhuanet.com/english/2018-12/21/c_137689956.htm
Xinhuanet (2018d) *Beijing to Build Technology Park for Developing Artificial Intelligence* http://www.xinhuanet.com/english/2018-01/03/c_136869144.htm
Xinhuanet (2019a) *China's Integrated Circuit Industry Sees Steady Growth: Newspaper* http://www.xinhuanet.com/english/2019-09/10/c_138380779.htm
Xinhuanet (2019b) *State Council Releases Vocational Education Reform Implementation Plan* http://www.xinhuanet.com/english/2019-02/13/c_137819109.htm
Xinhuanet (2019c) *Yangtze River — A Golden Economic Belt in Full Swing* http://www.xinhuanet.com/english/2019-01/05/c_137721655.htm
Xinhuanet (2019d) *IBM Partners with Shanghai to Build First AI Innovation Center in China* http://www.xinhuanet.com/english/2019-10/27/c_138506015.htm
Xinhuanet (2019e) *Xi and Putin — At Helm of China-Russia Relations* http://www.xinhuanet.com/english/2019-06/05/c_138118414.htm
Xinhuanet (2019f) *China, India Vow to Deepen Cooperation At 6th Strategic Economic Dialogue Held in India* http://www.xinhuanet.com/english/special/2019-09/10/c_138380768.htm
Xinhuanet (2019g) *Xi's Visit to Open New Chapter in China-Italy Ties, Says Ambassador* http://www.xinhuanet.com/english/2019-03/20/c_137910407.htm
Xinhuanet (2020a) *Commentary: China-EU Partnership to Be More Stable, Mature in Post-Pandemic Era* http://www.xinhuanet.com/english/2020-06/23/c_139161763.htm
Xinhuanet (2020b) *China-Russia Mutual Support Forges Impregnable Fortress Against 'Political Virus': FM* www.xinhuanet.com/english/2020-05/24/c_139084217.htm
Xinhuanet (2020c) *World's Biggest Trade Pact Signed, 'Victory of Multilateralism, Free Trade'* http://www.xinhuanet.com/english/2020-11/15/c_139518184.htm

Xinhuanet (2020d) *Nearly 2.93 mln HK Residents Show Support of National Security Legislation By Signing Petition* http://www.xinhuanet.com/english/2020-06/02/c_139105926.htm

Xue, G. (2020) *Non-traditional Security Cooperation Between China and Southeast Asia: Implications for Indo-Pacific Geopolitics*, International Affairs, Vol. 96, No. 1, pp. 29–48

Yang, G. (2005) *Environmental NGOs and Institutional Dynamics in China*, The China Quarterly, Vol. 181, pp. 46–66, doi:10.1017/S0305741005000032

Yang, A. and Taylor, M. (2010) *Relationship-building by Chinese ENGOs' Websites: Education, Not Activation*, Public Relations Review, Vol. 36, No. 4, pp. 342–351

Yang, K. and Yang, G. (2018) *Analysis of the Strategic Value of the Construction of the Djibouti Base*, Journal of Shijiazhuang University, Vol. 20, No. 2

Yazhuo Huang (2020) Progress in Theory and Practice of Government. Zhou Enlai School of Government, Nankai University, Tianjin, China. DOI: 10.4236/jss.2020.85014

Yi, H. *et al.* (2018) *Assessing the Quality of Upper-Secondary Vocational Education and Training: Evidence from China,* Comparative Education Review, March

Yu, X. (2011) *Transformation of Foreign Affairs and International Relations in China 1978–2008*, Brill

Yu, J. (2018) *China and Southeast Asia: Many Belts and Roads to Turn*, CIMB ASEAN Research Institute

Yue, H. (2017) *National Report on E-commerce Development in China*, Department of Policy, Research and Statistics Working Paper 17/2017, UNIDO

Yue, S. (2018) *Towards a Global Partnership Network*, Copenhagen Journal of Asian Studies, Vol. 36, No. 2, pp. 1–27

Zhang, H. (2010) *The Hukou System's Constraints On Migrant Workers' Job Mobility In Chinese Cities*, China Economic Review, Vol. 21, No. 1, pp. 51–64

Zhang, Q. (2012) *The Constitution of China — A Contextual Analysis*, Hart Publishing

Zhang, F. (2015) *Chinese Hegemony: Grand Strategy and International Institutions in East Asian History*, Stanford University Press

Zhang, L. and Chen, S. (2019) *China's Digital Economy: Opportunities and Risks,* WP/19/16 IMF Working Paper

Zhang, J. and Hu, M. (2020) *Chinese E-commerce Giants Alibaba, JD.com, Offer Support for Small and Medium Enterprises to aid in Coronavirus Recovery*, South China Morning Post

Zhang, P. and Pi, J. (2016) *Hukou system reforms and skilled-unskilled wage inequality in China*, China Economic Review, Vol. 41, No. C, pp. 90–113

Zhang, H. and Tesfaye, N. (2018) *Alignment of Belt and Road Initiative With Africa Agenda 2063*, Proceedings of the 3rd International Symposium on Asian B&R Conference on International Business Cooperation, Atlantis Press

Zhao, K. (2015) *The Motivation Behind China's Public Diplomacy*, The Chinese Journal of International Politics, Vol. 8, No. 2, pp. 167–196

Zheng, S. (2017) *China's Djibouti Military Base: 'Logistics Facility', Or Platform for Geopolitical Ambitions Overseas?* South China Morning Post

Zhong, N. and Zeng, G. (2006) *What We Have Learnt from SARS Epidemics in China* https://www.ncbi.nlm.nih.gov/pmc/articles/PMC1550436/

Zhou, B. (2015) *Explaining China's Intervention in the Korean War in 1950* http://www.inquiriesjournal.com/articles/1069/explaining-chinas-intervention-in-the-korean-war-in-1950

Zhu, H. and Walker, A. (2018) *Pension System Reform in China: Who Gets What Pensions?* Social Policy & Administration, Vol. 52, No. 7, pp. 1410–1424

Index

T

Lightning Source UK Ltd.
Milton Keynes UK
UKHW020312191021
392428UK00002B/175

9 781800 611269